Norihiro Yagi won the 32nd Akatsuka Award for his debut work, *UNDEADMAN*, which appeared in *Monthly Shonen Jump* magazine and produced two sequels. His first serialized manga was his comedy *Angel Densetsu* (Angel Legend), which appeared in *Monthly Shonen Jump* from 1992 to 2000. His epic saga, *Claymore*, has been running in the magazine since 2001.

In his spare time, Yagi enjoys things like the Japanese comedic duo *Downtown*, martial arts, games, driving, and hard rock music, but he doesn't consider these actual hobbies.

CLAYMORE VOL. 7
SHONEN JUMP ADVANCED Manga Edition

STORY AND ART BY
NORIHIRO YAGI

English Adaptation & Translation/Arashi Productions
Touch-up Art & Lettering/Sabrina Heep
Design/Izumi Evers
Editor/Jonathan Tarbox

Published by VIZ Media, LLC
P.O. Box 77010
San Francisco, CA 94107

10 9 8 7 6 5 4
First printing, April 2007
Fourth printing, May 2012

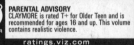

THE WORLD'S MOST
CUTTING-EDGE MANGA

SHONEN JUMP ADVANCED Manga Edition

Claymore

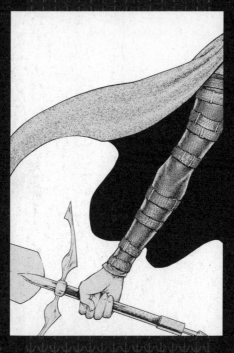

Vol. 7
Fit for Battle

Story and Art by **Norihiro Yagi**

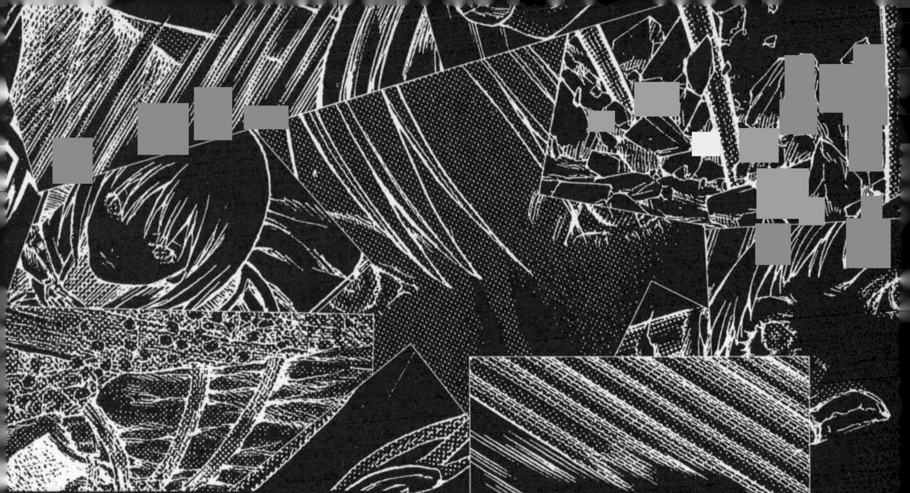

broadswords that they carried.

Clare is assigned to hunt an Awakened Being along with Ophelia, the number 4 warrior. When the Awakened Being grabs Raki, Clare releases her powers to their limits. Seeing Clare's extraordinary abilities, Ophelia becomes suspicious...

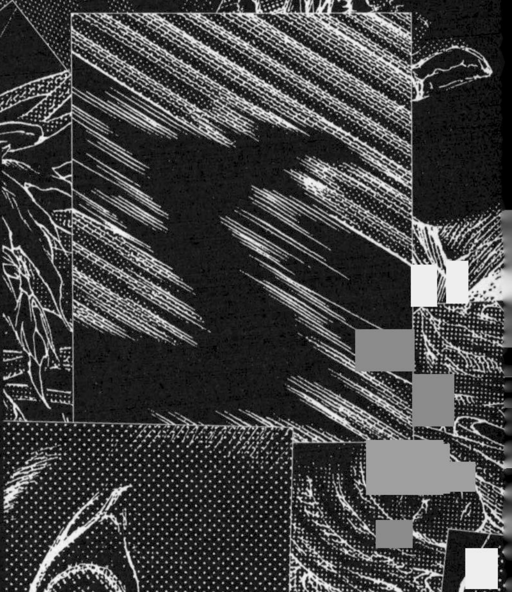

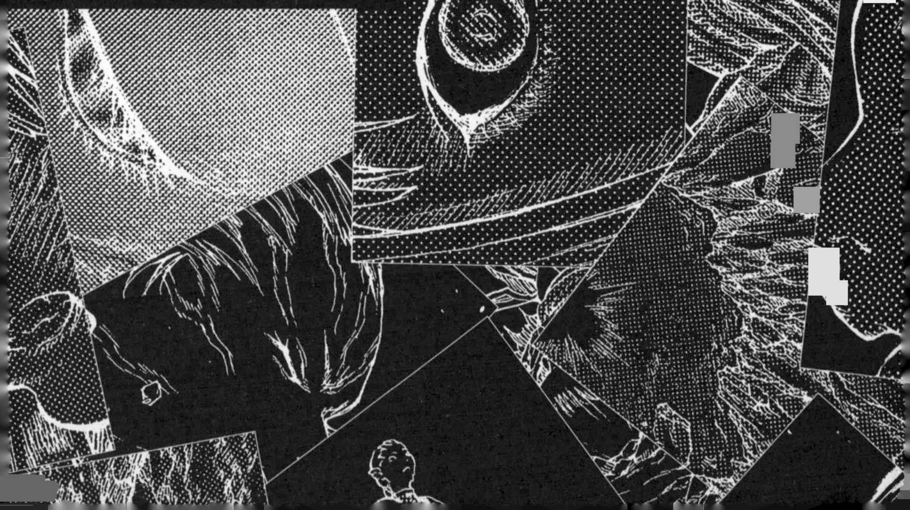

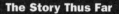

The Story Thus Far

Creatures known as Yoma have long preyed on humans, who were once powerless against their predators. But now mankind has developed female warriors who are half human and half monster, with silver eyes that can see the monsters' true form. These warriors came to be called Claymores after the immense

Claymore
クレイモア

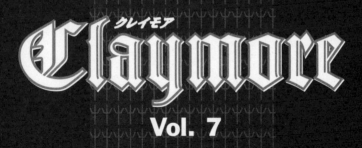

Vol. 7

CONTENTS

Scene 34: The Endless Gravestones, Part 4

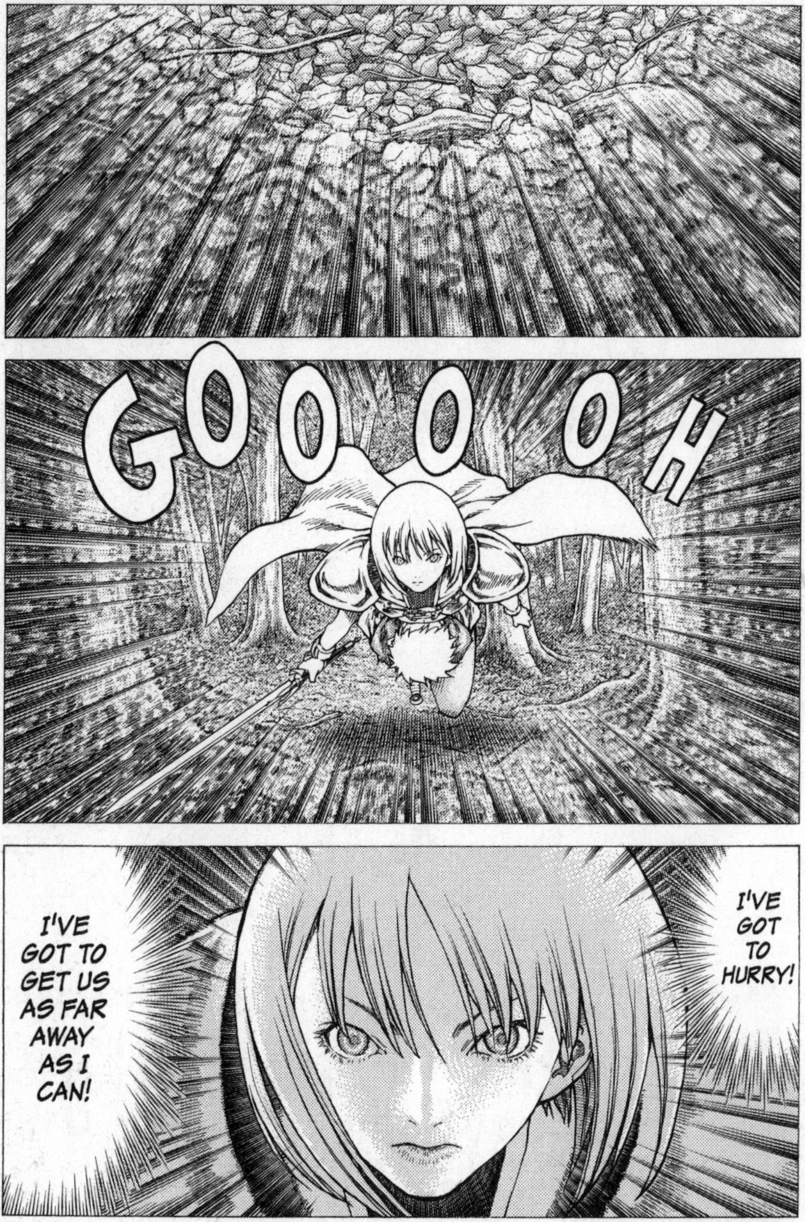
GOOOOH
I'VE GOT TO HURRY!
I'VE GOT TO GET US AS FAR AWAY AS I CAN!

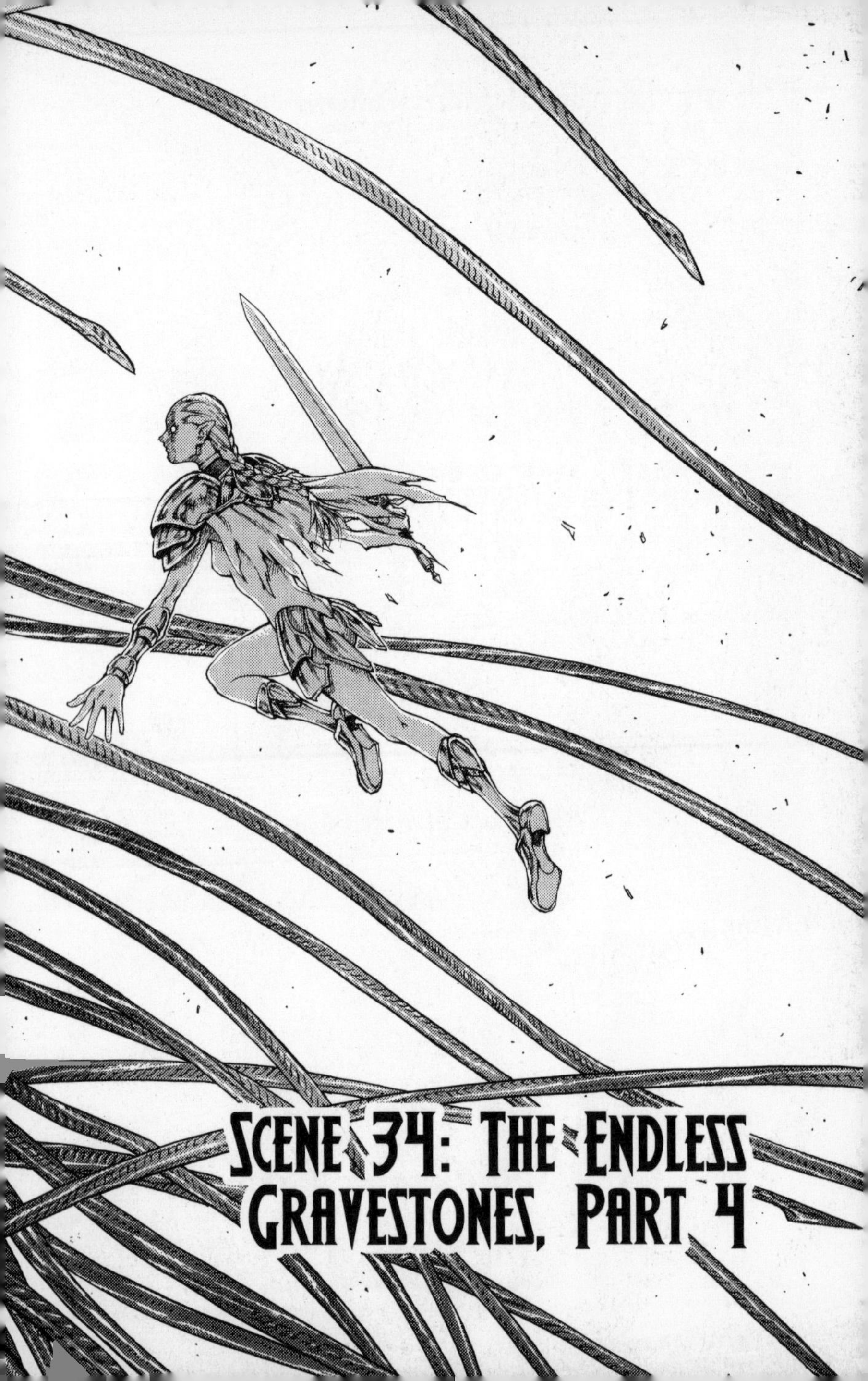
SCENE 34: THE ENDLESS GRAVESTONES, PART 4

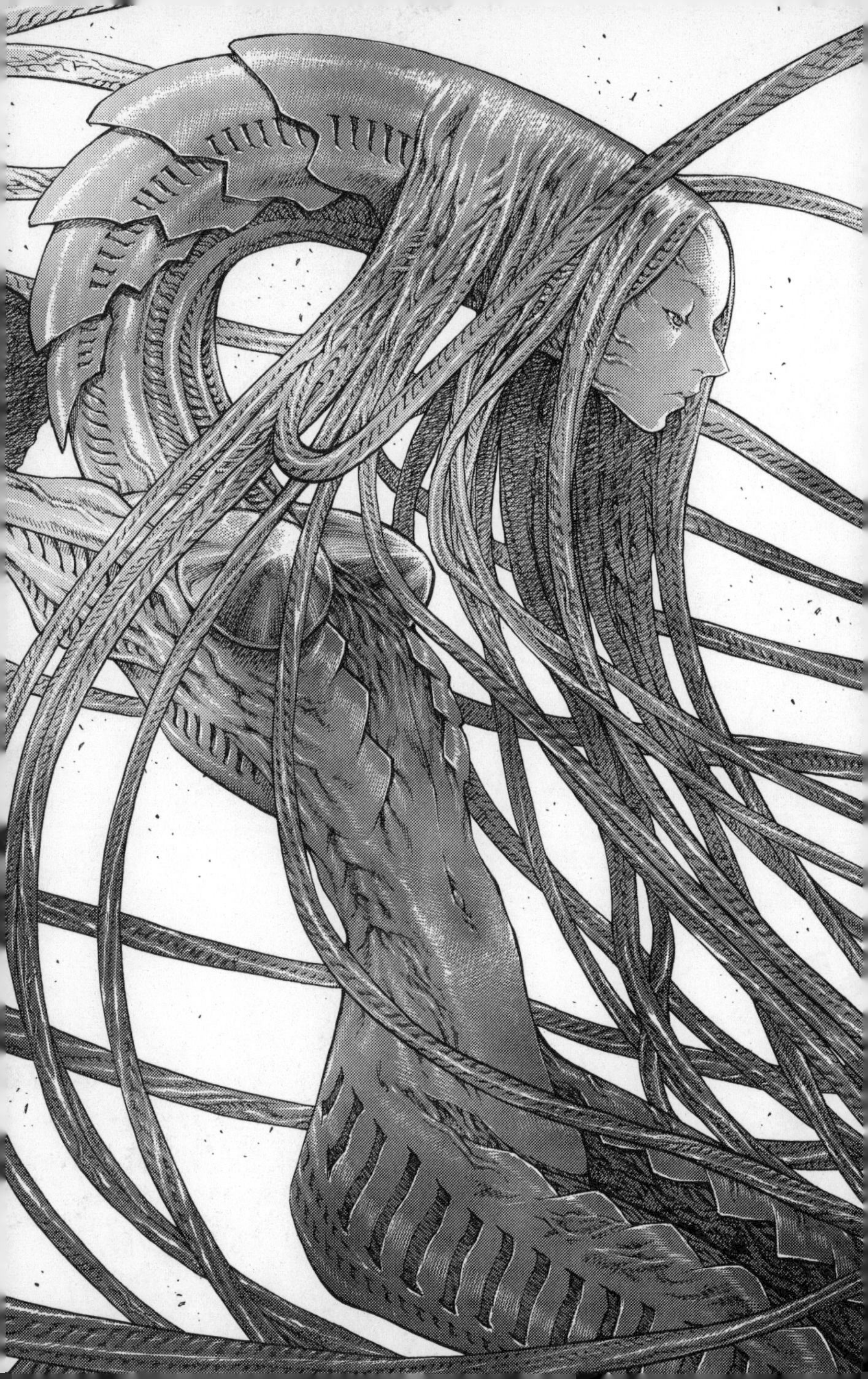

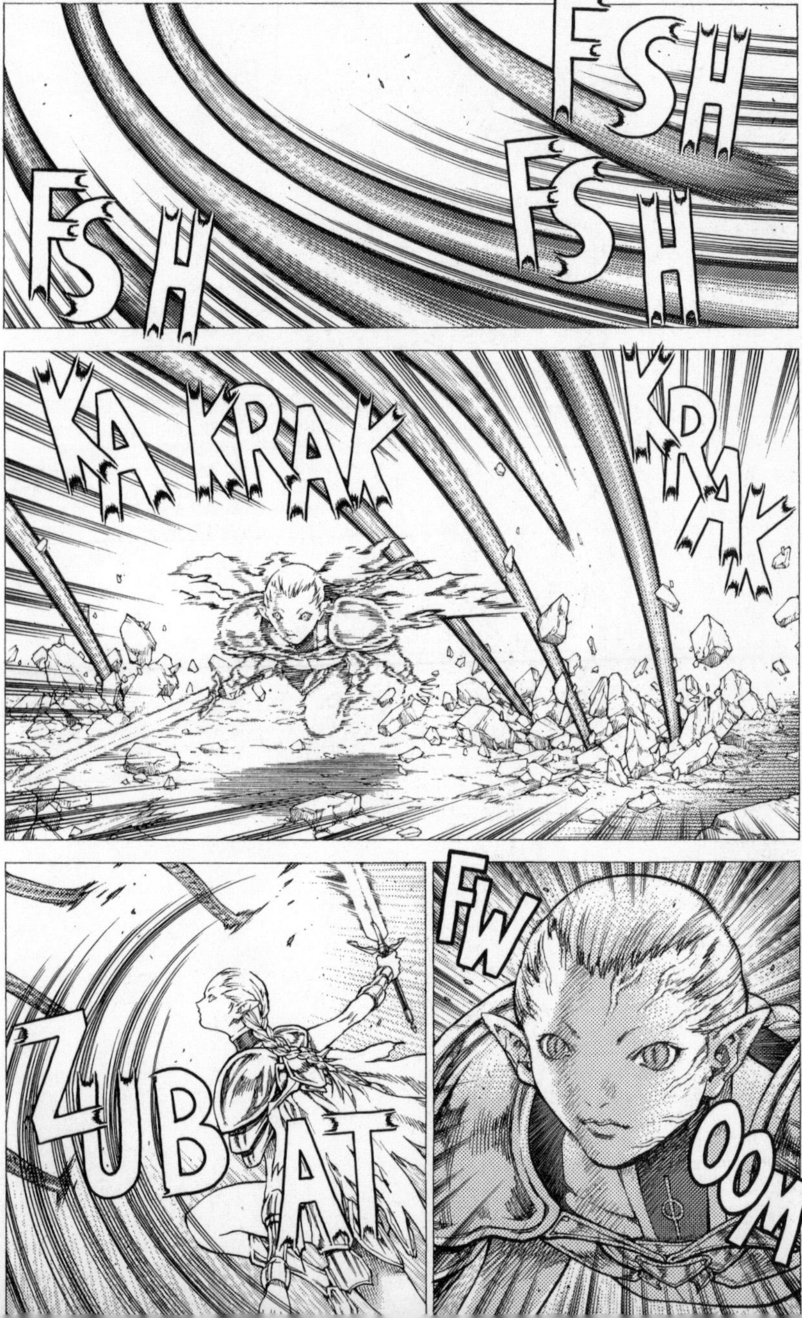
FSH
FSH
FSH
KRAK
KA KRAK
FWOOM
ZUBAT

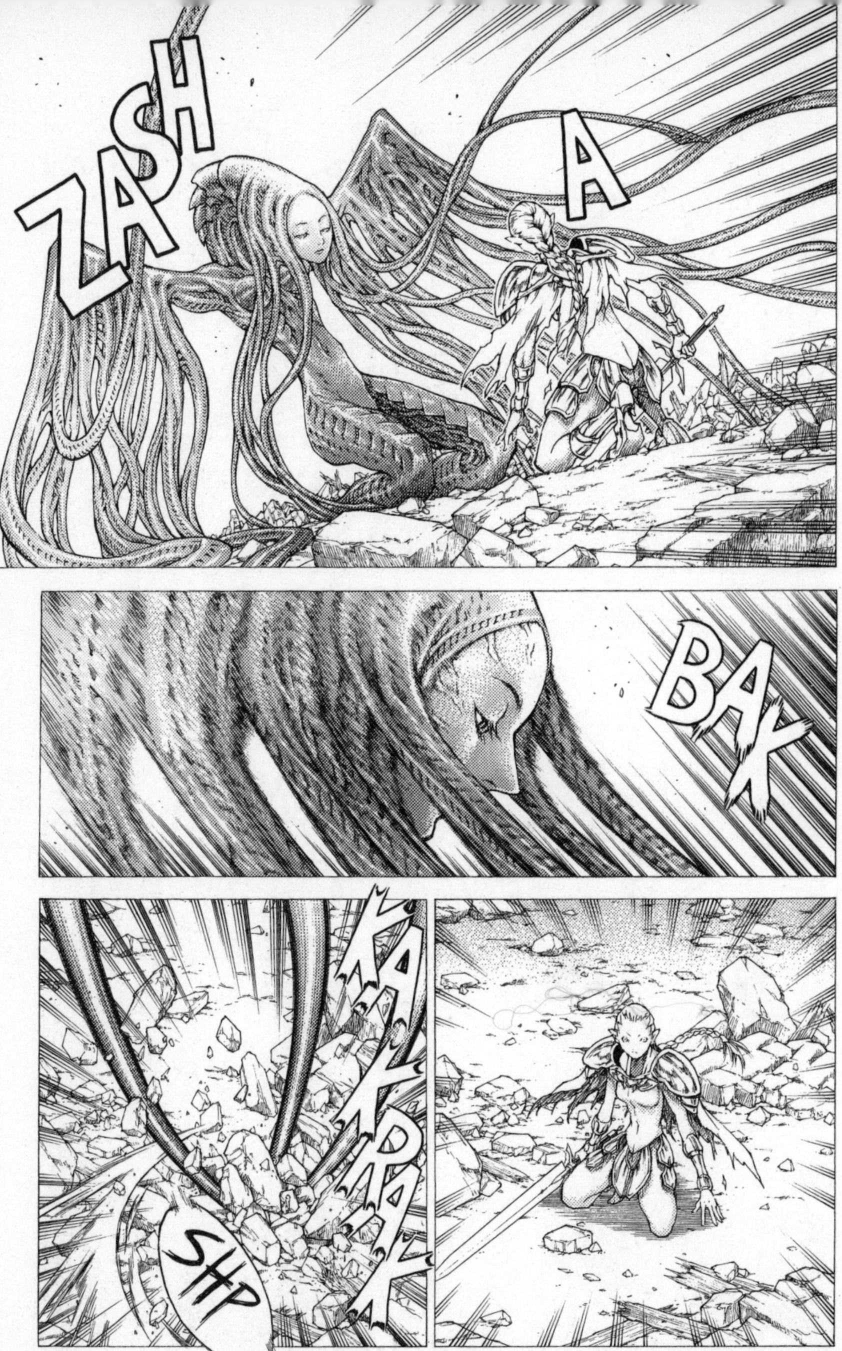
A
ZASH
BAK
KAKRAK
SHP

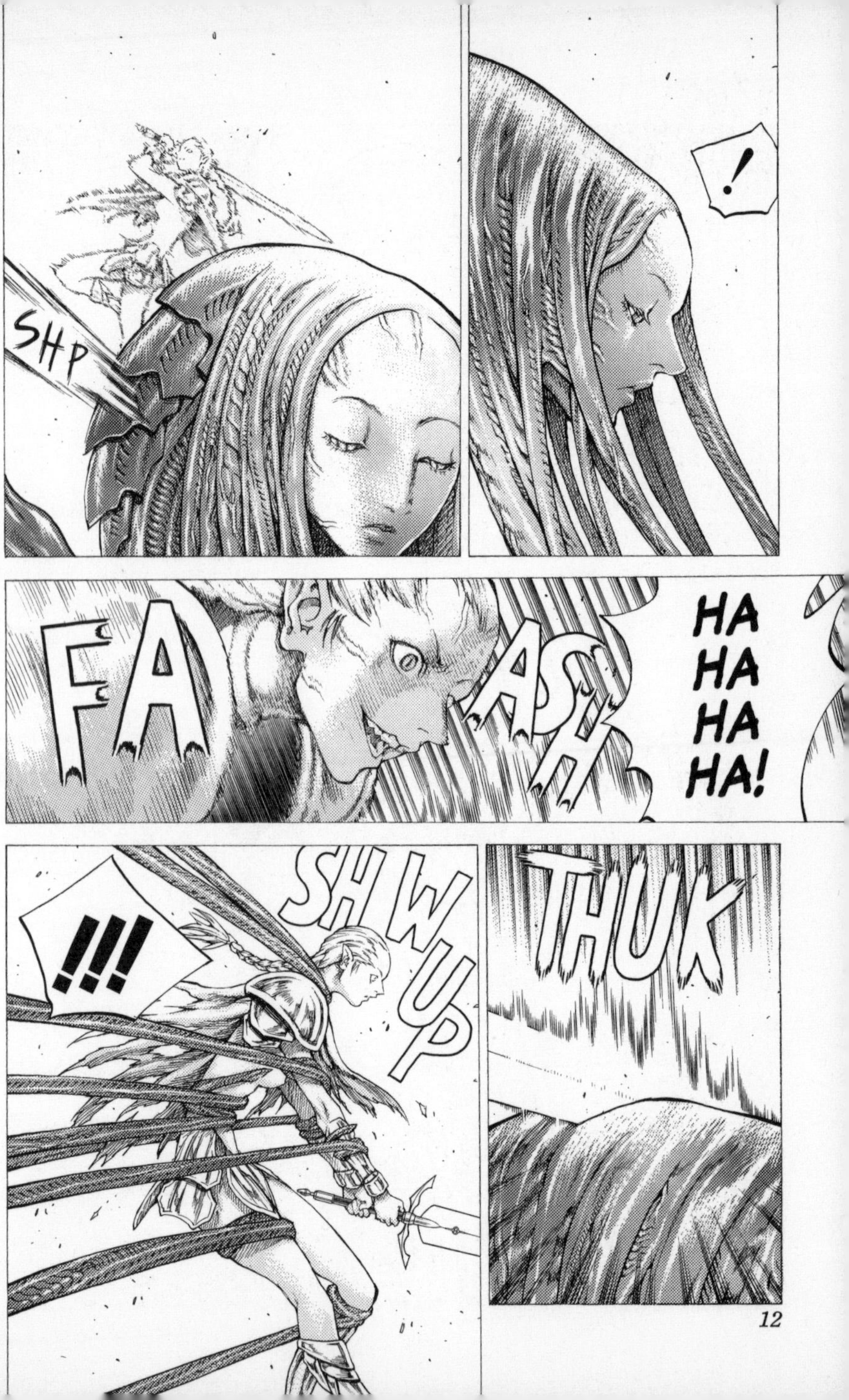
!
SHP
HA HA HA HA!
FASH
THUK
SHWUP
!!!

READ THIS WAY

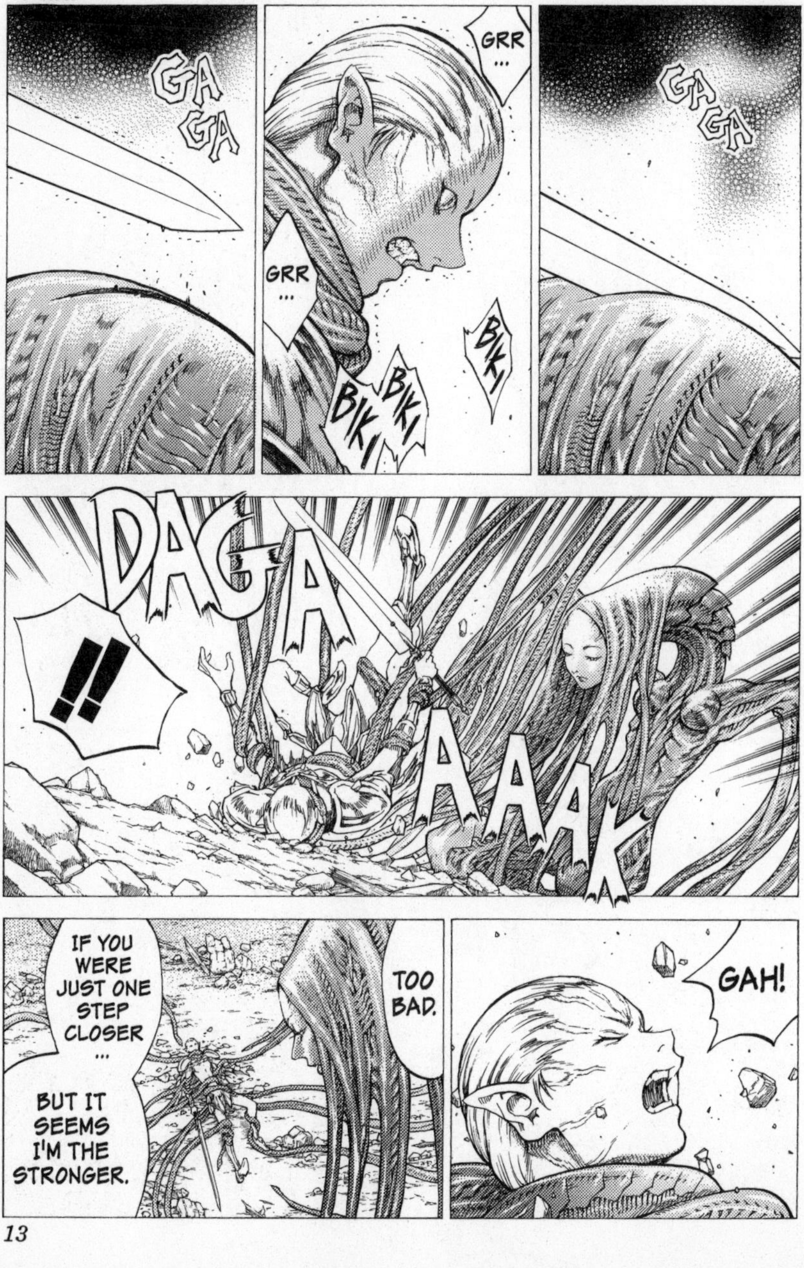
GAGA
GRR...
BIKI
BIKI BIKI
GRR...
GAGA
DAGA
AAAK
!!
GAH!
TOO BAD.
IF YOU WERE JUST ONE STEP CLOSER...
BUT IT SEEMS I'M THE STRONGER.

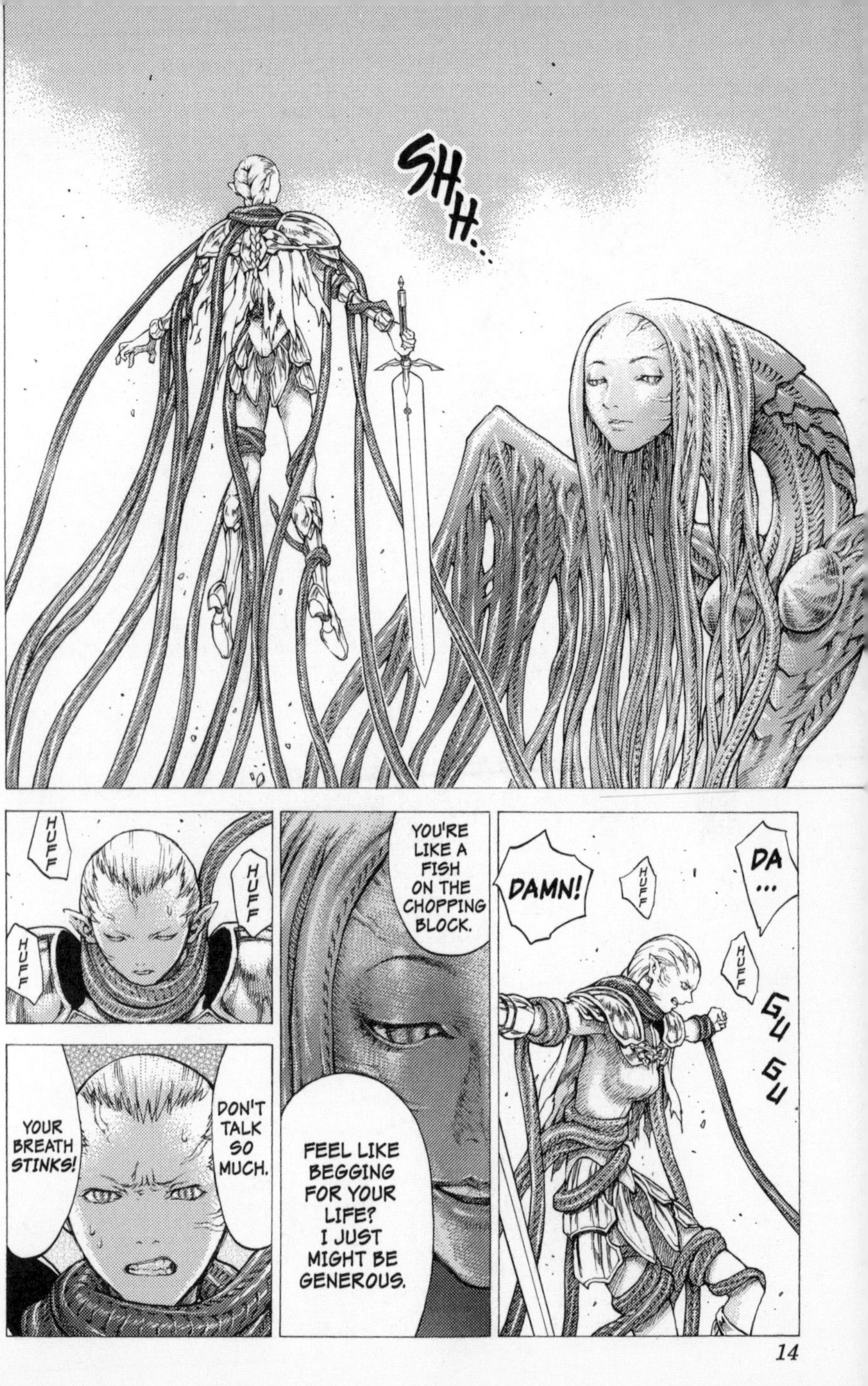
SHH...
DA...
HUFF
DAMN!
HUFF
GU GU
YOU'RE LIKE A FISH ON THE CHOPPING BLOCK.
FEEL LIKE BEGGING FOR YOUR LIFE? I JUST MIGHT BE GENEROUS.
HUFF
HUFF
HUFF
DON'T TALK SO MUCH.
YOUR BREATH STINKS!

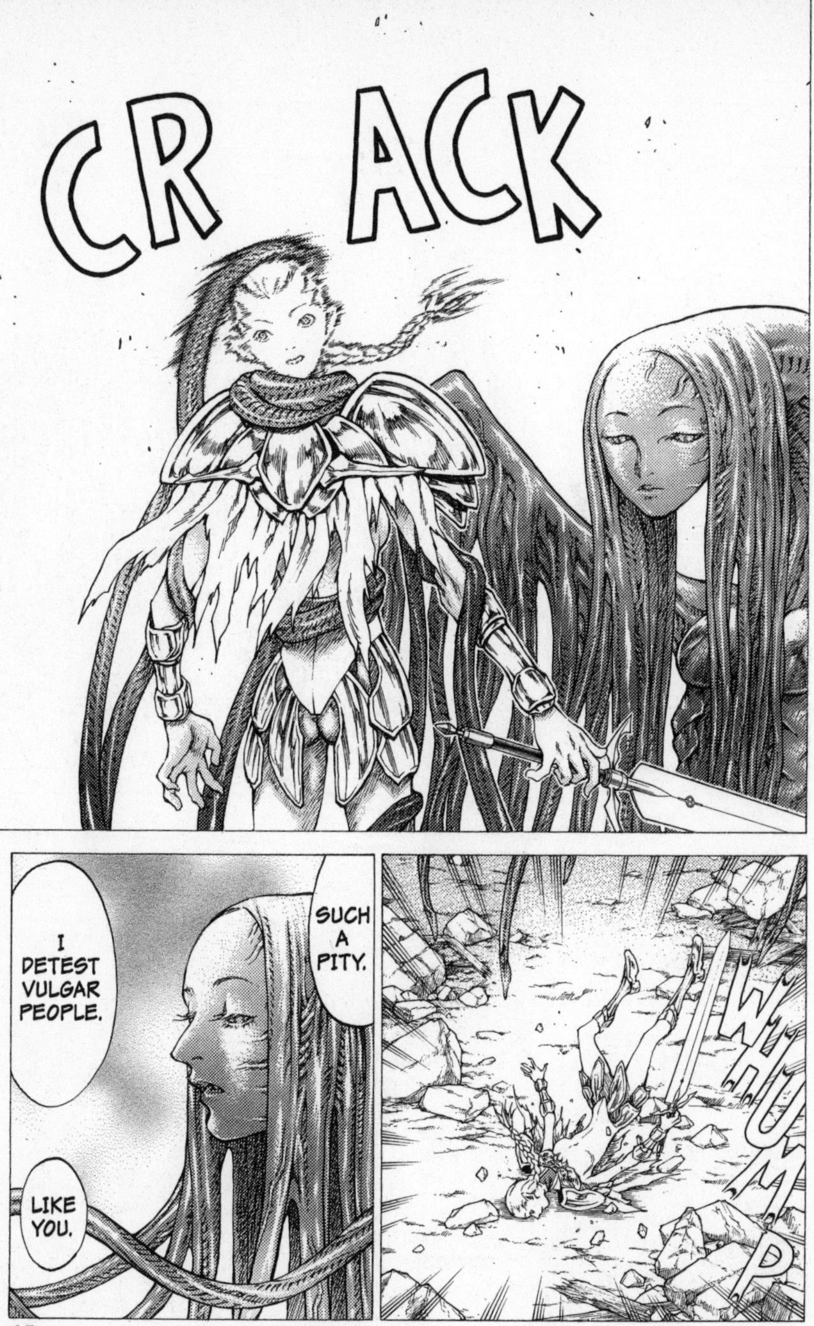
CR ACK
WHUMP
SUCH A PITY.
I DETEST VULGAR PEOPLE.
LIKE YOU.

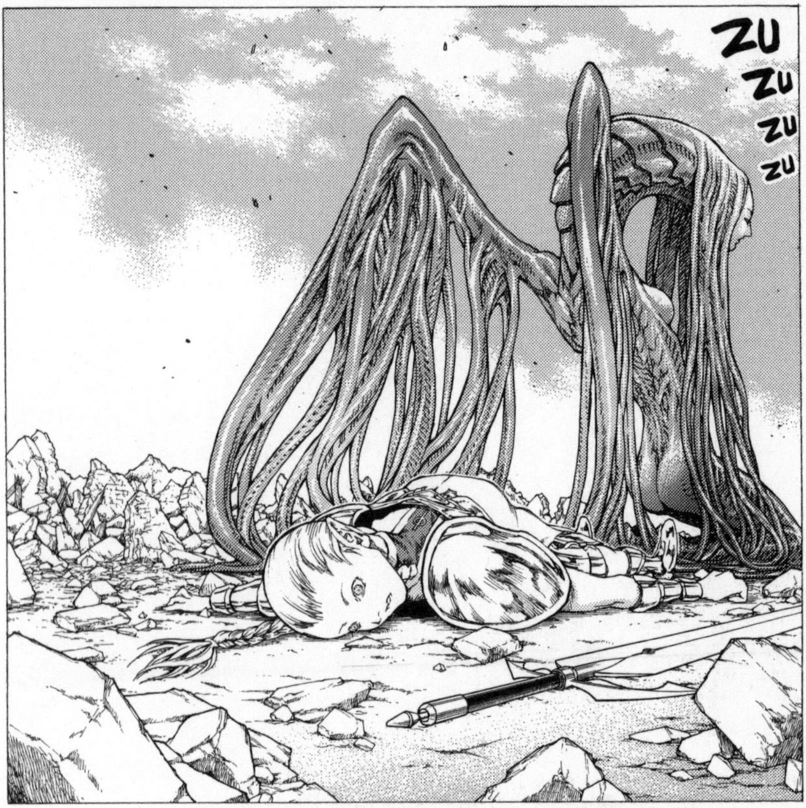
ZU ZU ZU ZU
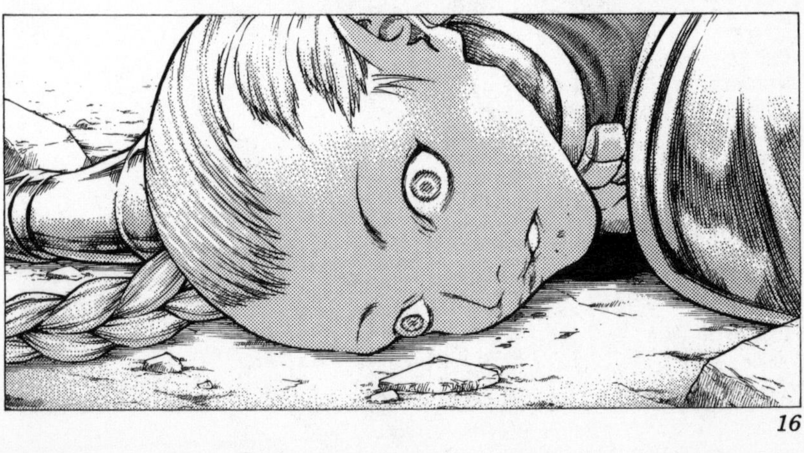

READ THIS WAY

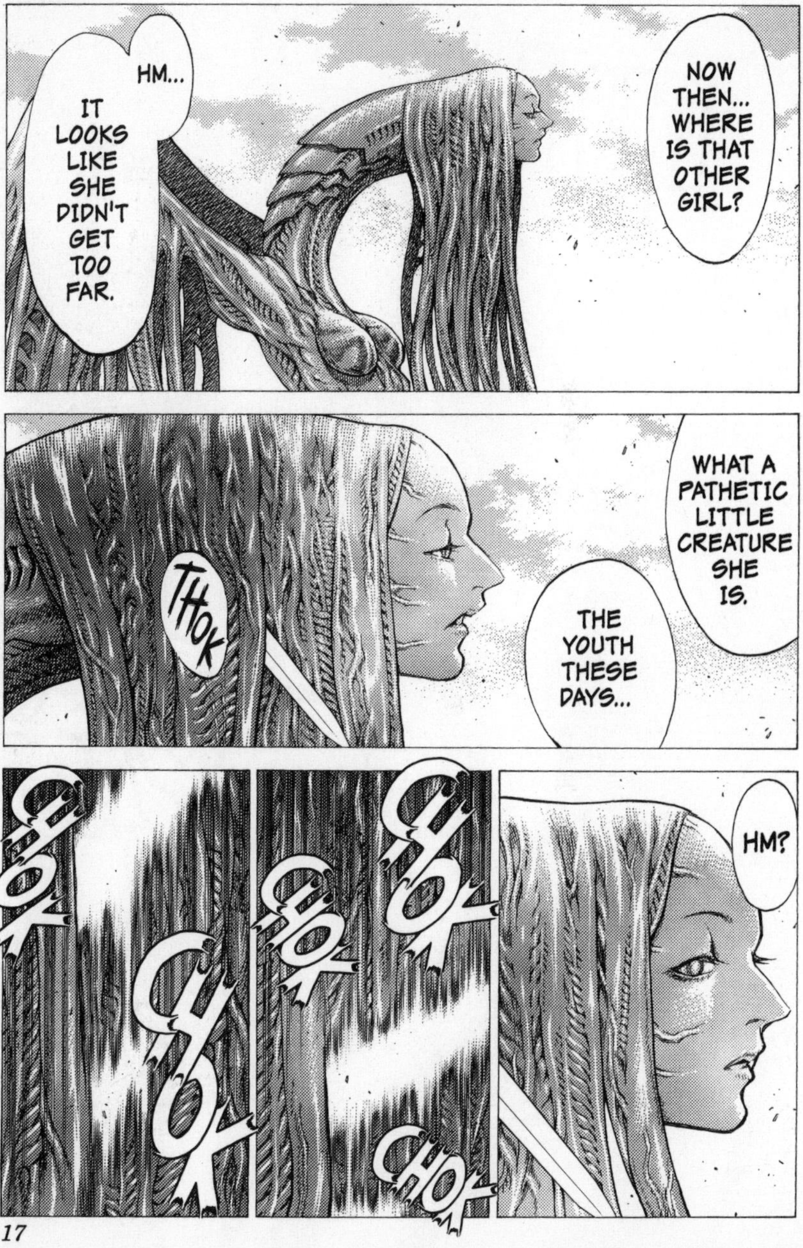
NOW THEN... WHERE IS THAT OTHER GIRL?
HM... IT LOOKS LIKE SHE DIDN'T GET TOO FAR.
WHAT A PATHETIC LITTLE CREATURE SHE IS.
THE YOUTH THESE DAYS...
THOK
HM?
CHOK
CHOK
CHOK
CHOK
CHOK
CHOK

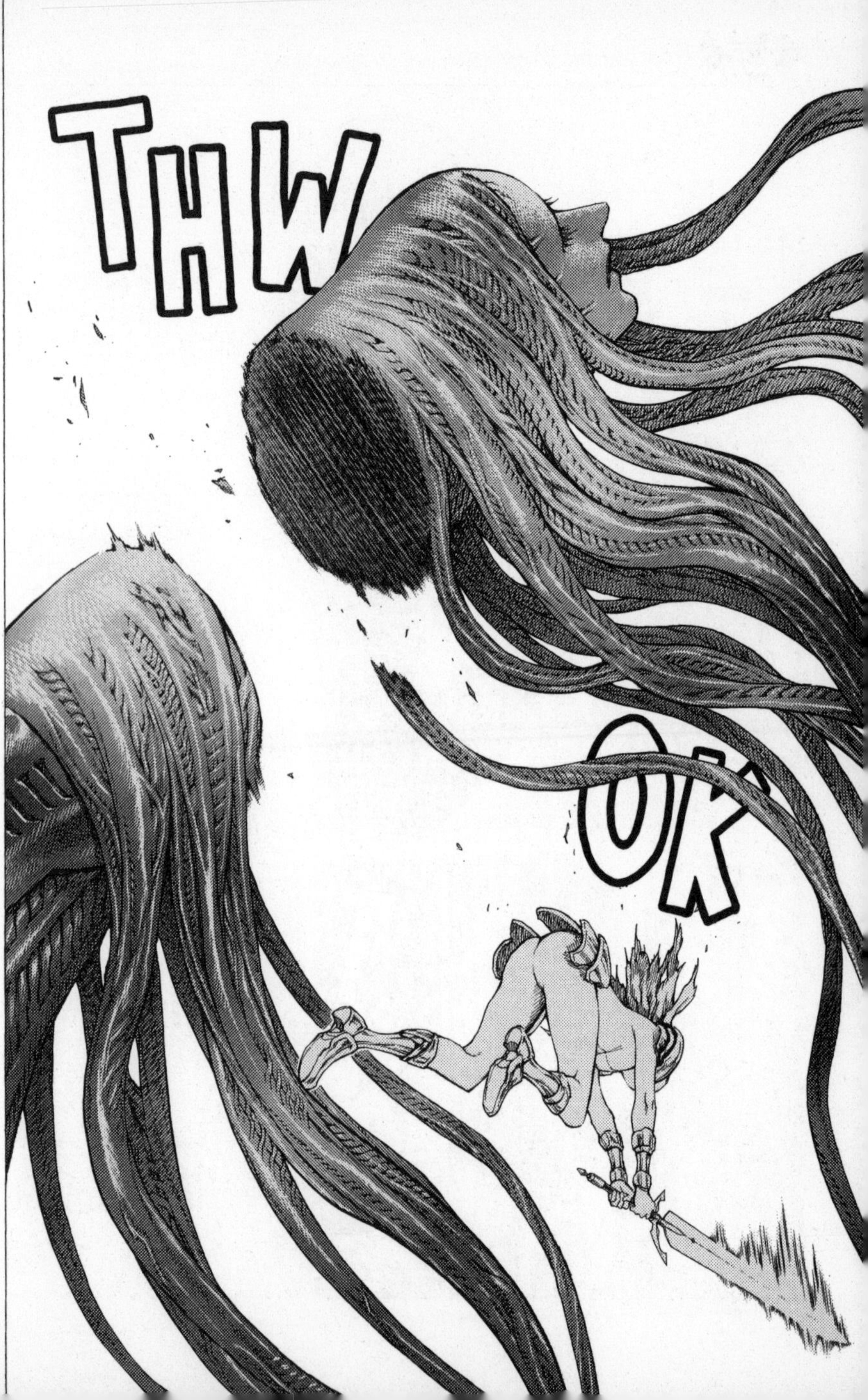
THWOK

READ THIS WAY

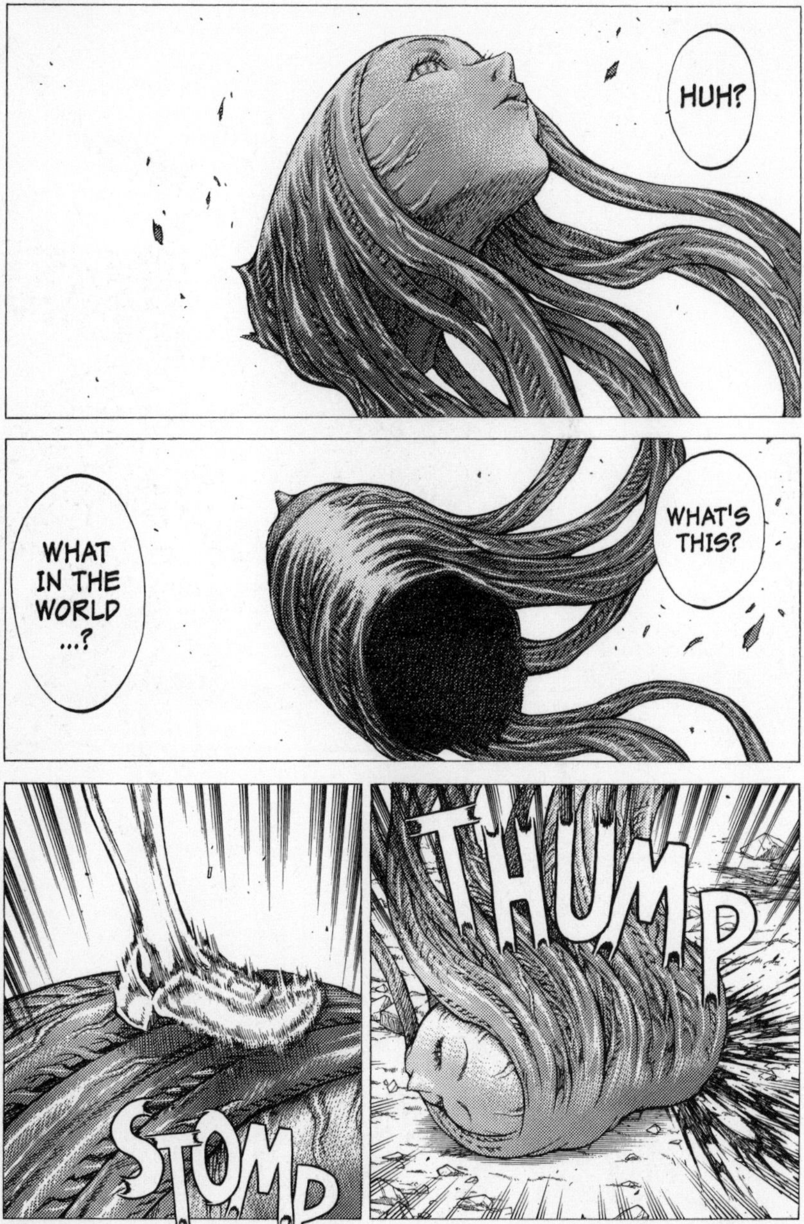
HUH?
WHAT'S THIS?
WHAT IN THE WORLD ...?
THUMP
STOMP

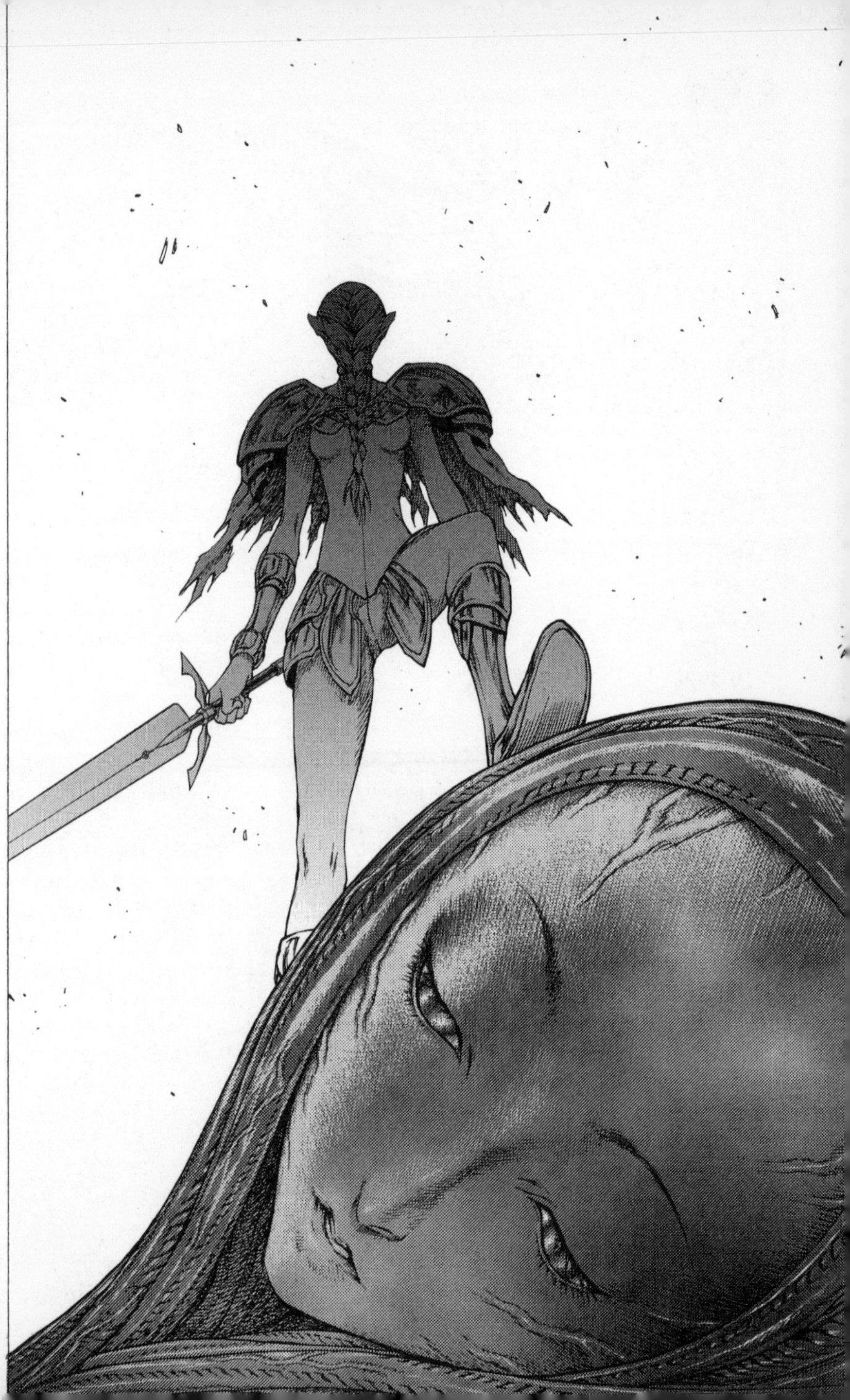

READ THIS WAY

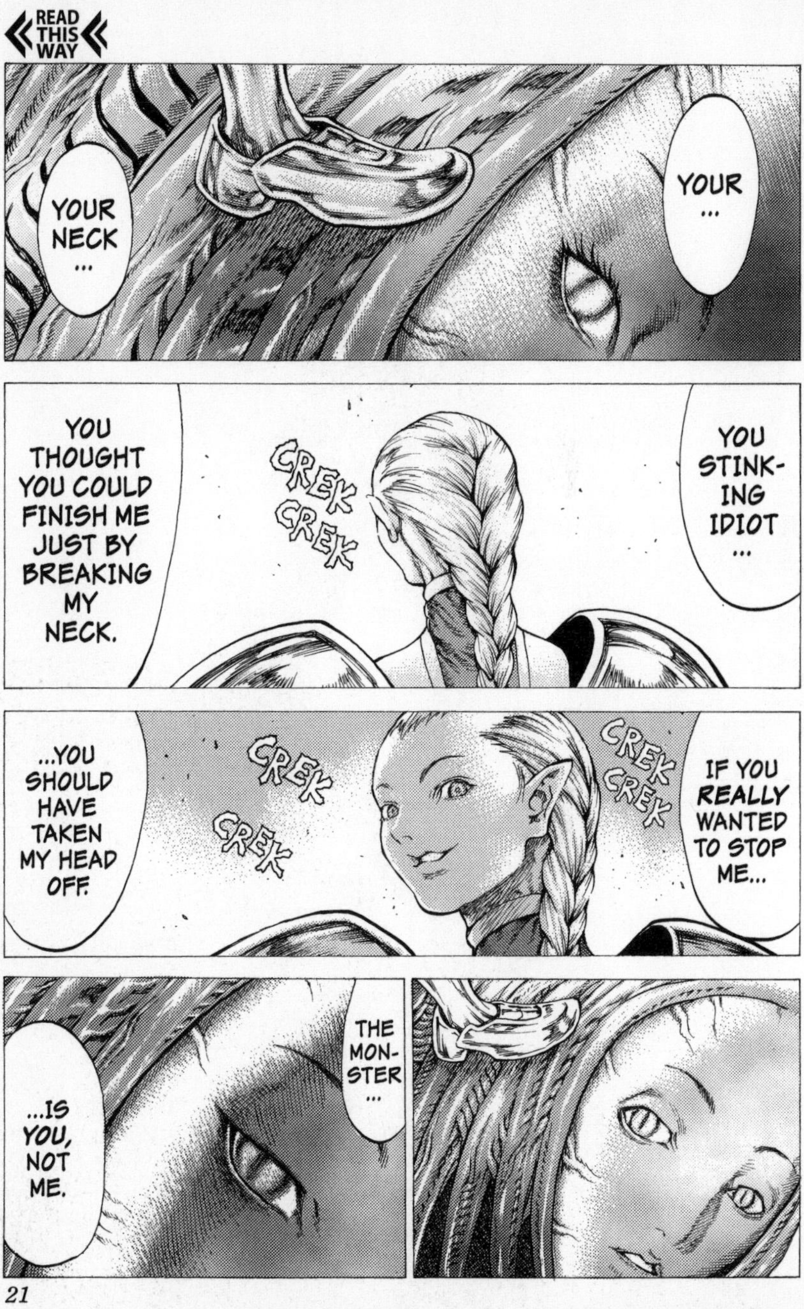
YOUR ...
YOUR NECK ...
YOU STINKING IDIOT ...
CREK CREK
YOU THOUGHT YOU COULD FINISH ME JUST BY BREAKING MY NECK.
IF YOU **REALLY** WANTED TO STOP ME...
CREK CREK
CREK
CREK
...YOU SHOULD HAVE TAKEN MY HEAD OFF.
THE MONSTER ...
...IS *YOU*, NOT ME.

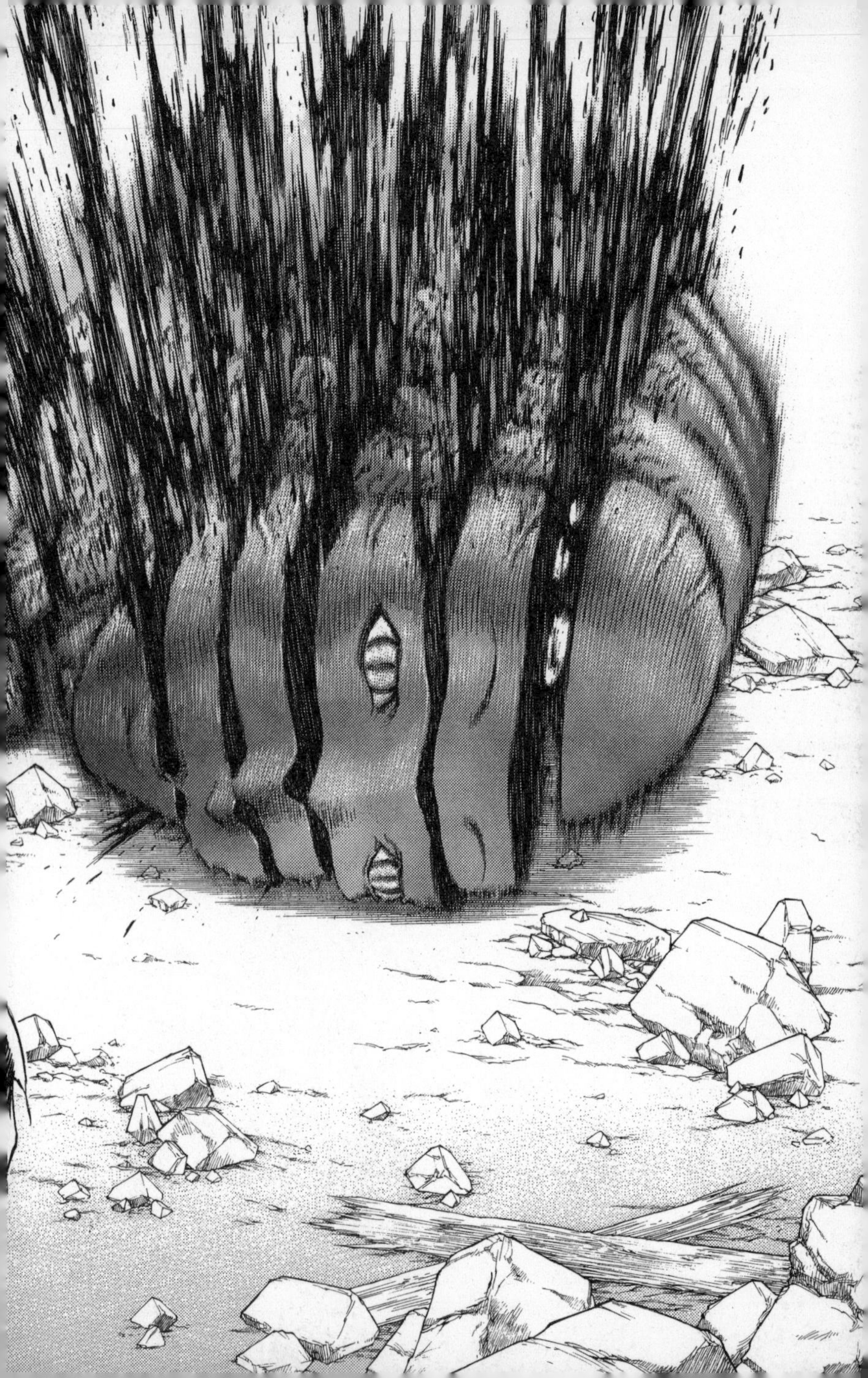

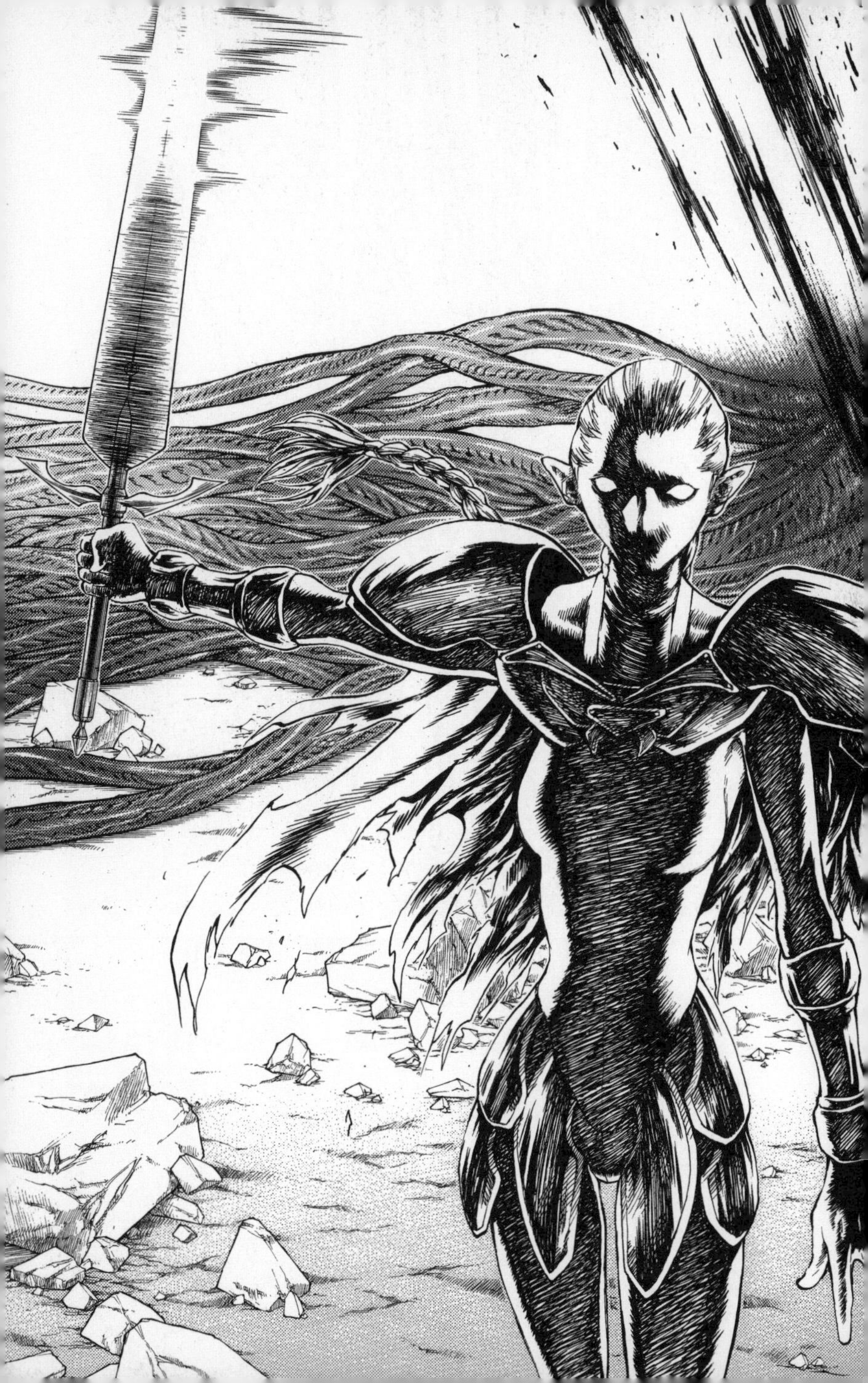

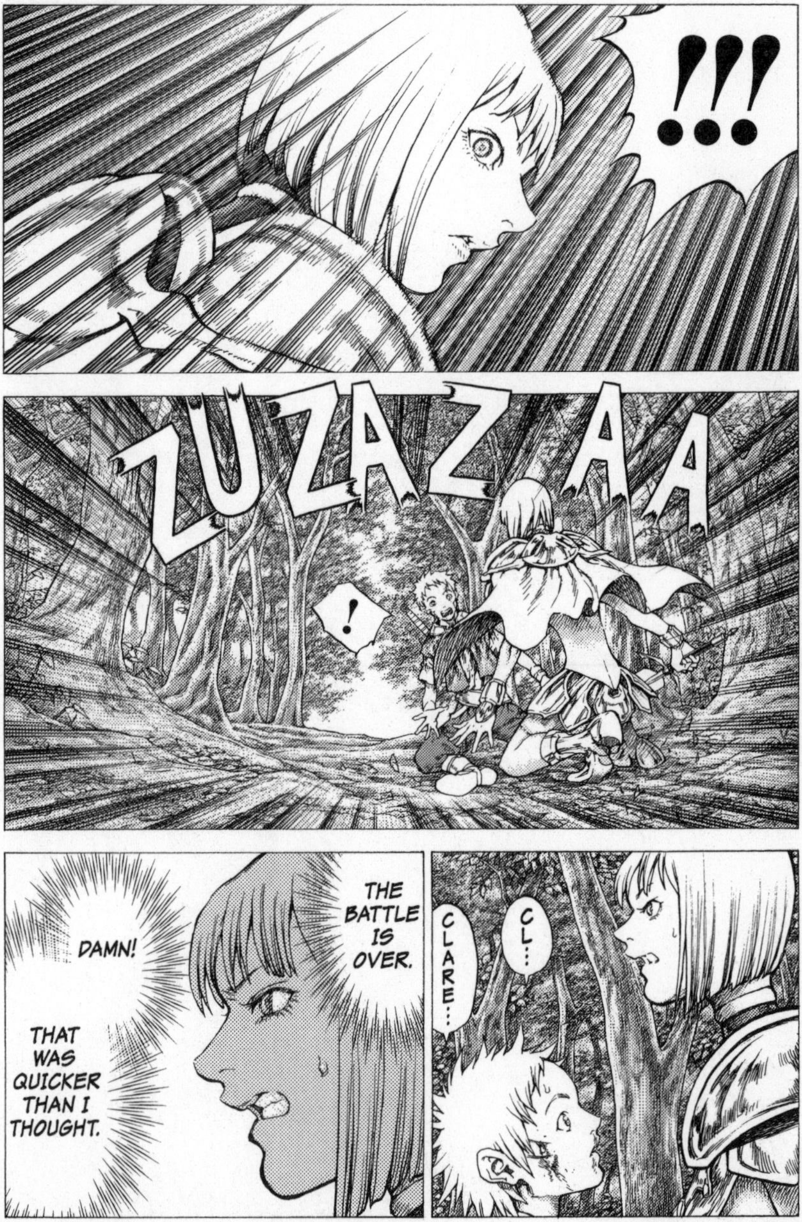
!!!
ZUZAZAA
!
CL...
CLARE...
THE BATTLE IS OVER.
DAMN!
THAT WAS QUICKER THAN I THOUGHT.

READ THIS WAY

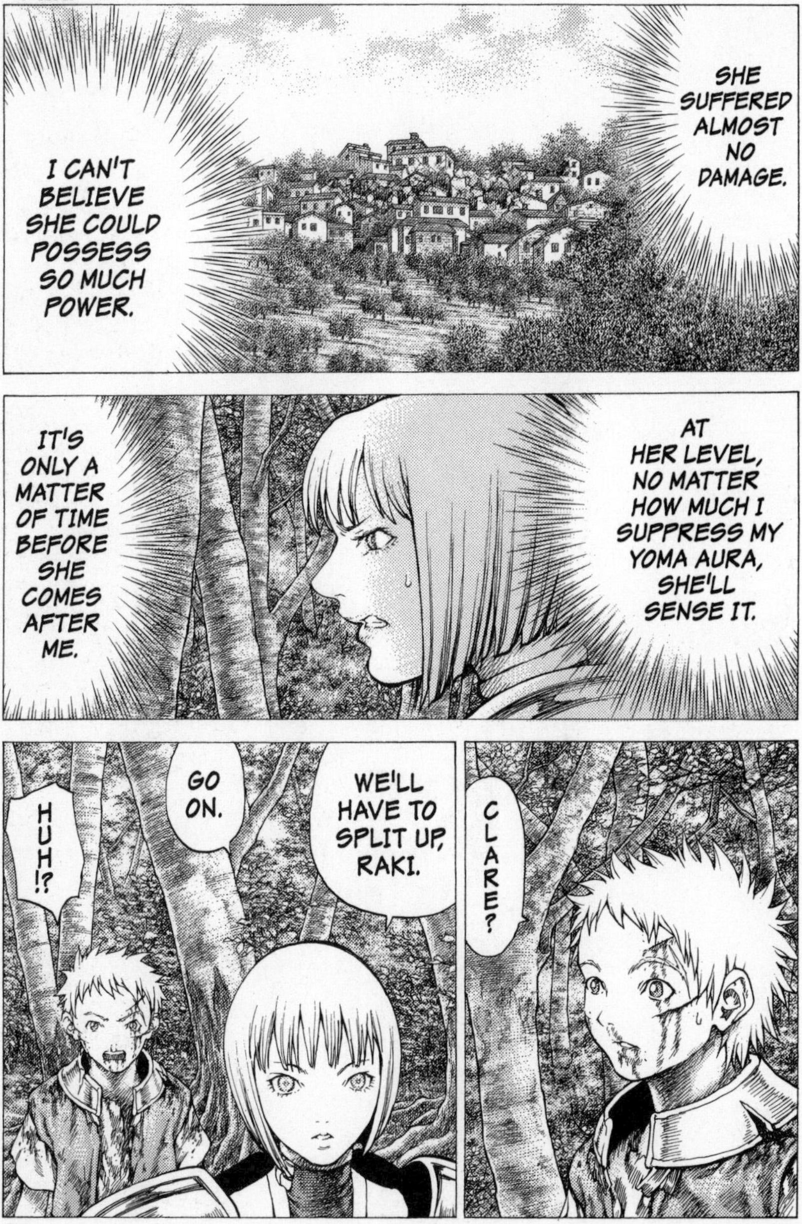

SHE SUFFERED ALMOST NO DAMAGE.
I CAN'T BELIEVE SHE COULD POSSESS SO MUCH POWER.
AT HER LEVEL, NO MATTER HOW MUCH I SUPPRESS MY YOMA AURA, SHE'LL SENSE IT.
IT'S ONLY A MATTER OF TIME BEFORE SHE COMES AFTER ME.
CLARE?
WE'LL HAVE TO SPLIT UP, RAKI.
GO ON.
HUH!?

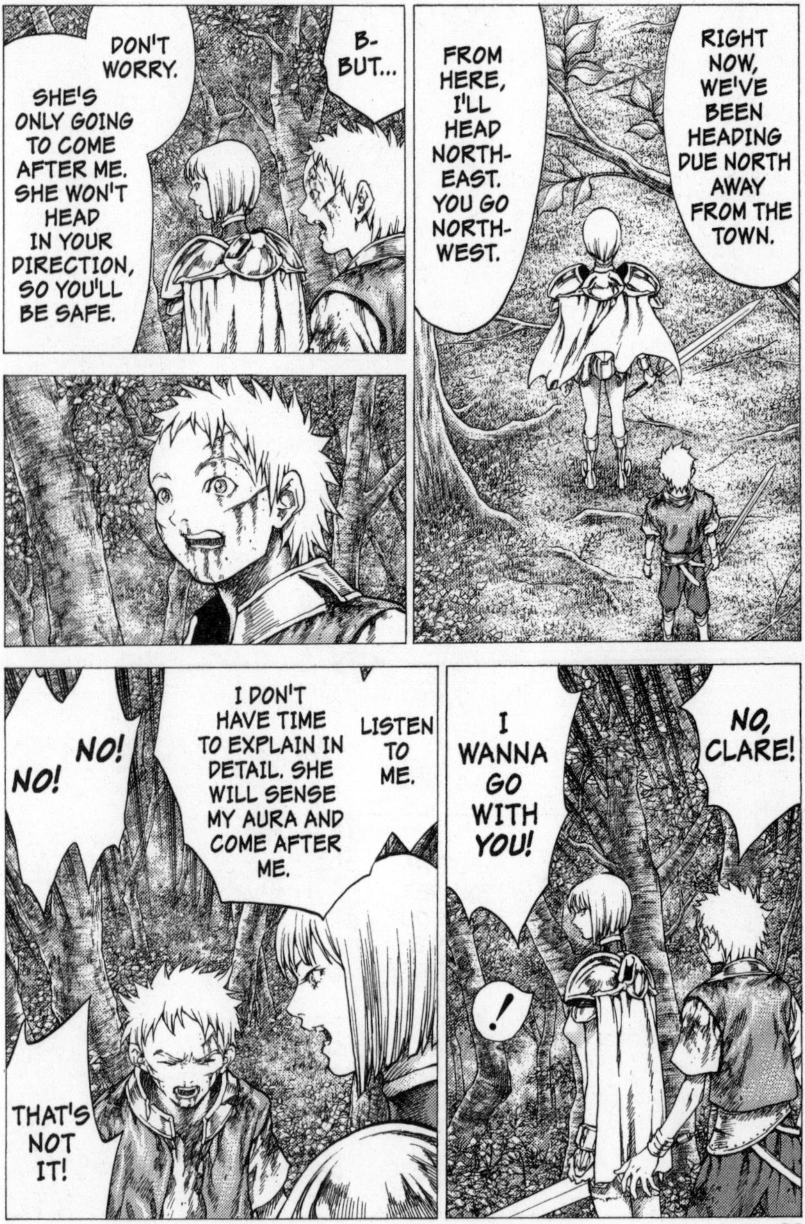
RIGHT NOW, WE'VE BEEN HEADING DUE NORTH AWAY FROM THE TOWN.
FROM HERE, I'LL HEAD NORTH-EAST. YOU GO NORTH-WEST.
B- BUT...
DON'T WORRY.
SHE'S ONLY GOING TO COME AFTER ME. SHE WON'T HEAD IN YOUR DIRECTION, SO YOU'LL BE SAFE.
NO, CLARE!
I WANNA GO WITH YOU!
!
LISTEN TO ME.
I DON'T HAVE TIME TO EXPLAIN IN DETAIL. SHE WILL SENSE MY AURA AND COME AFTER ME.
NO!
NO!
THAT'S NOT IT!

READ THIS WAY

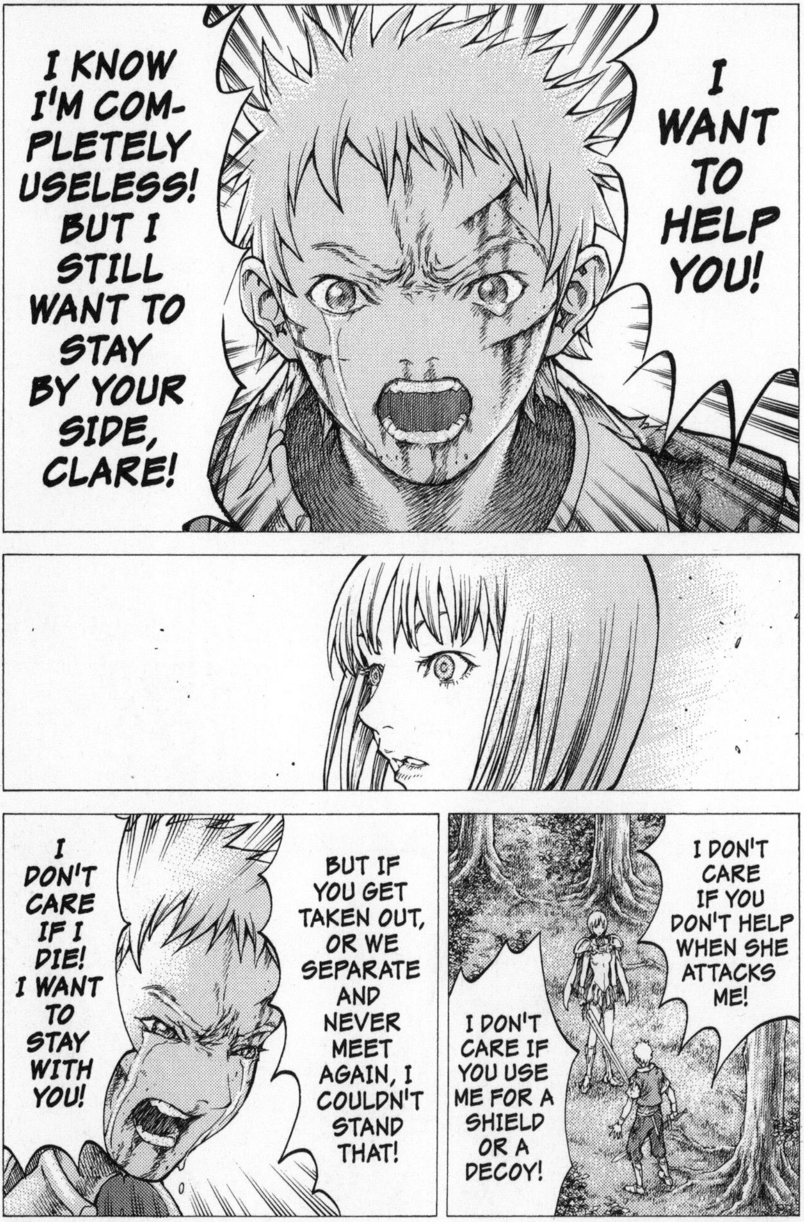

I WANT TO HELP YOU!
I KNOW I'M COMPLETELY USELESS! BUT I STILL WANT TO STAY BY YOUR SIDE, CLARE!
I DON'T CARE IF YOU DON'T HELP WHEN SHE ATTACKS ME!
I DON'T CARE IF YOU USE ME FOR A SHIELD OR A DECOY!
BUT IF YOU GET TAKEN OUT, OR WE SEPARATE AND NEVER MEET AGAIN, I COULDN'T STAND THAT!
I DON'T CARE IF I DIE! I WANT TO STAY WITH YOU!

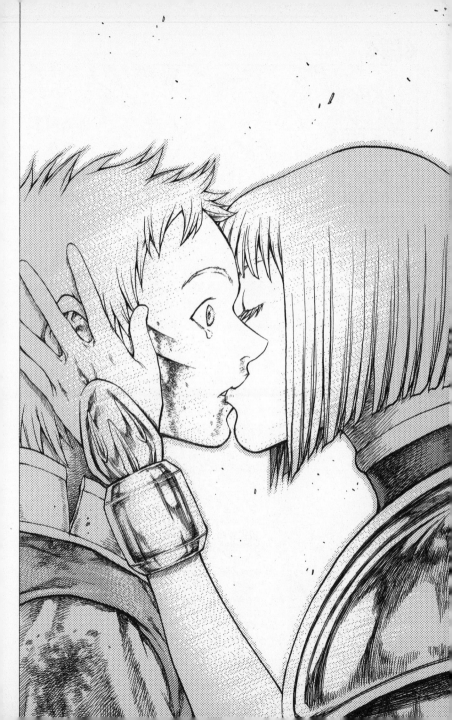

READ THIS WAY

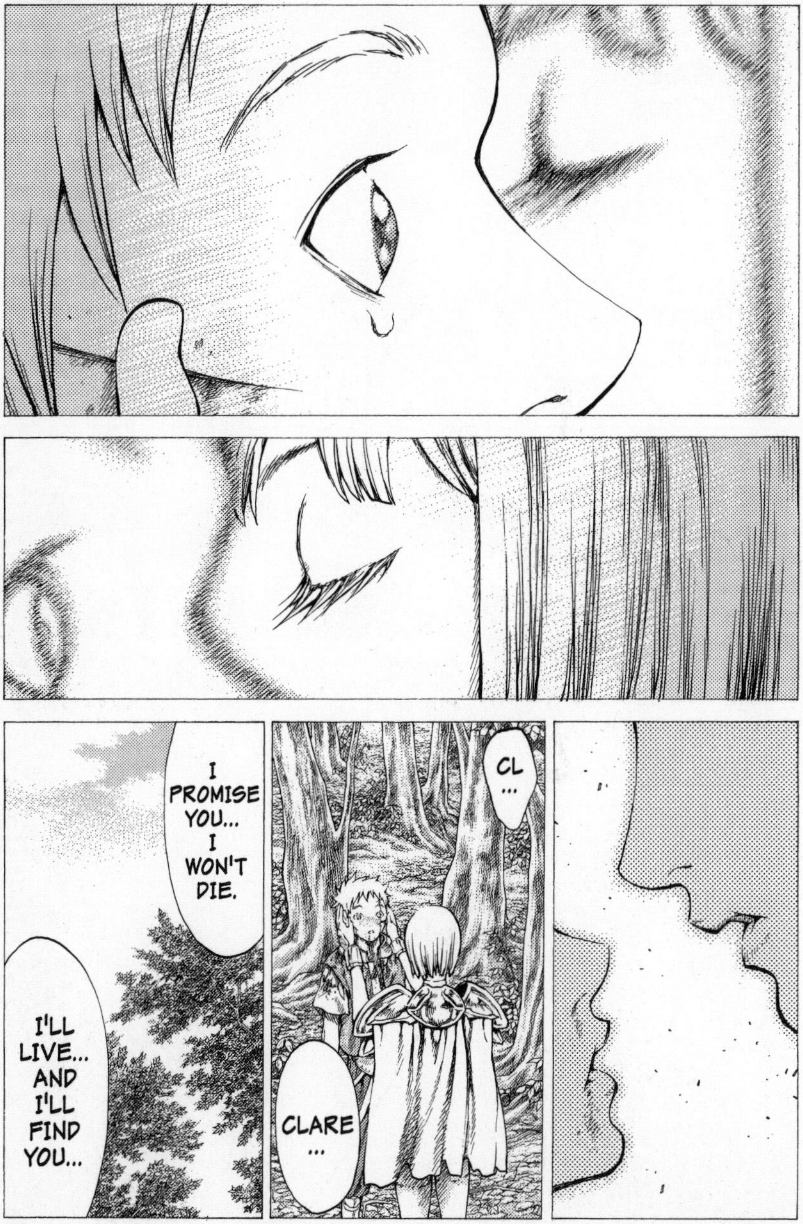
CL ...
CLARE ...
I PROMISE YOU... I WON'T DIE.
I'LL LIVE... AND I'LL FIND YOU...

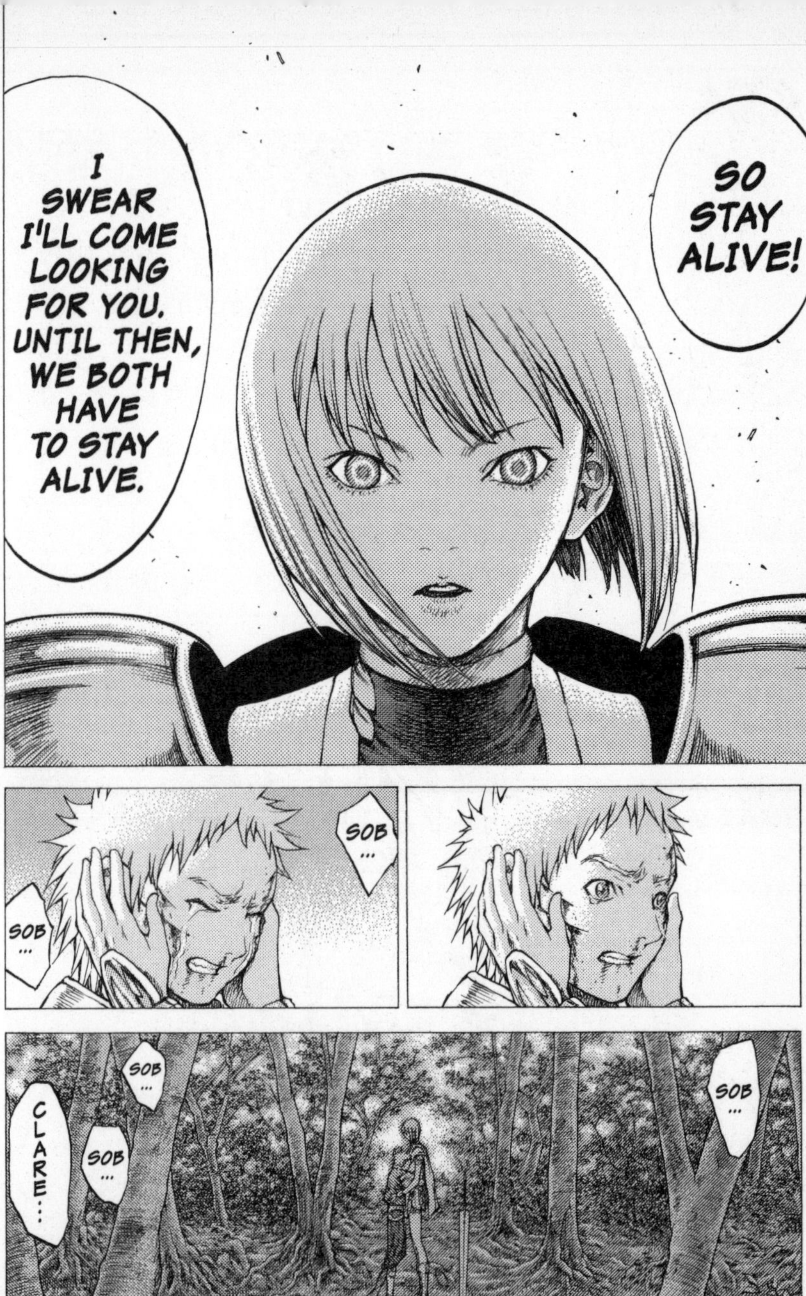
I SWEAR I'LL COME LOOKING FOR YOU. UNTIL THEN, WE BOTH HAVE TO STAY ALIVE.
SO STAY ALIVE!
SOB ...
SOB ...
SOB ...
SOB ...
CLARE...
SOB ...

READ THIS WAY

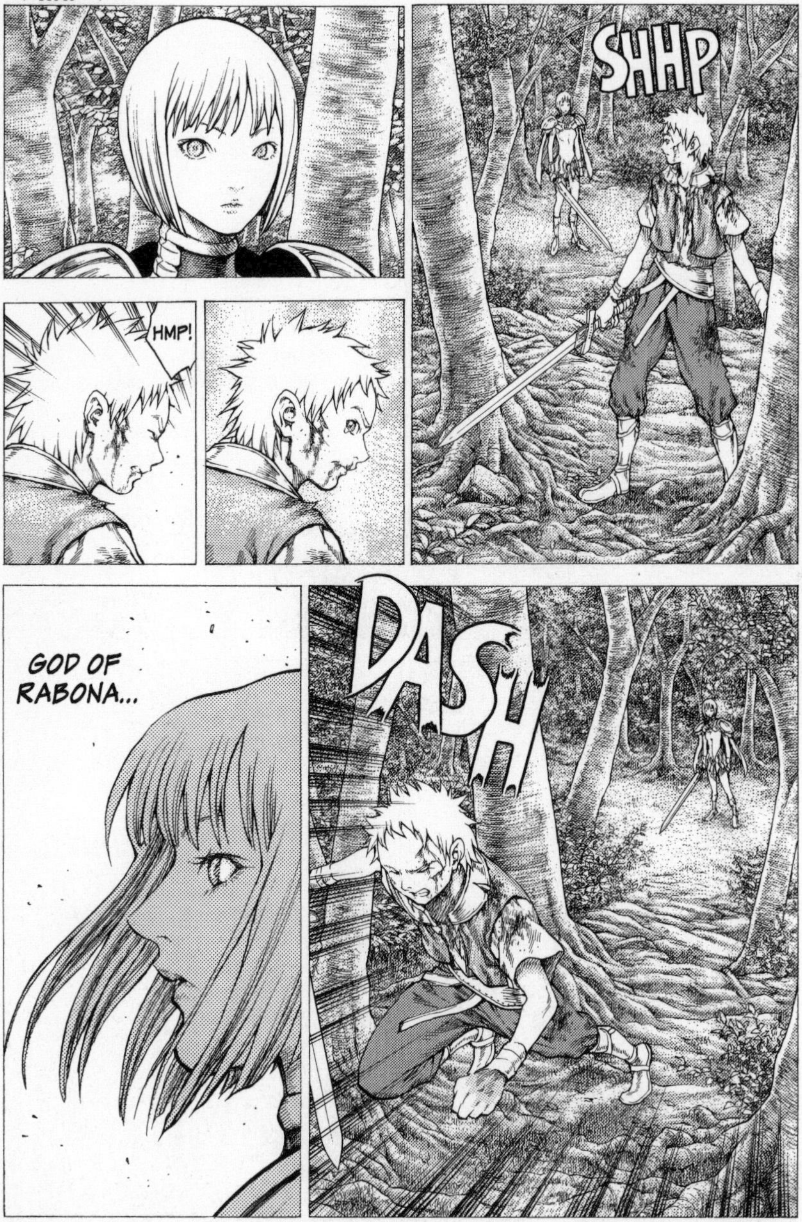
SHHP
HMP!
DASH
GOD OF RABONA...

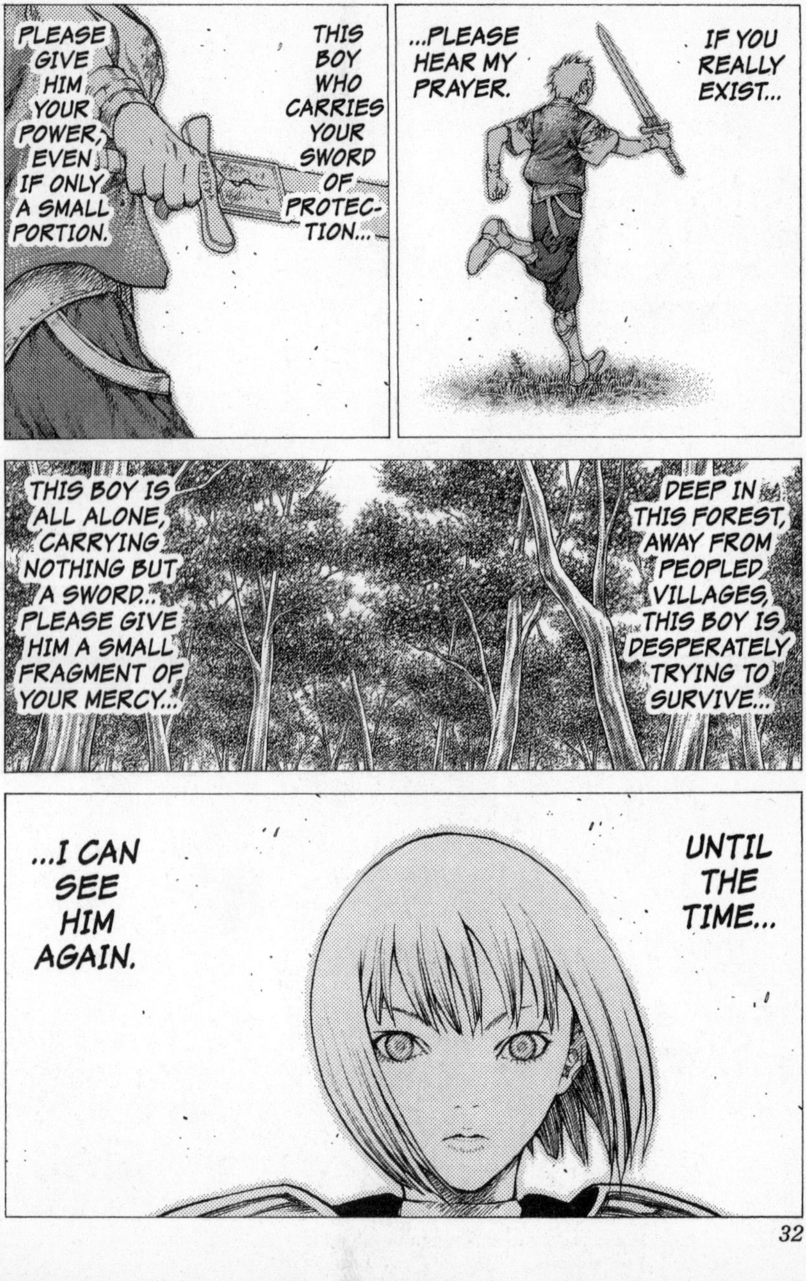
IF YOU REALLY EXIST...
...PLEASE HEAR MY PRAYER.
THIS BOY WHO CARRIES YOUR SWORD OF PROTECTION...
PLEASE GIVE HIM YOUR POWER, EVEN IF ONLY A SMALL PORTION.
DEEP IN THIS FOREST, AWAY FROM PEOPLED VILLAGES, THIS BOY IS DESPERATELY TRYING TO SURVIVE...
THIS BOY IS ALL ALONE, CARRYING NOTHING BUT A SWORD... PLEASE GIVE HIM A SMALL FRAGMENT OF YOUR MERCY...
UNTIL THE TIME...
...I CAN SEE HIM AGAIN.

READ THIS WAY

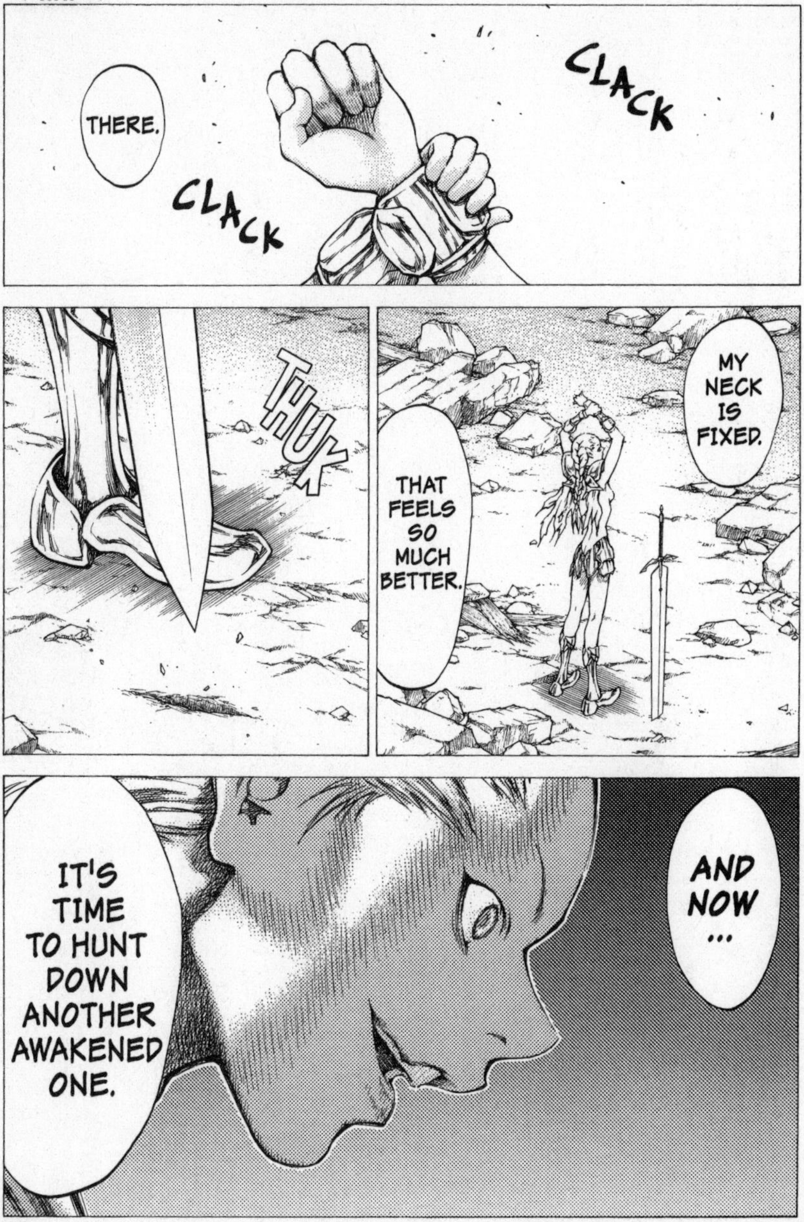
CLACK
THERE.
CLACK
MY NECK IS FIXED.
THAT FEELS SO MUCH BETTER.
THUK
AND NOW...
IT'S TIME TO HUNT DOWN ANOTHER AWAKENED ONE.

クレイモア
Claymore™

Scene 35: The Endless Gravestones, Part 5

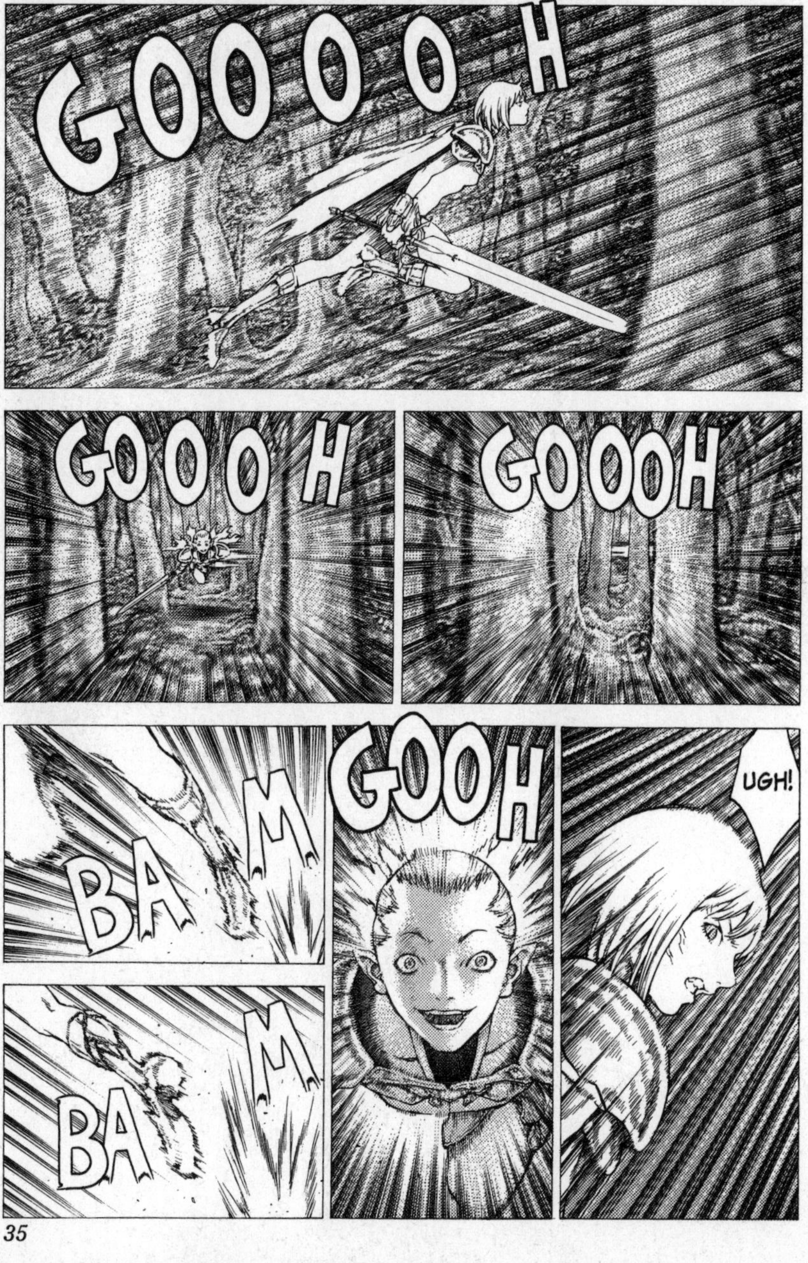
GOOOOH
GOOOH
GOOOH
UGH!
GOOH
BAM
BAM

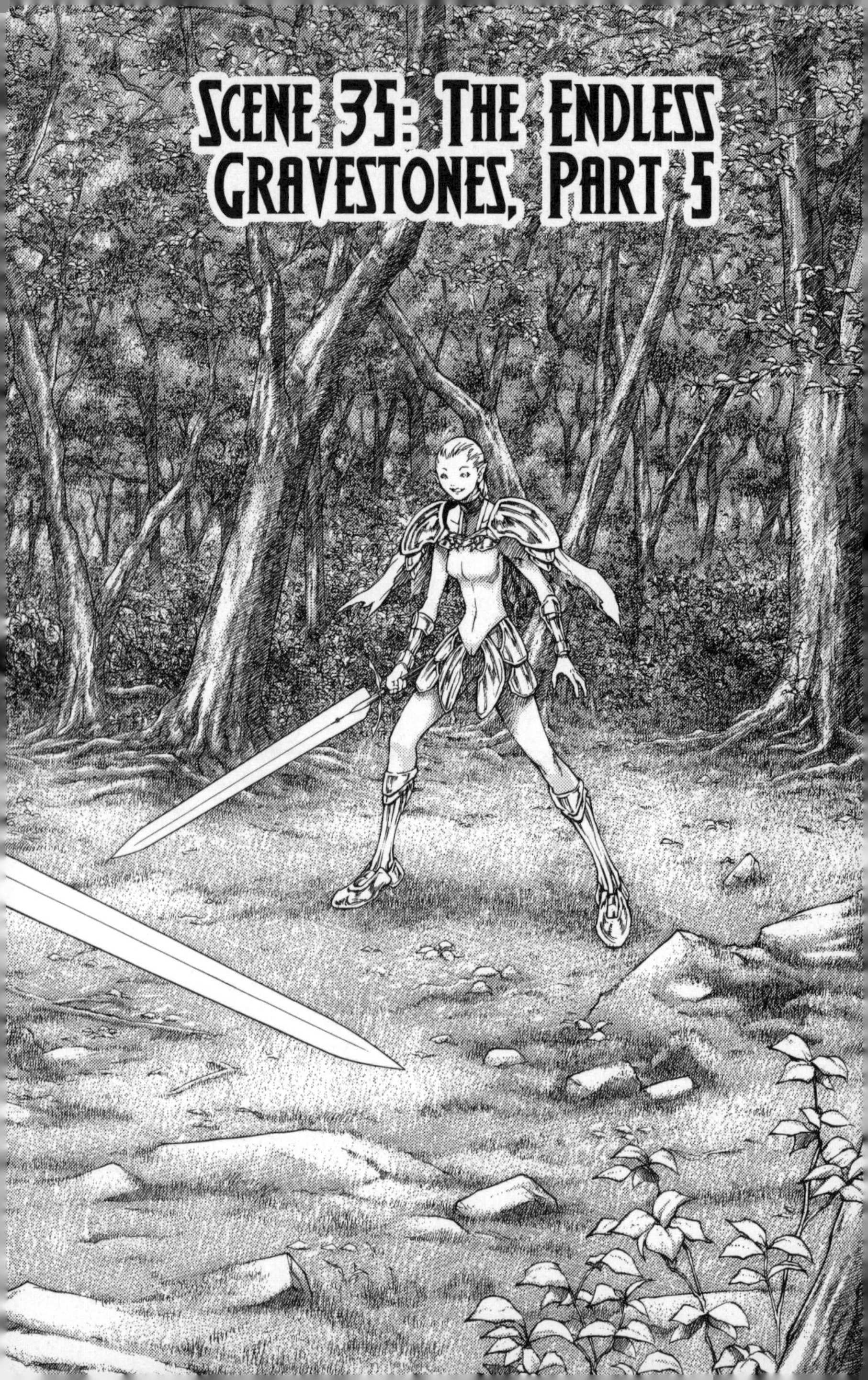
Scene 35: The Endless
Gravestones, Part 5

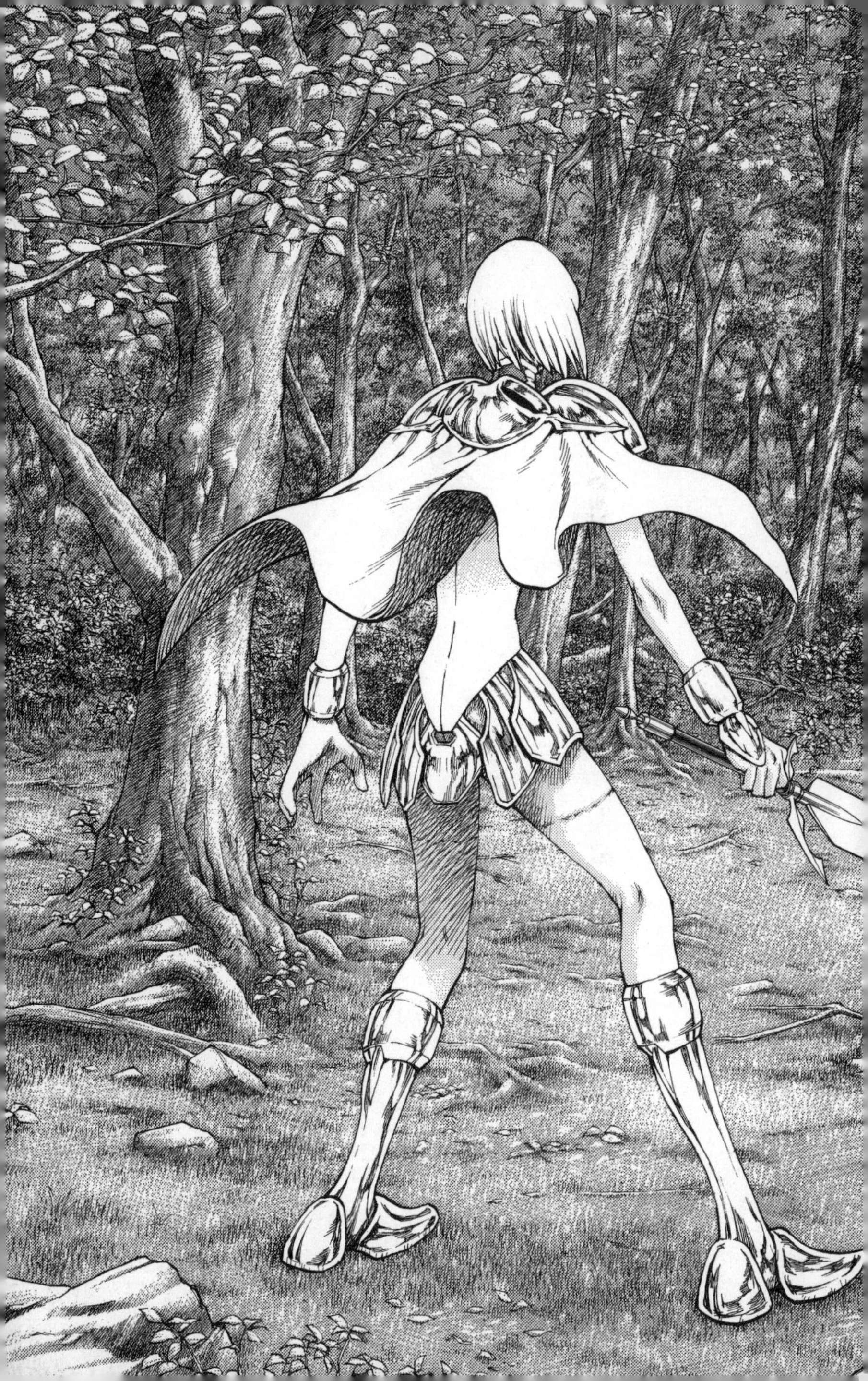

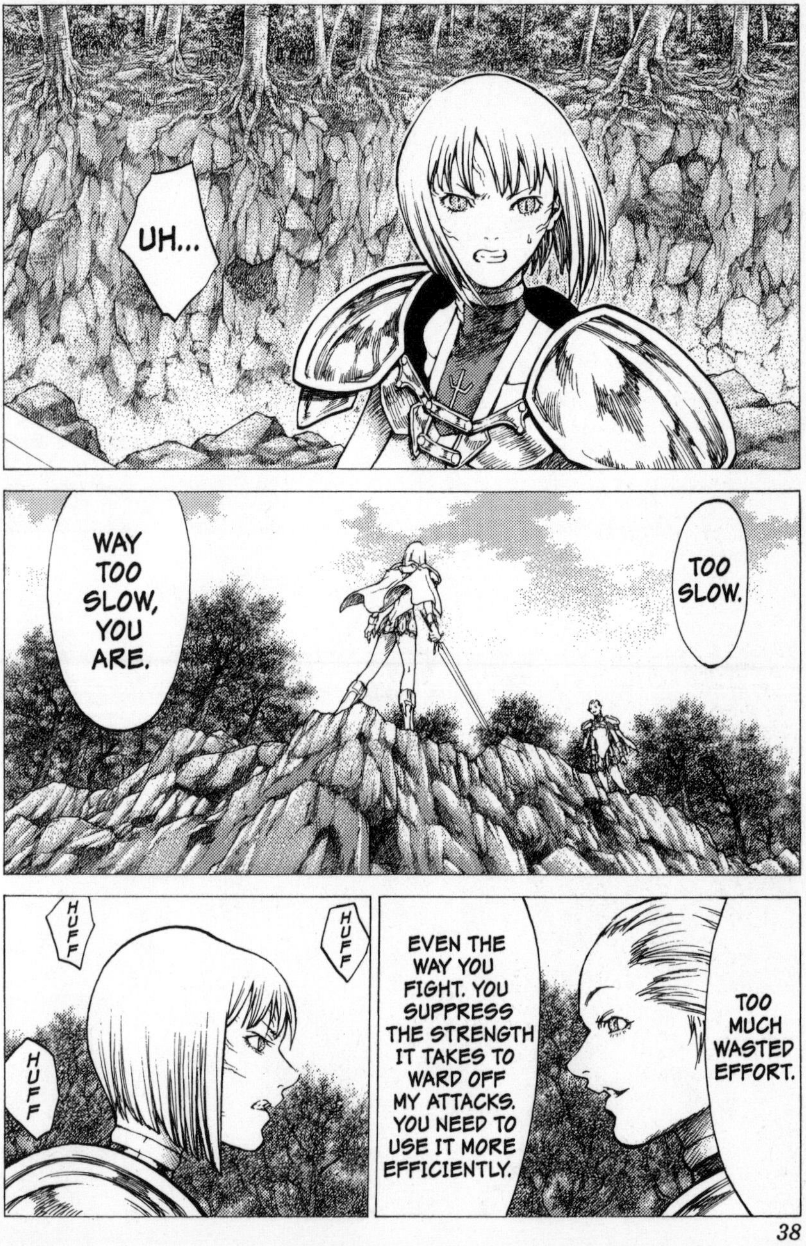
UH...
TOO SLOW.
WAY TOO SLOW, YOU ARE.
TOO MUCH WASTED EFFORT.
EVEN THE WAY YOU FIGHT. YOU SUPPRESS THE STRENGTH IT TAKES TO WARD OFF MY ATTACKS. YOU NEED TO USE IT MORE EFFICIENTLY.
HUFF
HUFF
HUFF

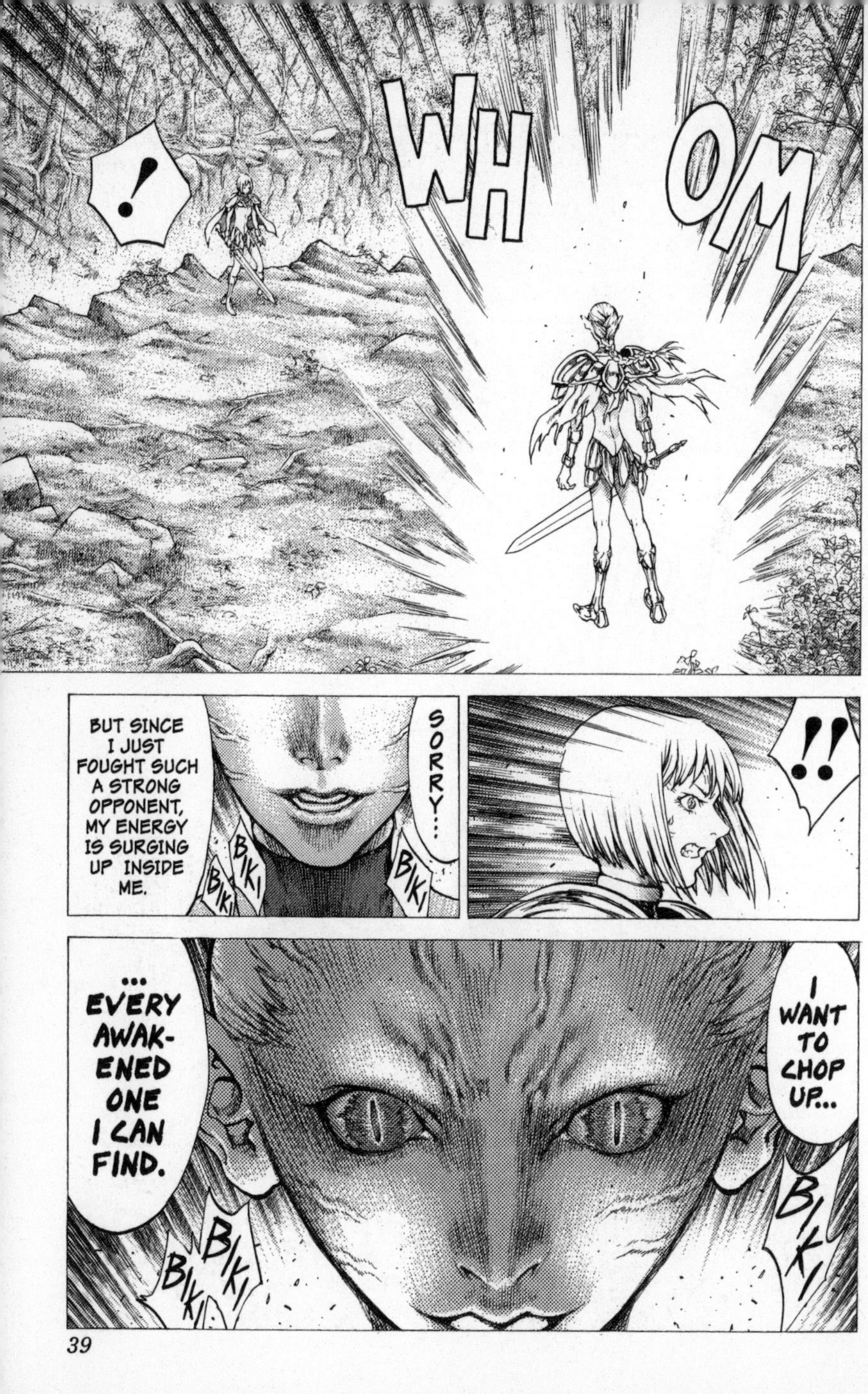
WH OM
!
!!
SORRY...
BUT SINCE I JUST FOUGHT SUCH A STRONG OPPONENT, MY ENERGY IS SURGING UP INSIDE ME.
BIKI
BIKI BIKI
I WANT TO CHOP UP...
...EVERY AWAKENED ONE I CAN FIND.
BIKI
BIKI BIKI

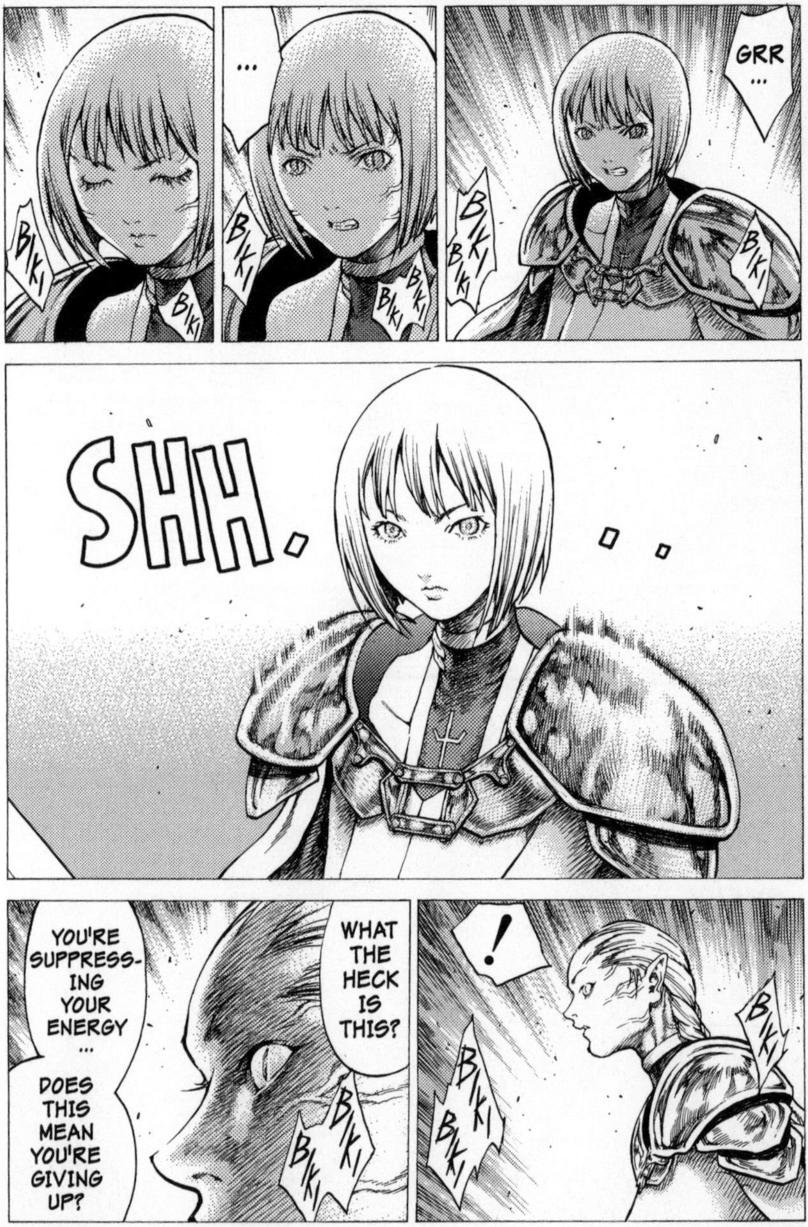
GRR ...
BIKI
BIKI
BIKI
BIKI
...
BIKI
BIKI
BIKI
BIKI
SHH. . .
!
BIKI
BIKI
BIKI
WHAT THE HECK IS THIS?
YOU'RE SUPPRESS-ING YOUR ENERGY ...
DOES THIS MEAN YOU'RE GIVING UP?
BIKI
BIKI

READ THIS WAY

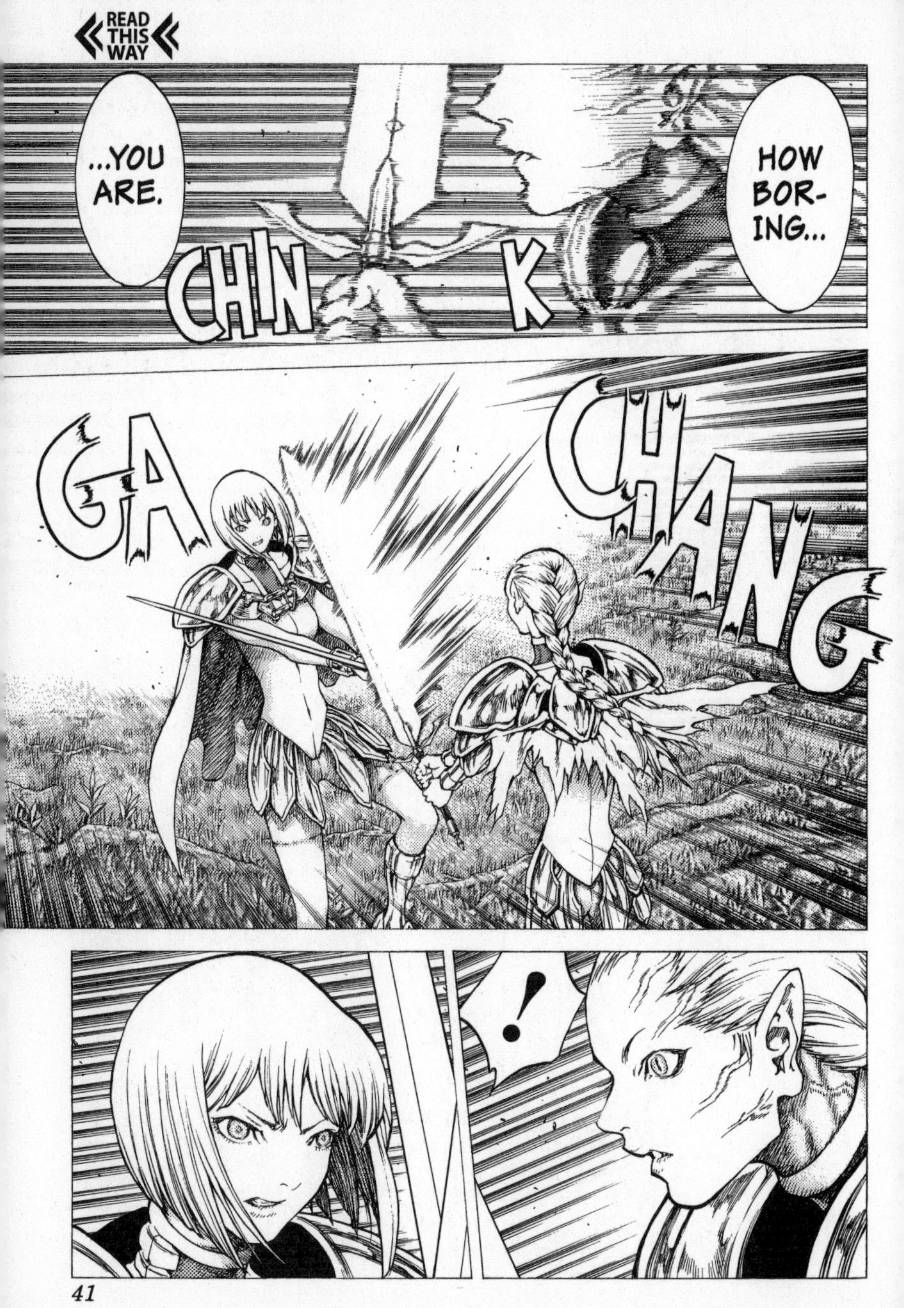
HOW BOR-ING...
CHIN K
...YOU ARE.
GA CHANG
!

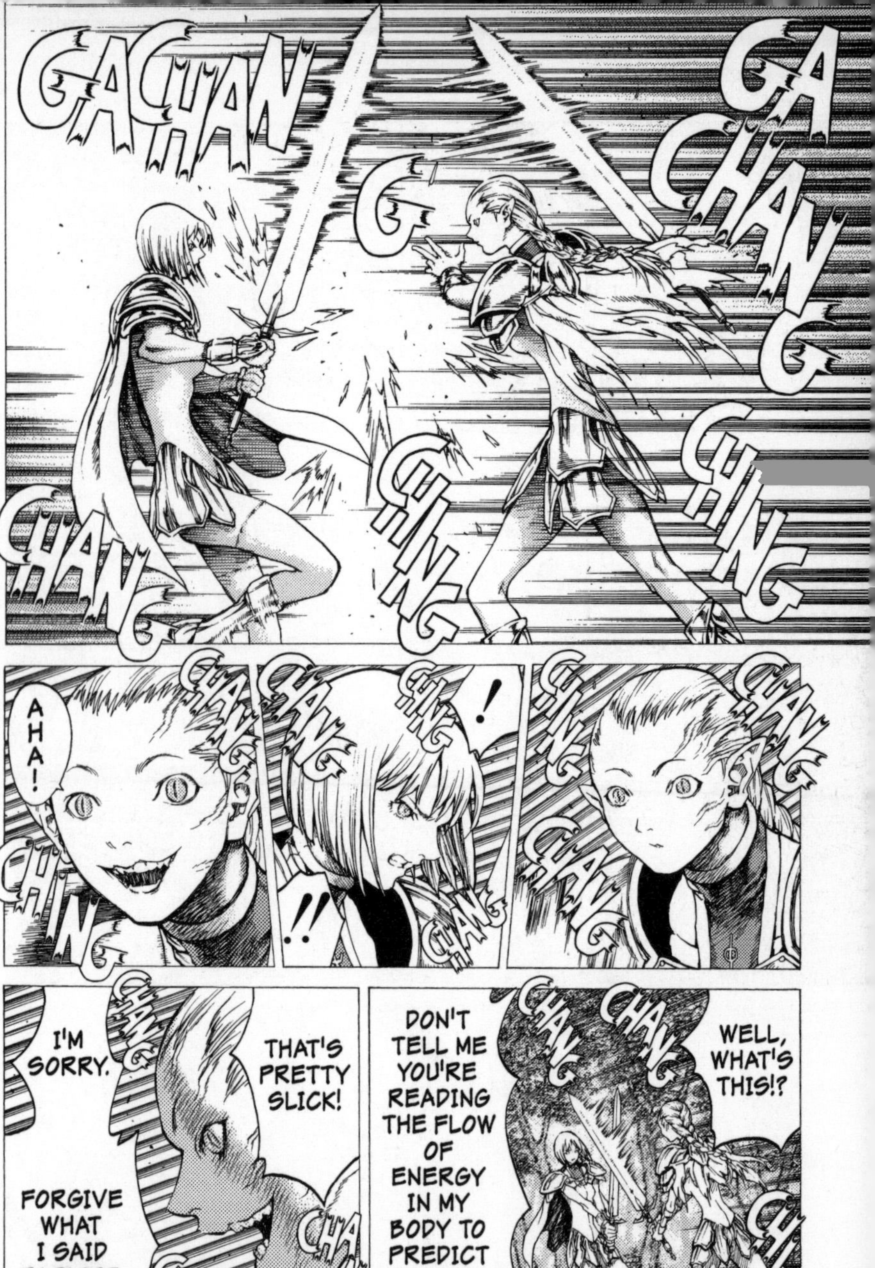
GA CHANG
G
CHING
CHING
GACHAN
CHANG
CHANG
CHING
CHANG
CHANG
CHING
!
CHANG
!!
CHANG
CHANG
AHA!
CHING
WELL, WHAT'S THIS!?
CHANG
CHANG
CHING
DON'T TELL ME YOU'RE READING THE FLOW OF ENERGY IN MY BODY TO PREDICT MY MOVEMENTS!
THAT'S PRETTY SLICK!
CHANG
CHANG
I'M SORRY.
FORGIVE WHAT I SAID EARLIER.
CHING

READ THIS WAY

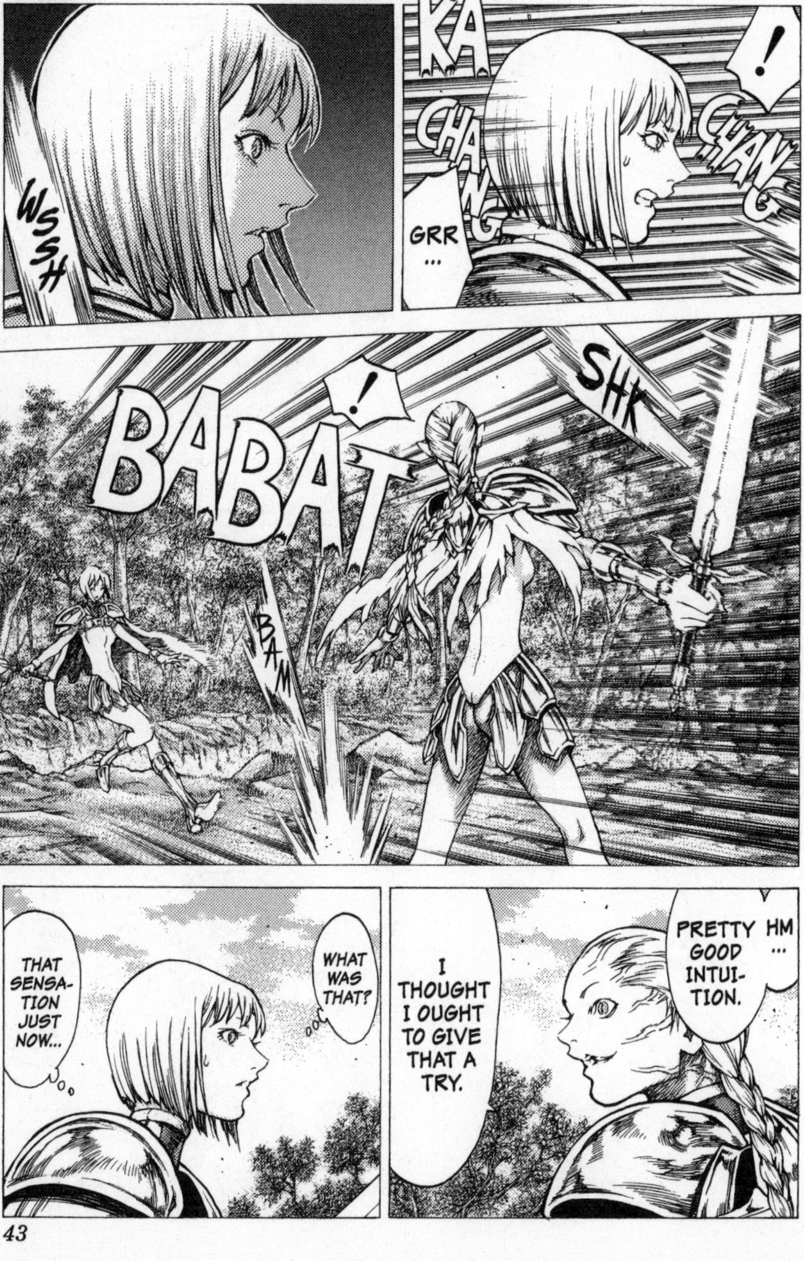
!
CHANG
KA
CHANG
GRR ...
WSSH
SHK
!
BABAT
BAM
HM ...
PRETTY GOOD INTUITION.
I THOUGHT I OUGHT TO GIVE THAT A TRY.
WHAT WAS THAT?
THAT SENSATION JUST NOW...

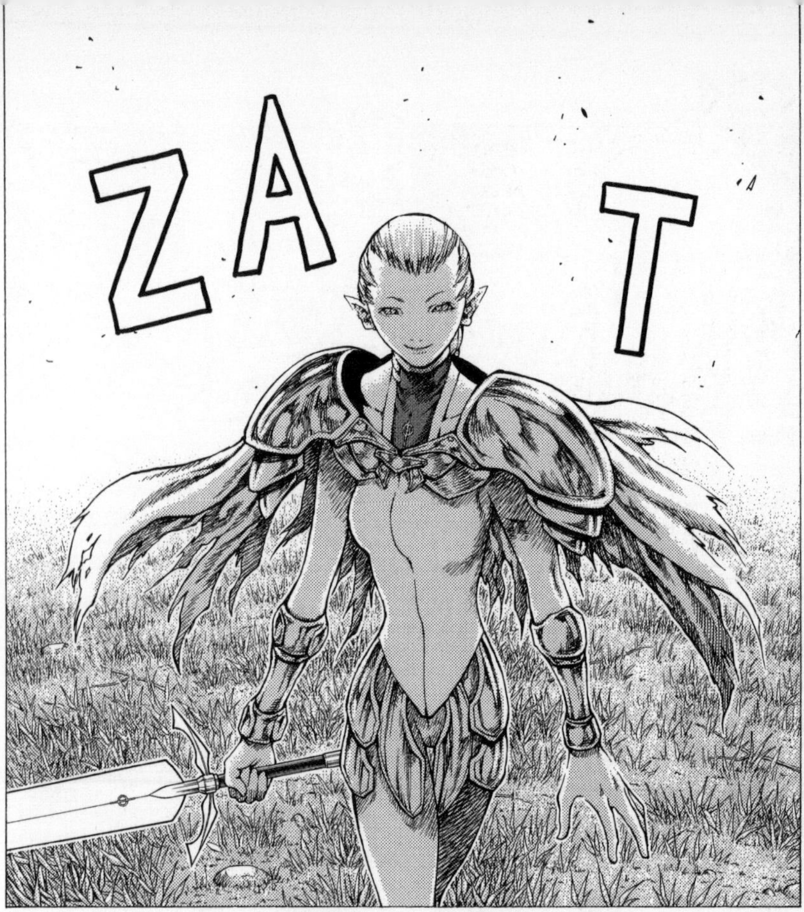
ZAT

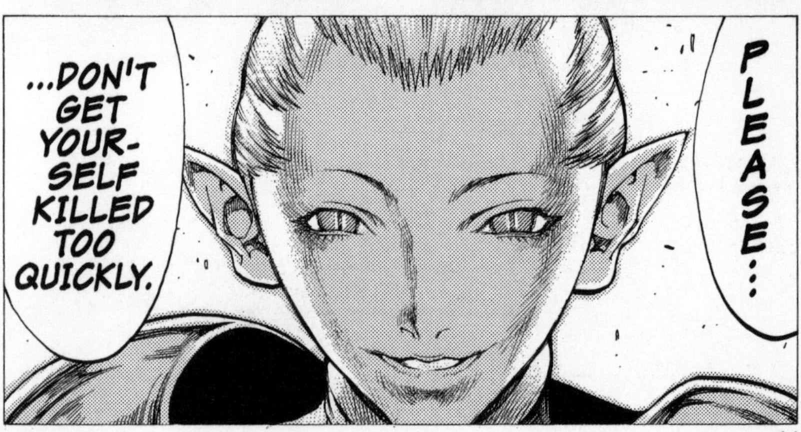
PLEASE...
...DON'T GET YOUR-SELF KILLED TOO QUICKLY.

READ THIS WAY

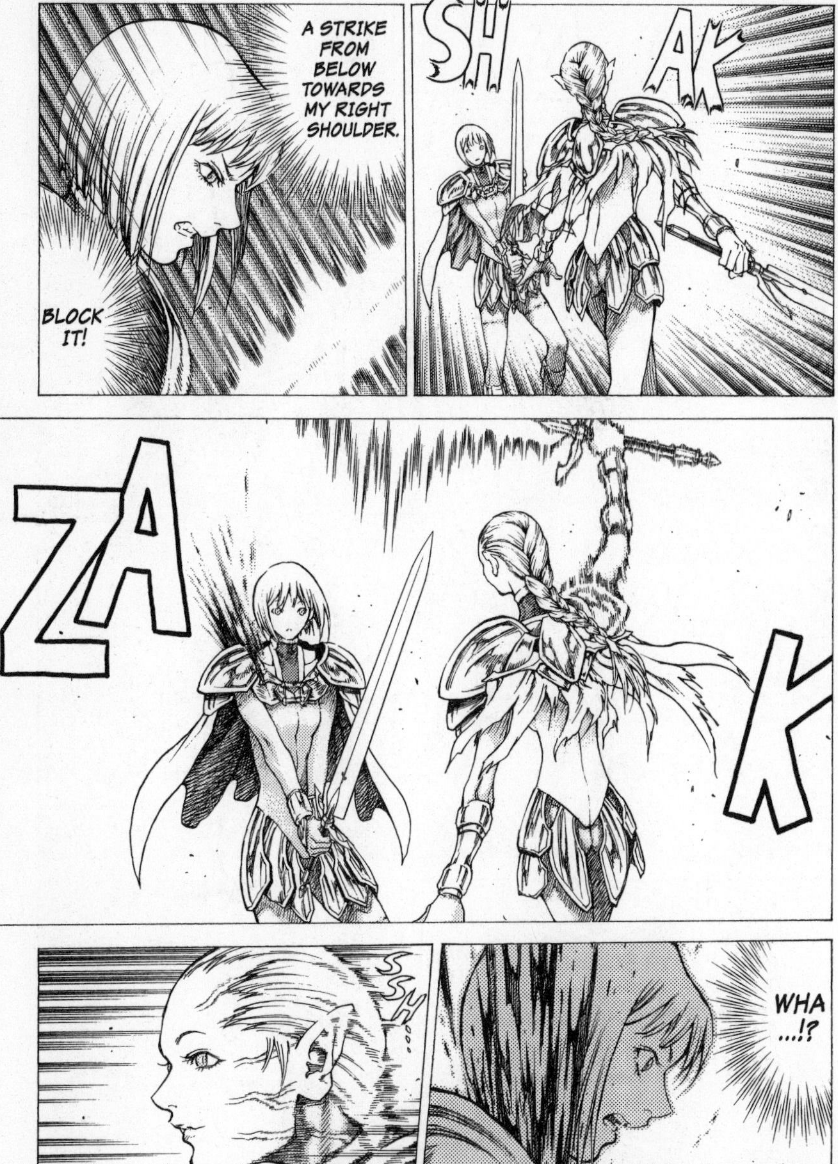
SHAK
A STRIKE FROM BELOW TOWARDS MY RIGHT SHOULDER.
BLOCK IT!
ZAK
WHA ...!?
SSH...

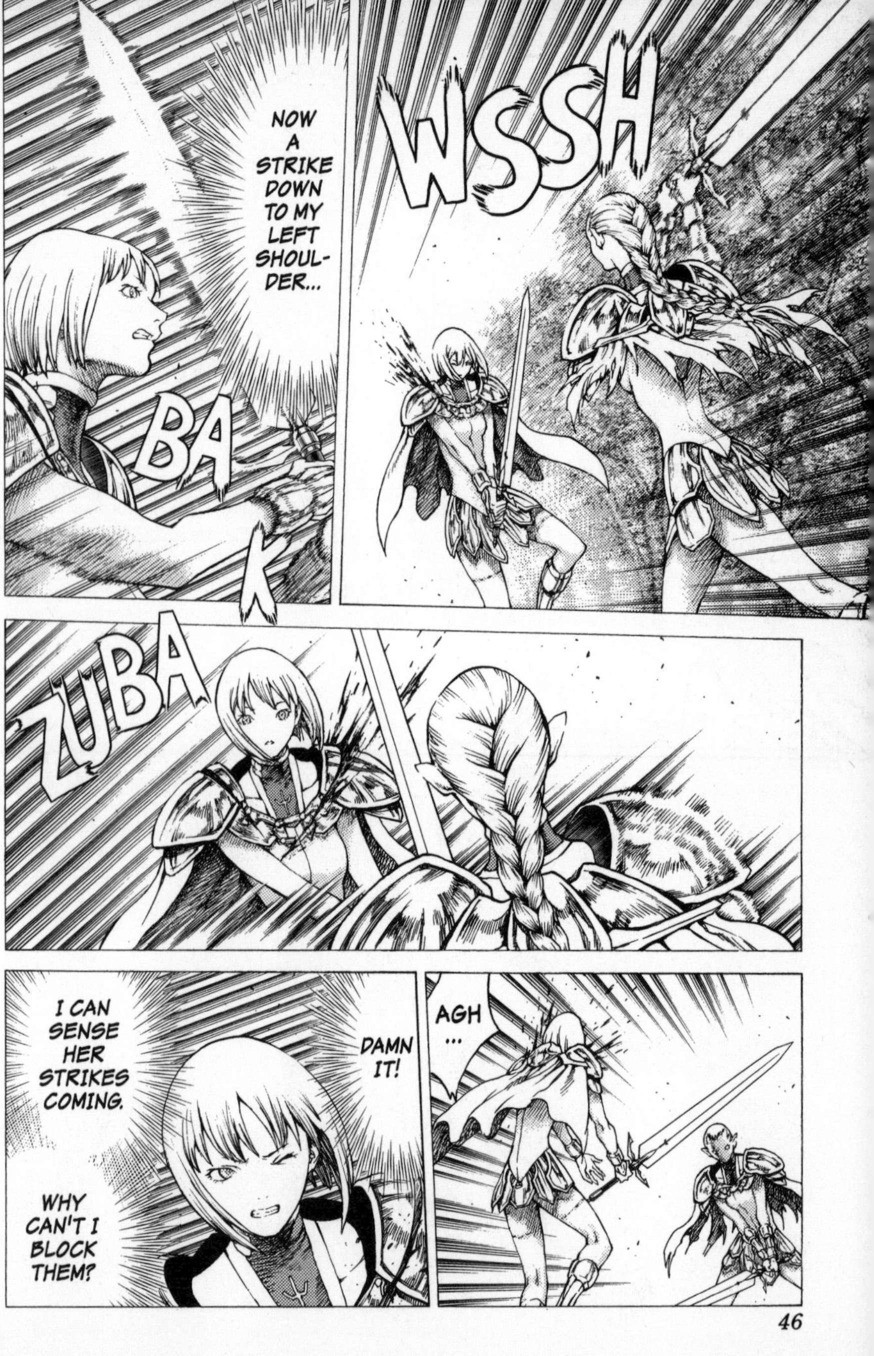
WSSH
NOW A STRIKE DOWN TO MY LEFT SHOULDER...
BAK
ZUBA
AGH...
DAMN IT!
I CAN SENSE HER STRIKES COMING.
WHY CAN'T I BLOCK THEM?

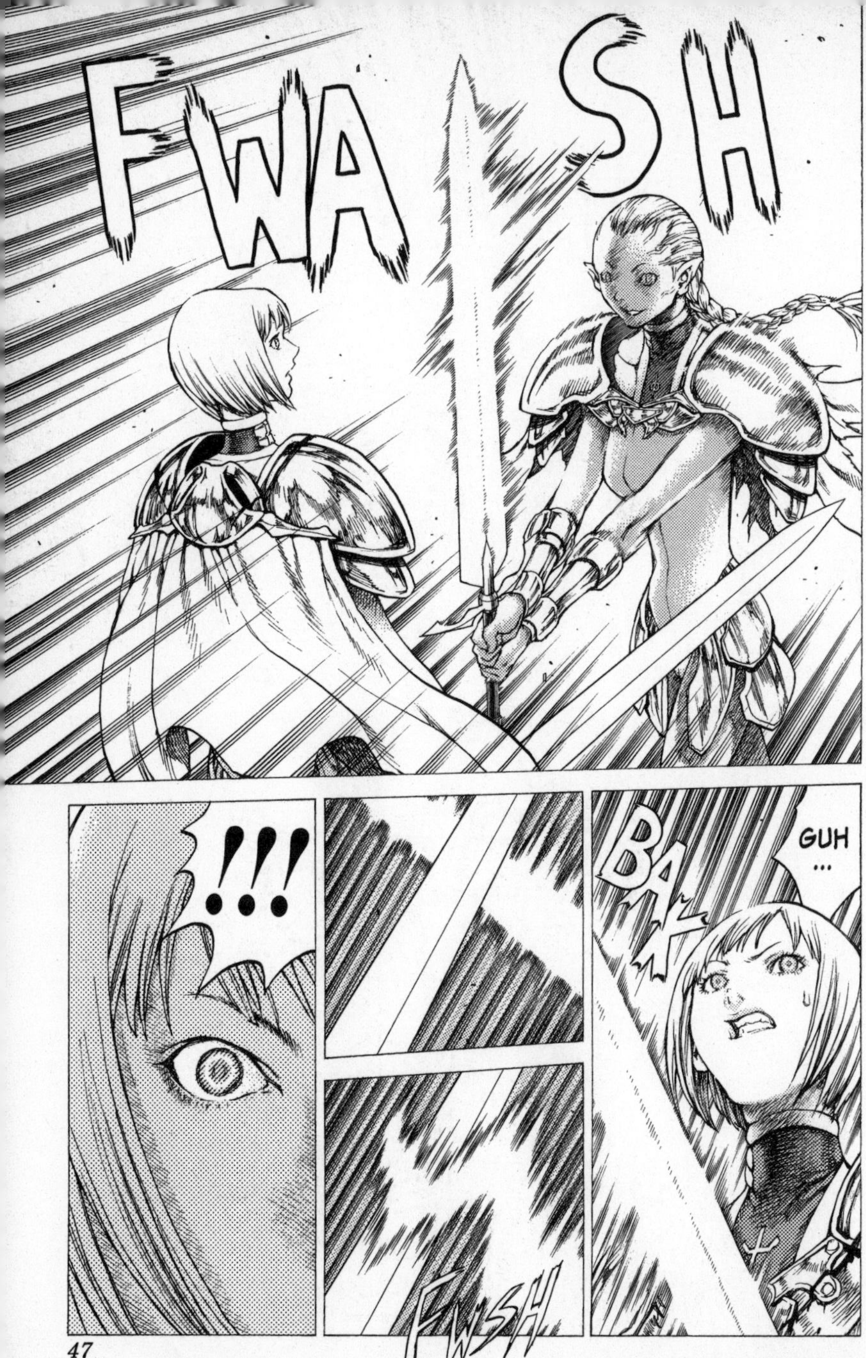
FWASH
BAK
GUH ...
FWSH
!!!

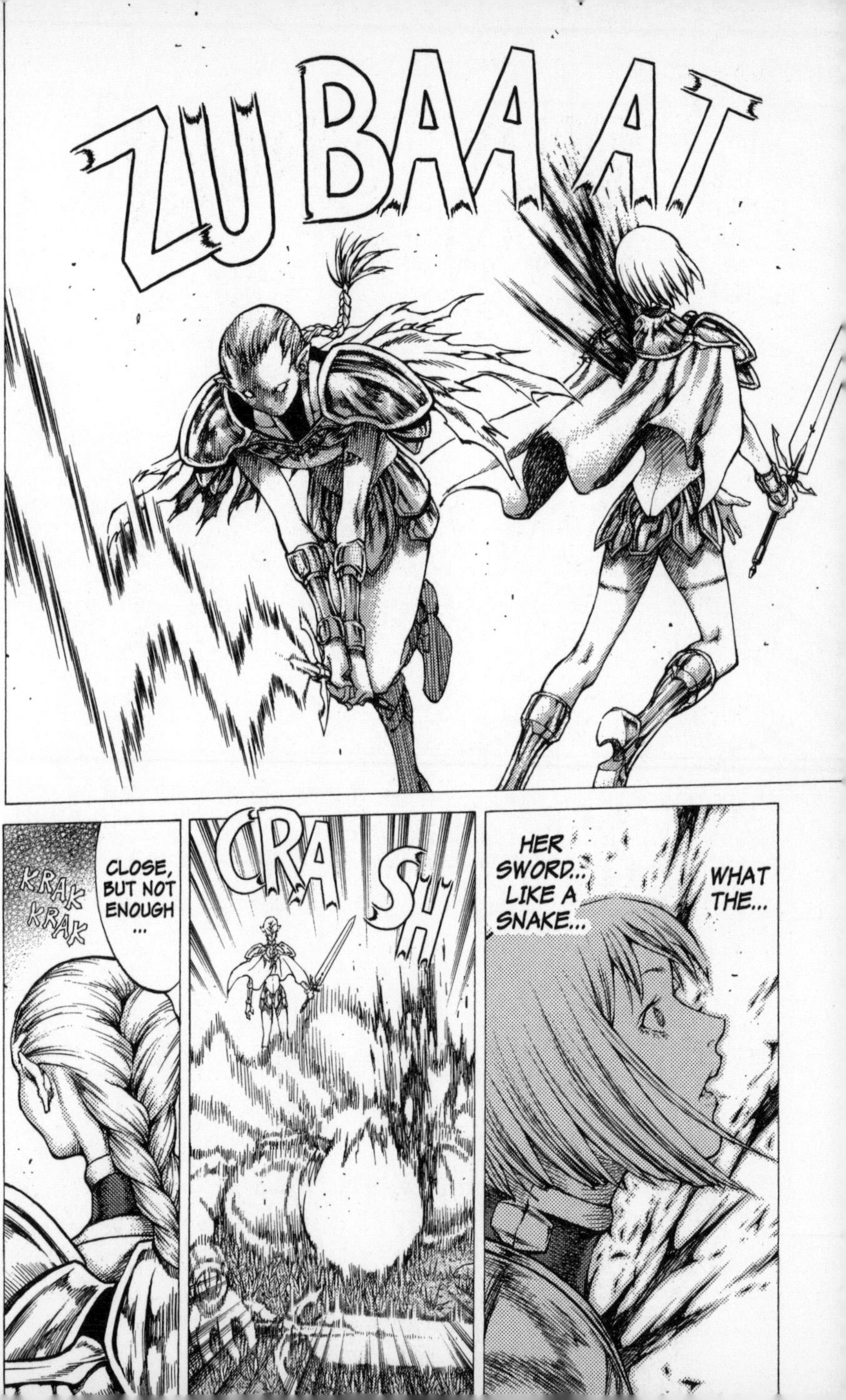
ZUBAAAT
WHAT THE...
HER SWORD... LIKE A SNAKE...
CRASH
CLOSE, BUT NOT ENOUGH ...
KRAK KRAK

READ THIS WAY

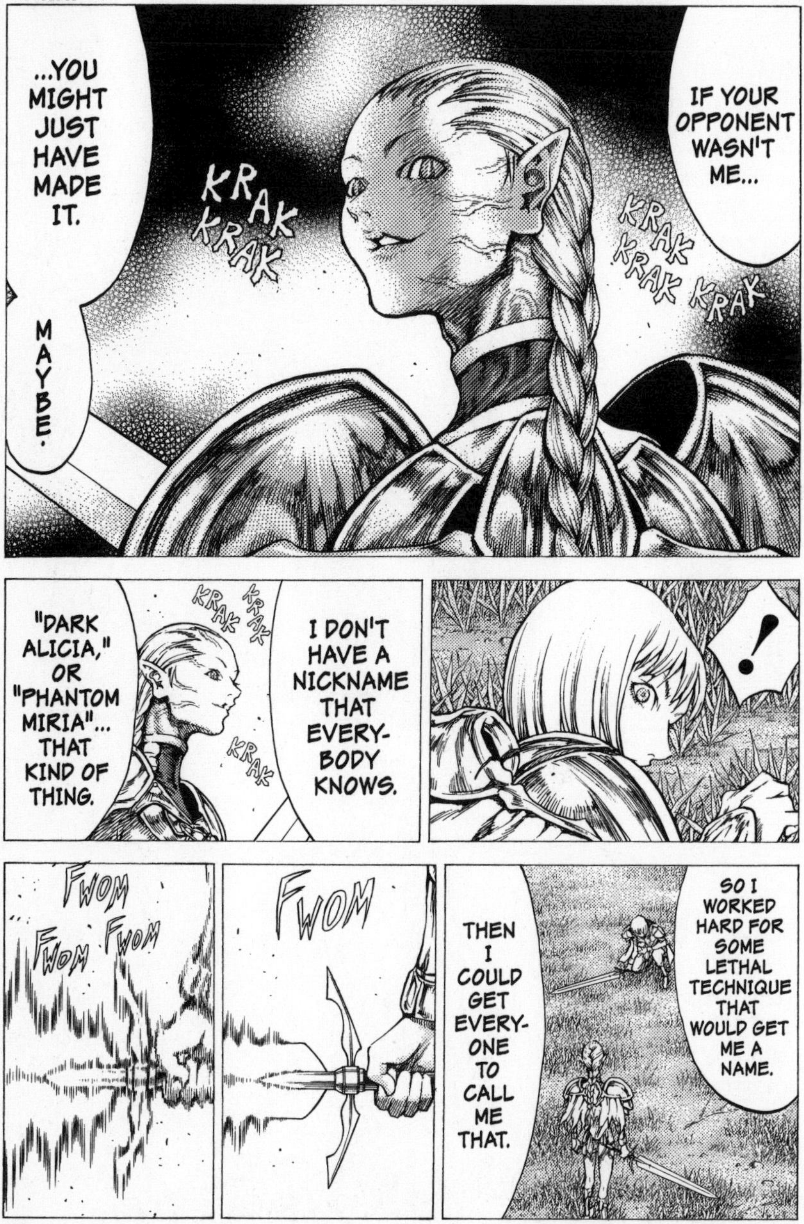
IF YOUR OPPONENT WASN'T ME...
KRAK KRAK KRAK KRAK
KRAK KRAK
...YOU MIGHT JUST HAVE MADE IT.
MAYBE.
!
KRAK KRAK
I DON'T HAVE A NICKNAME THAT EVERYBODY KNOWS.
"DARK ALICIA," OR "PHANTOM MIRIA"... THAT KIND OF THING.
KRAK
SO I WORKED HARD FOR SOME LETHAL TECHNIQUE THAT WOULD GET ME A NAME.
THEN I COULD GET EVERYONE TO CALL ME THAT.
FWOM
FWOM
FWOM FWOM

THIS IS CALLED THE "RIPPLING SWORD."
FWOM
FWOM
FWOM
FWOM
"RIPPLING OPHELIA"... GREAT NAME, DON'T YOU THINK?
BUT IT'S NOT TOO WELL KNOWN YET.
FWOM
FWOM
FWOM
BECAUSE MOST OF THE PEOPLE WHO'VE SEEN IT ARE DEAD.

READ THIS WAY

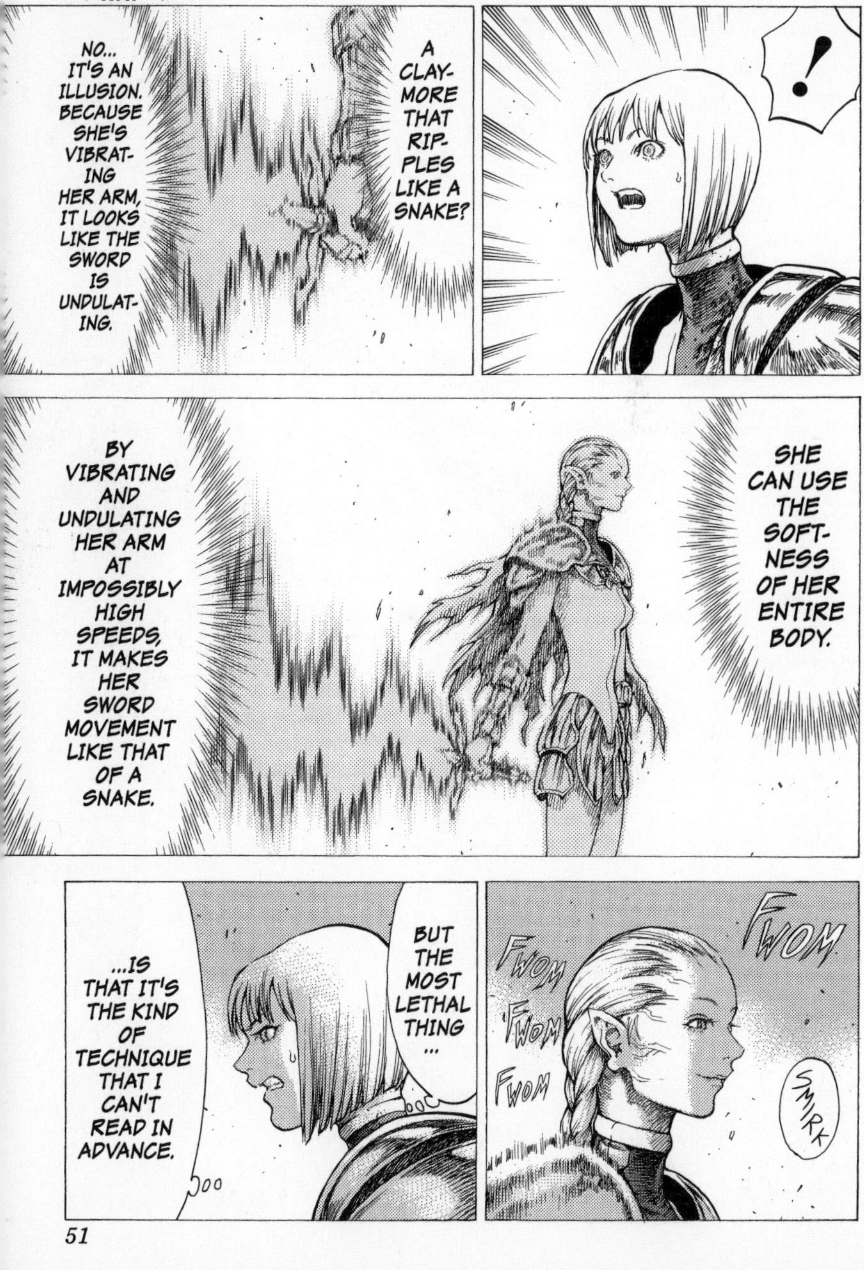

!
A CLAYMORE THAT RIPPLES LIKE A SNAKE?
NO... IT'S AN ILLUSION. BECAUSE SHE'S VIBRATING HER ARM, IT LOOKS LIKE THE SWORD IS UNDULATING.
SHE CAN USE THE SOFTNESS OF HER ENTIRE BODY.
BY VIBRATING AND UNDULATING HER ARM AT IMPOSSIBLY HIGH SPEEDS, IT MAKES HER SWORD MOVEMENT LIKE THAT OF A SNAKE.
FWOM
FWOM
FWOM
FWOM
SMIRK
BUT THE MOST LETHAL THING...
...IS THAT IT'S THE KIND OF TECHNIQUE THAT I CAN'T READ IN ADVANCE.

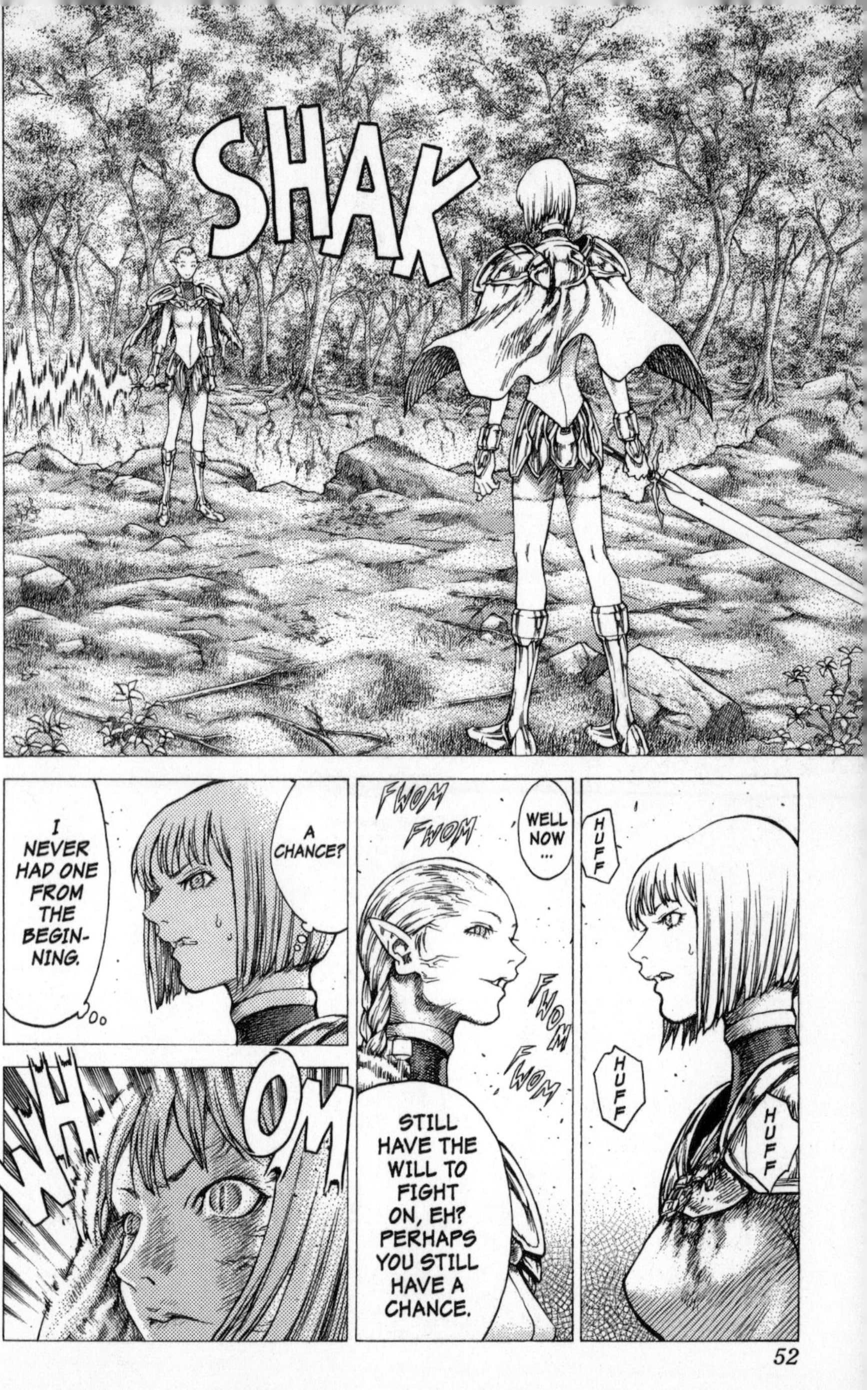
SHAK
HUFF
HUFF
HUFF
FWOM FWOM
WELL NOW ...
FWOM FWOM
STILL HAVE THE WILL TO FIGHT ON, EH? PERHAPS YOU STILL HAVE A CHANCE.
A CHANCE?
I NEVER HAD ONE FROM THE BEGIN-NING.
WHOM

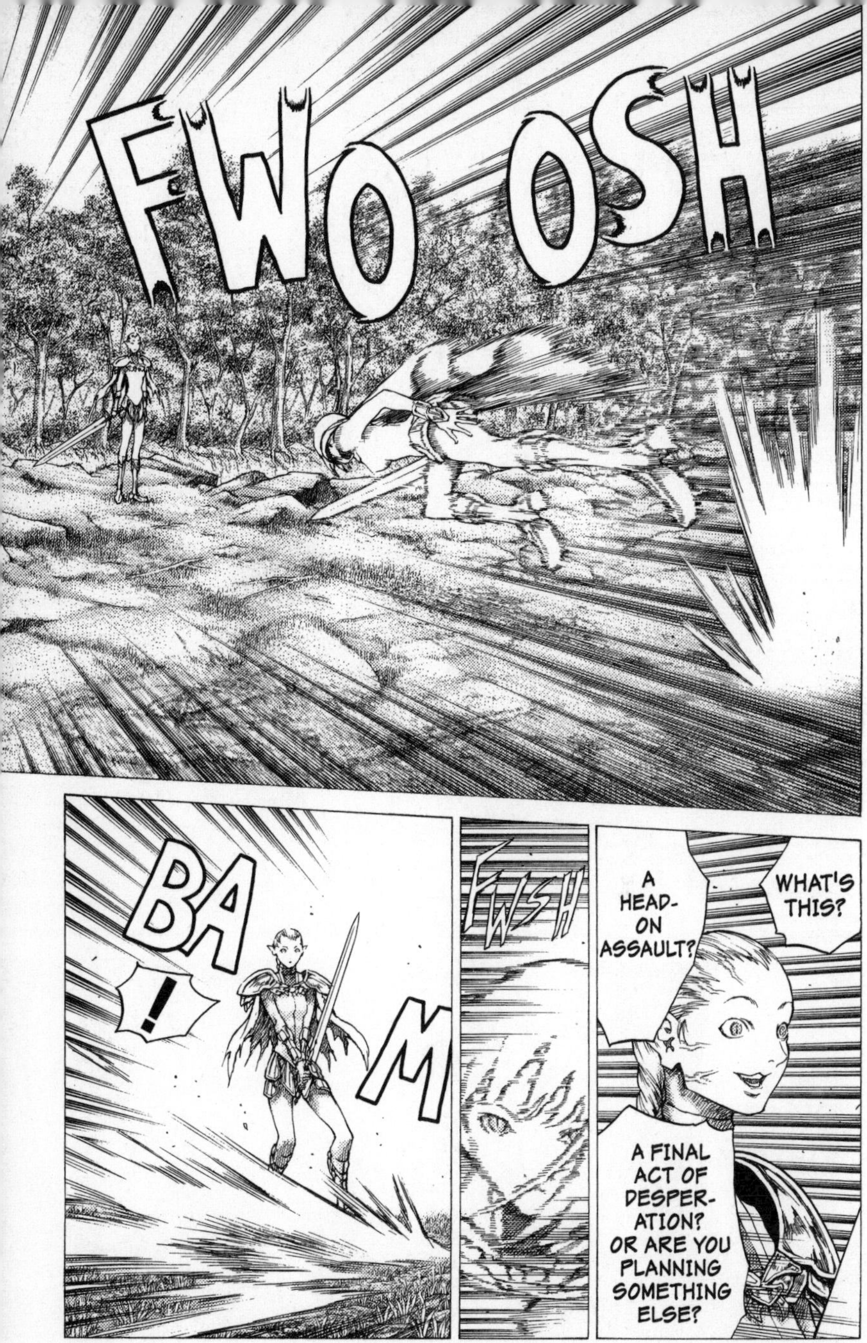
FWOOSH
WHAT'S THIS?
A HEAD-ON ASSAULT?
A FINAL ACT OF DESPERATION? OR ARE YOU PLANNING SOMETHING ELSE?
FWSH
BAM
!

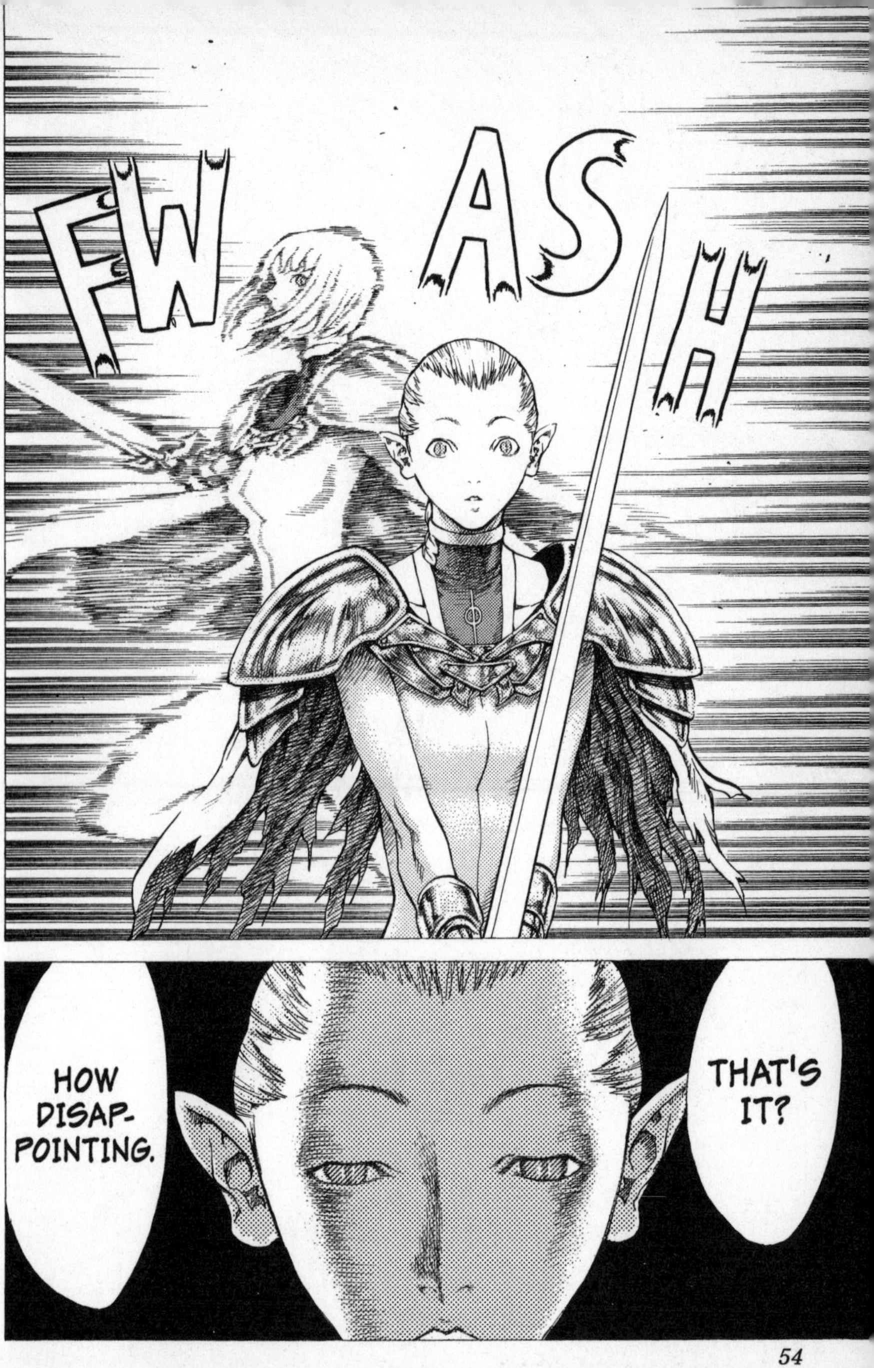
FWASH
THAT'S IT?
HOW DISAP-POINTING.

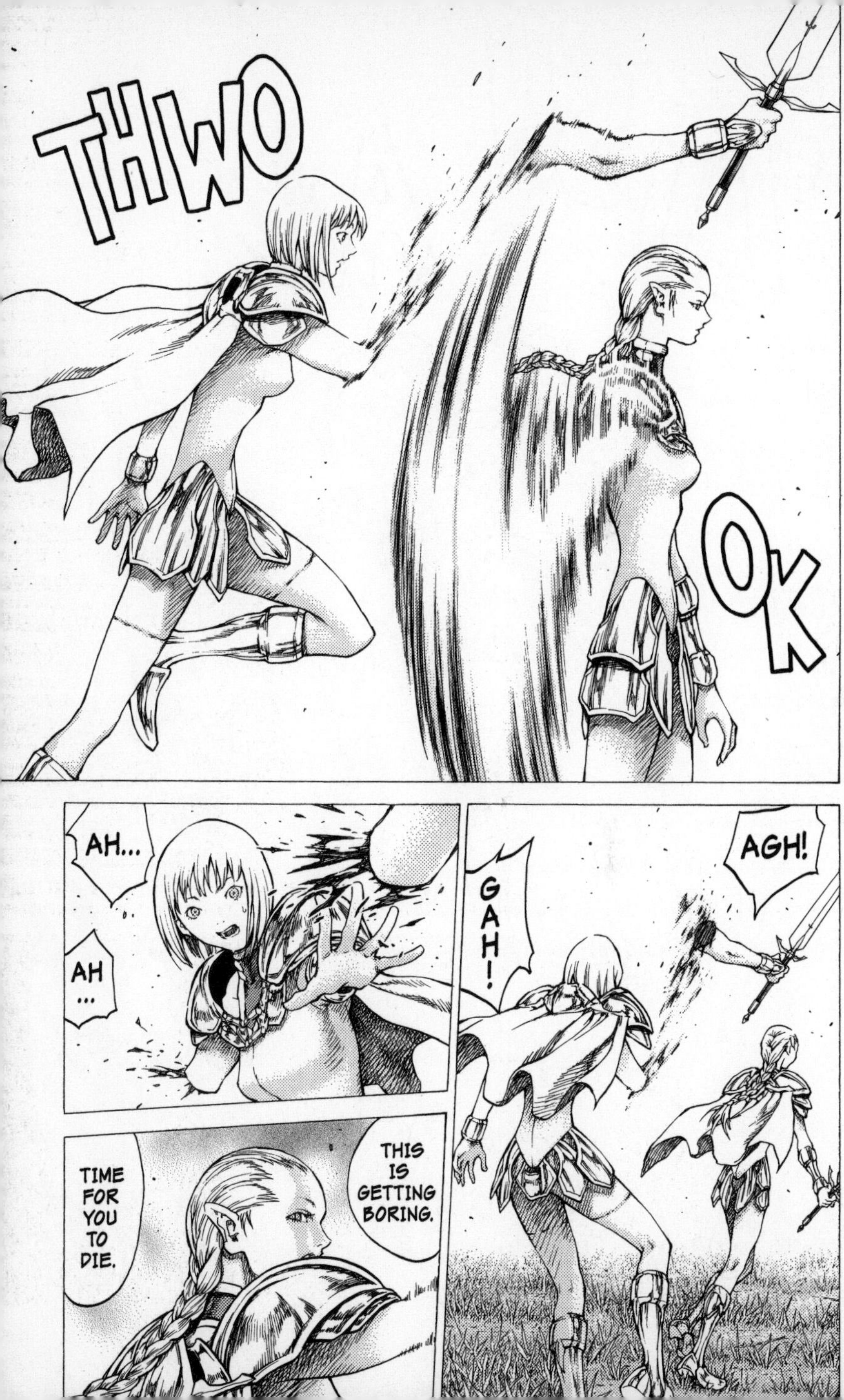
THWO
OK
AGH!
GAH!
AH...
AH ...
THIS IS GETTING BORING.
TIME FOR YOU TO DIE.

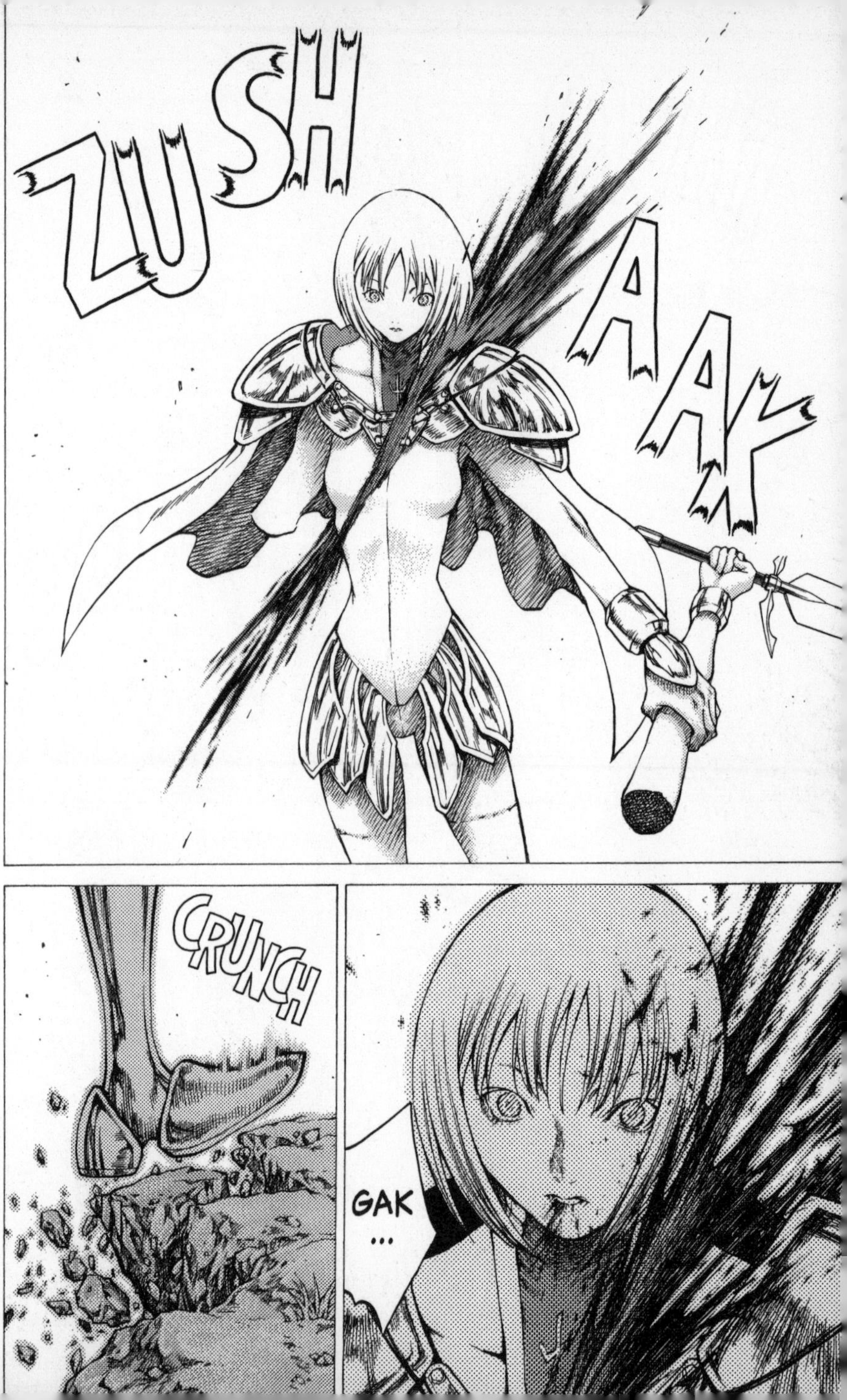
ZUSH
AAAK
GAK ...
CRUNCH

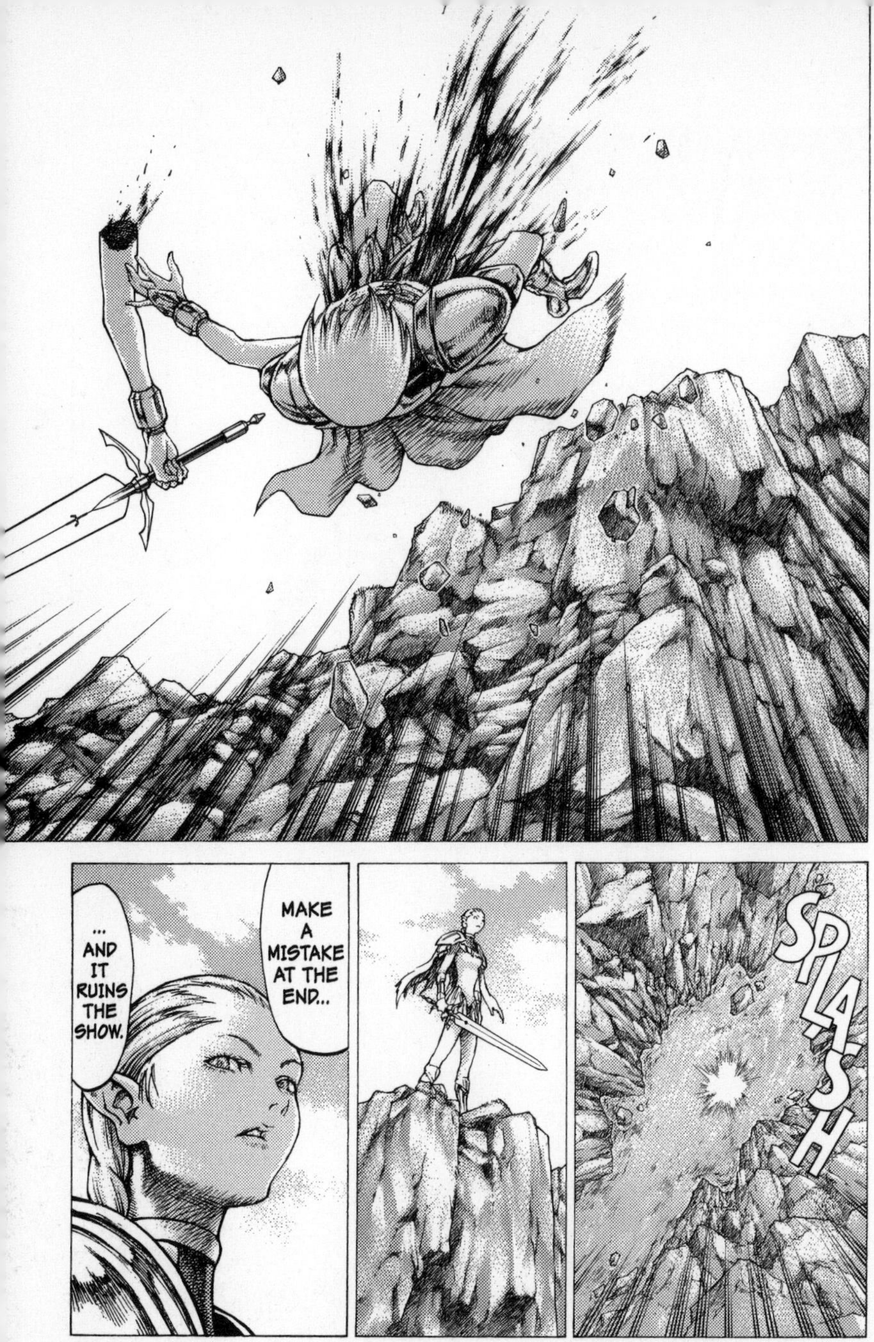
SPLASH
MAKE A MISTAKE AT THE END...
...AND IT RUINS THE SHOW.

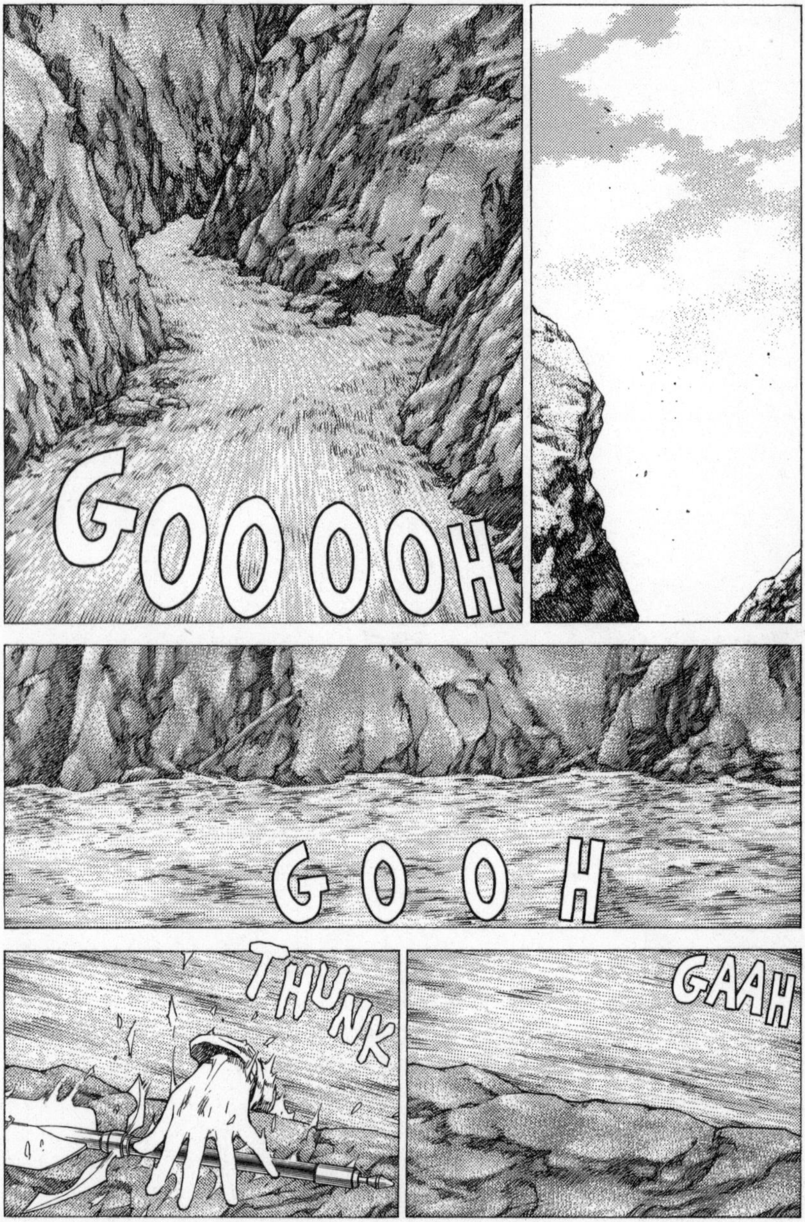
GOOOOH
GOOOH
GAAH
THUNK

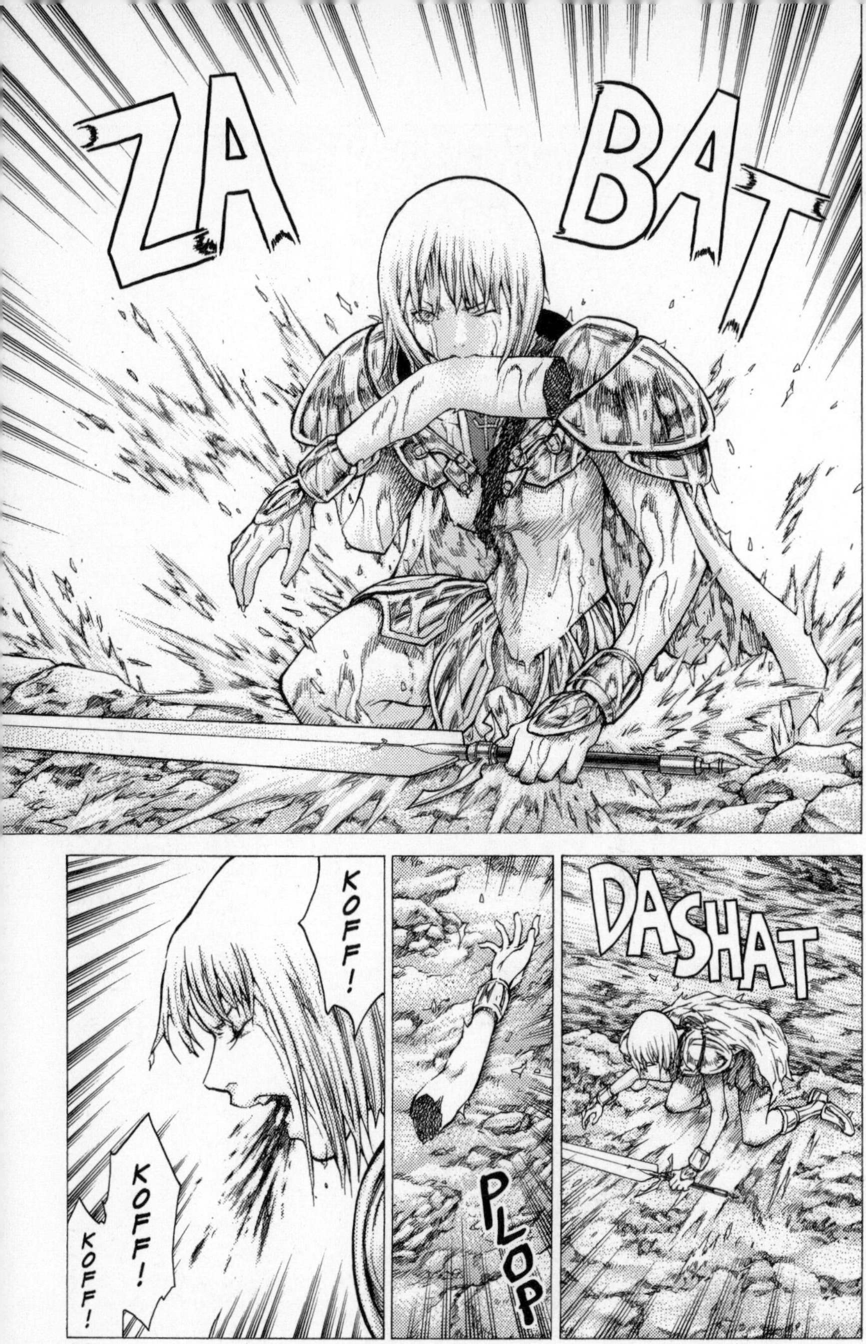
ZA BAT
DASHAT
PLOP
KOFF!
KOFF!
KOFF!

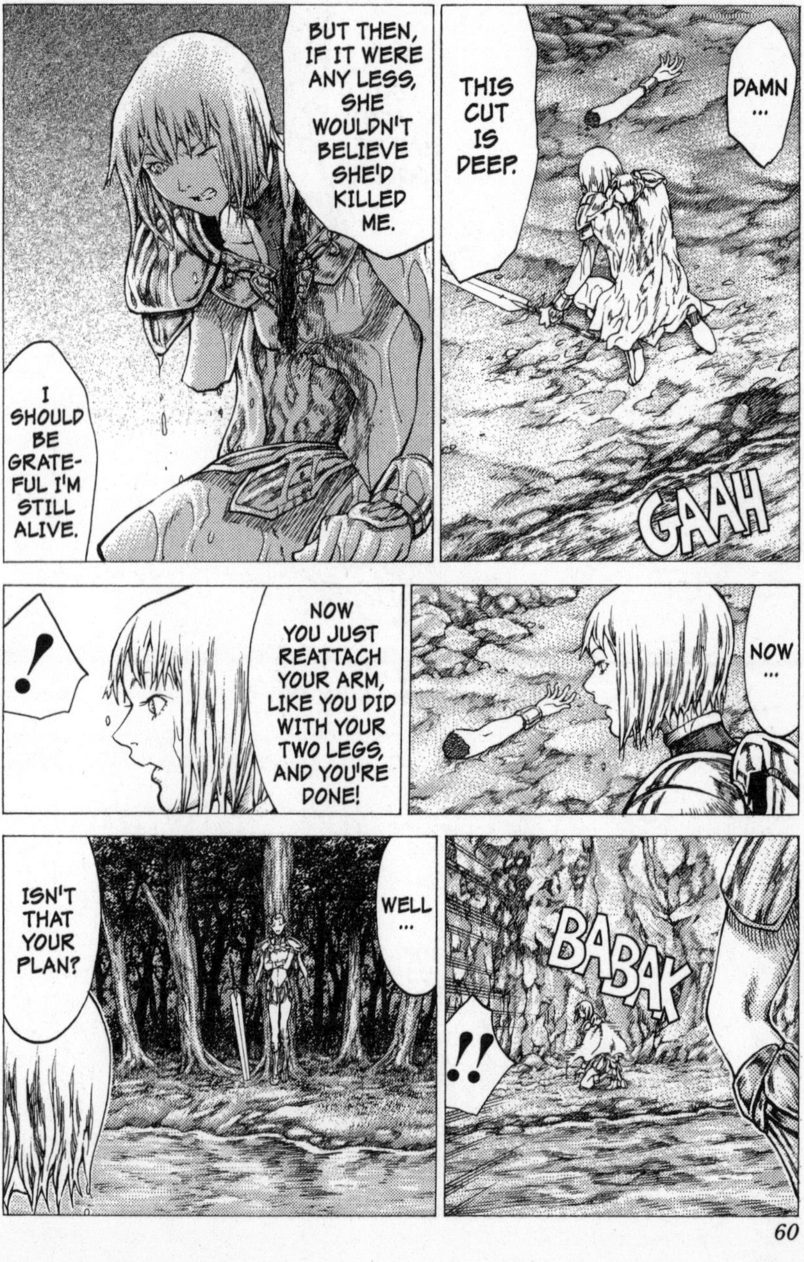
DAMN ...
THIS CUT IS DEEP.
GAAH
BUT THEN, IF IT WERE ANY LESS, SHE WOULDN'T BELIEVE SHE'D KILLED ME.
I SHOULD BE GRATE-FUL I'M STILL ALIVE.
NOW ...
NOW YOU JUST REATTACH YOUR ARM, LIKE YOU DID WITH YOUR TWO LEGS, AND YOU'RE DONE!
!
BABAK
!!
WELL ...
ISN'T THAT YOUR PLAN?

READ THIS WAY

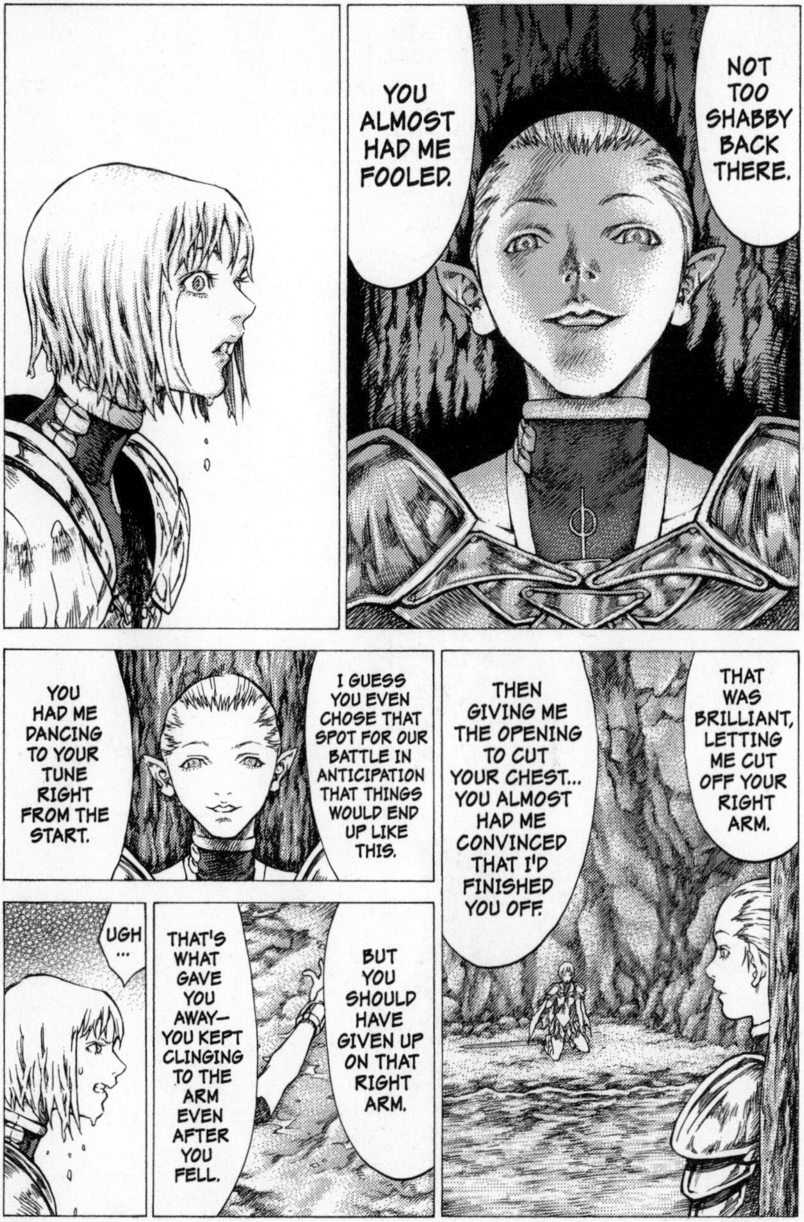

NOT TOO SHABBY BACK THERE.
YOU ALMOST HAD ME FOOLED.
THAT WAS BRILLIANT, LETTING ME CUT OFF YOUR RIGHT ARM.
THEN GIVING ME THE OPENING TO CUT YOUR CHEST... YOU ALMOST HAD ME CONVINCED THAT I'D FINISHED YOU OFF.
I GUESS YOU EVEN CHOSE THAT SPOT FOR OUR BATTLE IN ANTICIPATION THAT THINGS WOULD END UP LIKE THIS.
YOU HAD ME DANCING TO YOUR TUNE RIGHT FROM THE START.
BUT YOU SHOULD HAVE GIVEN UP ON THAT RIGHT ARM.
THAT'S WHAT GAVE YOU AWAY— YOU KEPT CLINGING TO THE ARM EVEN AFTER YOU FELL.
UGH ...

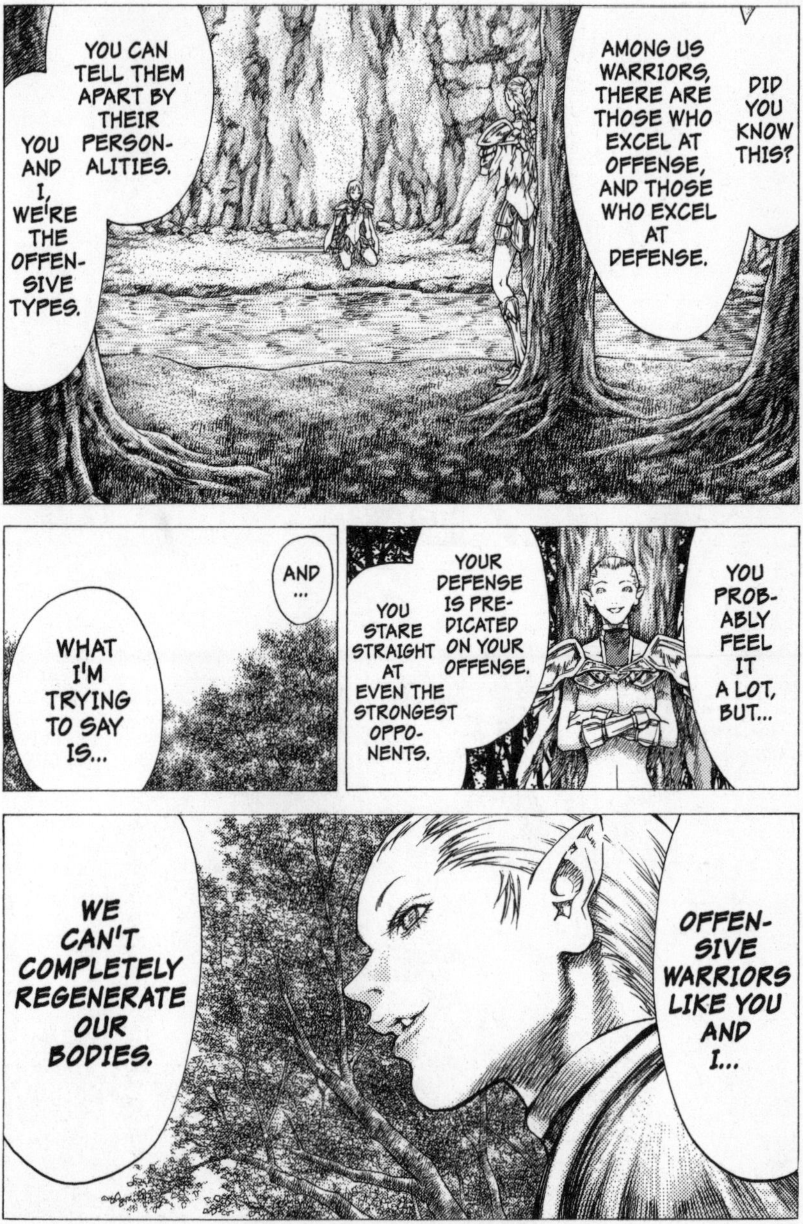
DID YOU KNOW THIS?
AMONG US WARRIORS, THERE ARE THOSE WHO EXCEL AT OFFENSE, AND THOSE WHO EXCEL AT DEFENSE.
YOU CAN TELL THEM APART BY THEIR PERSONALITIES.
YOU AND I, WE'RE THE OFFENSIVE TYPES.
YOU PROBABLY FEEL IT A LOT, BUT...
YOUR DEFENSE IS PREDICATED ON YOUR OFFENSE.
YOU STARE STRAIGHT AT EVEN THE STRONGEST OPPONENTS.
AND...
WHAT I'M TRYING TO SAY IS...
OFFENSIVE WARRIORS LIKE YOU AND I...
WE CAN'T COMPLETELY REGENERATE OUR BODIES.

READ THIS WAY

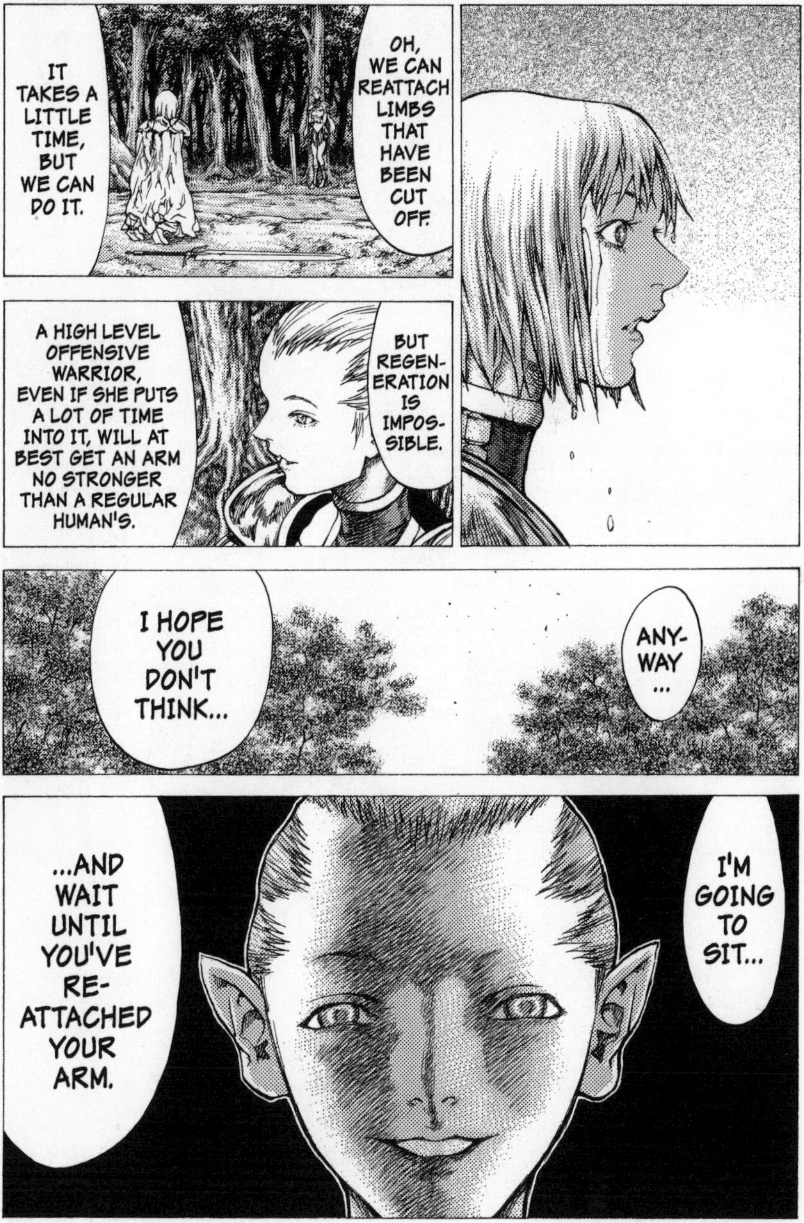
OH, WE CAN REATTACH LIMBS THAT HAVE BEEN CUT OFF.
IT TAKES A LITTLE TIME, BUT WE CAN DO IT.
BUT REGEN-ERATION IS IMPOS-SIBLE.
A HIGH LEVEL OFFENSIVE WARRIOR, EVEN IF SHE PUTS A LOT OF TIME INTO IT, WILL AT BEST GET AN ARM NO STRONGER THAN A REGULAR HUMAN'S.
ANY-WAY ...
I HOPE YOU DON'T THINK...
I'M GOING TO SIT...
...AND WAIT UNTIL YOU'VE RE-ATTACHED YOUR ARM.

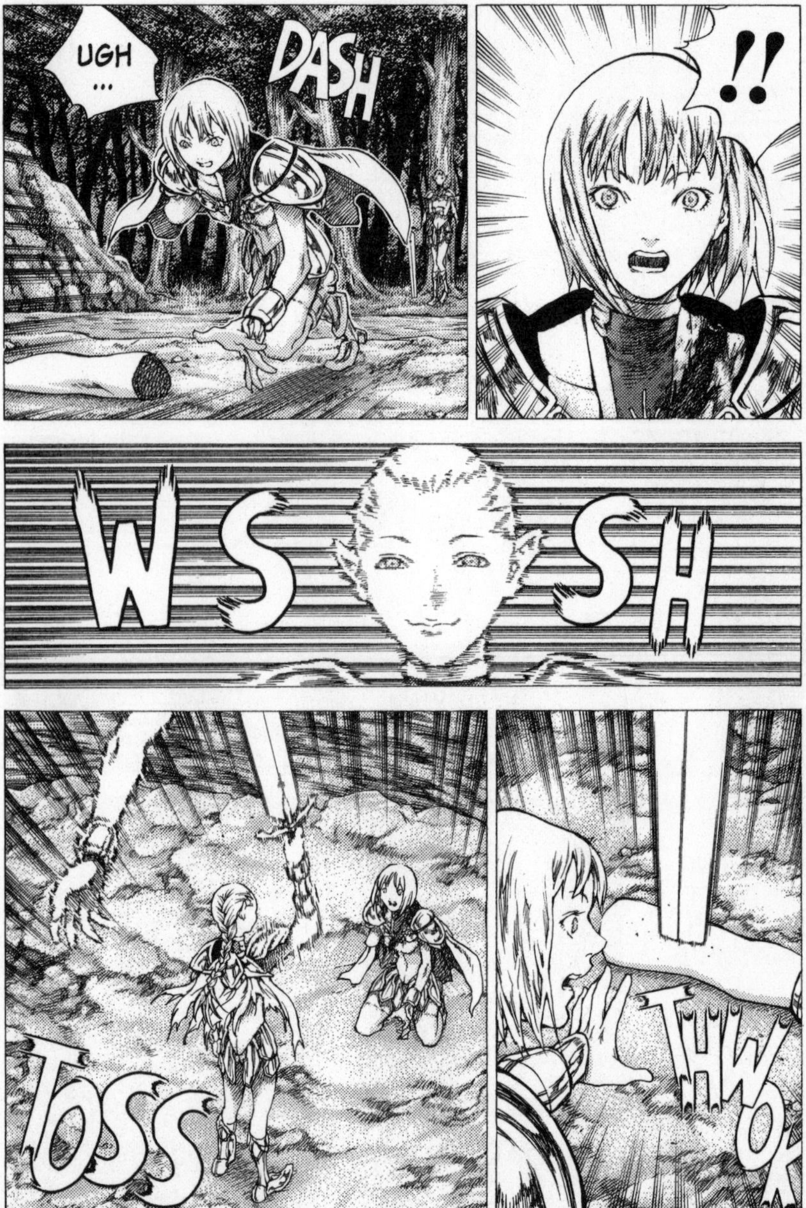
!!
UGH ...
DASH
WSSH
THWOK
TOSS

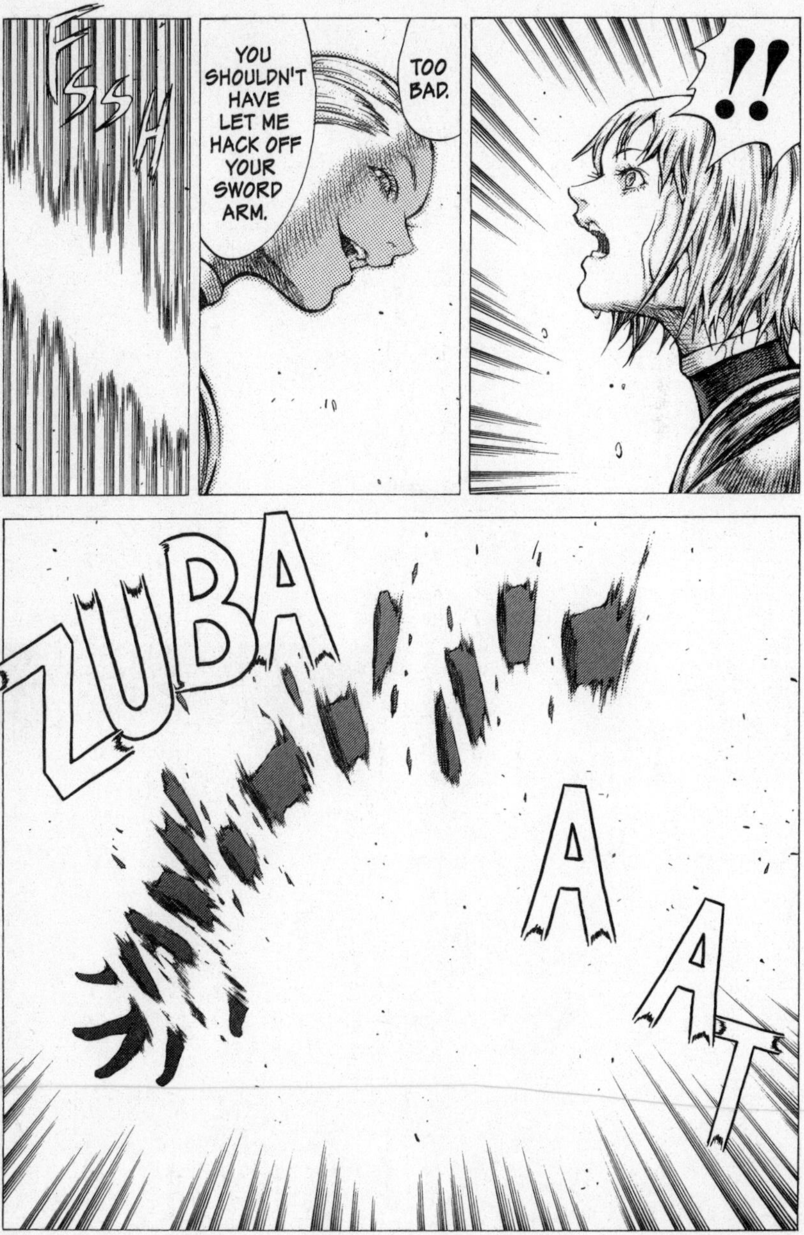
!!
TOO BAD.
YOU SHOULDN'T HAVE LET ME HACK OFF YOUR SWORD ARM.
FSSH
ZUBA
A
A
T

クレイモア
Claymore™

Scene 36: The Endless Gravestones, Part 6

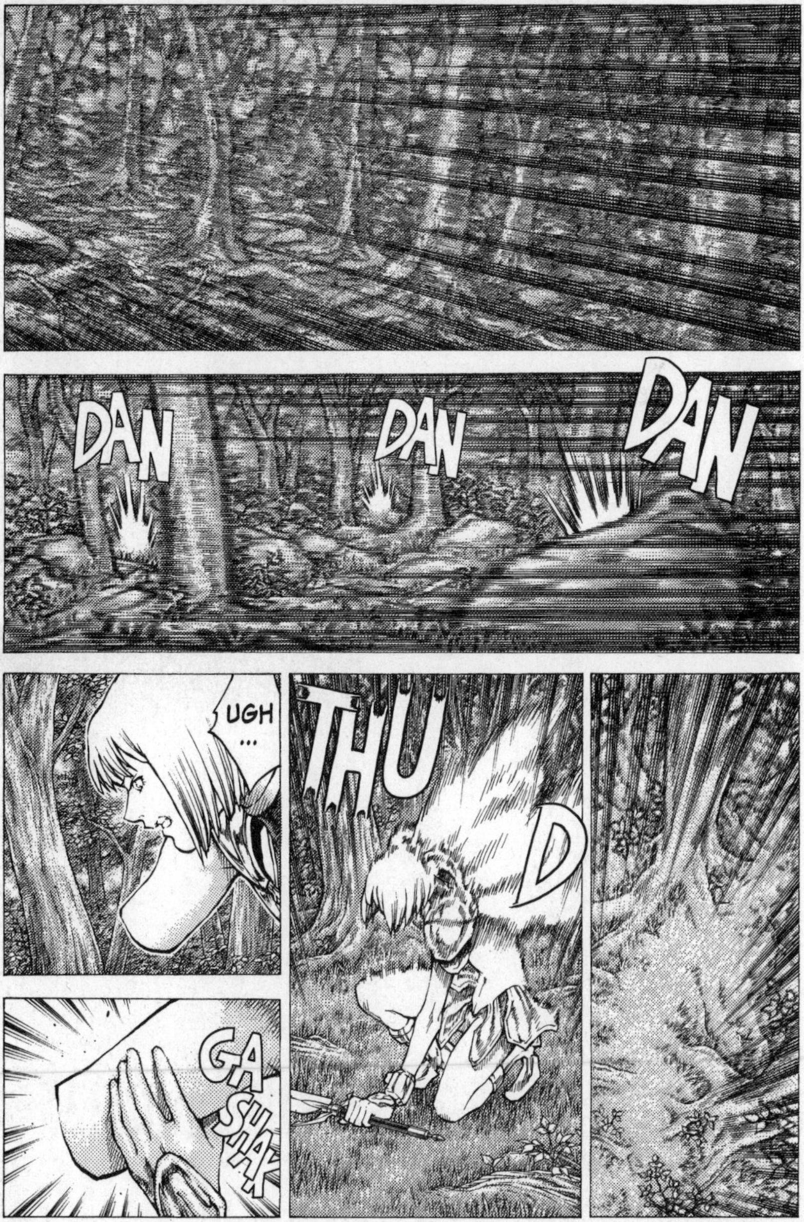
DAN
DAN
DAN
THUD
UGH ...
GASHAK

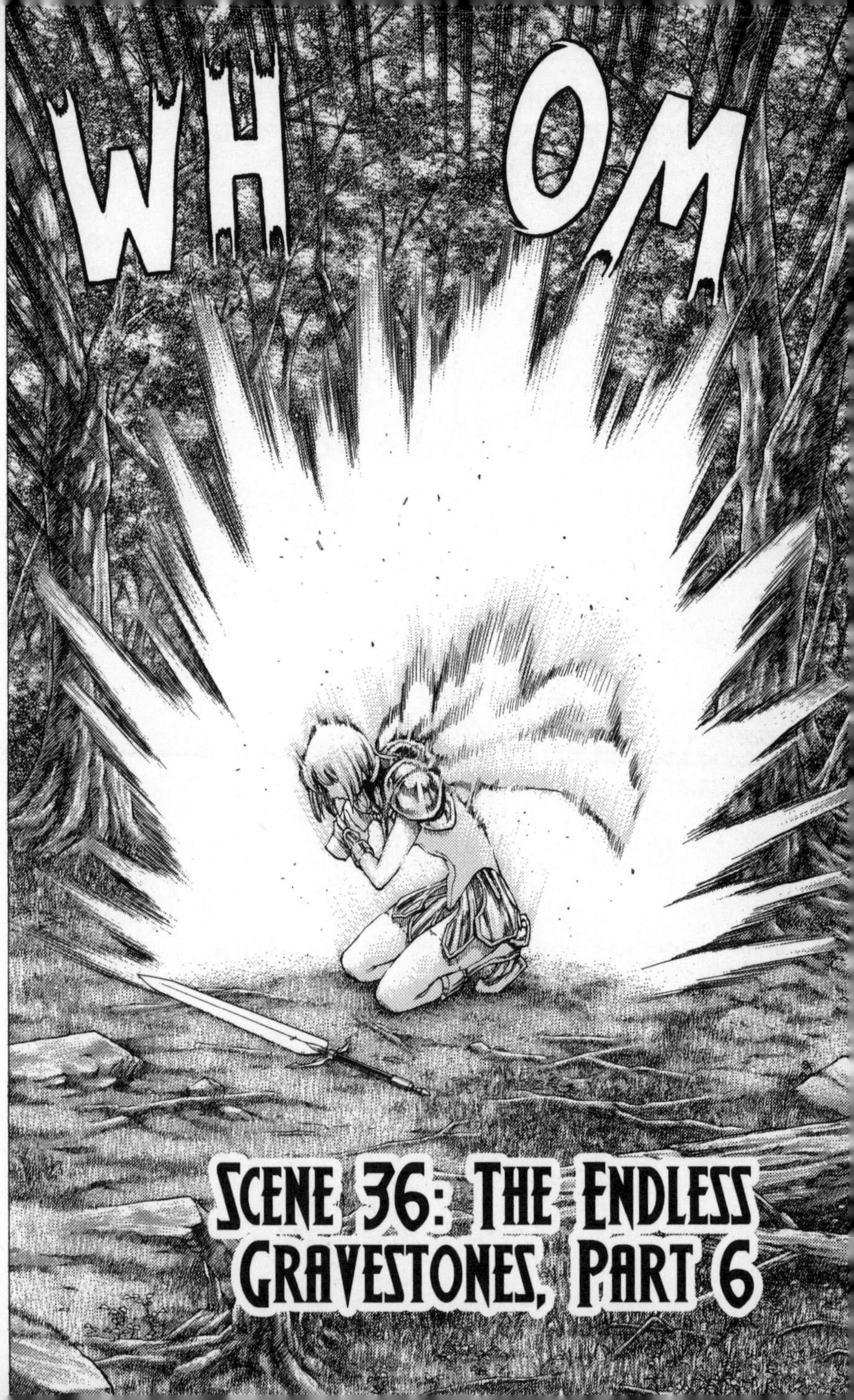
WH OM
Scene 36: The Endless Gravestones, Part 6

READ THIS WAY

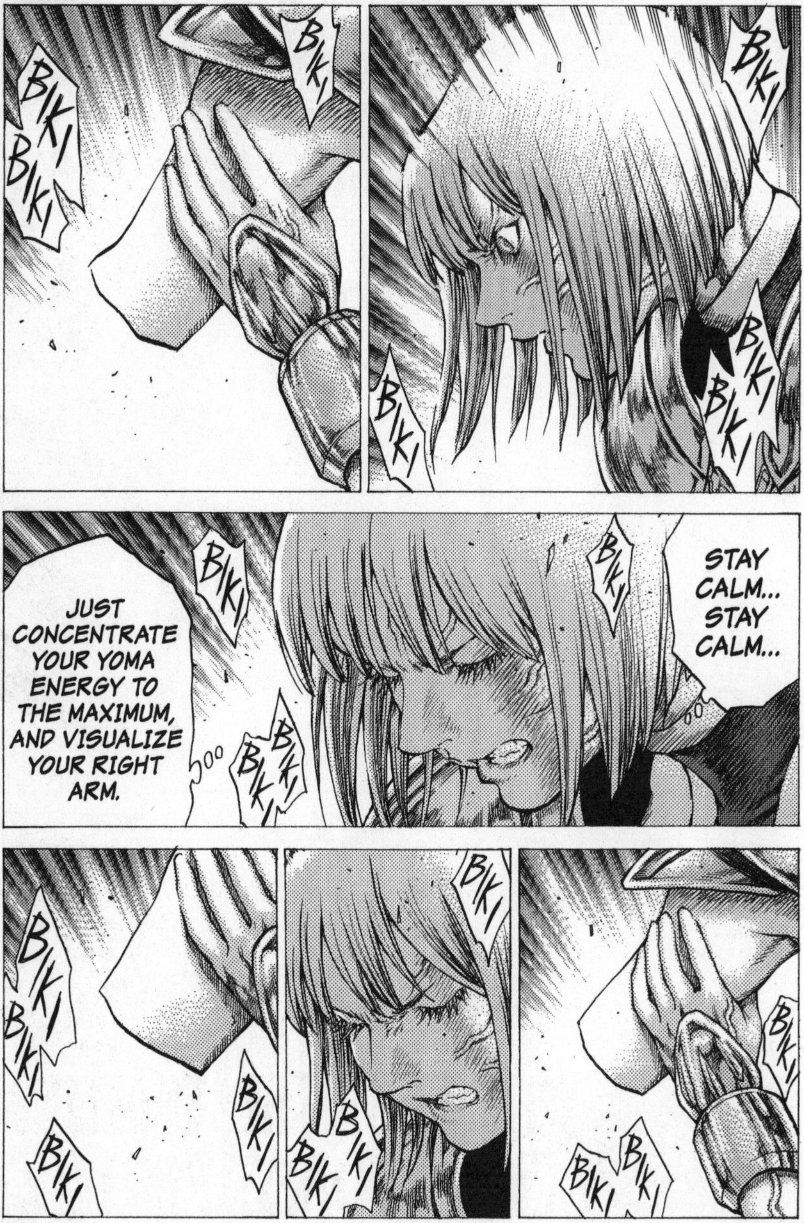
BIKI
BIKI
BIKI BIKI
BIKI
BIKI
BIKI BIKI
STAY CALM... STAY CALM...
BIKI
BIKI
JUST CONCENTRATE YOUR YOMA ENERGY TO THE MAXIMUM, AND VISUALIZE YOUR RIGHT ARM.
BIKI BIKI
BIKI
BIKI BIKI
BIKI
BIKI
BIKI BIKI
BIKI BIKI
BIKI

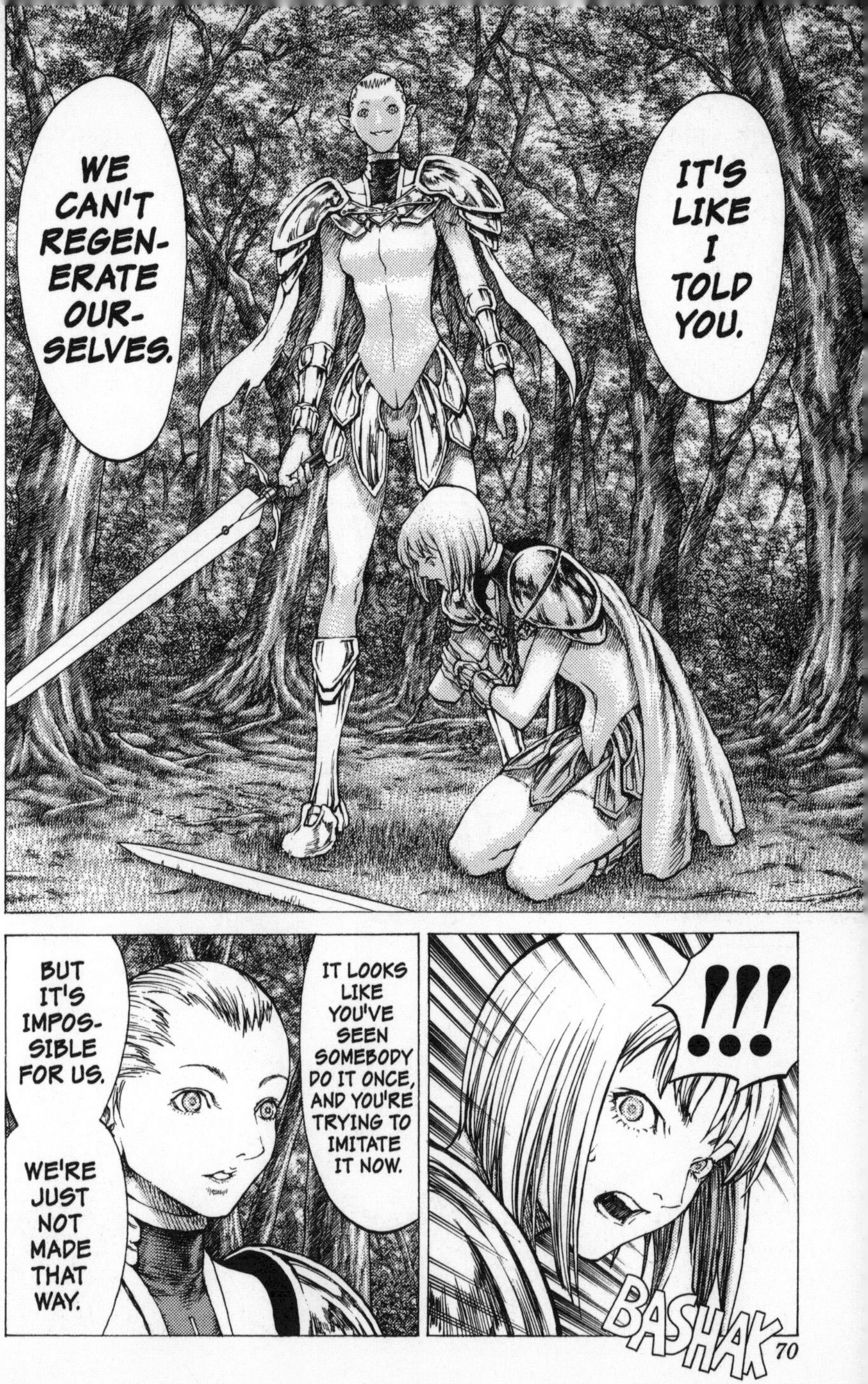
IT'S LIKE I TOLD YOU.
WE CAN'T REGEN- ERATE OUR- SELVES.
!!!
BASHAK
IT LOOKS LIKE YOU'VE SEEN SOMEBODY DO IT ONCE, AND YOU'RE TRYING TO IMITATE IT NOW.
BUT IT'S IMPOS- SIBLE FOR US.
WE'RE JUST NOT MADE THAT WAY.

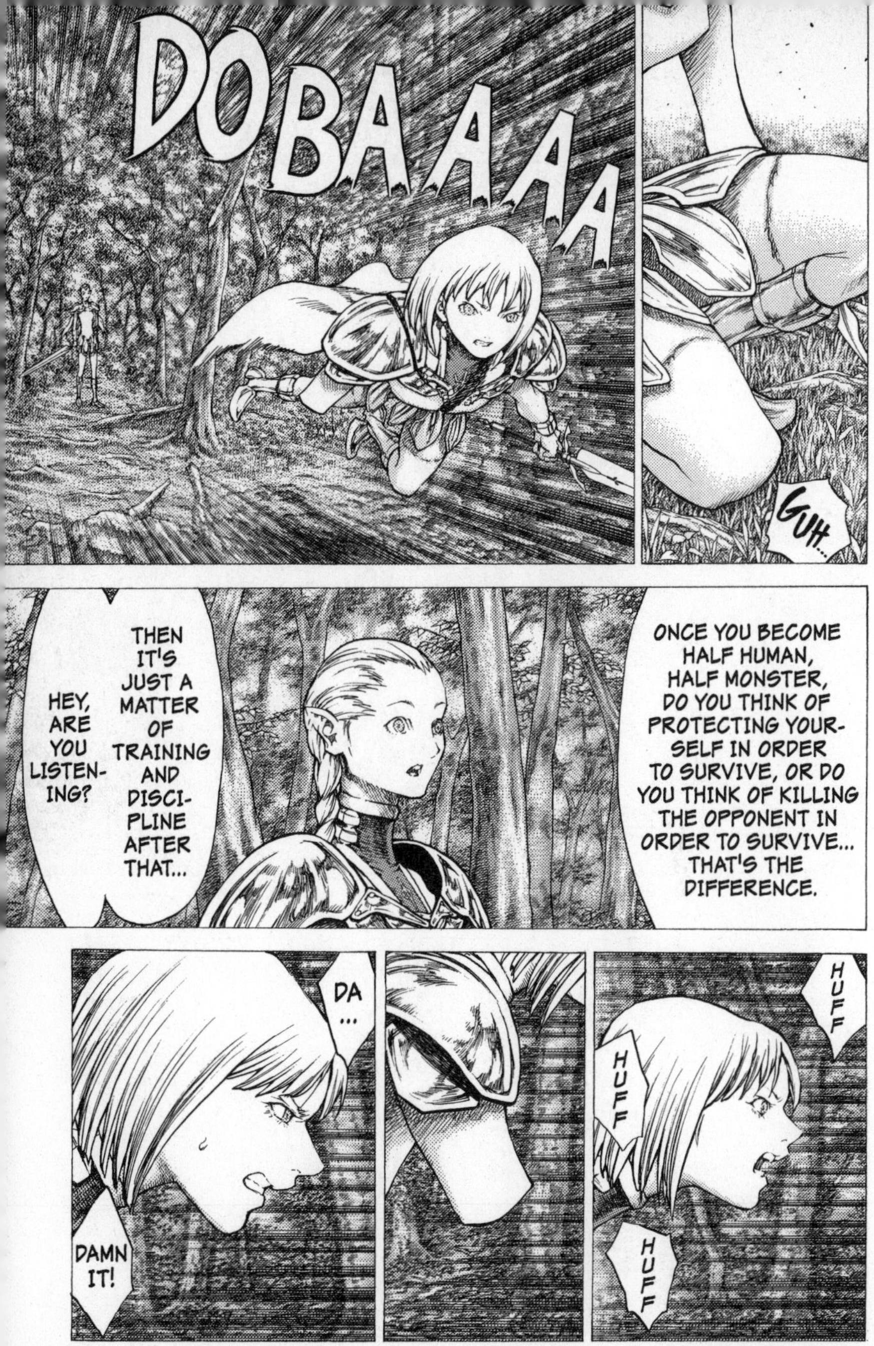
GUH...
DOBAAAA
ONCE YOU BECOME HALF HUMAN, HALF MONSTER, DO YOU THINK OF PROTECTING YOURSELF IN ORDER TO SURVIVE, OR DO YOU THINK OF KILLING THE OPPONENT IN ORDER TO SURVIVE... THAT'S THE DIFFERENCE.
THEN IT'S JUST A MATTER OF TRAINING AND DISCIPLINE AFTER THAT...
HEY, ARE YOU LISTENING?
HUFF
HUFF
HUFF
DA...
DAMN IT!

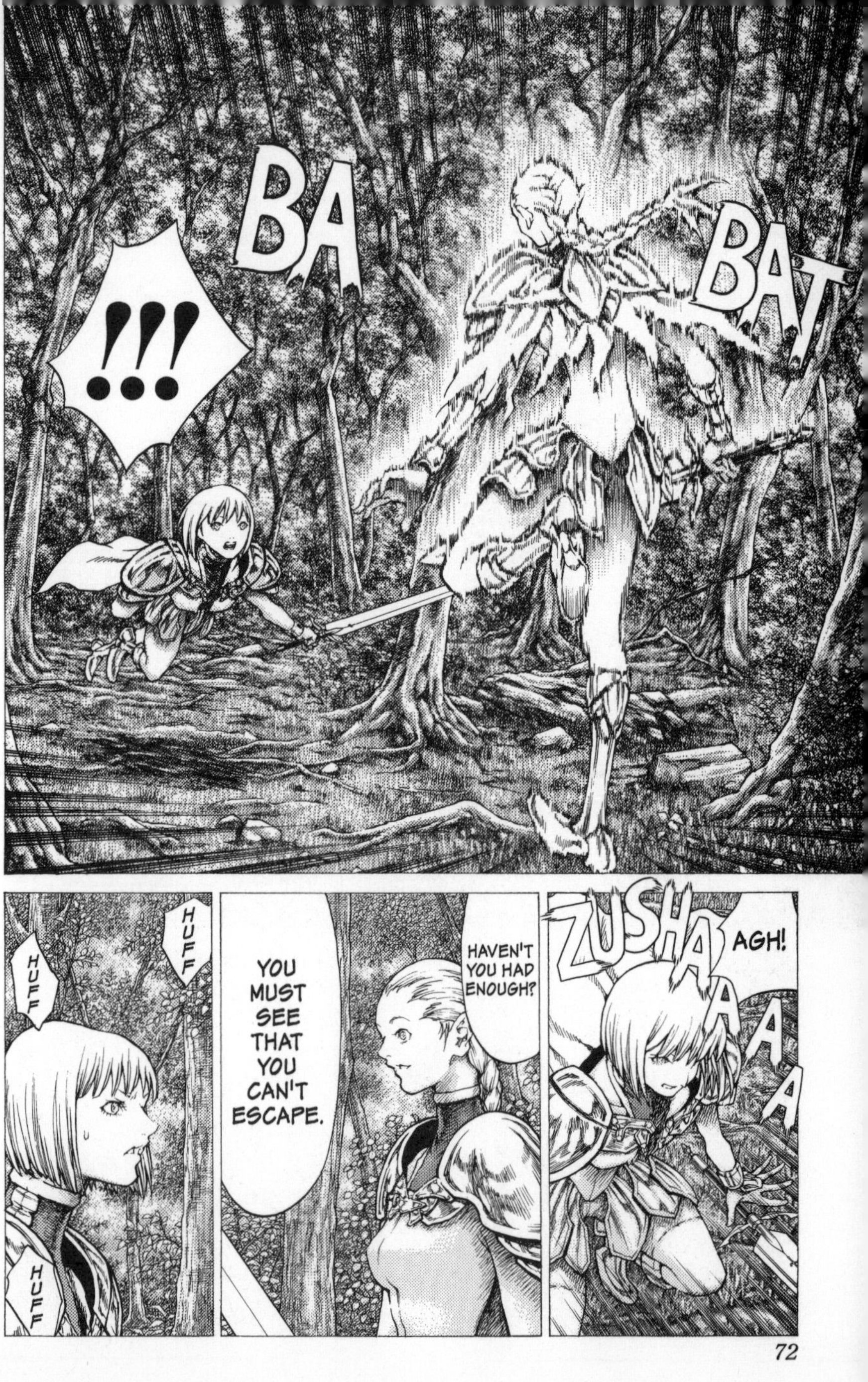
BA
BAT
!!!
ZUSHAAAAA
AGH!
HAVEN'T YOU HAD ENOUGH?
YOU MUST SEE THAT YOU CAN'T ESCAPE.
HUFF
HUFF
HUFF

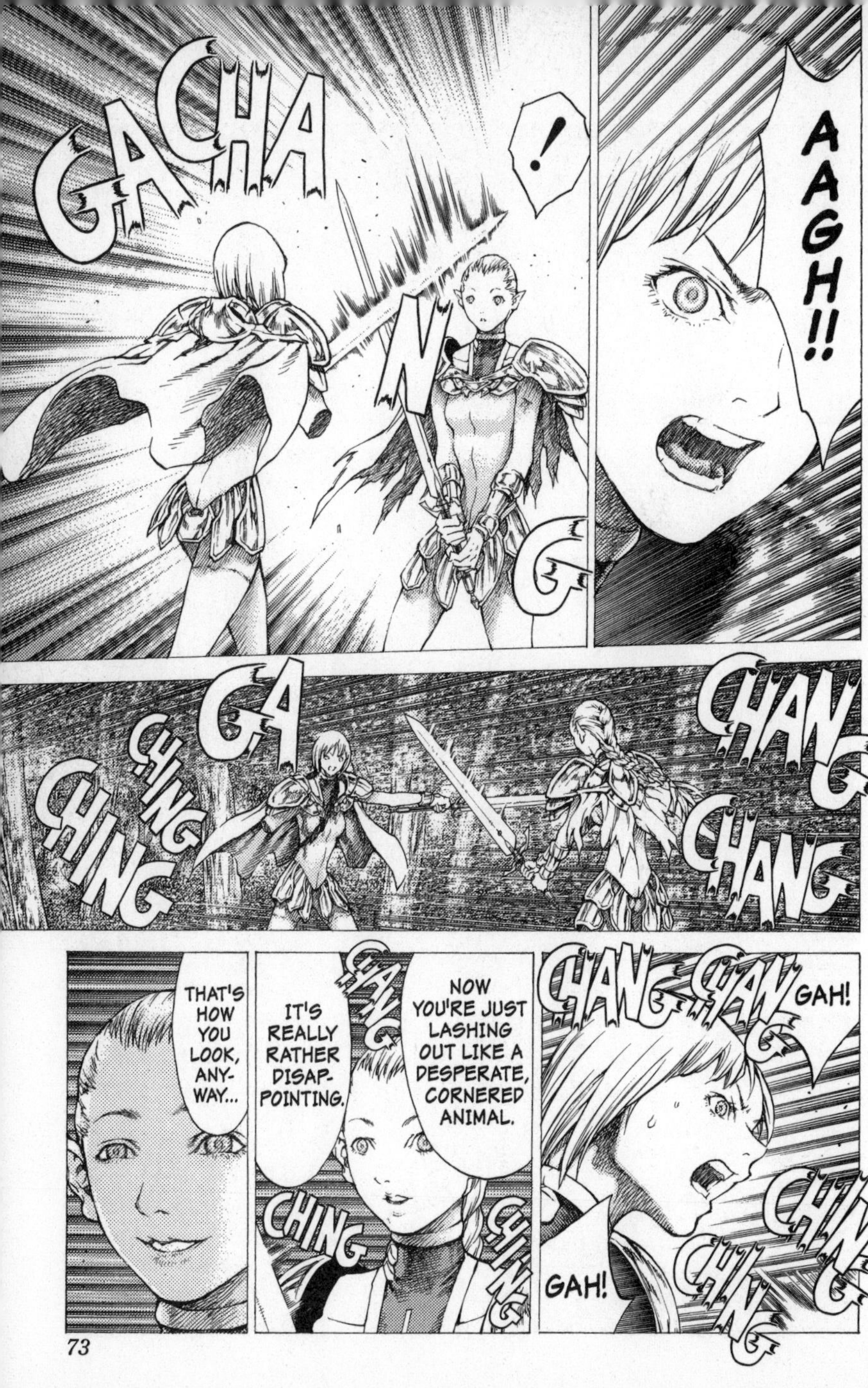
AAGH!!
!
GACHA
N
G
CHANG
CHANG
GA
CHING
CHING
CHANG CHANG
GAH!
CHING
CHING
GAH!
NOW YOU'RE JUST LASHING OUT LIKE A DESPERATE, CORNERED ANIMAL.
CHANG
IT'S REALLY RATHER DISAP-POINTING.
CHING
CHING
THAT'S HOW YOU LOOK, ANY-WAY...

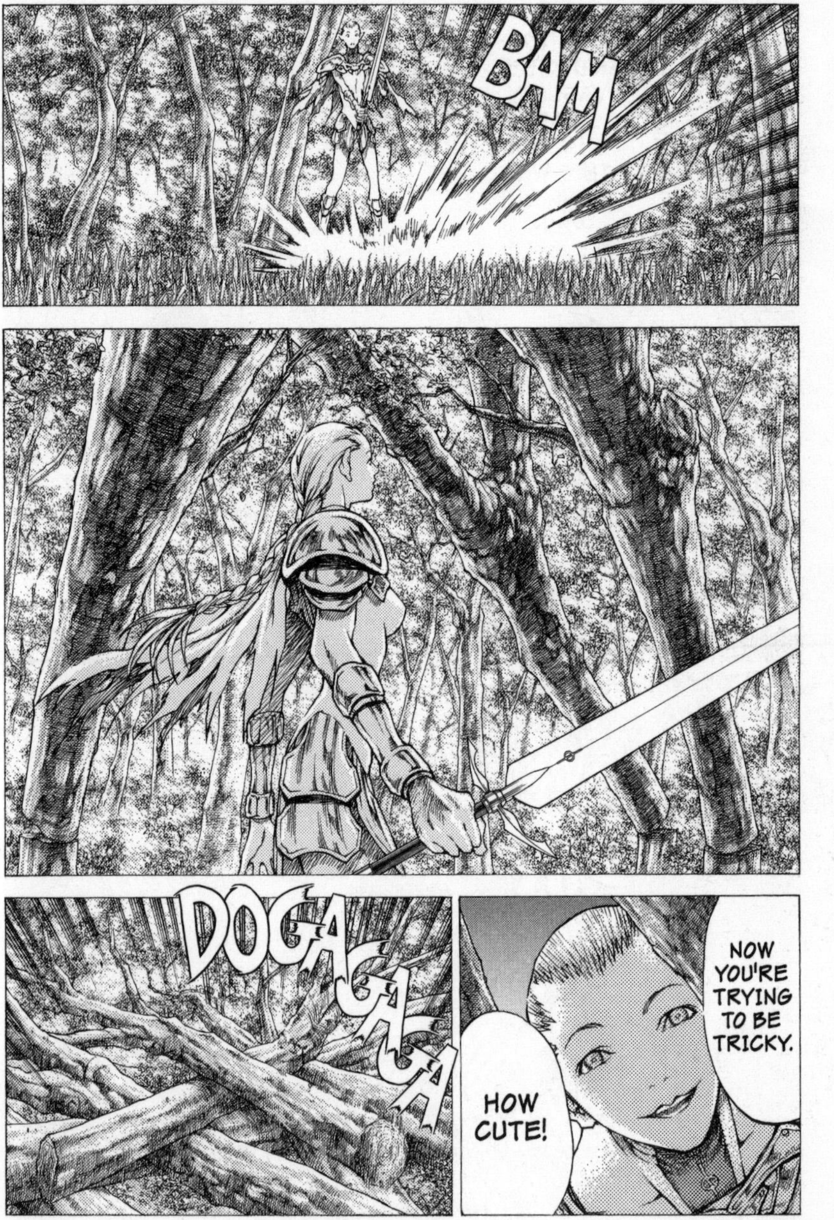
BAM
NOW YOU'RE TRYING TO BE TRICKY.
HOW CUTE!
DOGAGAGA

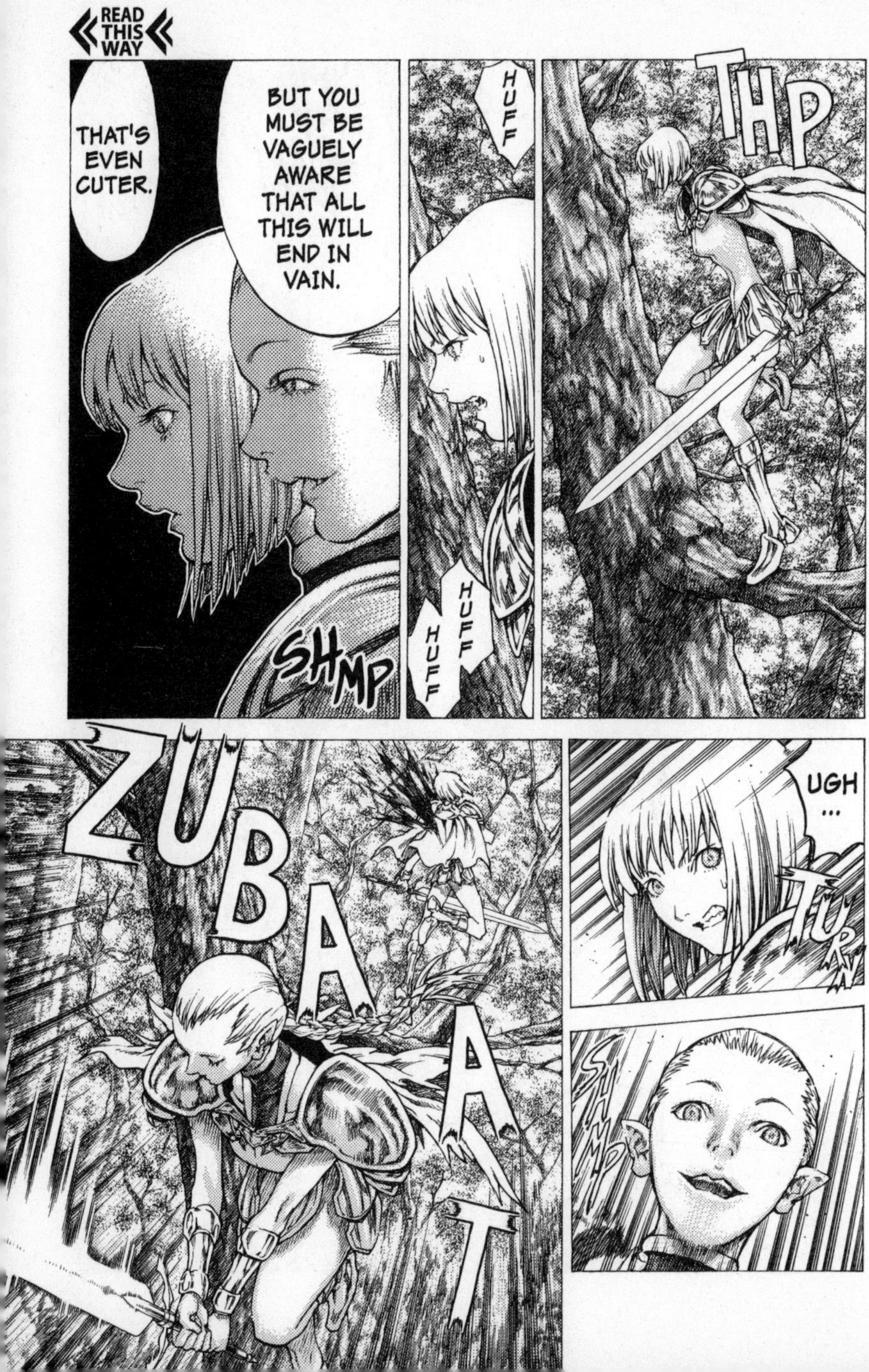
READ THIS WAY
THP
HUFF
HUFF
HUFF
BUT YOU MUST BE VAGUELY AWARE THAT ALL THIS WILL END IN VAIN.
THAT'S EVEN CUTER.
SHMP
UGH ...
TURN
SHMP
ZUBAAT

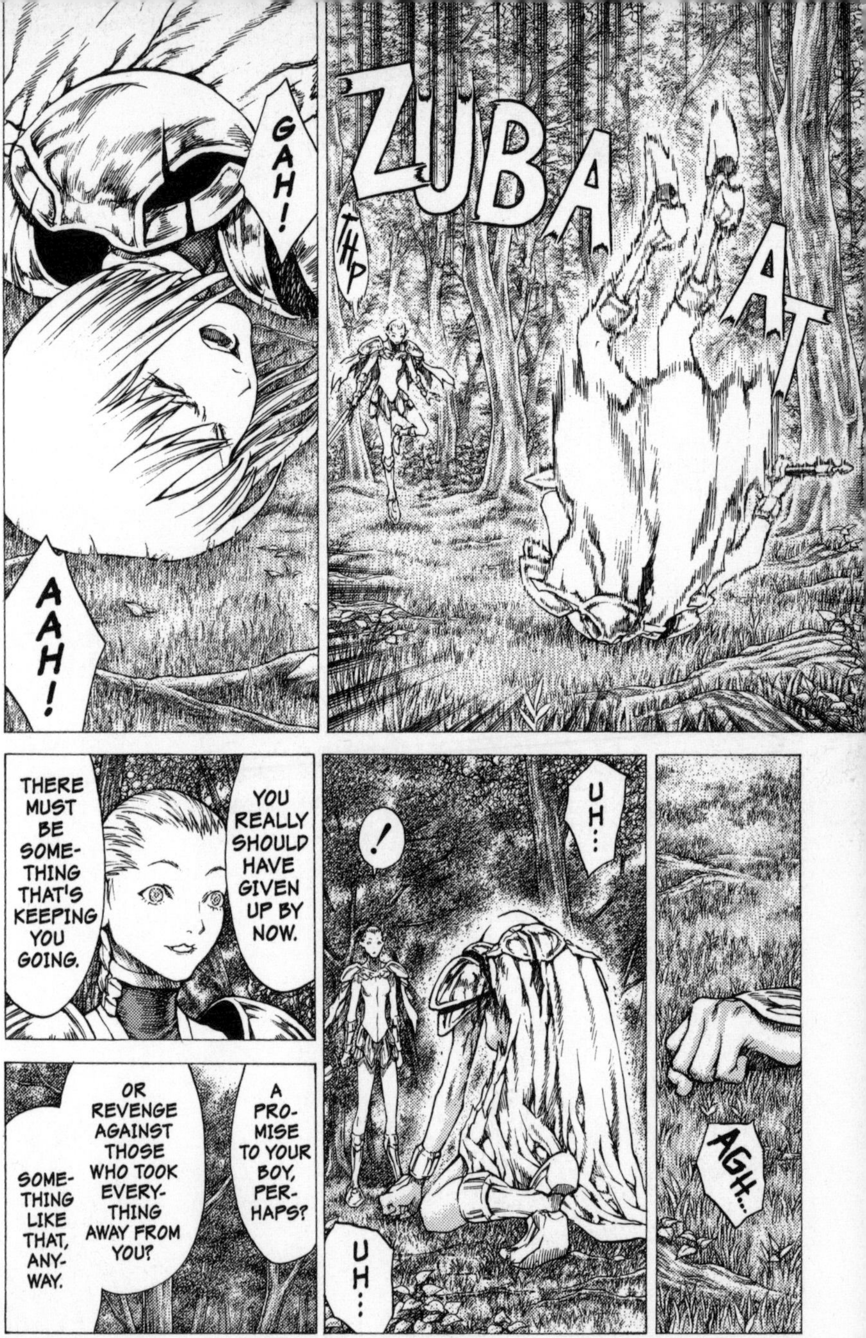
ZUBA
AT
THP
GAH!
AAH!
AGH...
UH...
!
UH...
YOU REALLY SHOULD HAVE GIVEN UP BY NOW.
THERE MUST BE SOME-THING THAT'S KEEPING YOU GOING.
A PRO-MISE TO YOUR BOY, PER-HAPS?
OR REVENGE AGAINST THOSE WHO TOOK EVERY-THING AWAY FROM YOU?
SOME-THING LIKE THAT, ANY-WAY.

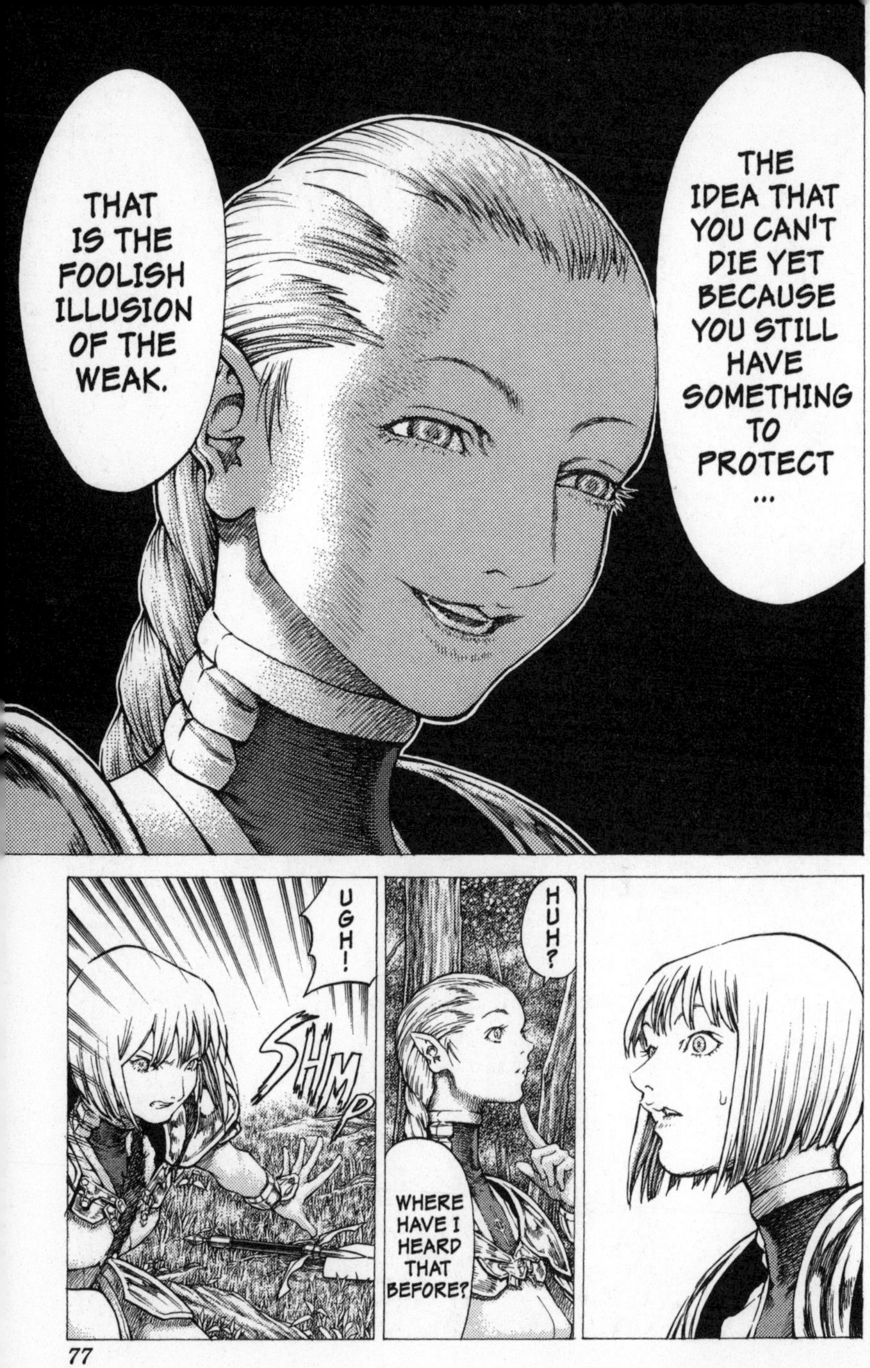
THE IDEA THAT YOU CAN'T DIE YET BECAUSE YOU STILL HAVE SOMETHING TO PROTECT ...
THAT IS THE FOOLISH ILLUSION OF THE WEAK.
HUH?
WHERE HAVE I HEARD THAT BEFORE?
UGH!
SHMP

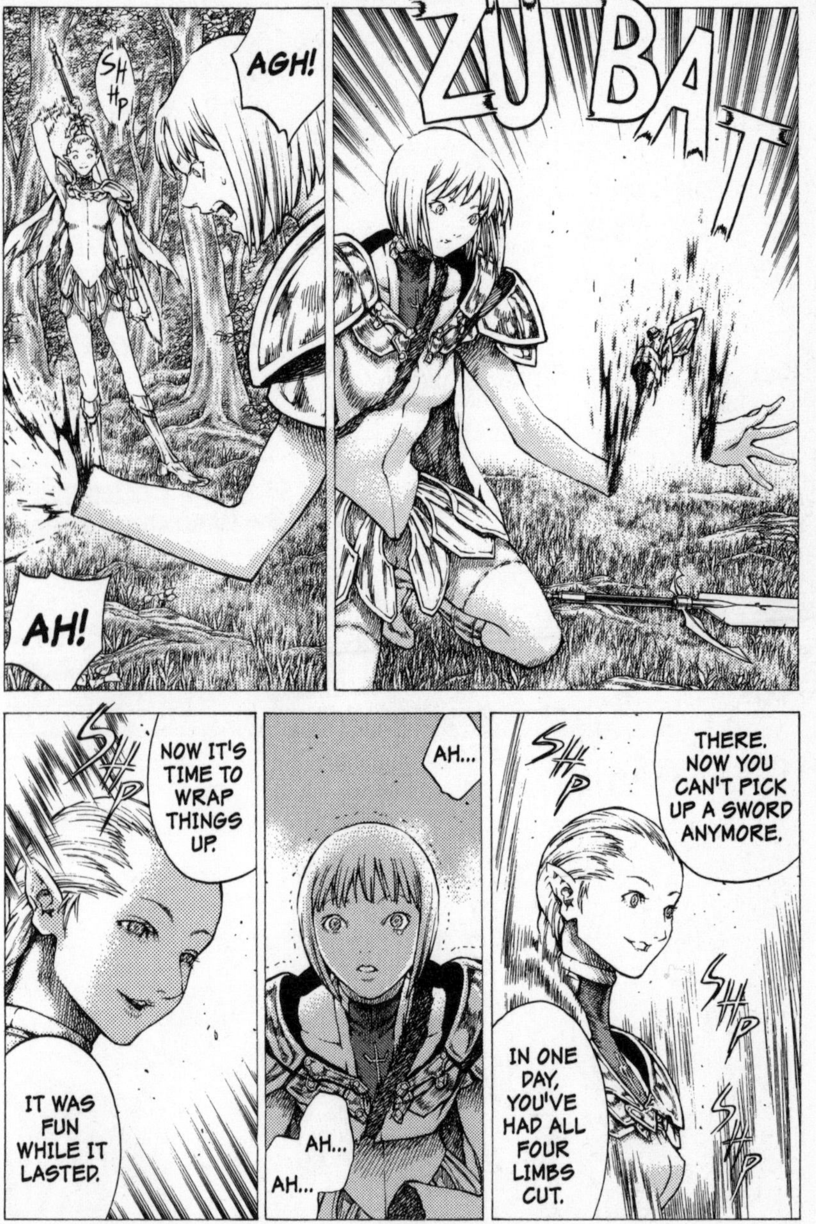
ZU BAT
AGH!
SHHP
AH!
THERE. NOW YOU CAN'T PICK UP A SWORD ANYMORE.
SHHP
SHHP
IN ONE DAY, YOU'VE HAD ALL FOUR LIMBS CUT.
SHHP
AH...
AH...
AH...
NOW IT'S TIME TO WRAP THINGS UP.
SHHP
IT WAS FUN WHILE IT LASTED.

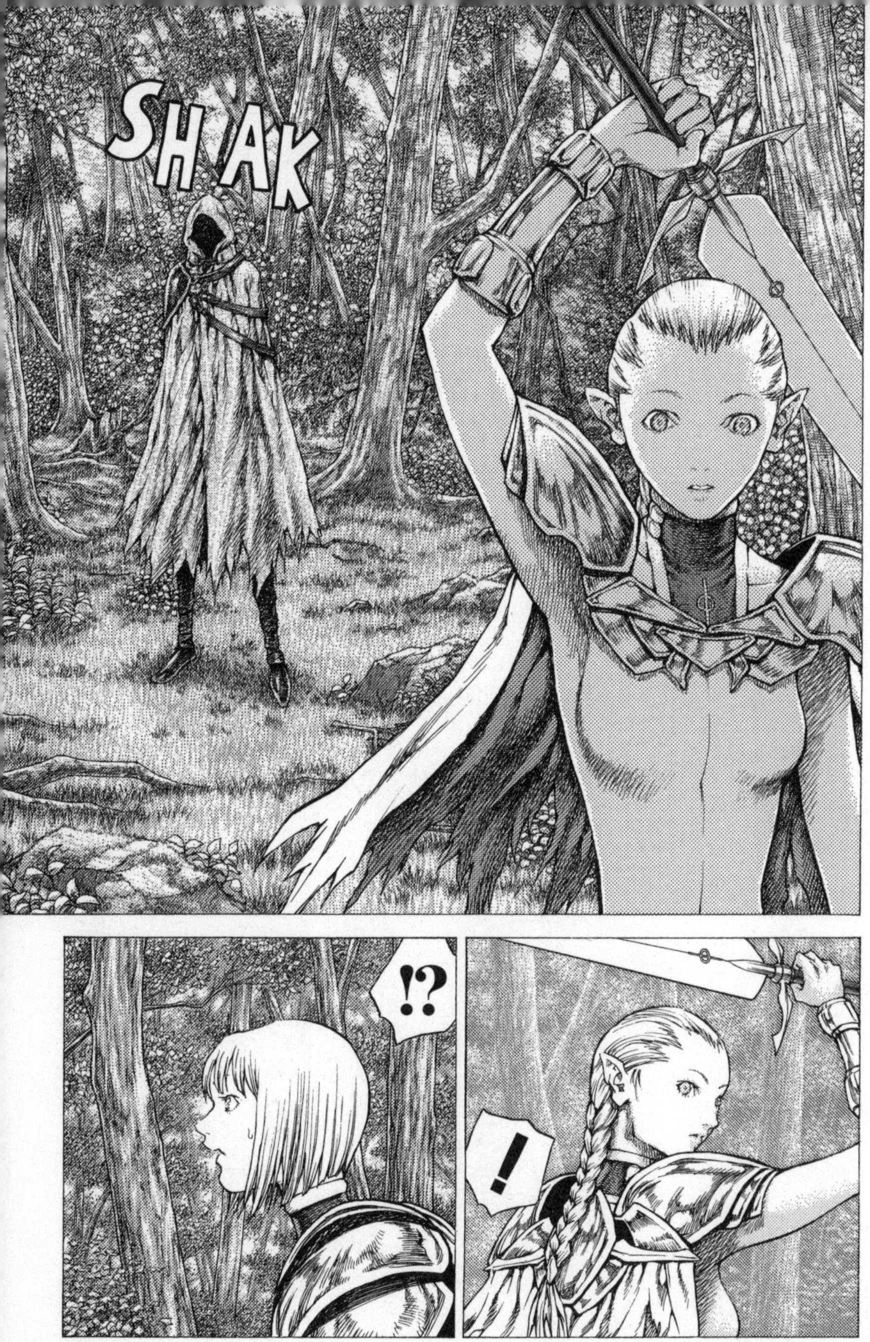
SHAK
!
!?

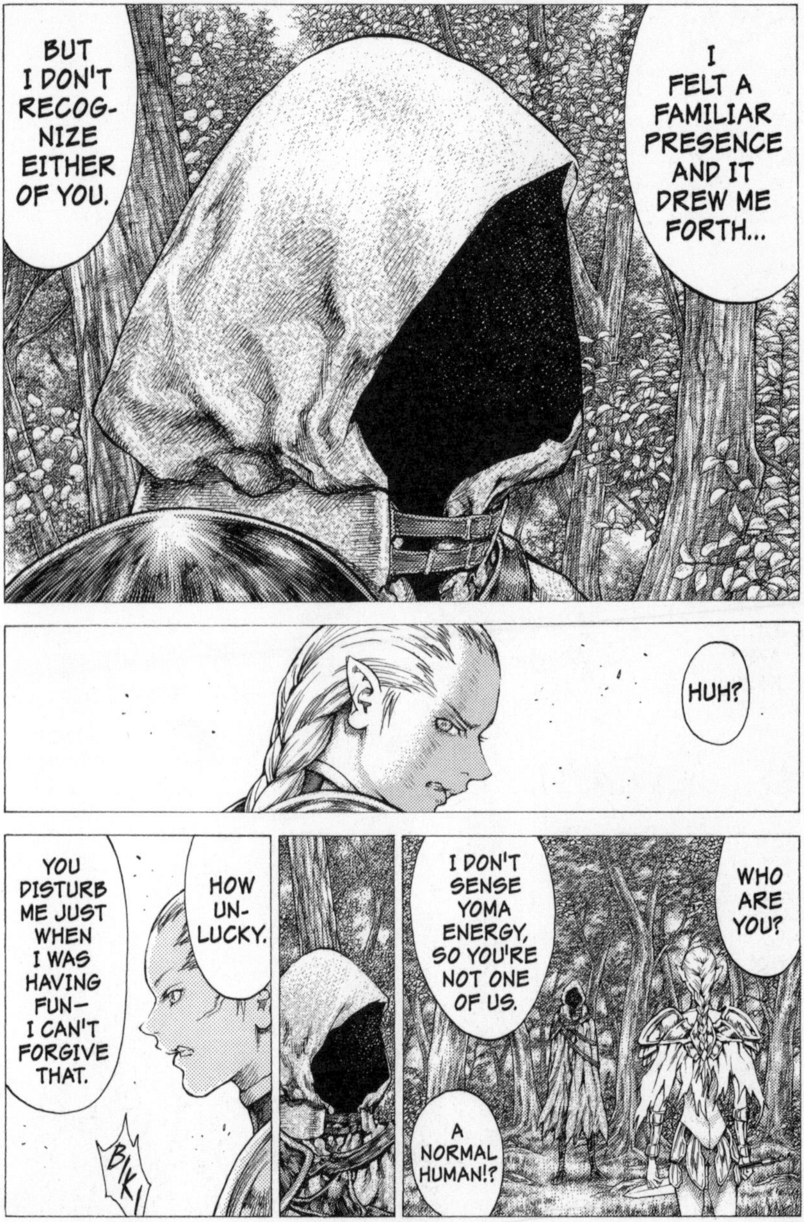
I FELT A FAMILIAR PRESENCE AND IT DREW ME FORTH...
BUT I DON'T RECOG-NIZE EITHER OF YOU.
HUH?
WHO ARE YOU?
I DON'T SENSE YOMA ENERGY, SO YOU'RE NOT ONE OF US.
A NORMAL HUMAN!?
HOW UN-LUCKY.
YOU DISTURB ME JUST WHEN I WAS HAVING FUN— I CAN'T FORGIVE THAT.
BIKI

READ THIS WAY

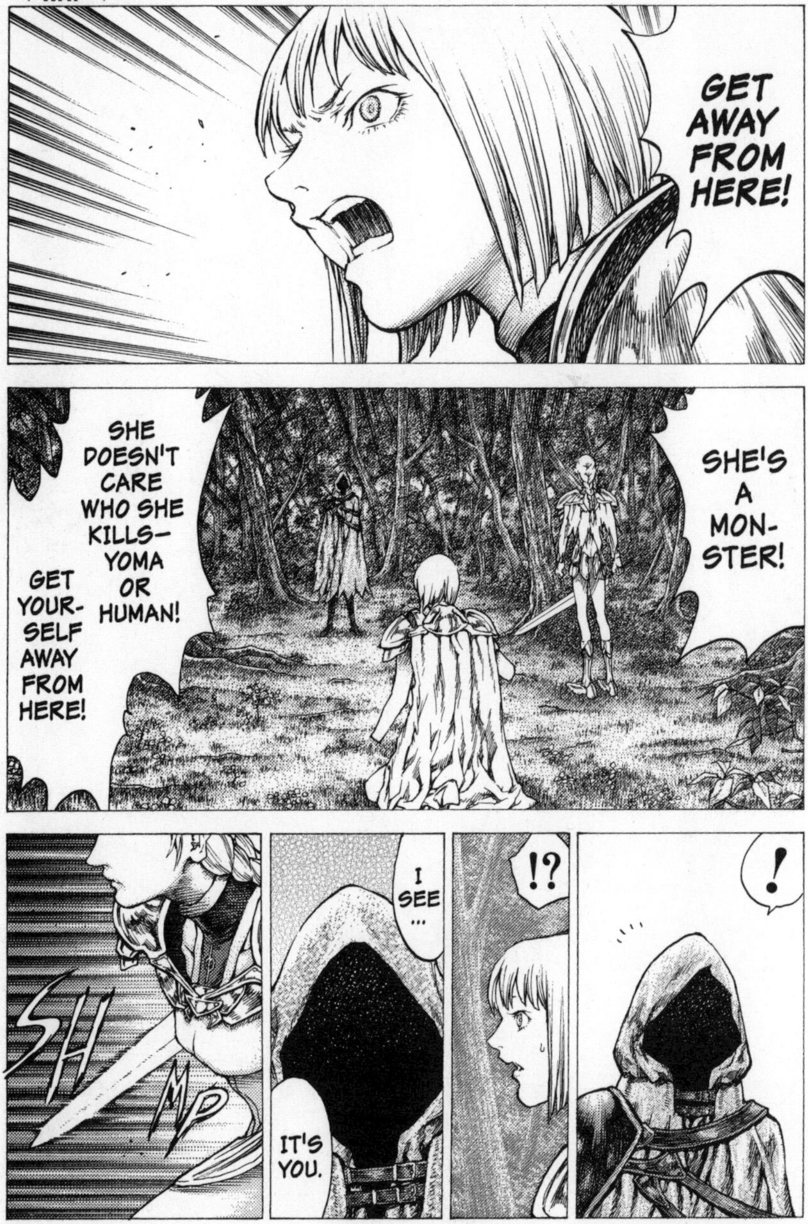
GET AWAY FROM HERE!
SHE'S A MON-STER!
SHE DOESN'T CARE WHO SHE KILLS— YOMA OR HUMAN!
GET YOUR-SELF AWAY FROM HERE!
!
!?
I SEE...
IT'S YOU.
SHMP

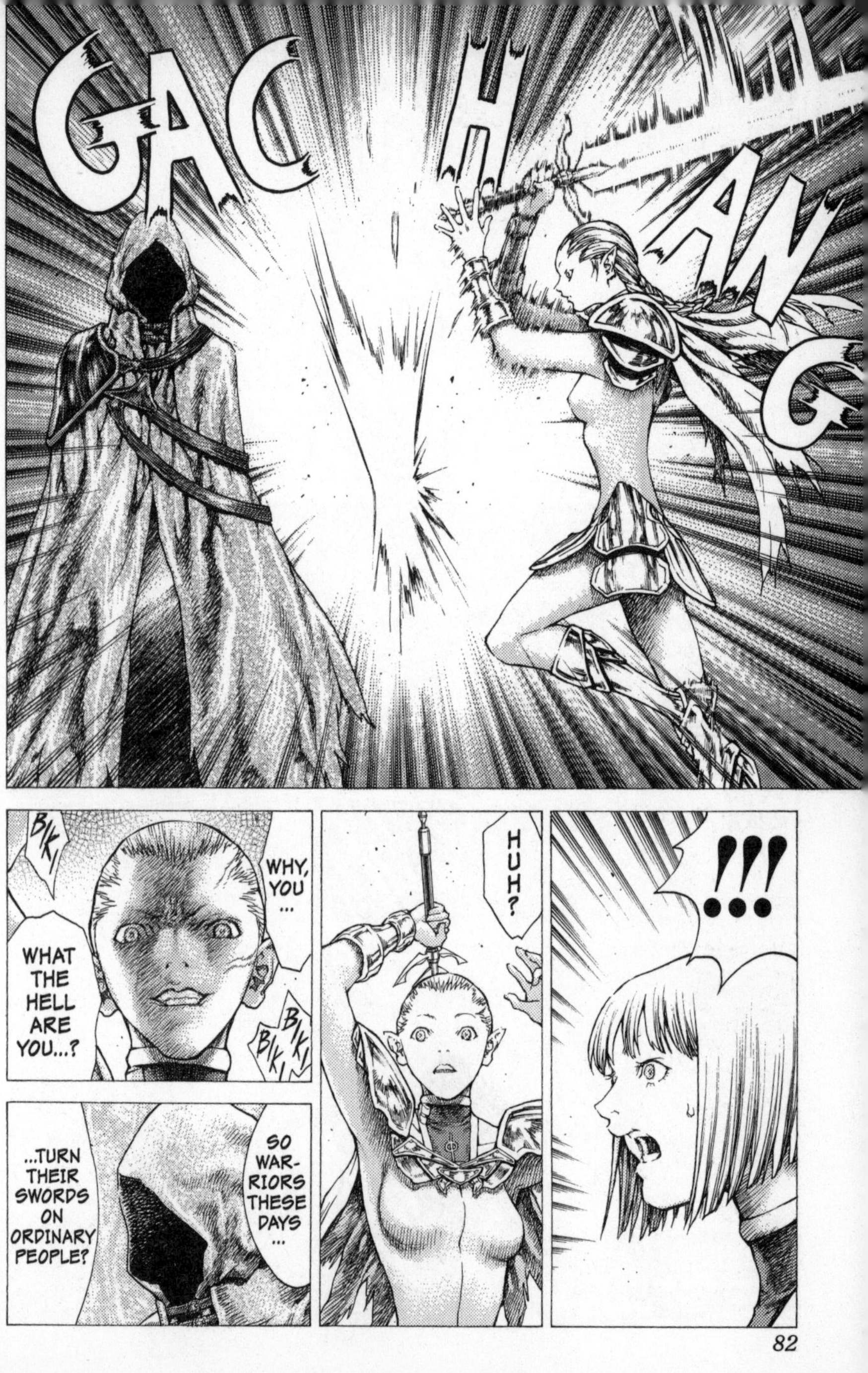
GACHANG
!!!
HUH?
WHY, YOU...
BIKI
WHAT THE HELL ARE YOU...?
BIKI BIKI
SO WARRIORS THESE DAYS...
...TURN THEIR SWORDS ON ORDINARY PEOPLE?

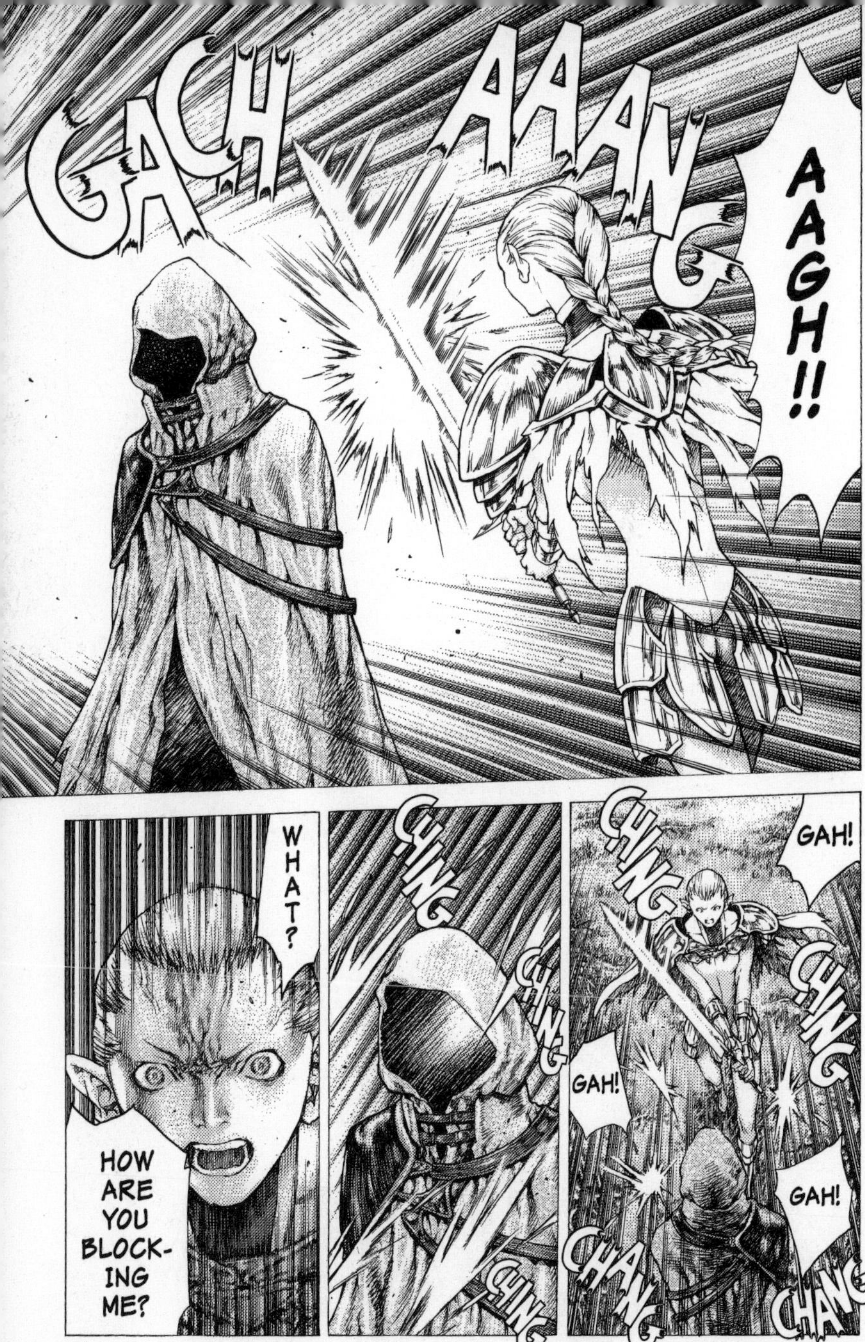
AAGH!!
GACH AAAANG
GAH!
CHING CHING
CHING CHING
GAH!
GAH!
CHANG CHANG
CHANG
CHING
CHING CHING
CHING
WHAT?
HOW ARE YOU BLOCKING-ING ME?

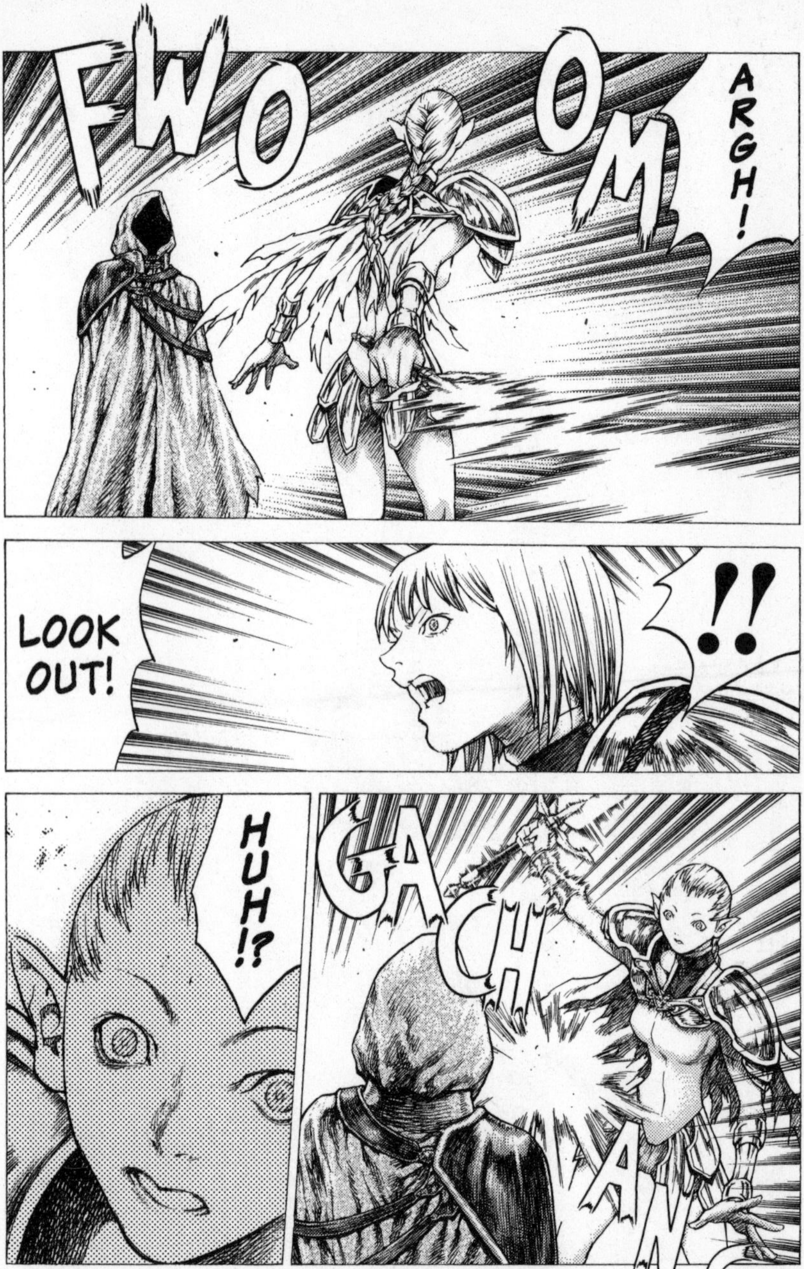
ARGH!
FWOOM
!!
LOOK OUT!
GACHANG
HUH!?

READ THIS WAY

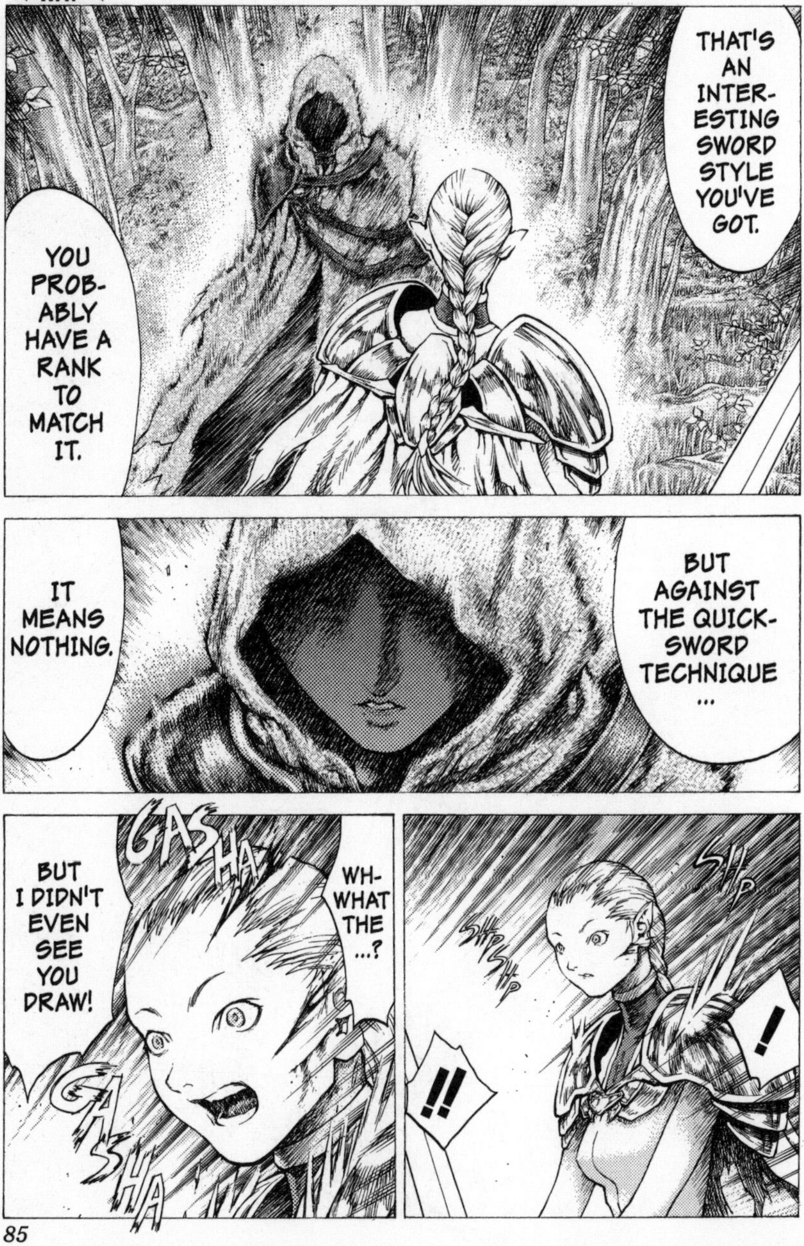

THAT'S AN INTER-ESTING SWORD STYLE YOU'VE GOT.
YOU PROB-ABLY HAVE A RANK TO MATCH IT.
BUT AGAINST THE QUICK-SWORD TECHNIQUE ...
IT MEANS NOTHING.
SHP
SHPSHP
!
!!
GASHA
WH-WHAT THE ...?
BUT I DIDN'T EVEN SEE YOU DRAW!
GASHA

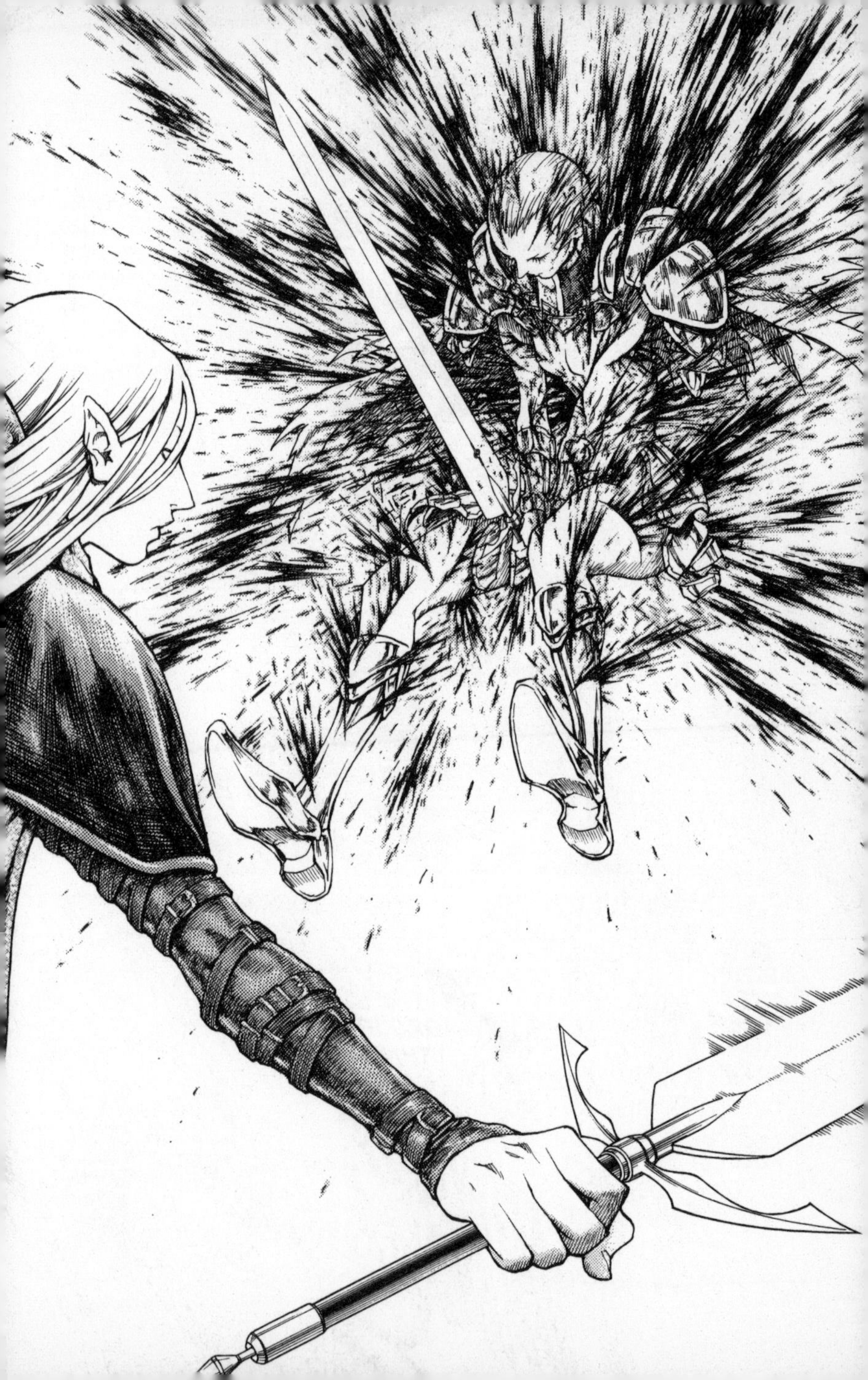

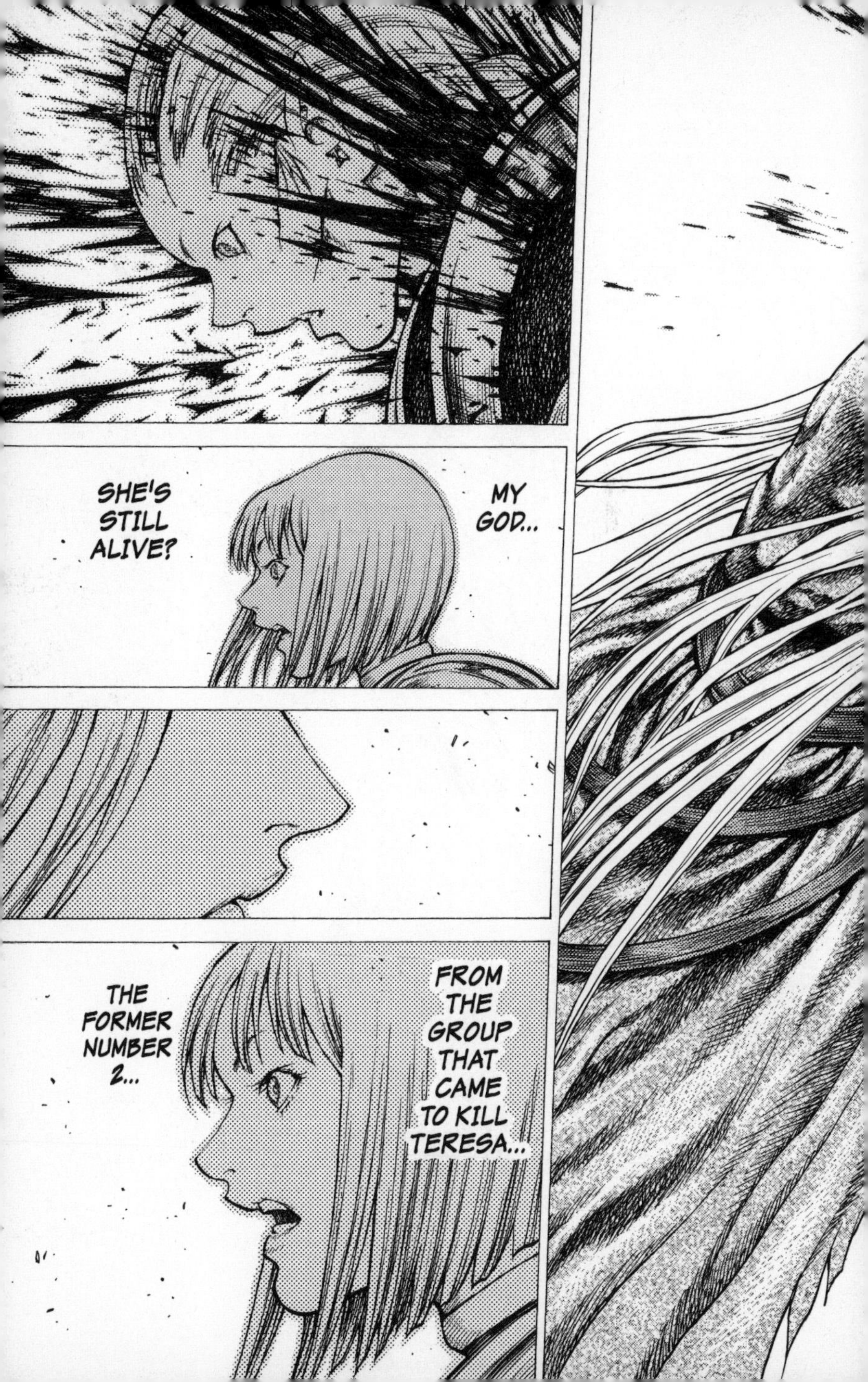
MY GOD...
SHE'S STILL ALIVE?
FROM THE GROUP THAT CAME TO KILL TERESA...
THE FORMER NUMBER 2...

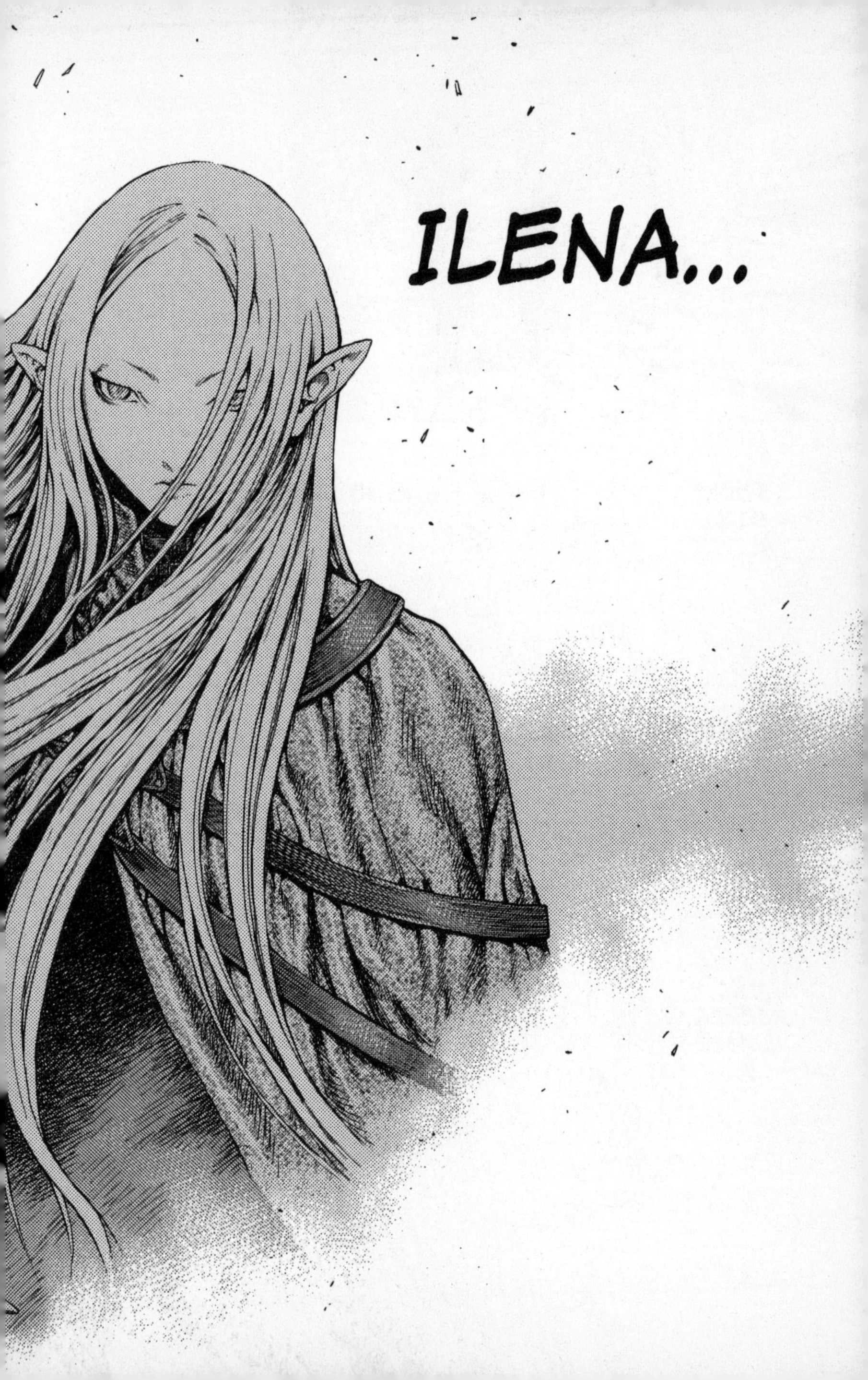
ILENA...

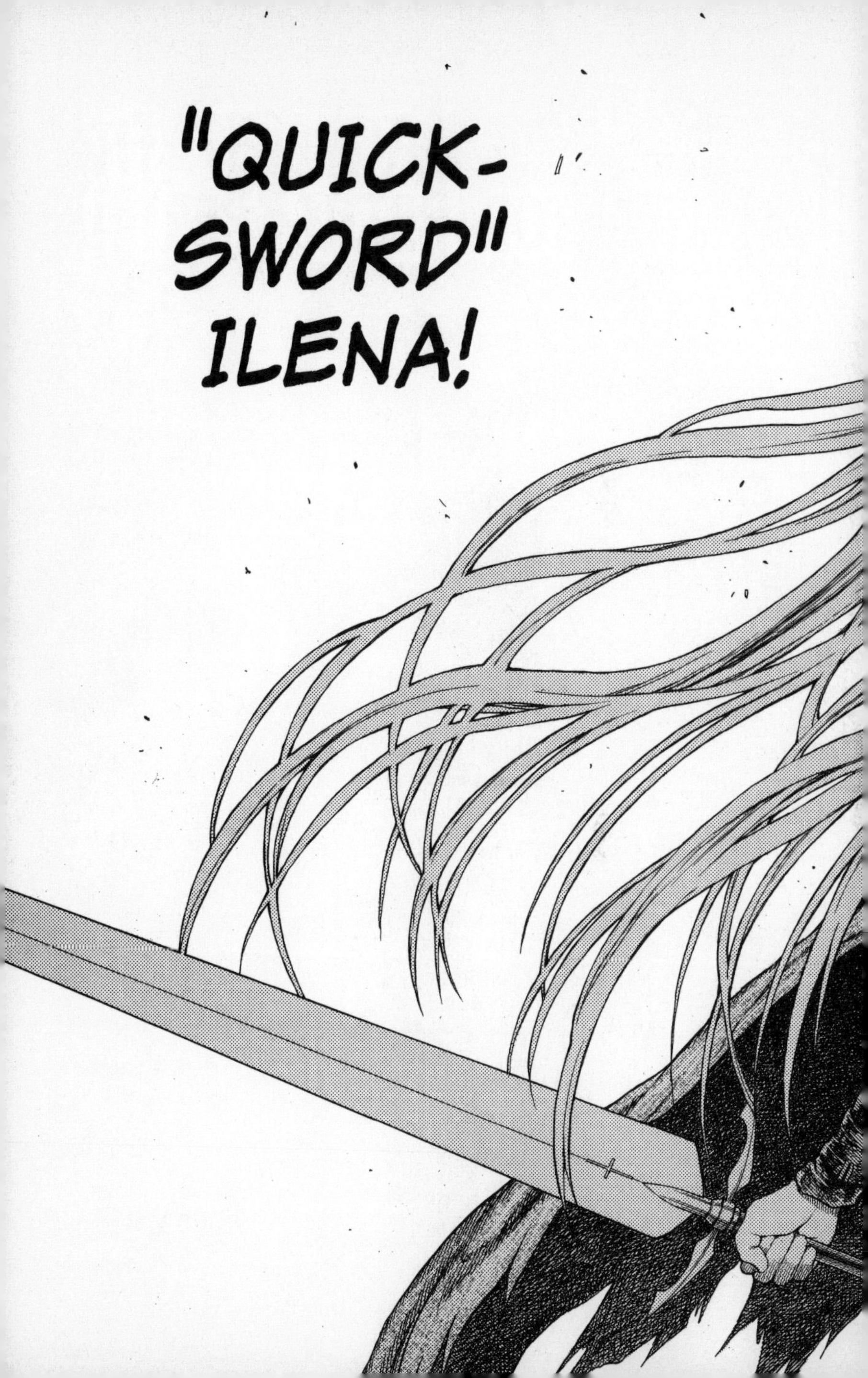
"QUICK-SWORD" ILENA!

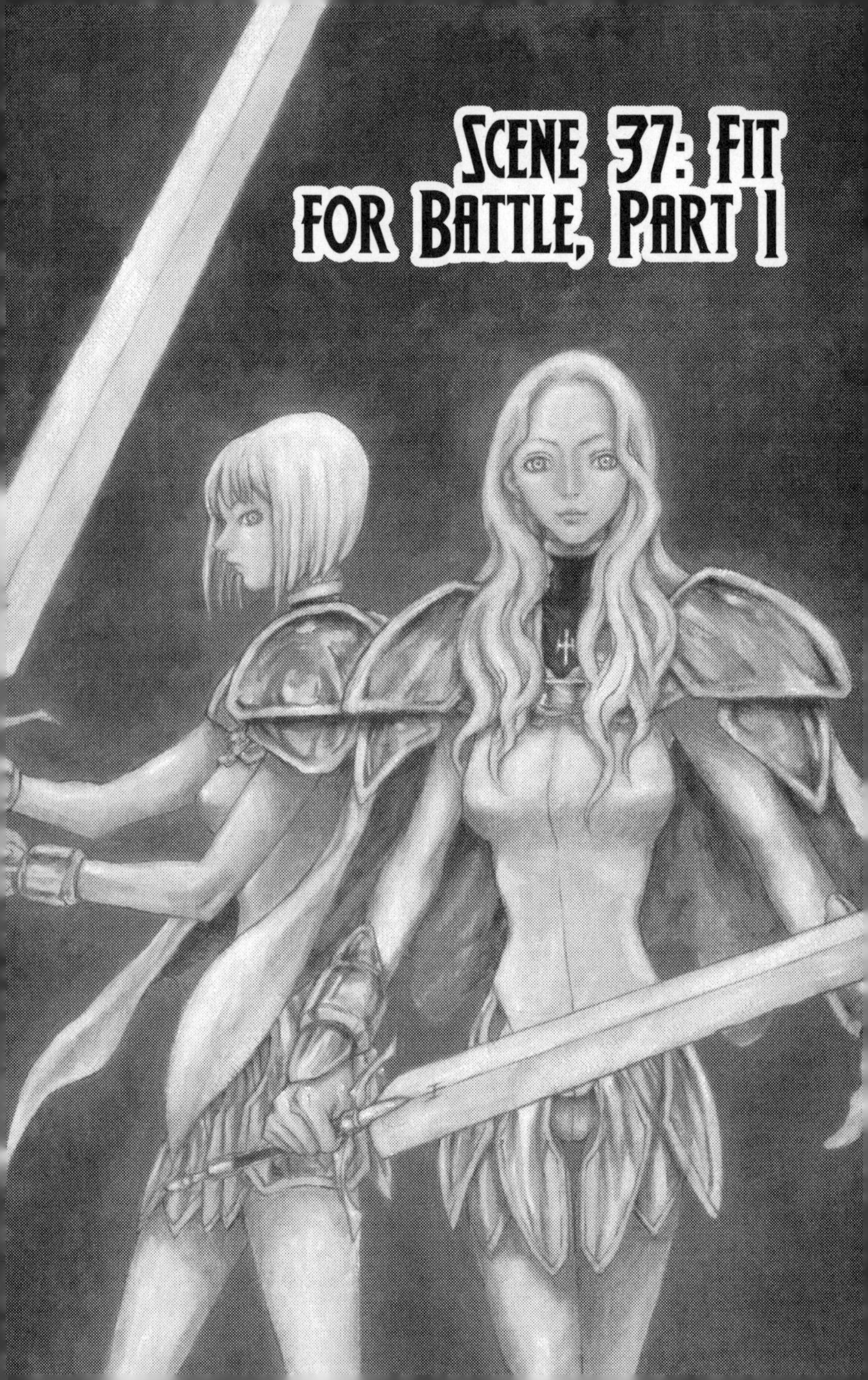
Scene 37: Fit
for Battle, Part 1

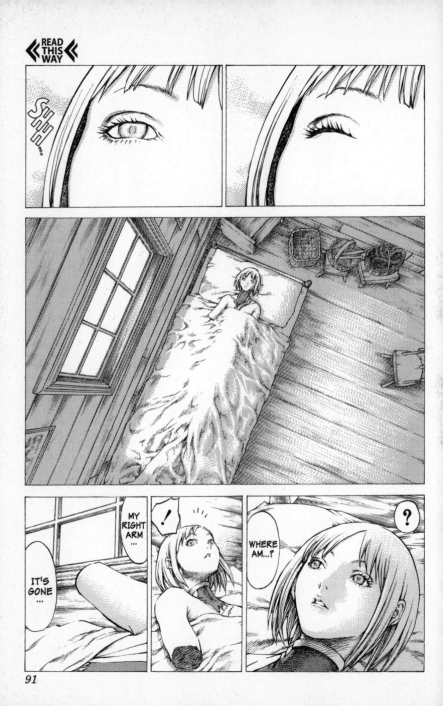

SHH...

MY
RIGHT
ARM
...

!

?

IT'S
GONE
...

WHERE
AM...?

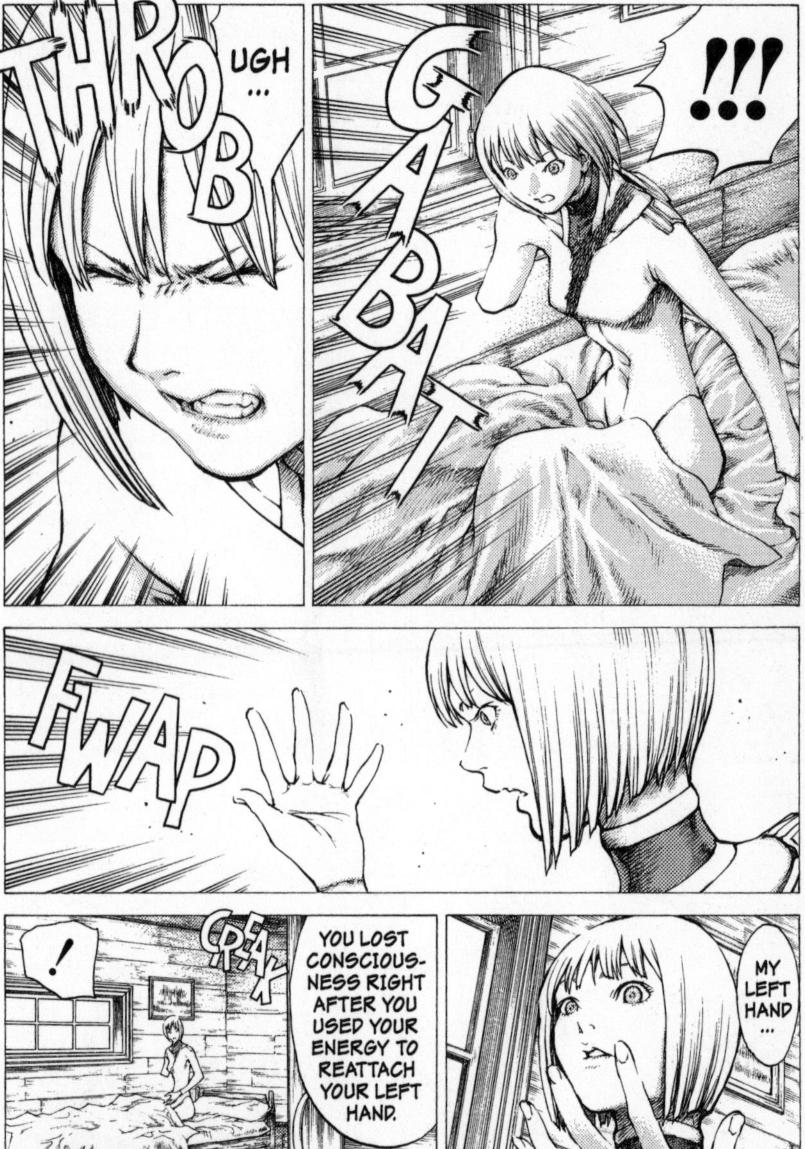
!!!
GABAT
UGH ...
THROB
FWAP
MY LEFT HAND ...
YOU LOST CONSCIOUSNESS RIGHT AFTER YOU USED YOUR ENERGY TO REATTACH YOUR LEFT HAND.
CREAK
!

READ THIS WAY

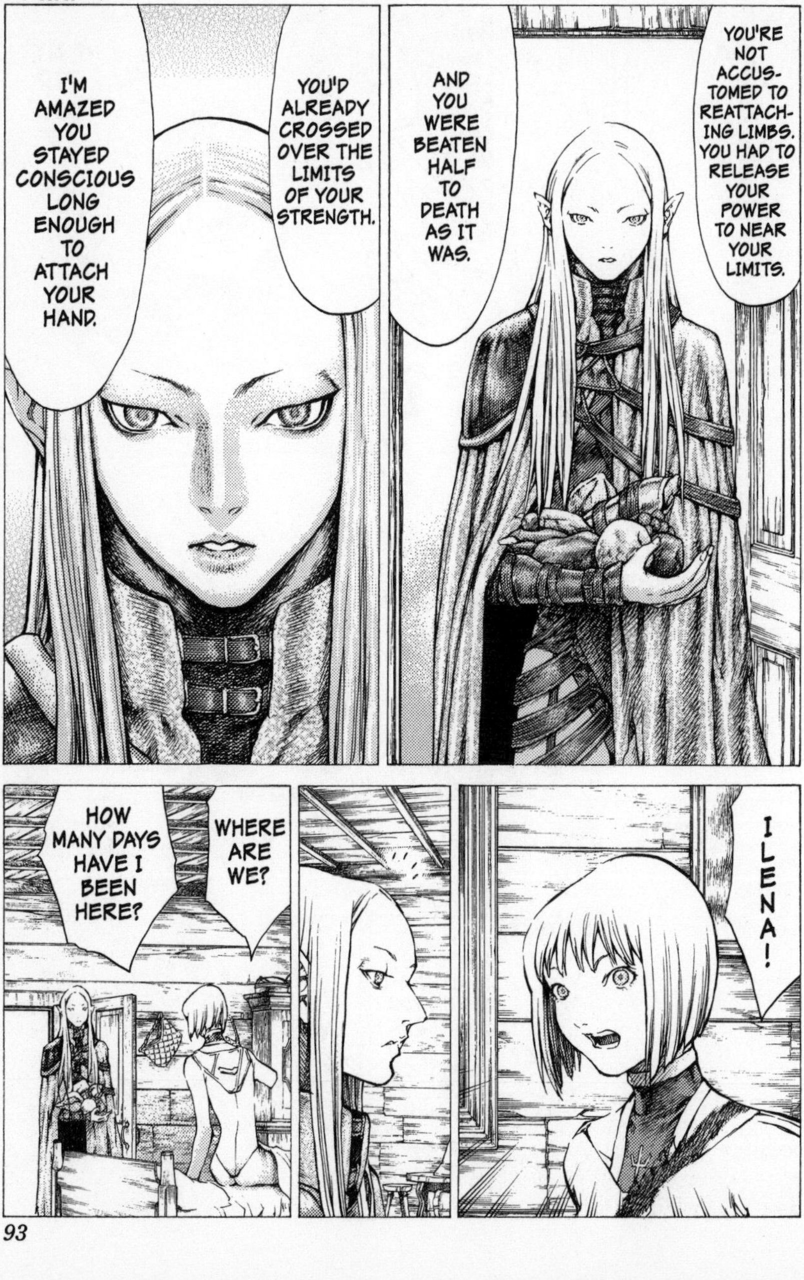
YOU'RE NOT ACCUS-TOMED TO REATTACH-ING LIMBS. YOU HAD TO RELEASE YOUR POWER TO NEAR YOUR LIMITS.
AND YOU WERE BEATEN HALF TO DEATH AS IT WAS.
YOU'D ALREADY CROSSED OVER THE LIMITS OF YOUR STRENGTH.
I'M AMAZED YOU STAYED CONSCIOUS LONG ENOUGH TO ATTACH YOUR HAND.
ILENA!
WHERE ARE WE?
HOW MANY DAYS HAVE I BEEN HERE?

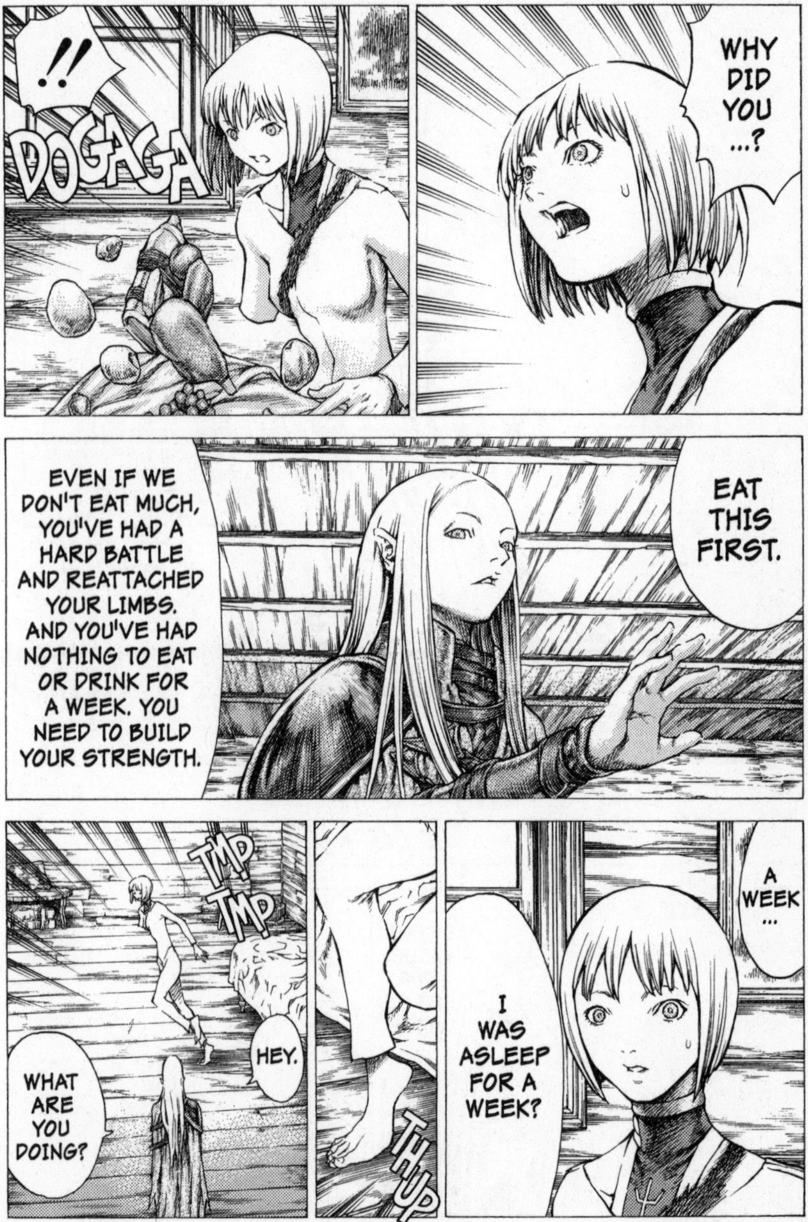
WHY DID YOU ...?
!!
DOGAGA
EAT THIS FIRST.
EVEN IF WE DON'T EAT MUCH, YOU'VE HAD A HARD BATTLE AND REATTACHED YOUR LIMBS. AND YOU'VE HAD NOTHING TO EAT OR DRINK FOR A WEEK. YOU NEED TO BUILD YOUR STRENGTH.
A WEEK ...
I WAS ASLEEP FOR A WEEK?
THUP
TMP TMP
HEY.
WHAT ARE YOU DOING?

READ THIS WAY

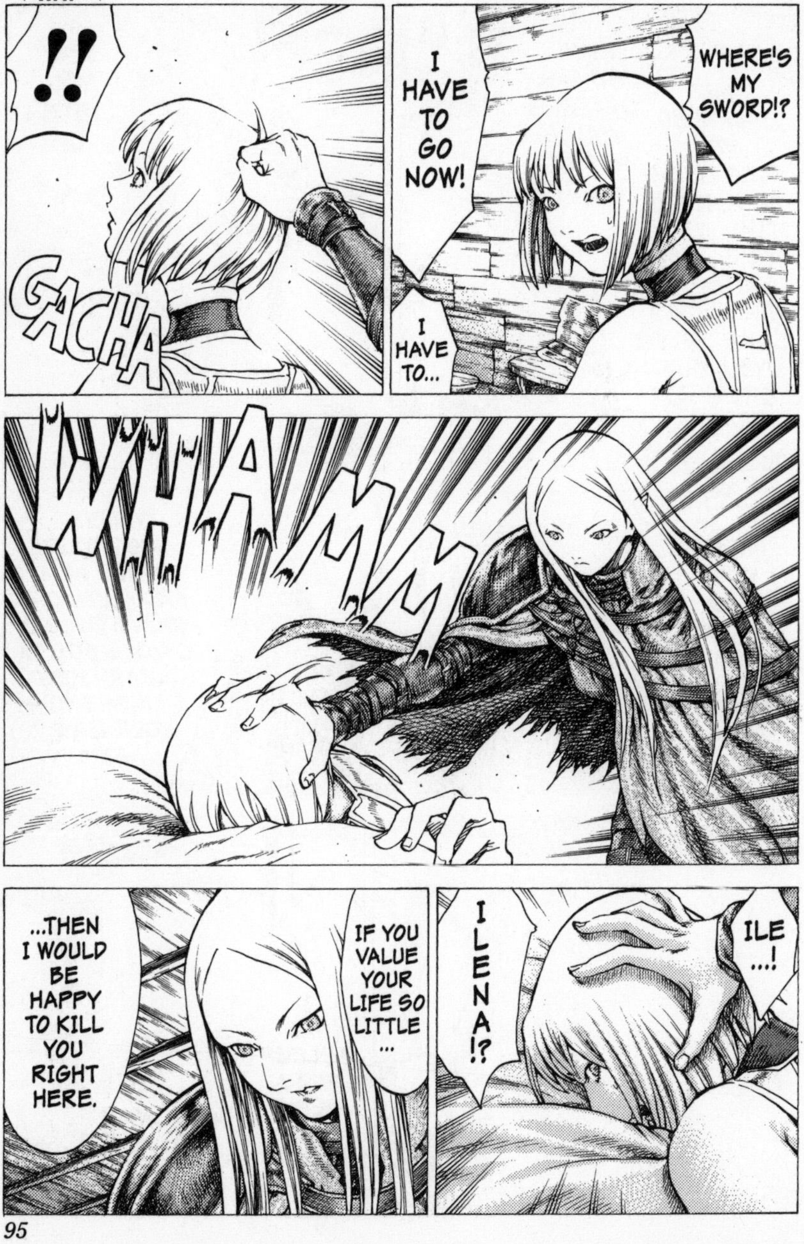
WHERE'S MY SWORD!?
I HAVE TO GO NOW!
I HAVE TO...
!!
GACHA
WHAMM
ILE ...!
ILENA!?
IF YOU VALUE YOUR LIFE SO LITTLE ...
...THEN I WOULD BE HAPPY TO KILL YOU RIGHT HERE.

NOW YOU LISTEN UP.
UGH ...
THAT WOMAN CHASING YOU IS STILL ALIVE.
SHE DAMAGED YOU THIS MUCH, SO FOR THE TIME BEING SHE'LL BE SATISFIED AND WON'T COME AFTER YOU, BUT SHE'S NOT DEAD.
UMH ...
YOU'VE LOST YOUR SWORD ARM. FROM NOW ON, YOU'VE GOT NO CHOICE BUT TO LEARN HOW TO FIGHT WITH YOUR OTHER ARM.
RIGHT NOW, YOU COULDN'T EVEN KILL A SINGLE YOMA.
UGH ...
GRR...

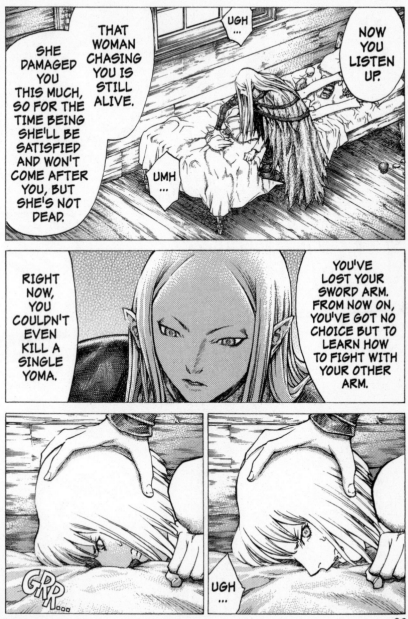

READ THIS WAY

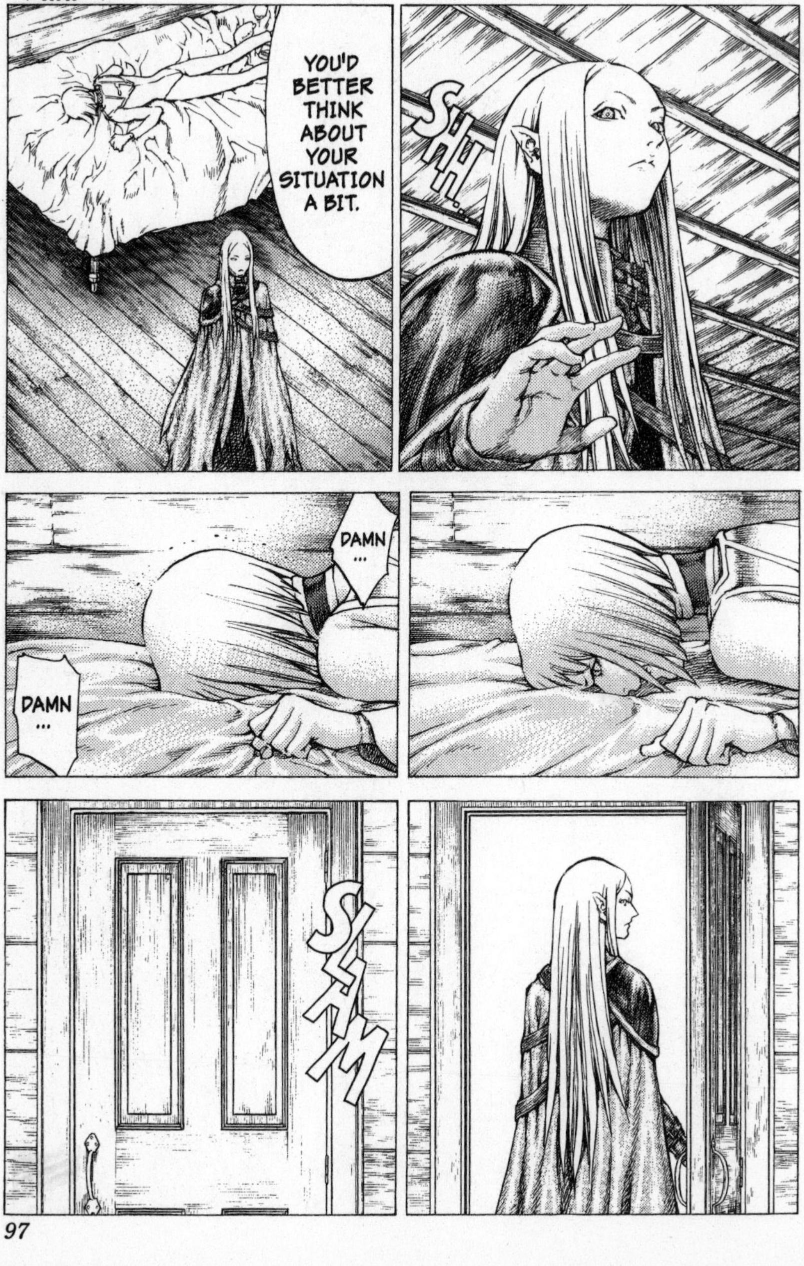
SH...
YOU'D BETTER THINK ABOUT YOUR SITUATION A BIT.
DAMN ...
DAMN ...
SLAM

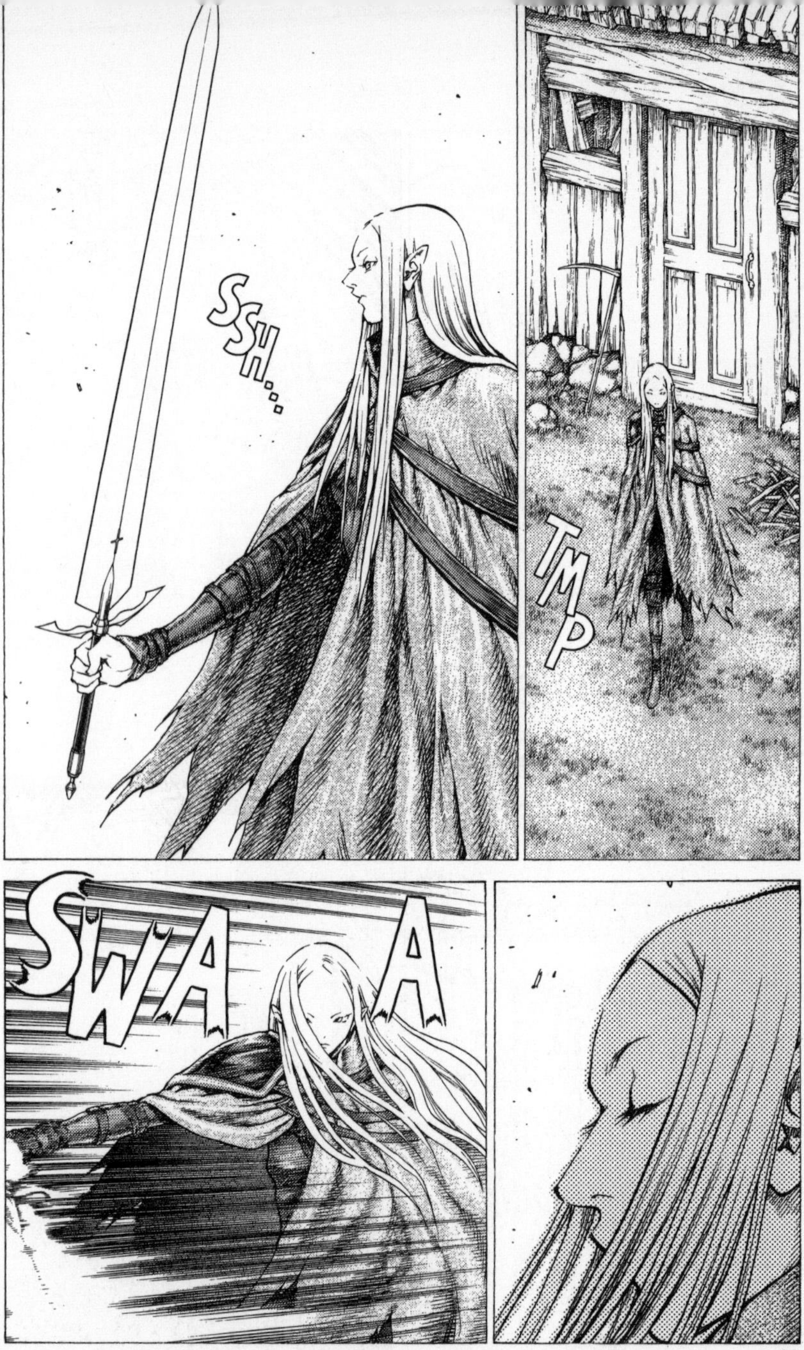
TMP
SSH...
SWAA

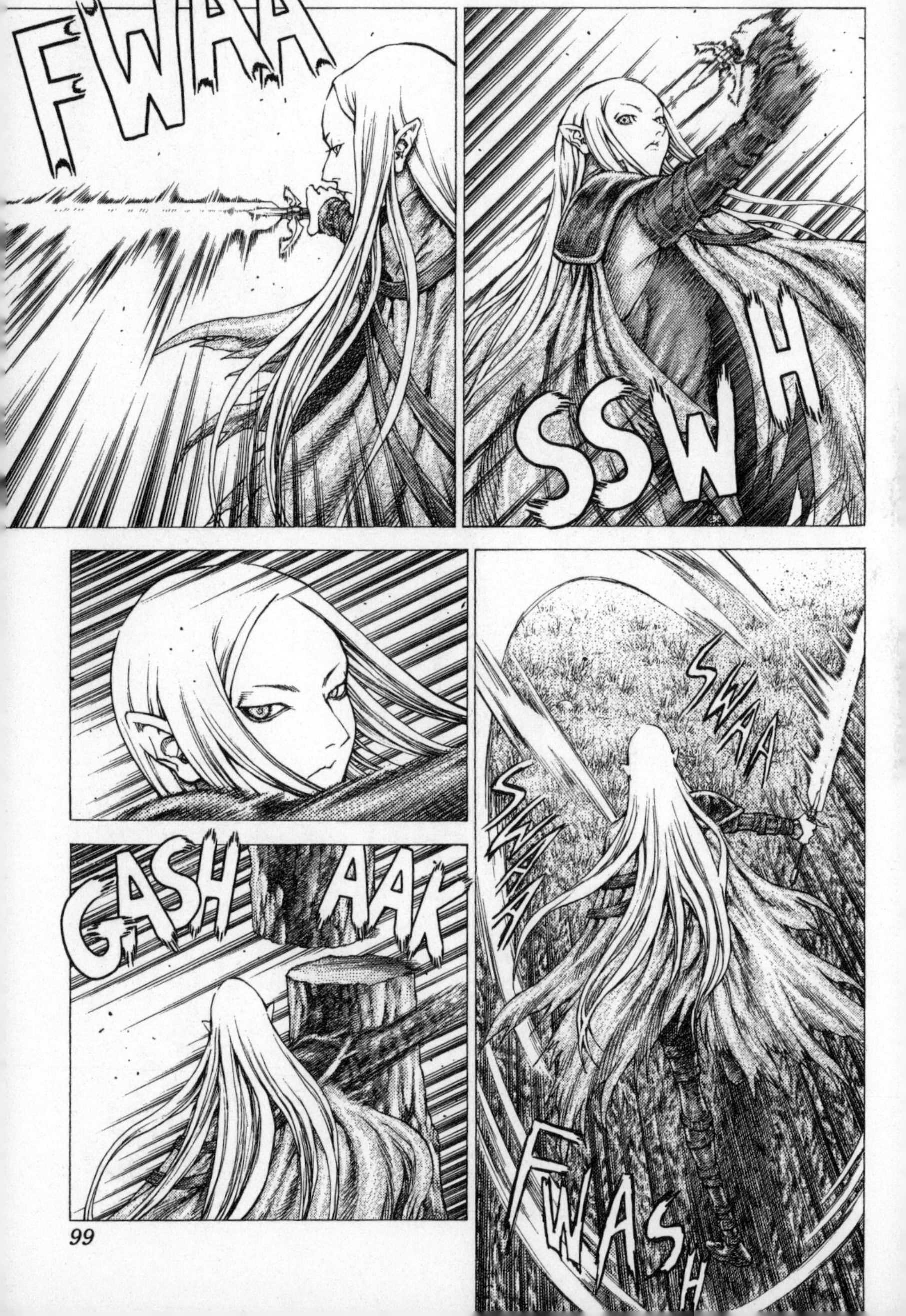
SSWH
FWAA
SWAA
SWAA
FWASH
GASH
AAK

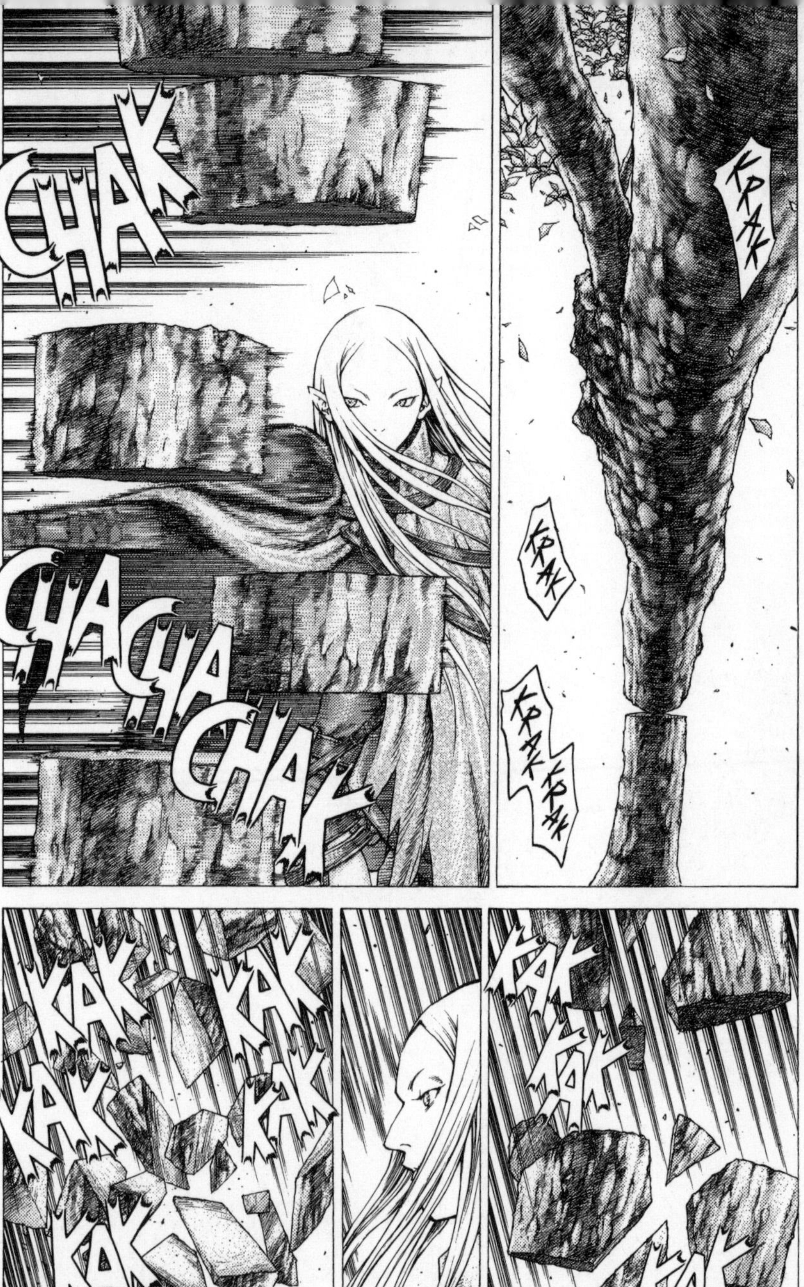
KRAK
KRAK
KRAK KRAK
CHAK
CHACHA CHAK
KAK KAK
KAK
KAK KAK
KAK KAK
KAK

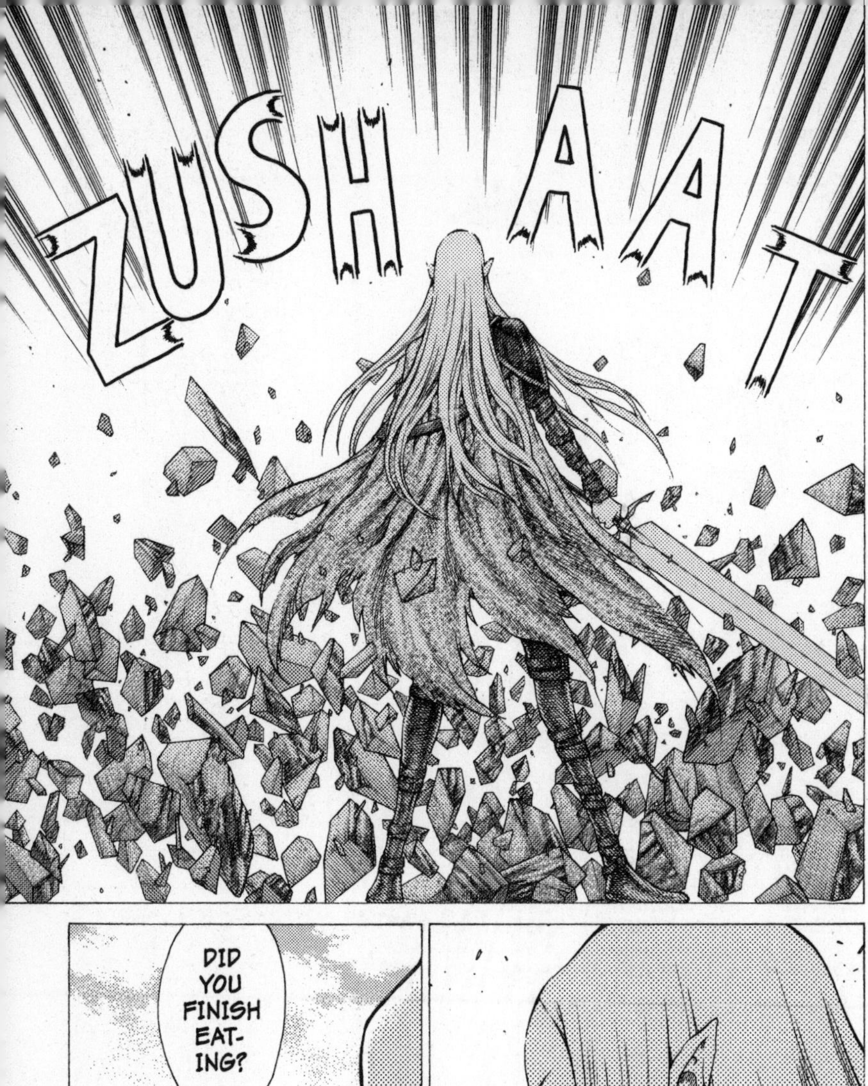
ZUSHAAT

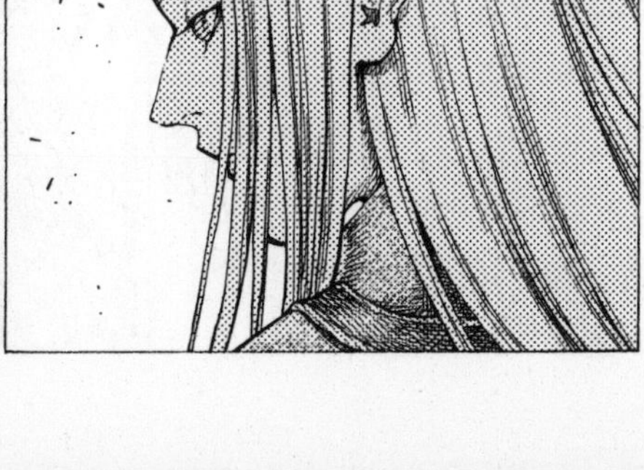

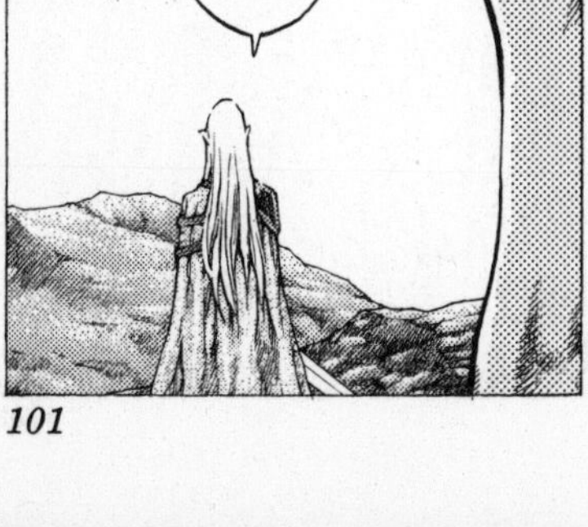
DID YOU FINISH EAT-ING?

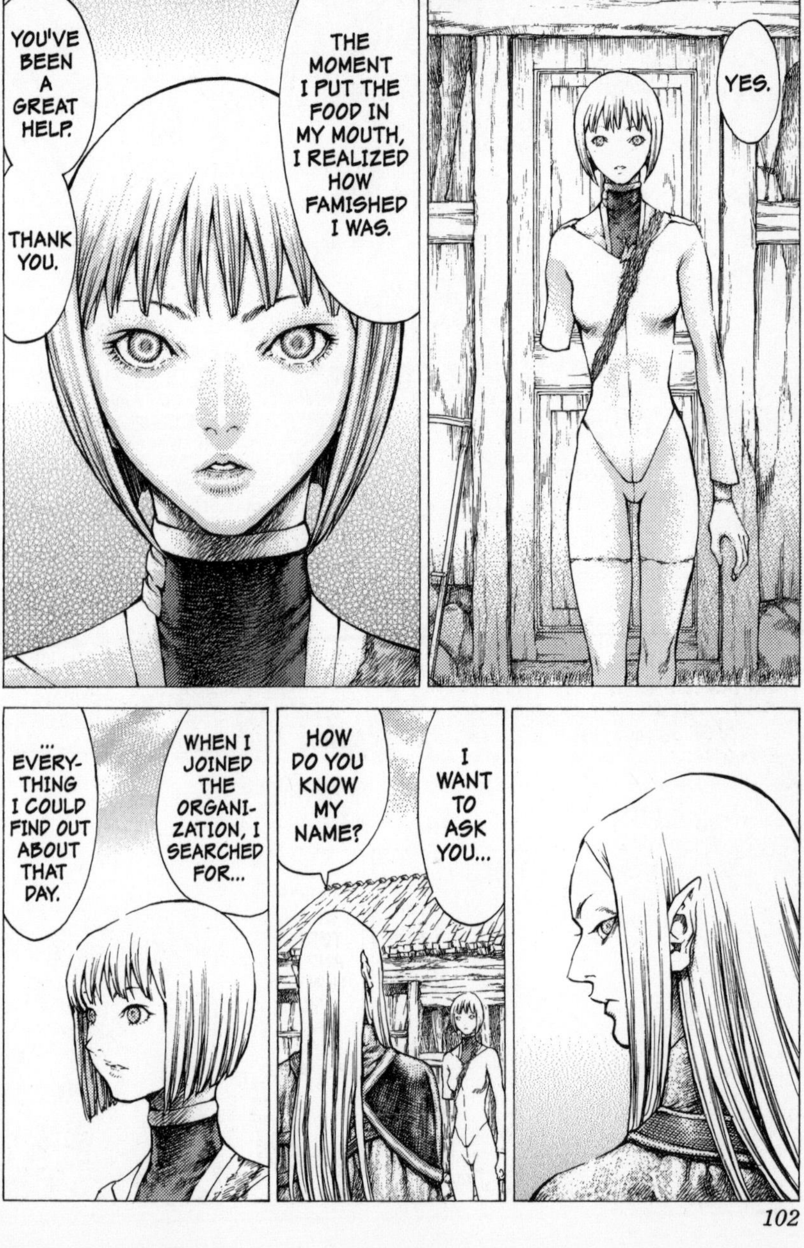
YES.
THE MOMENT I PUT THE FOOD IN MY MOUTH, I REALIZED HOW FAMISHED I WAS.
YOU'VE BEEN A GREAT HELP.
THANK YOU.
I WANT TO ASK YOU...
HOW DO YOU KNOW MY NAME?
WHEN I JOINED THE ORGANI-ZATION, I SEARCHED FOR...
... EVERY-THING I COULD FIND OUT ABOUT THAT DAY.

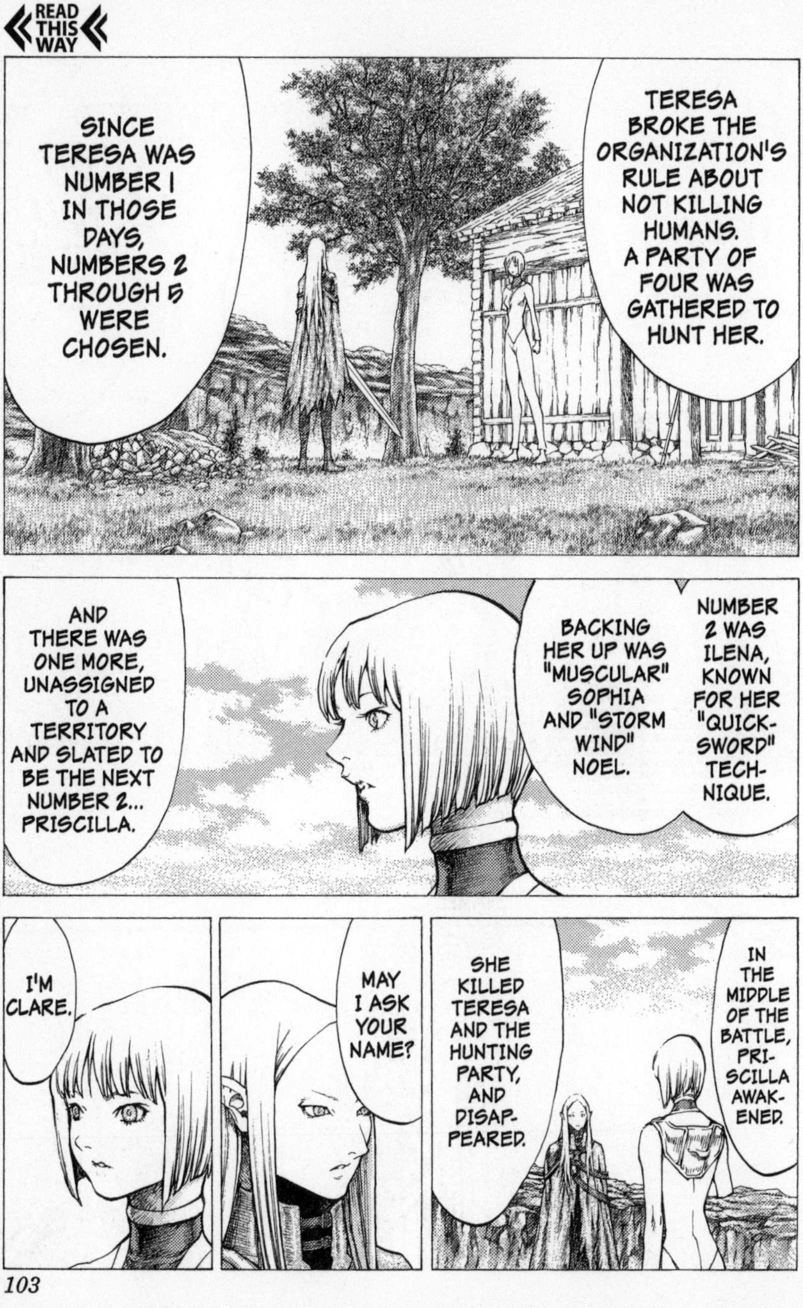
READ THIS WAY
TERESA BROKE THE ORGANIZATION'S RULE ABOUT NOT KILLING HUMANS. A PARTY OF FOUR WAS GATHERED TO HUNT HER.
SINCE TERESA WAS NUMBER 1 IN THOSE DAYS, NUMBERS 2 THROUGH 5 WERE CHOSEN.
NUMBER 2 WAS ILENA, KNOWN FOR HER "QUICK-SWORD" TECHNIQUE.
BACKING HER UP WAS "MUSCULAR" SOPHIA AND "STORM WIND" NOEL.
AND THERE WAS ONE MORE, UNASSIGNED TO A TERRITORY AND SLATED TO BE THE NEXT NUMBER 2... PRISCILLA.
IN THE MIDDLE OF THE BATTLE, PRISCILLA AWAKENED.
SHE KILLED TERESA AND THE HUNTING PARTY, AND DISAPPEARED.
MAY I ASK YOUR NAME?
I'M CLARE.

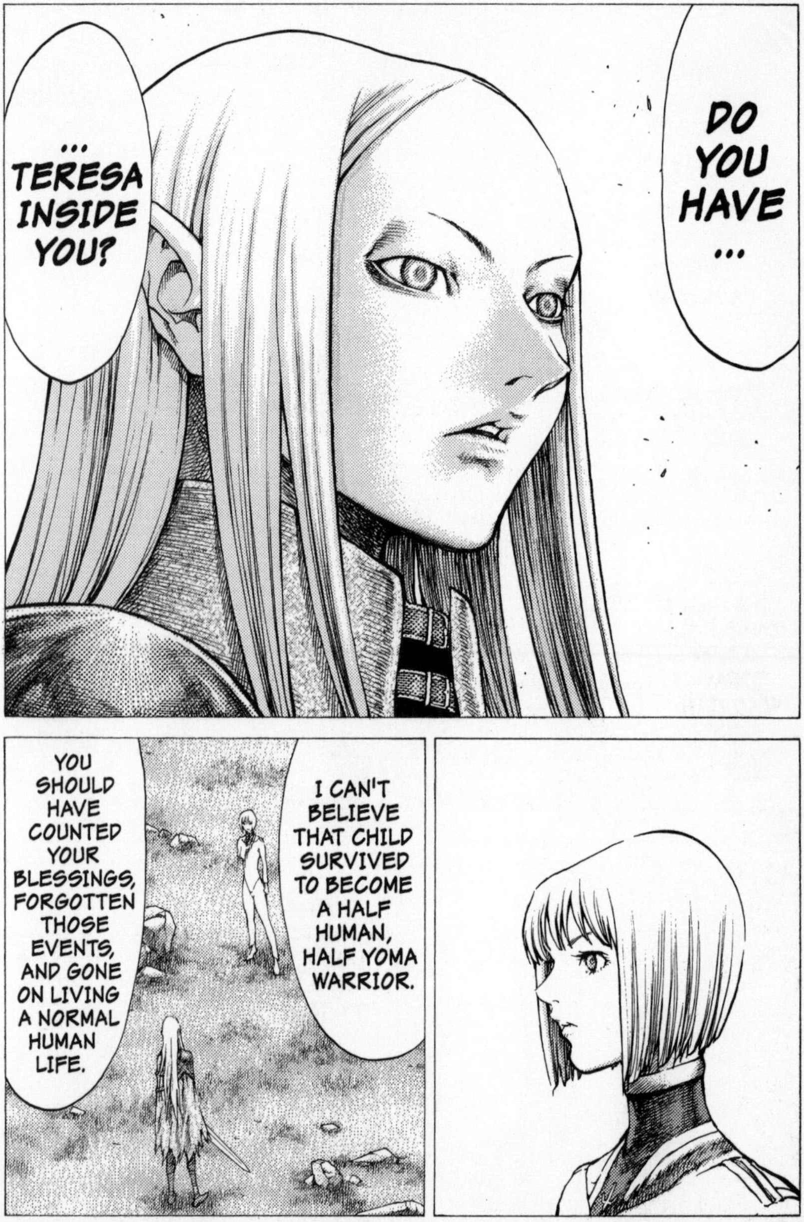
DO YOU HAVE ...
... TERESA INSIDE YOU?
I CAN'T BELIEVE THAT CHILD SURVIVED TO BECOME A HALF HUMAN, HALF YOMA WARRIOR.
YOU SHOULD HAVE COUNTED YOUR BLESSINGS, FORGOTTEN THOSE EVENTS, AND GONE ON LIVING A NORMAL HUMAN LIFE.

READ THIS WAY

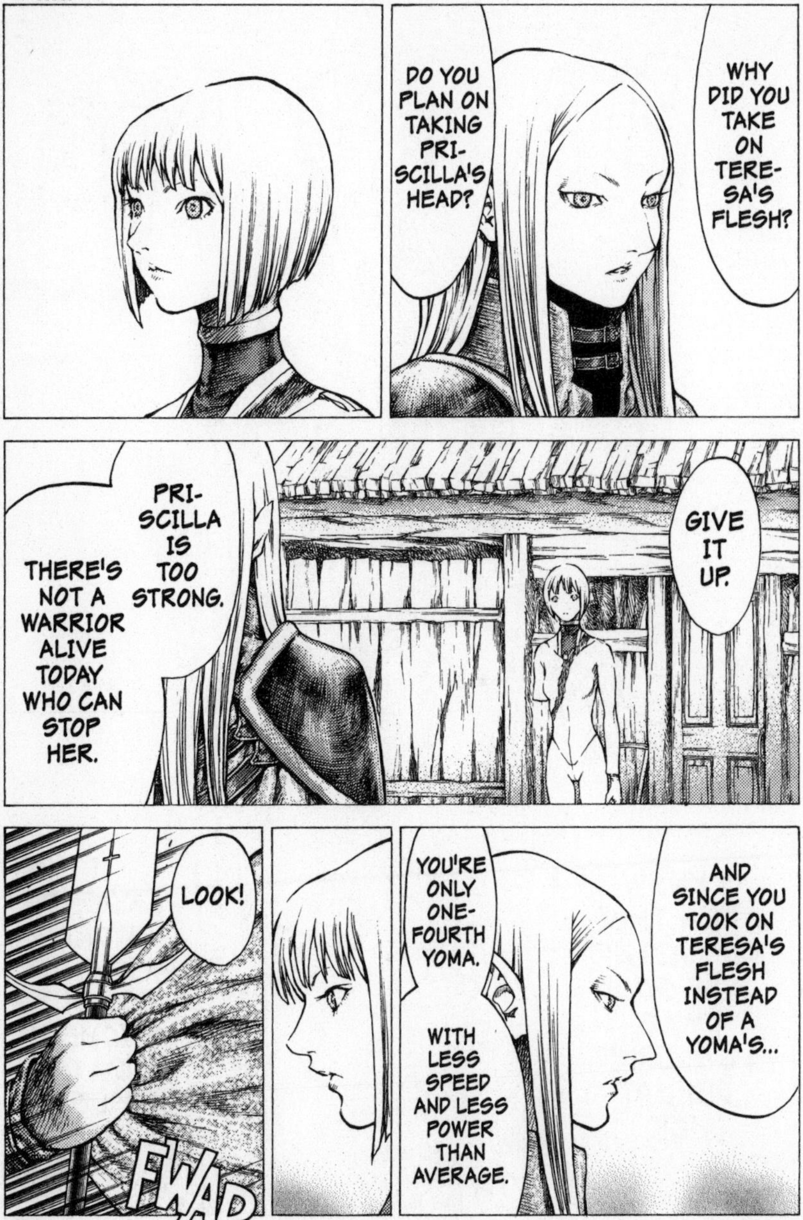
WHY DID YOU TAKE ON TERESA'S FLESH?
DO YOU PLAN ON TAKING PRISCILLA'S HEAD?
GIVE IT UP.
PRISCILLA IS TOO STRONG.
THERE'S NOT A WARRIOR ALIVE TODAY WHO CAN STOP HER.
AND SINCE YOU TOOK ON TERESA'S FLESH INSTEAD OF A YOMA'S...
YOU'RE ONLY ONE-FOURTH YOMA.
WITH LESS SPEED AND LESS POWER THAN AVERAGE.
LOOK!
FWAP

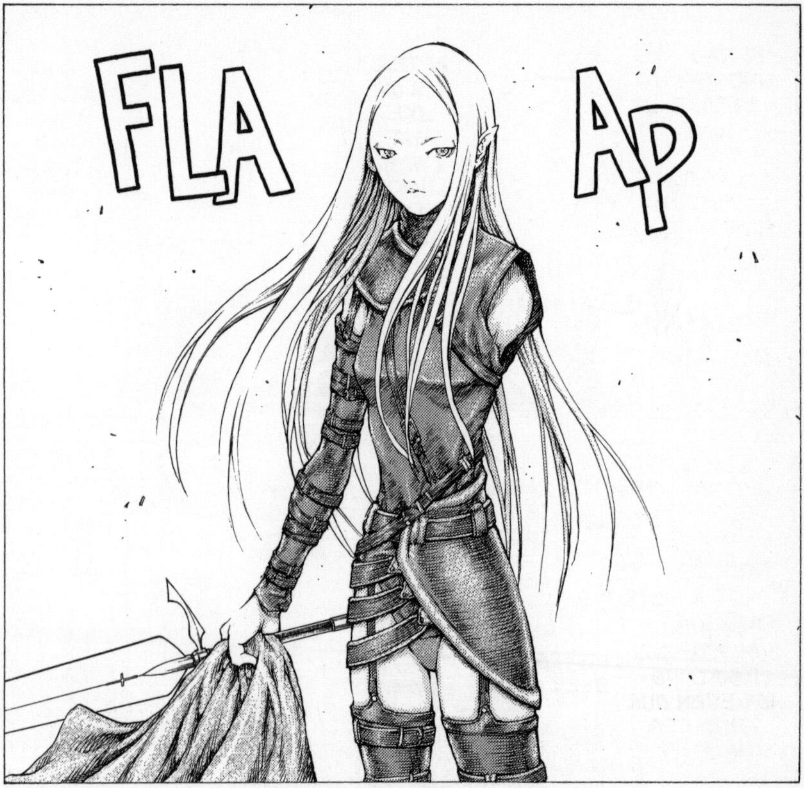
FLAAP

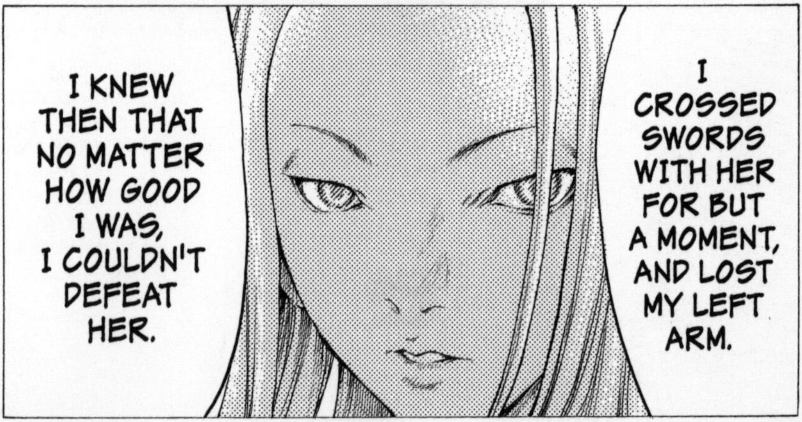
I CROSSED SWORDS WITH HER FOR BUT A MOMENT, AND LOST MY LEFT ARM.
I KNEW THEN THAT NO MATTER HOW GOOD I WAS, I COULDN'T DEFEAT HER.

READ THIS WAY

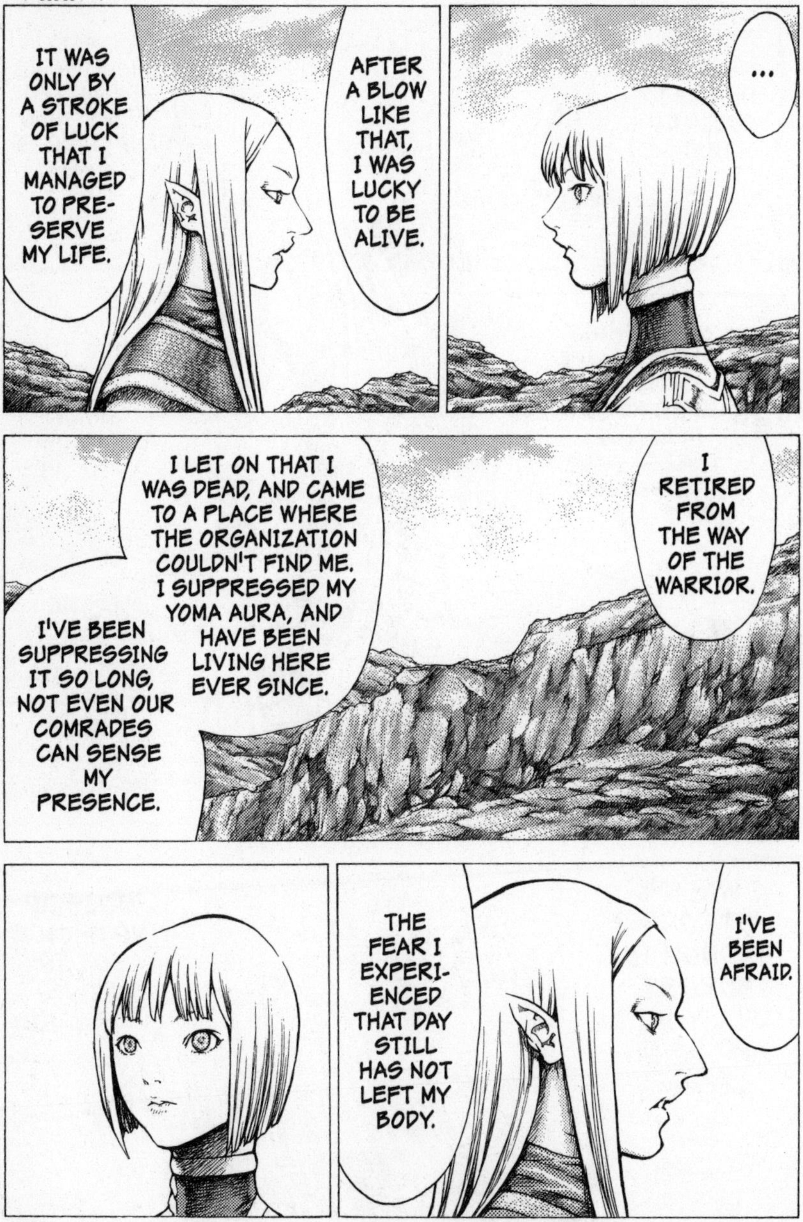
...
AFTER A BLOW LIKE THAT, I WAS LUCKY TO BE ALIVE.
IT WAS ONLY BY A STROKE OF LUCK THAT I MANAGED TO PRE-SERVE MY LIFE.
I RETIRED FROM THE WAY OF THE WARRIOR.
I LET ON THAT I WAS DEAD, AND CAME TO A PLACE WHERE THE ORGANIZATION COULDN'T FIND ME. I SUPPRESSED MY YOMA AURA, AND HAVE BEEN LIVING HERE EVER SINCE.
I'VE BEEN SUPPRESSING IT SO LONG, NOT EVEN OUR COMRADES CAN SENSE MY PRESENCE.
I'VE BEEN AFRAID.
THE FEAR I EXPERI-ENCED THAT DAY STILL HAS NOT LEFT MY BODY.

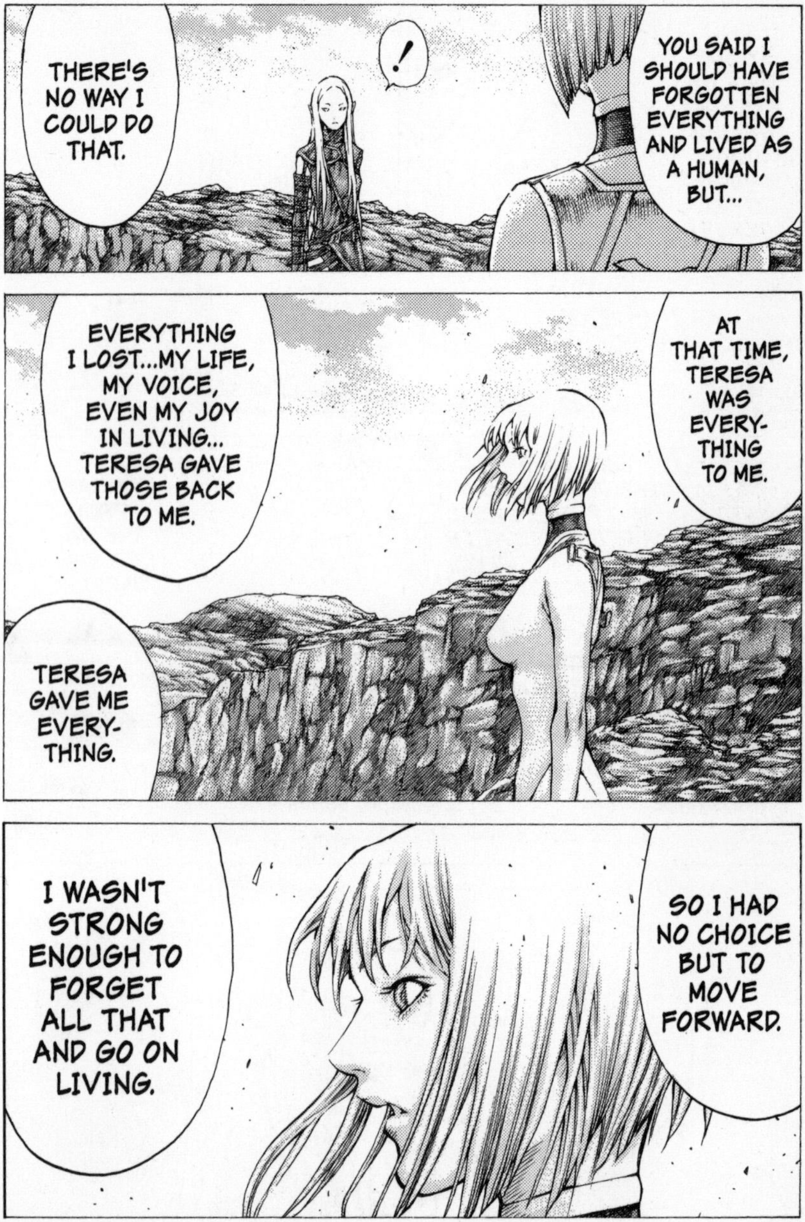
YOU SAID I SHOULD HAVE FORGOTTEN EVERYTHING AND LIVED AS A HUMAN, BUT...
!
THERE'S NO WAY I COULD DO THAT.
AT THAT TIME, TERESA WAS EVERYTHING TO ME.
EVERYTHING I LOST...MY LIFE, MY VOICE, EVEN MY JOY IN LIVING... TERESA GAVE THOSE BACK TO ME.
TERESA GAVE ME EVERYTHING.
SO I HAD NO CHOICE BUT TO MOVE FORWARD.
I WASN'T STRONG ENOUGH TO FORGET ALL THAT AND GO ON LIVING.

READ THIS WAY

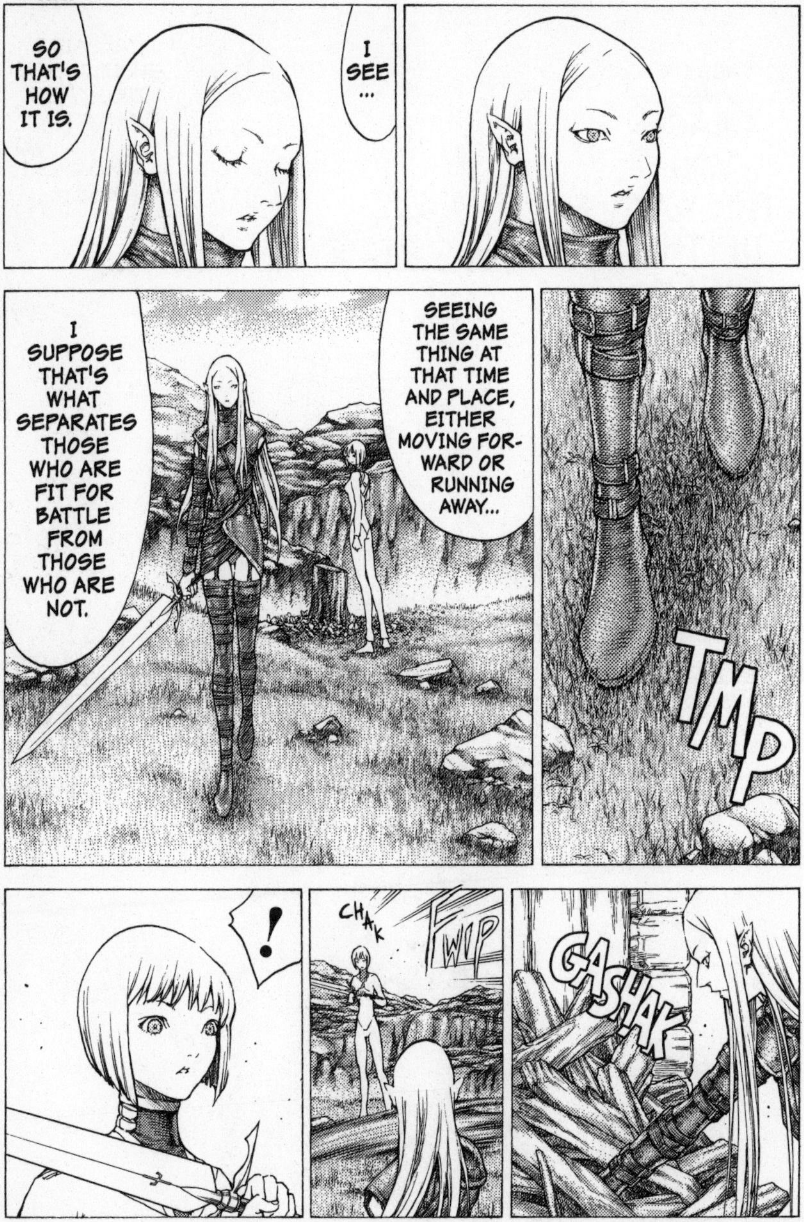
I SEE ...
SO THAT'S HOW IT IS.
TMP
SEEING THE SAME THING AT THAT TIME AND PLACE, EITHER MOVING FORWARD OR RUNNING AWAY...
I SUPPOSE THAT'S WHAT SEPARATES THOSE WHO ARE FIT FOR BATTLE FROM THOSE WHO ARE NOT.
GASHAK
FWIP
CHAK
!

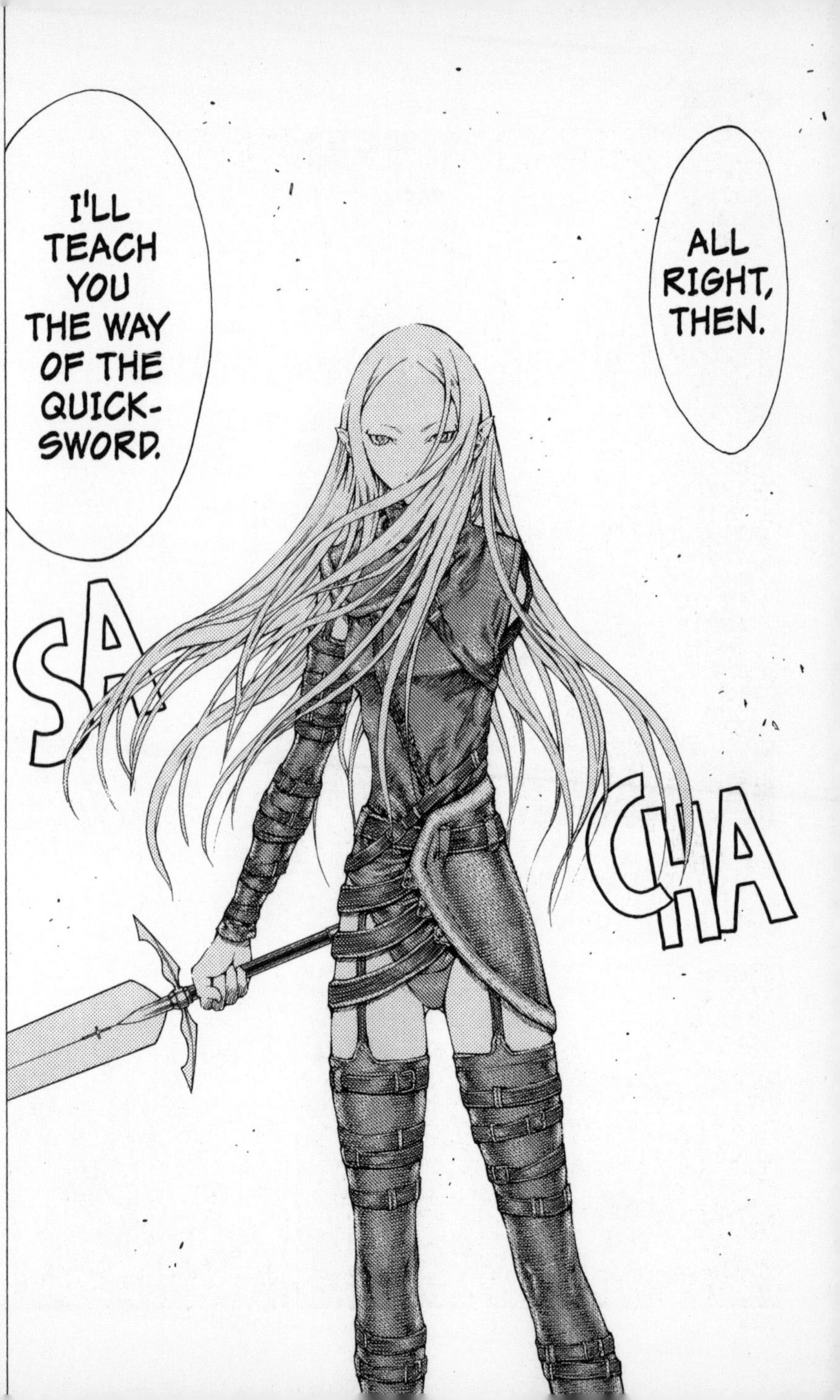
ALL RIGHT, THEN.
I'LL TEACH YOU THE WAY OF THE QUICK-SWORD.
SA
CHA

READ THIS WAY

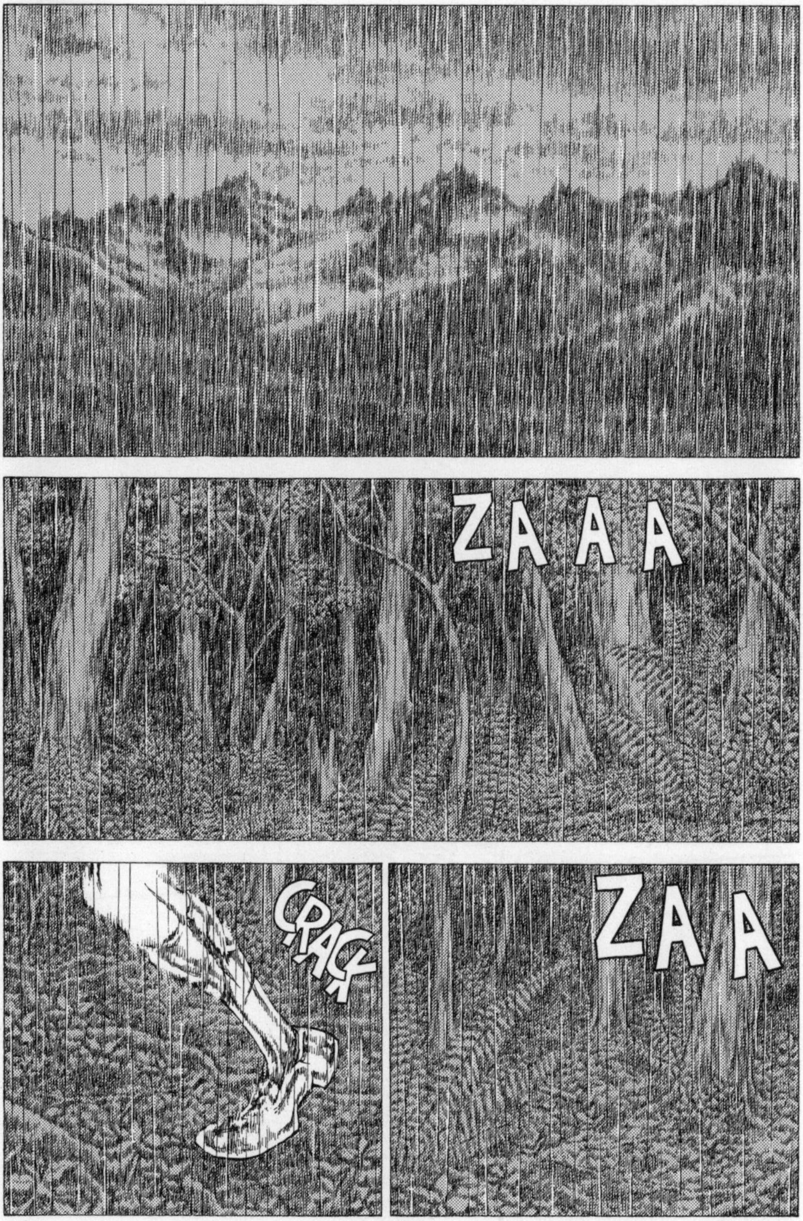
ZAAA
ZAA
CRACK

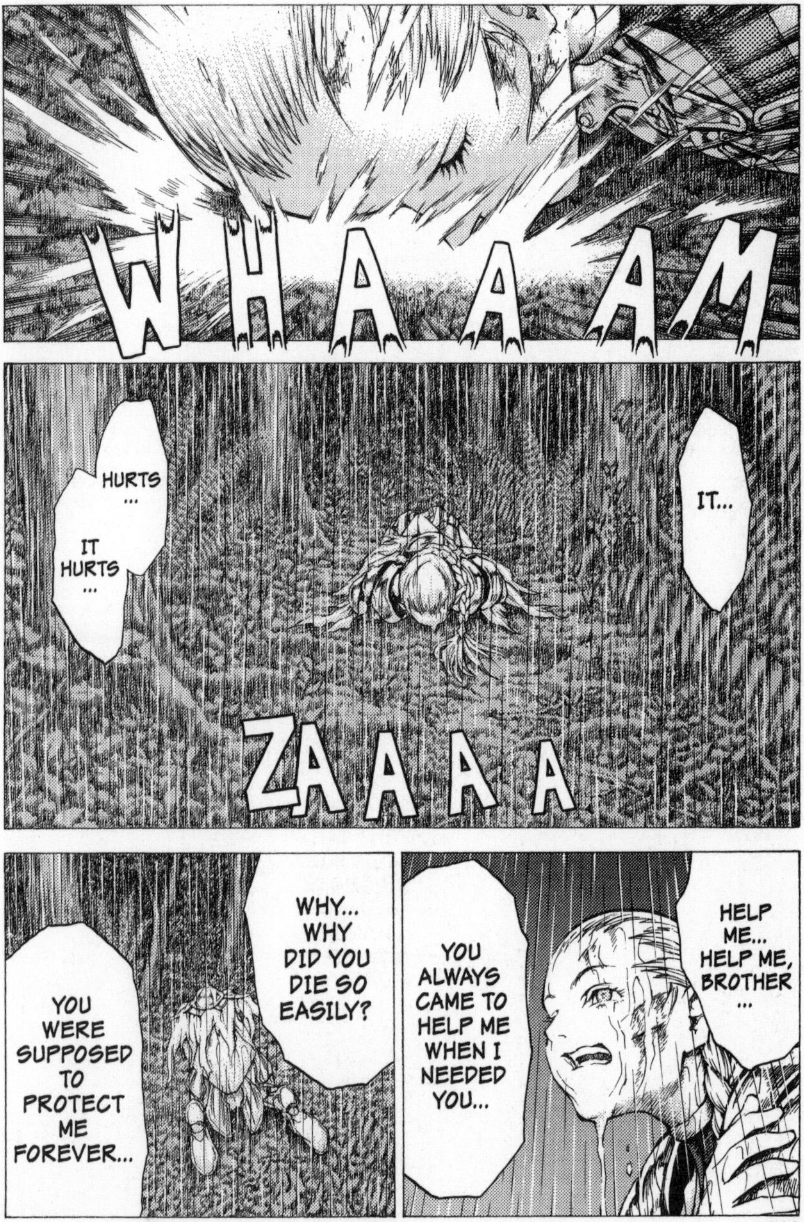
WHAAAM
IT...
HURTS... IT HURTS...
ZAAAA
HELP ME... HELP ME, BROTHER...
YOU ALWAYS CAME TO HELP ME WHEN I NEEDED YOU...
WHY... WHY DID YOU DIE SO EASILY?
YOU WERE SUPPOSED TO PROTECT ME FOREVER...

READ THIS WAY

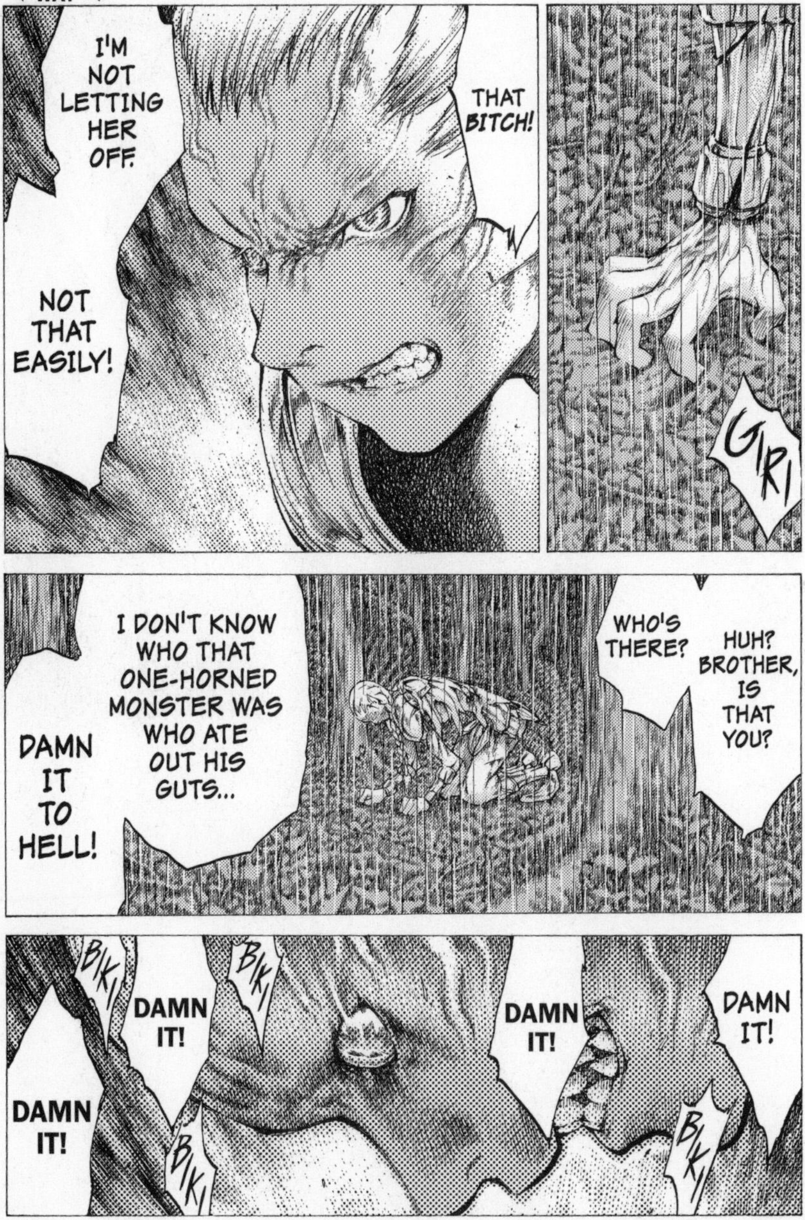
GIRI
THAT BITCH!
I'M NOT LETTING HER OFF.
NOT THAT EASILY!
HUH? BROTHER, IS THAT YOU?
WHO'S THERE?
I DON'T KNOW WHO THAT ONE-HORNED MONSTER WAS WHO ATE OUT HIS GUTS...
DAMN IT TO HELL!
DAMN IT!
BIKI
DAMN IT!
BIKI
DAMN IT!
BIKI
BIKI
DAMN IT!

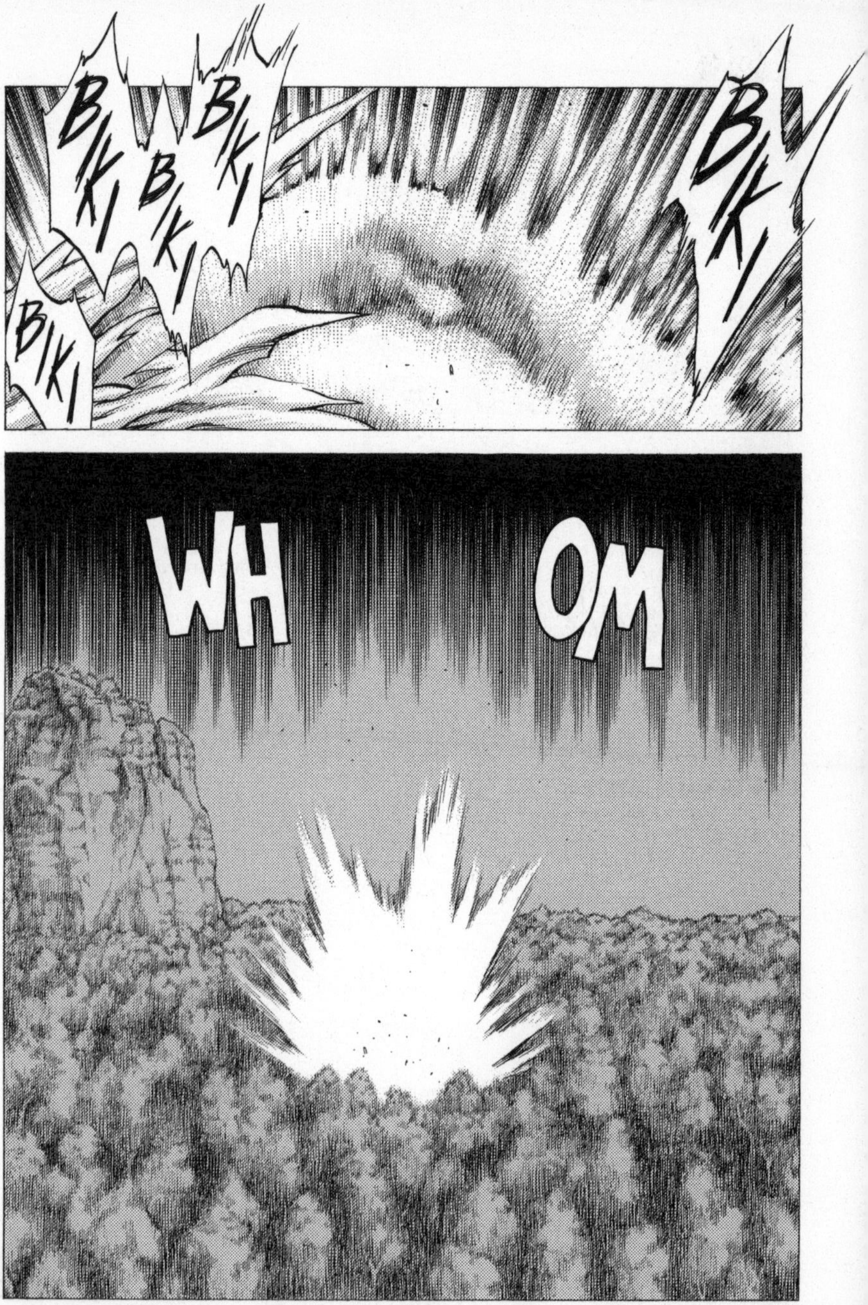
BIKI
BIKI
BIKI
BIKI
BIKI
WH OM

READ THIS WAY

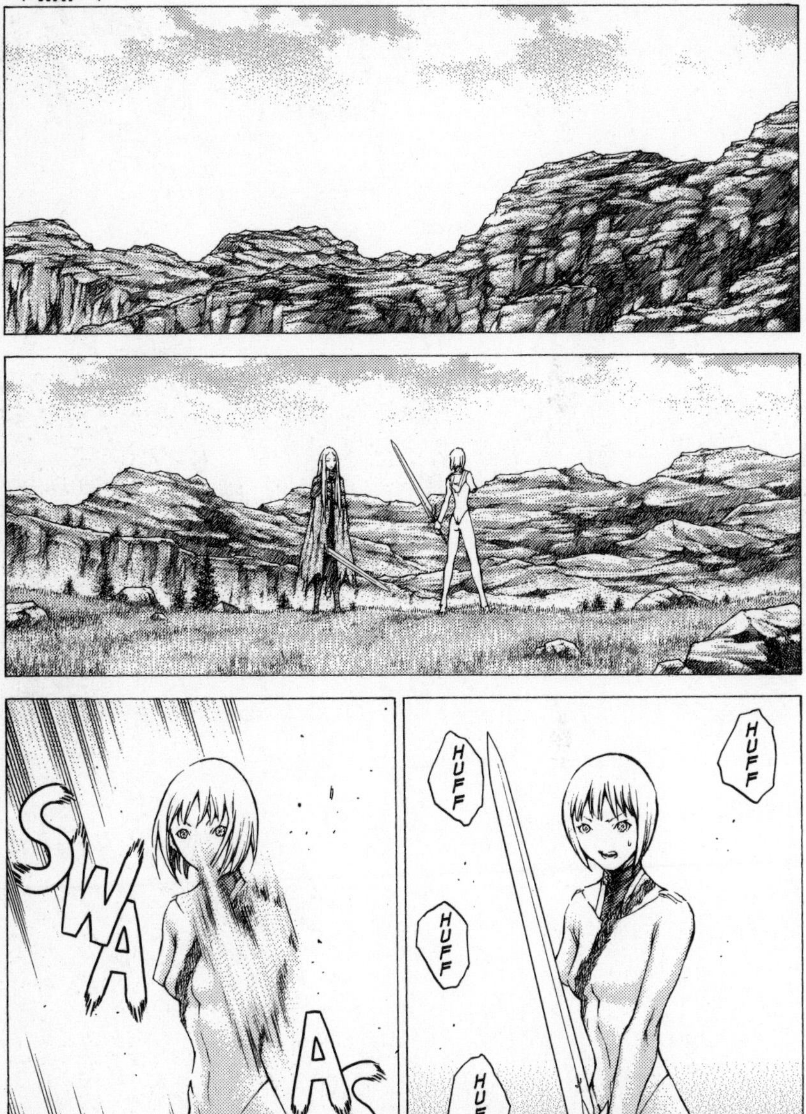
HUFF
HUFF
HUFF
HUFF
SWASH

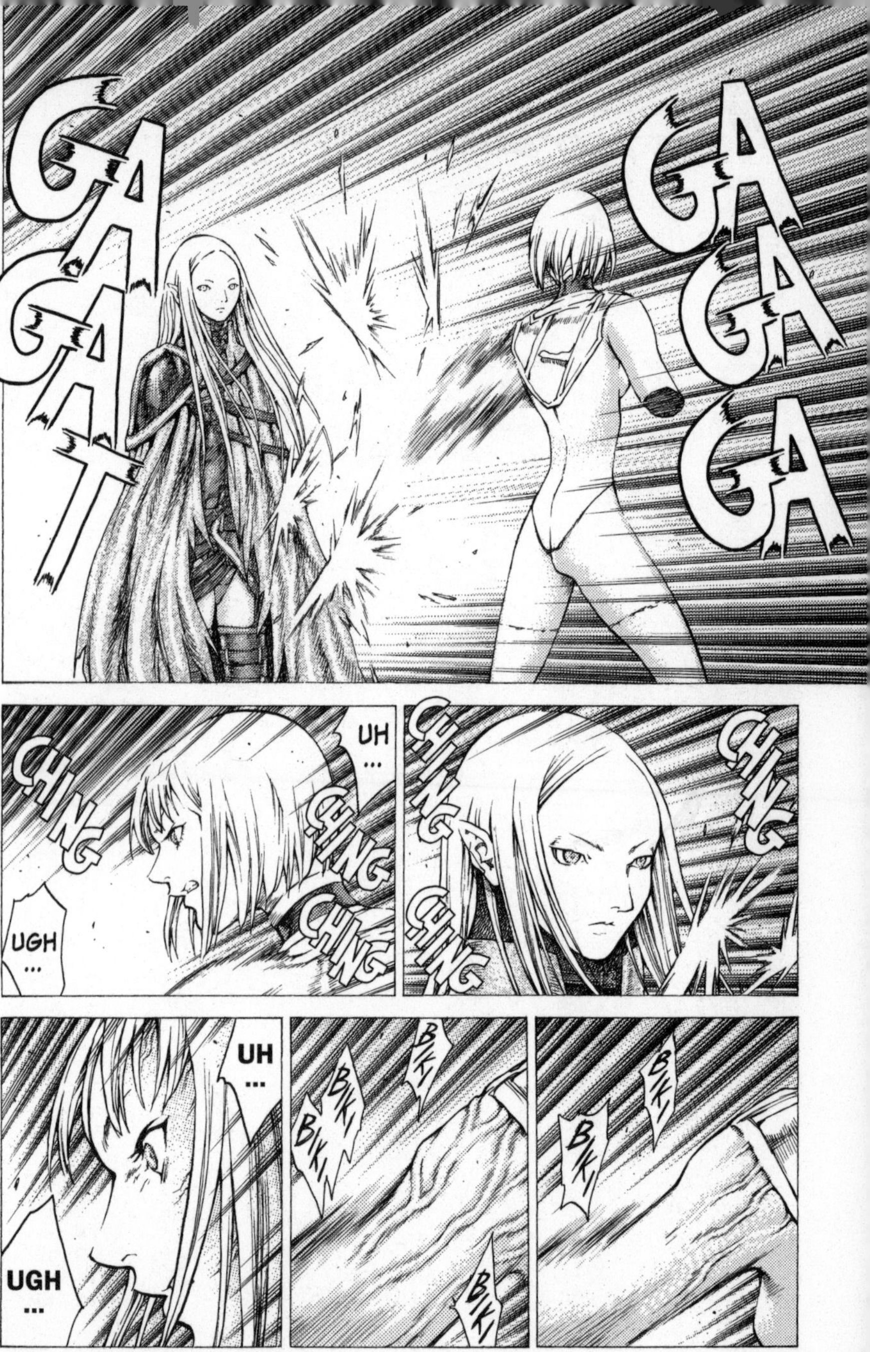
GAGAGAGA
GAGAGAT
CHING
CHING
CHING
UH...
CHING
CHING
UGH...
BIKI
BIKI
BIKI
BIKI
BIKI
BIKI
UH...
UGH...

READ THIS WAY

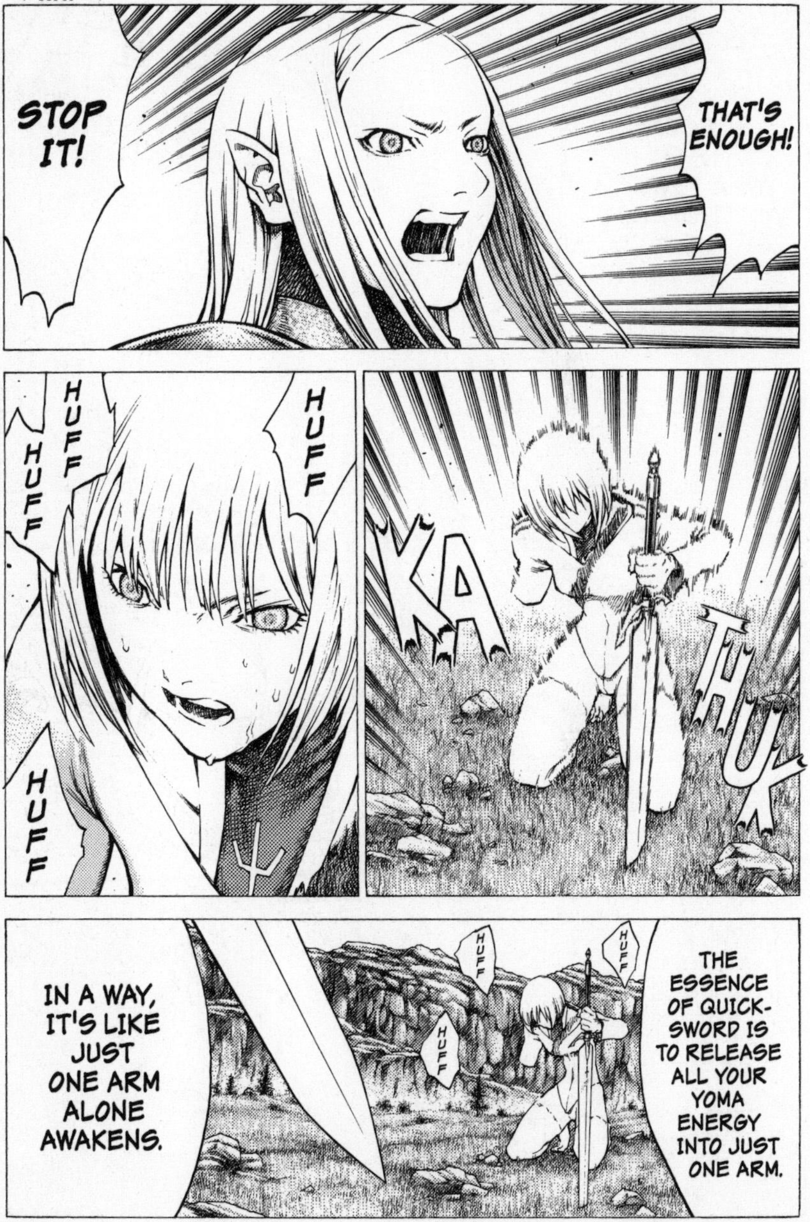
THAT'S ENOUGH!
STOP IT!
KA
THUK
HUFF
HUFF HUFF
HUFF
THE ESSENCE OF QUICK-SWORD IS TO RELEASE ALL YOUR YOMA ENERGY INTO JUST ONE ARM.
HUFF
HUFF
HUFF
IN A WAY, IT'S LIKE JUST ONE ARM ALONE AWAKENS.

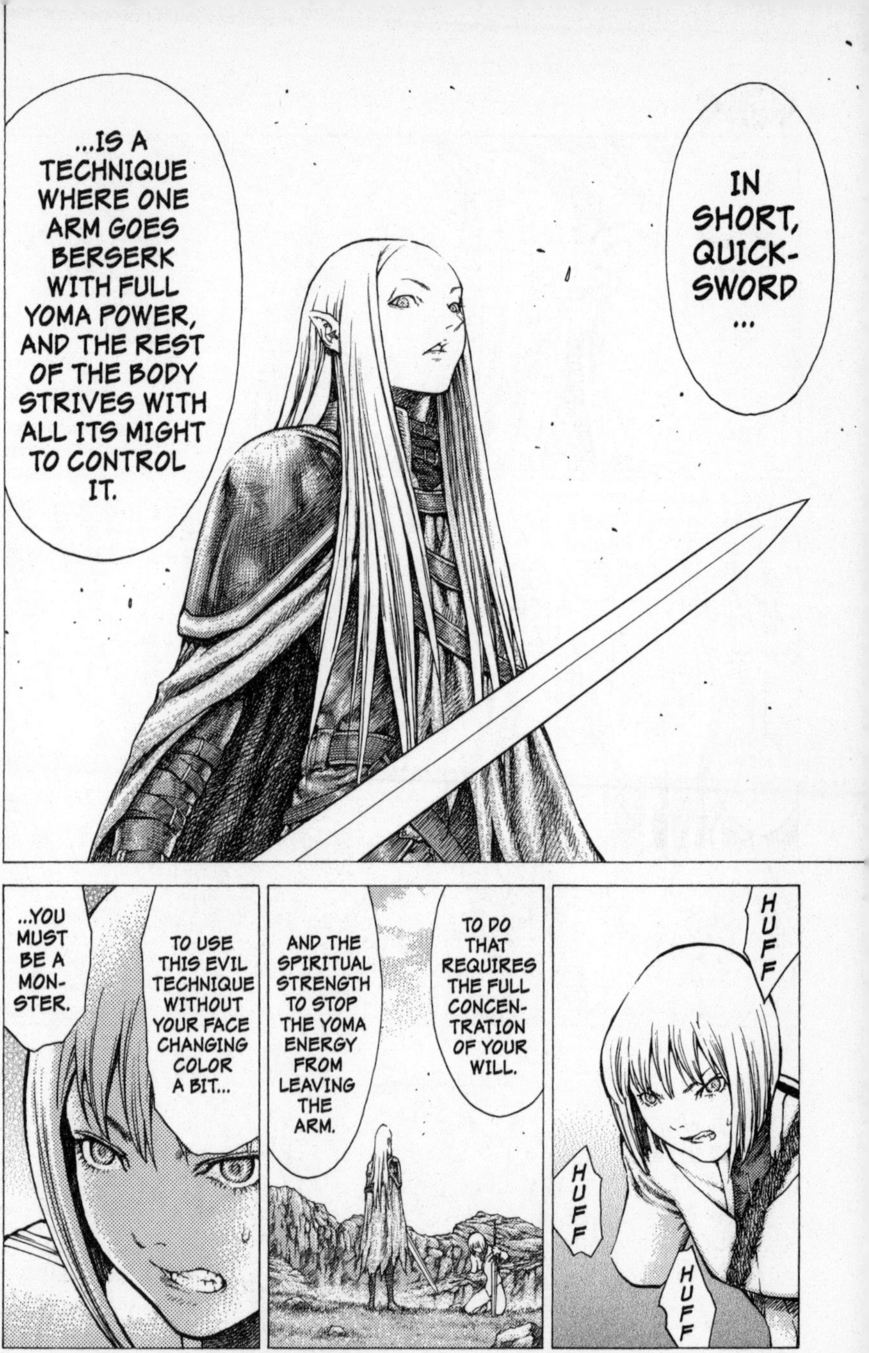
IN SHORT, QUICK-SWORD...
...IS A TECHNIQUE WHERE ONE ARM GOES BERSERK WITH FULL YOMA POWER, AND THE REST OF THE BODY STRIVES WITH ALL ITS MIGHT TO CONTROL IT.
HUFF
HUFF
HUFF
TO DO THAT REQUIRES THE FULL CONCENTRATION OF YOUR WILL.
AND THE SPIRITUAL STRENGTH TO STOP THE YOMA ENERGY FROM LEAVING THE ARM.
TO USE THIS EVIL TECHNIQUE WITHOUT YOUR FACE CHANGING COLOR A BIT...
...YOU MUST BE A MONSTER.

READ THIS WAY

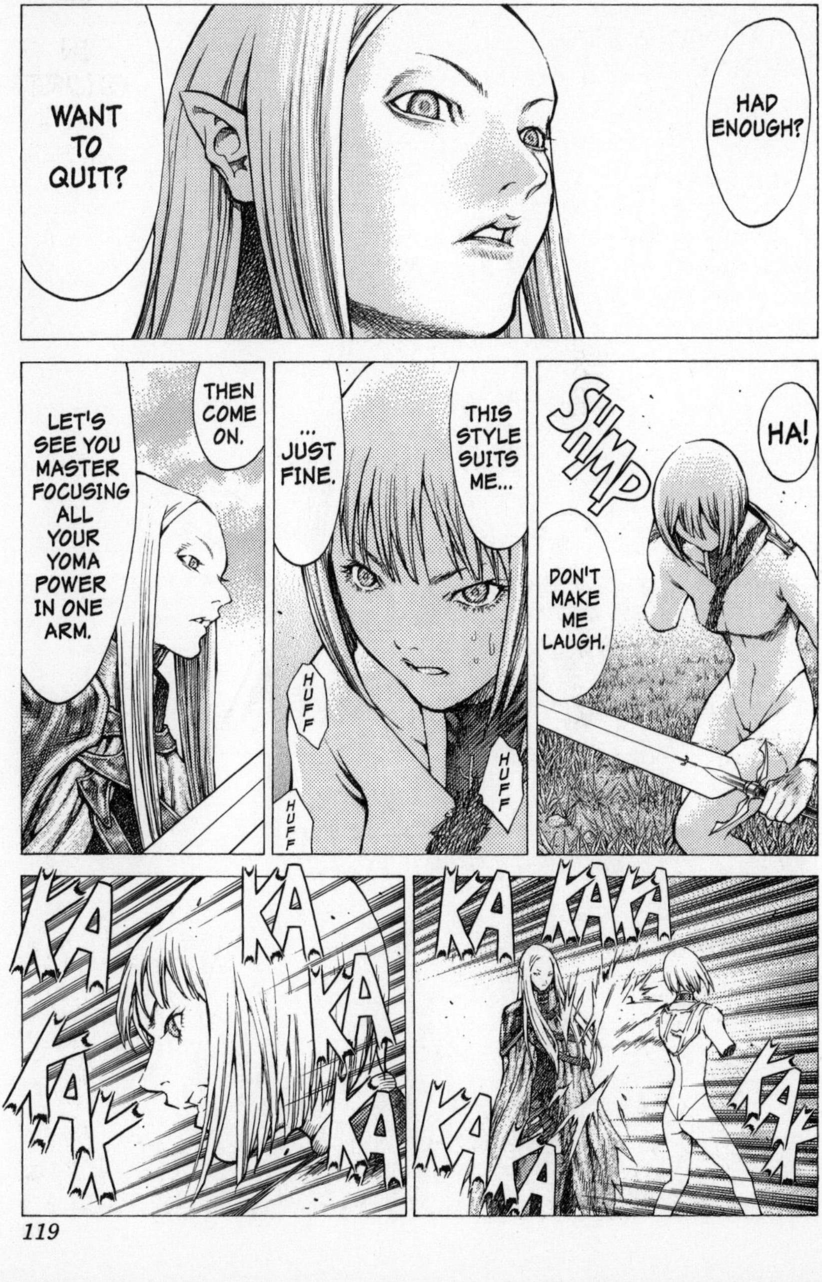

HAD ENOUGH?
WANT TO QUIT?
HA!
SHMP
DON'T MAKE ME LAUGH.
THIS STYLE SUITS ME...
... JUST FINE.
HUFF
HUFF
HUFF
THEN COME ON.
LET'S SEE YOU MASTER FOCUSING ALL YOUR YOMA POWER IN ONE ARM.
KA KAKA
KA
KAKAKA
KA
KA
KA
KA
KA

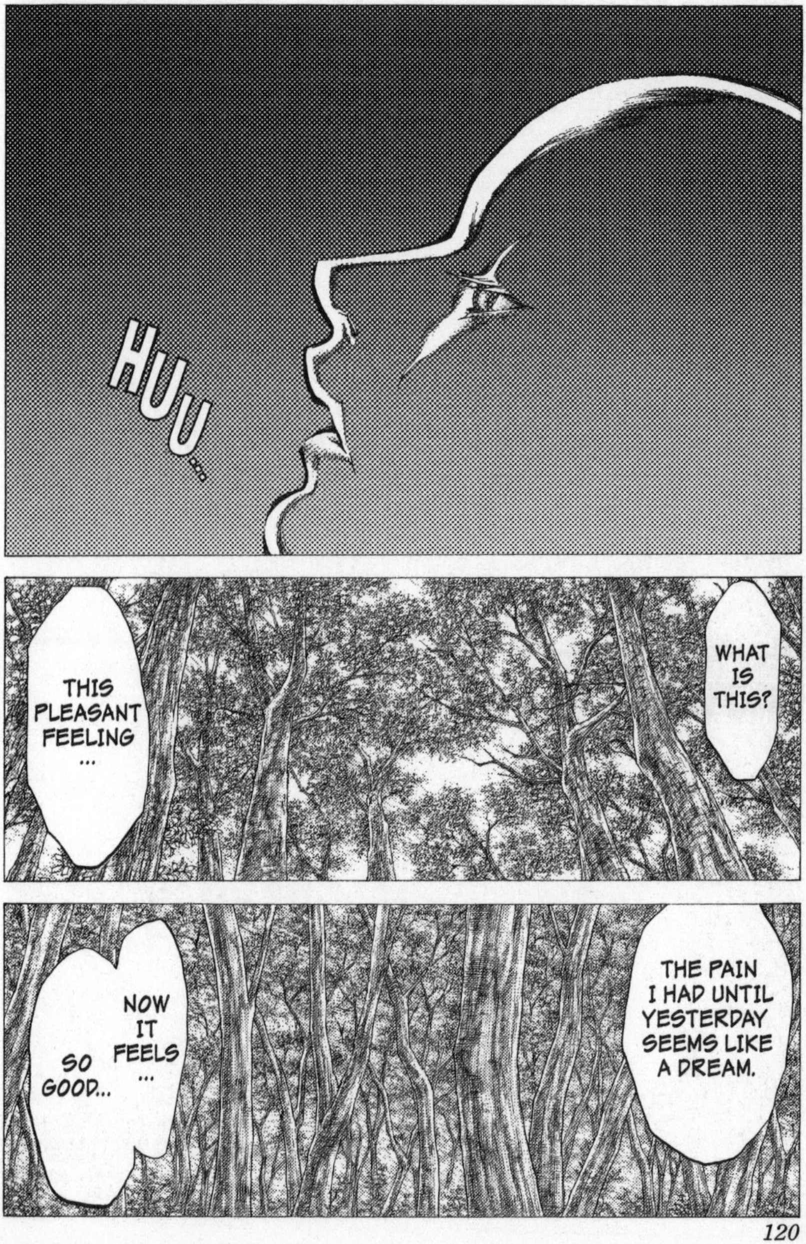
HUU...
WHAT IS THIS?
THIS PLEASANT FEELING...
THE PAIN I HAD UNTIL YESTERDAY SEEMS LIKE A DREAM.
NOW IT FEELS...
SO GOOD...

READ THIS WAY

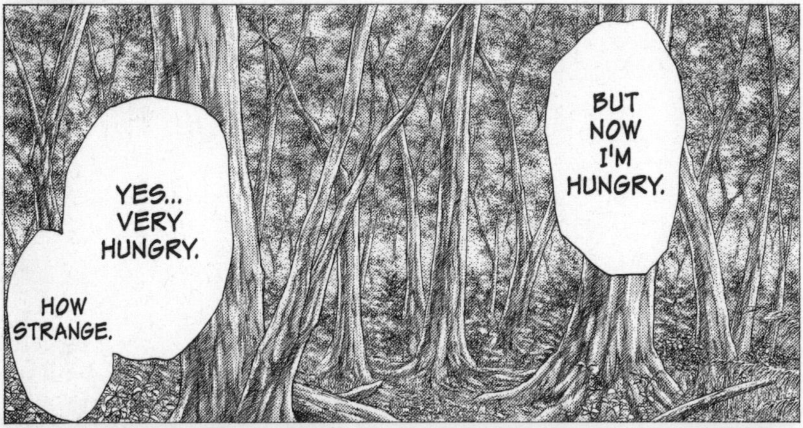
BUT NOW I'M HUNGRY.
YES... VERY HUNGRY.
HOW STRANGE.

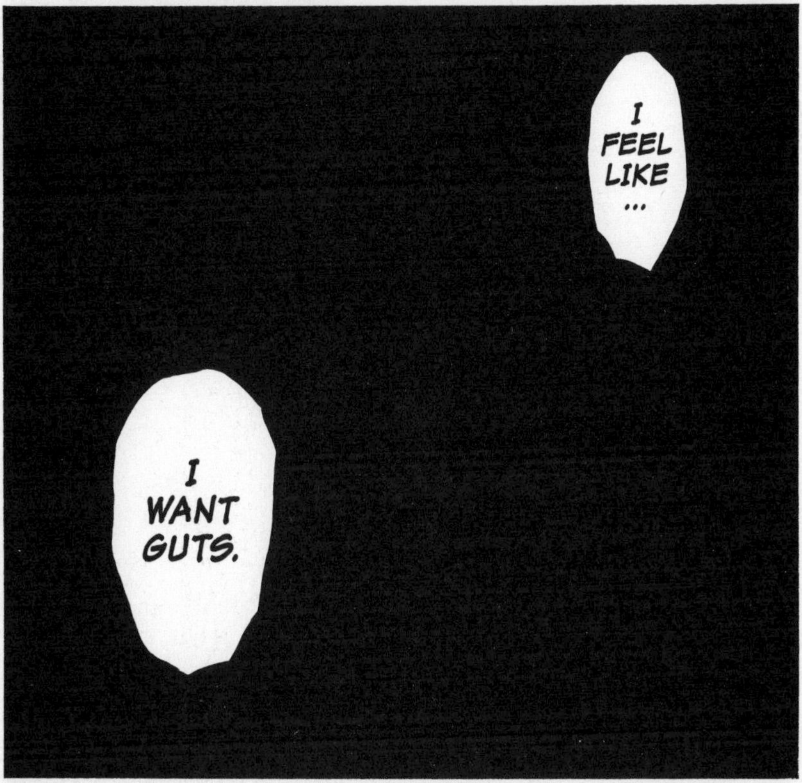
I FEEL LIKE ...
I WANT GUTS.

クレイモア
Claymore™

SCENE 38: FIT FOR BATTLE, PART 2

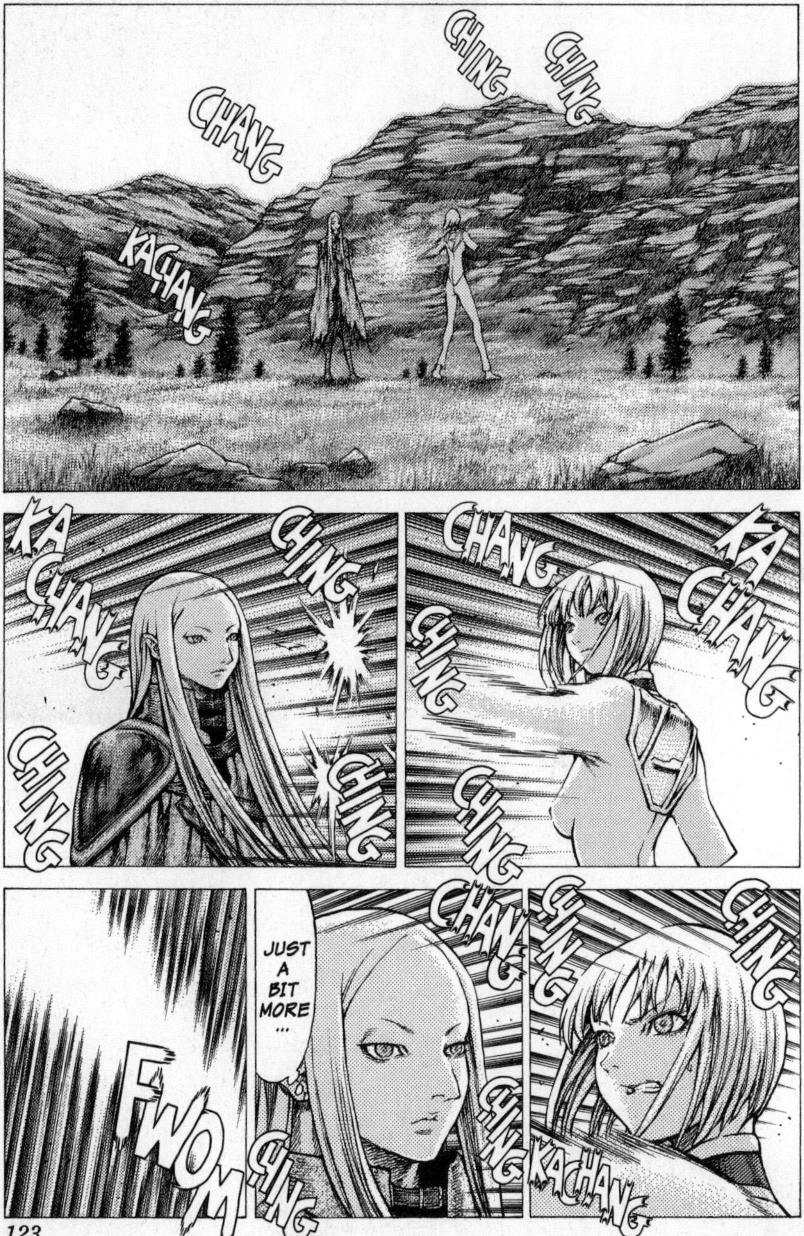
CHING
CHING
CHANG
KACHANG
KA CHANG
CHANG
CHING CHING
CHING CHING
CHING
KA CHANG
CHING
CHING CHING
CHING
CHING
KACHANG
CHANG
CHING
JUST A BIT MORE ...
CHING
FWOM

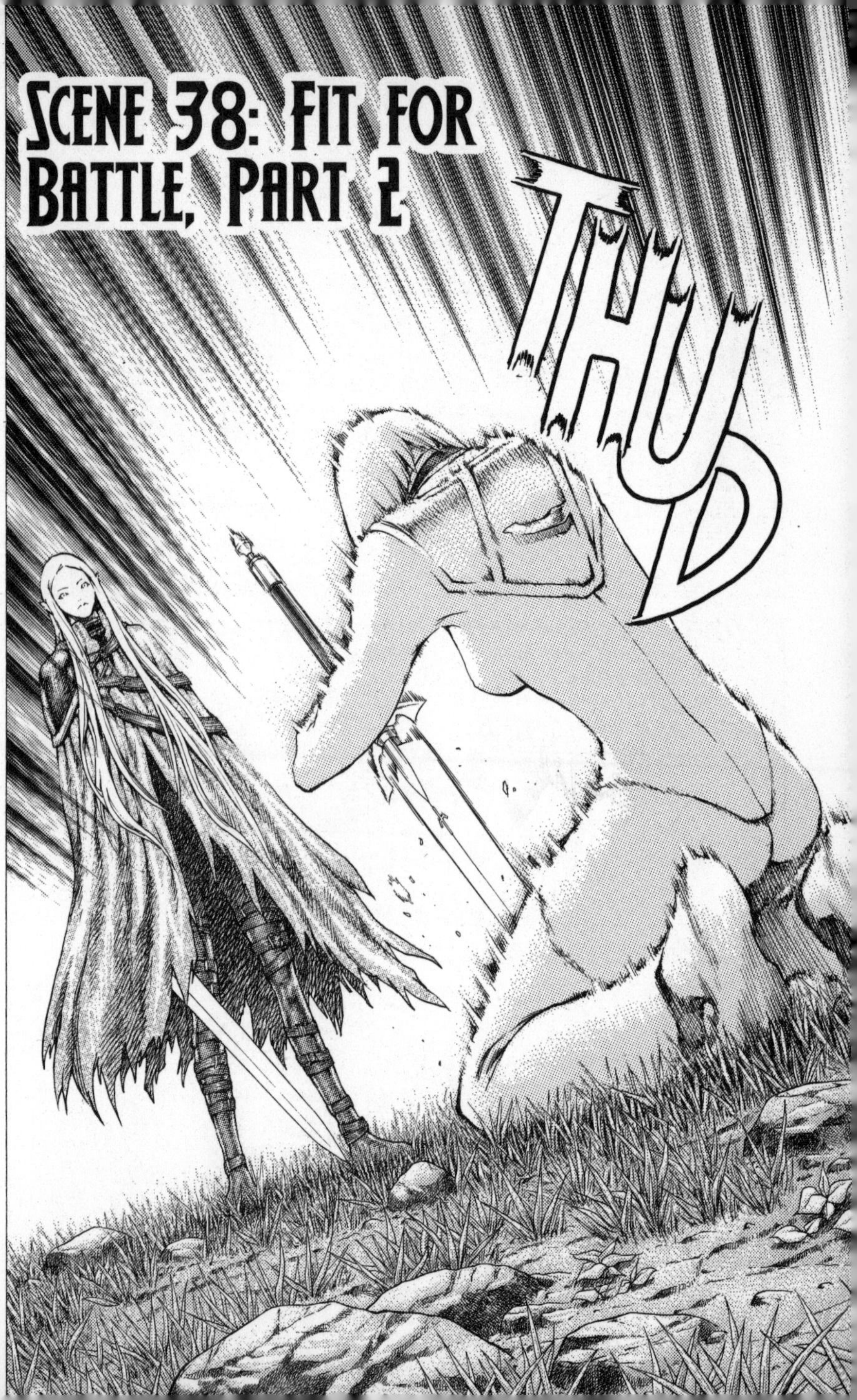
SCENE 38: FIT FOR BATTLE, PART 2
THUD

READ THIS WAY

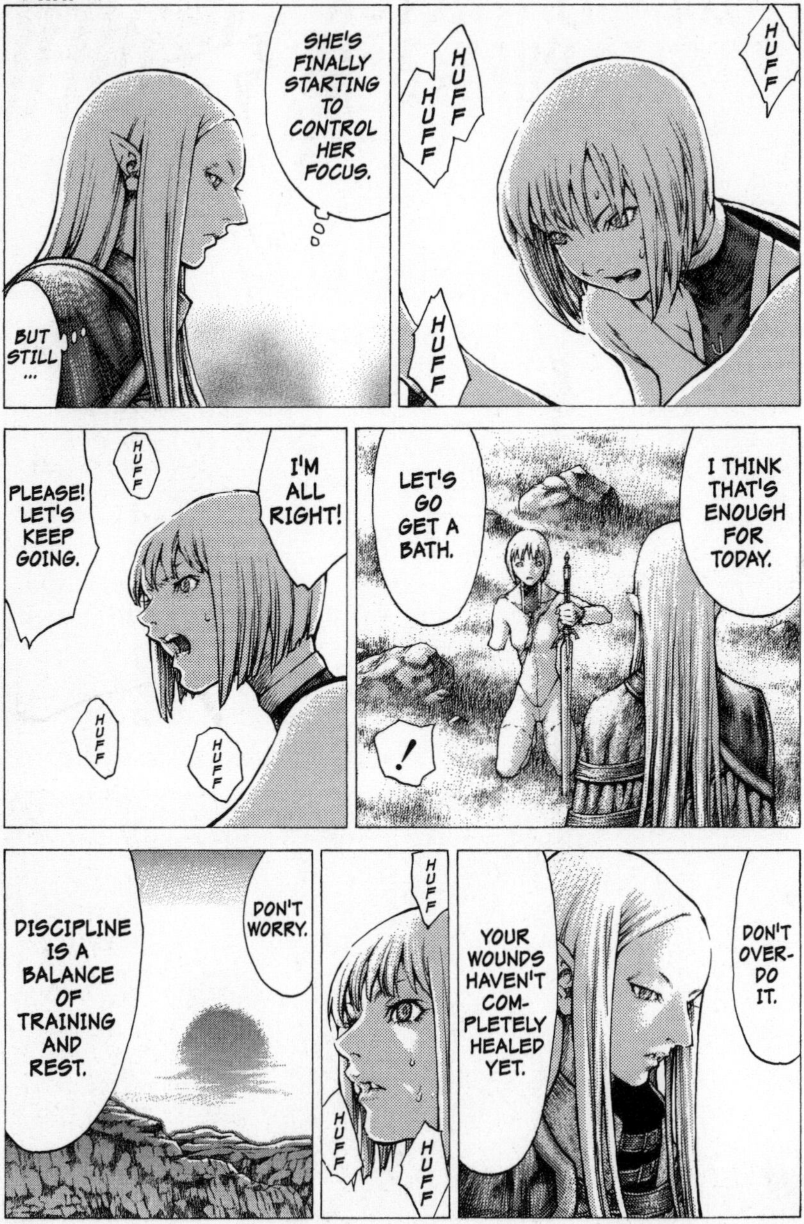
HUFF
HUFF
HUFF
HUFF
SHE'S FINALLY STARTING TO CONTROL HER FOCUS.
BUT STILL...
I THINK THAT'S ENOUGH FOR TODAY.
LET'S GO GET A BATH.
!
I'M ALL RIGHT!
HUFF
PLEASE! LET'S KEEP GOING.
HUFF
HUFF
DON'T OVER-DO IT.
YOUR WOUNDS HAVEN'T COM-PLETELY HEALED YET.
HUFF
DON'T WORRY.
HUFF
HUFF
DISCIPLINE IS A BALANCE OF TRAINING AND REST.

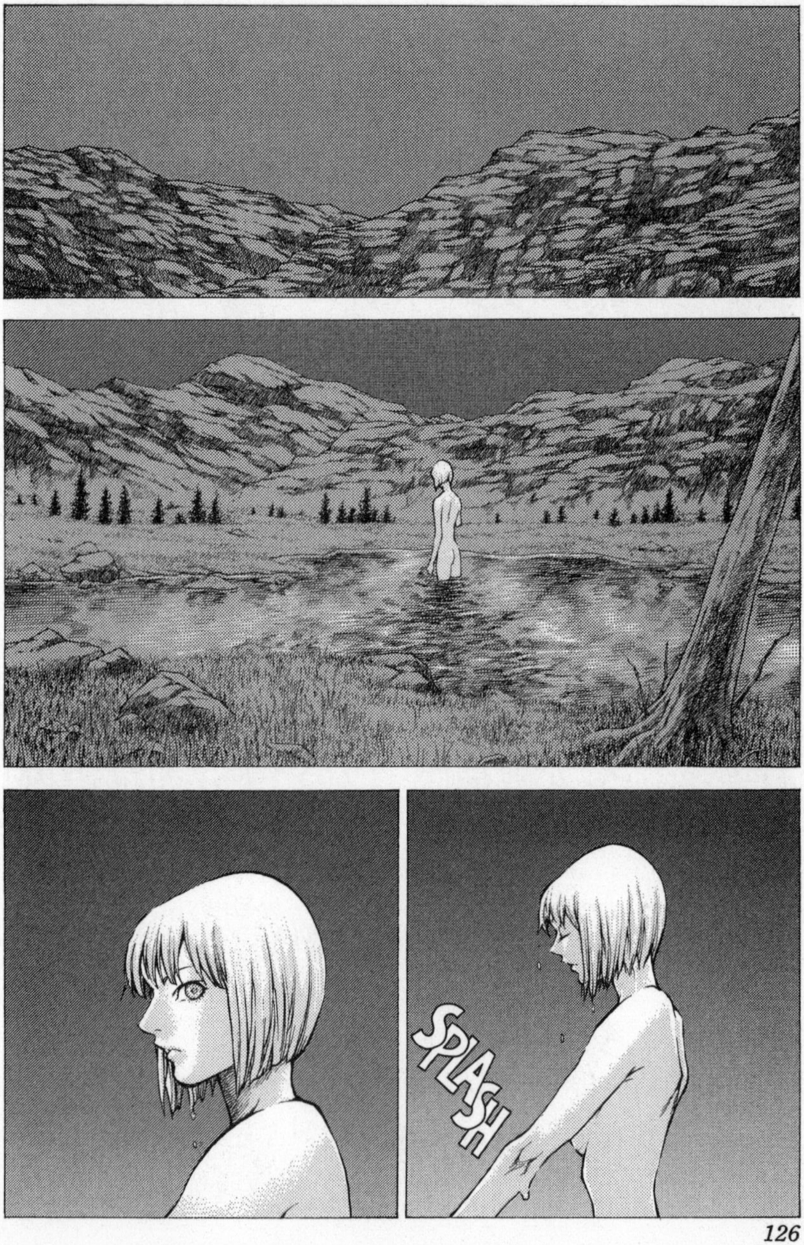
SPLASH

READ THIS WAY

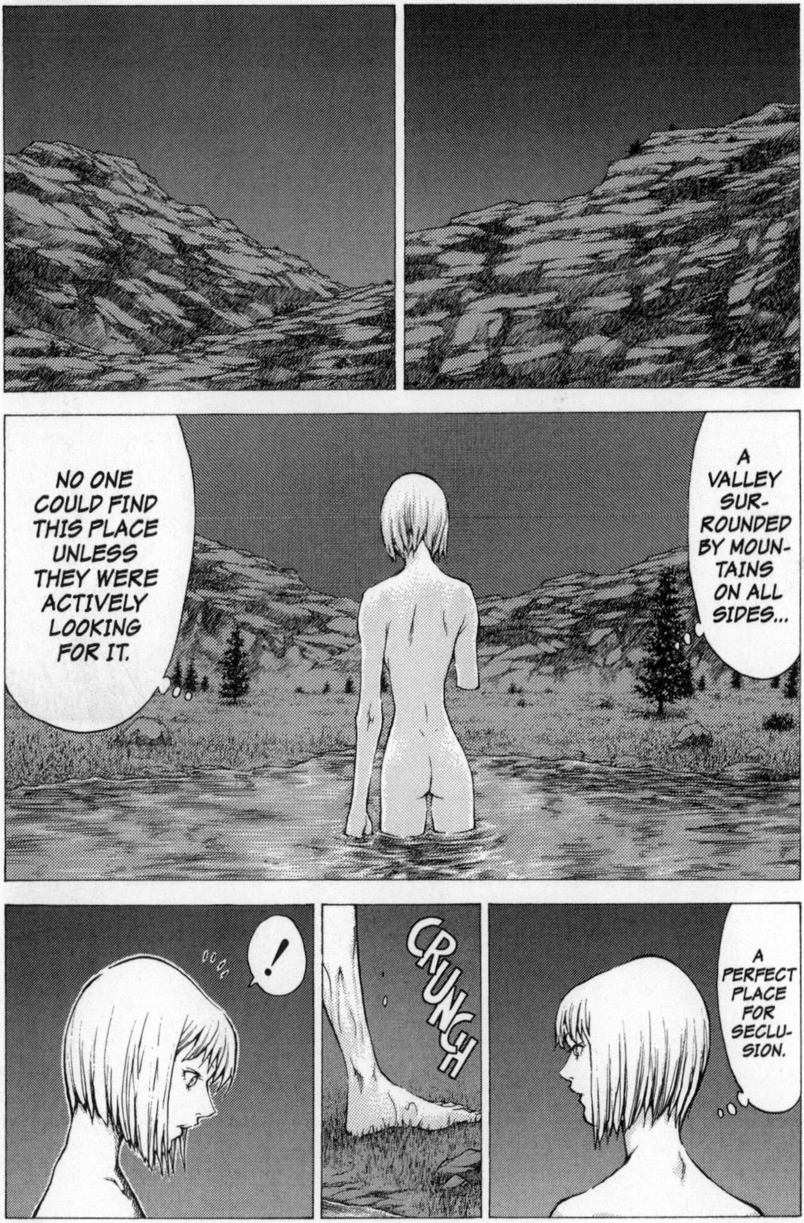
A VALLEY SURROUNDED BY MOUNTAINS ON ALL SIDES...
NO ONE COULD FIND THIS PLACE UNLESS THEY WERE ACTIVELY LOOKING FOR IT.
A PERFECT PLACE FOR SECLUSION.
CRUNCH
!

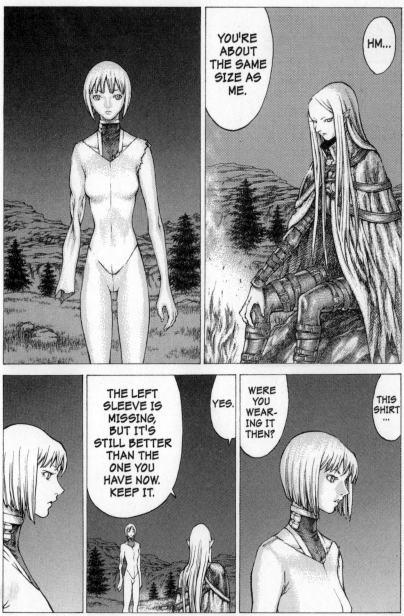

HM...
YOU'RE ABOUT THE SAME SIZE AS ME.
THIS SHIRT...
WERE YOU WEAR-ING IT THEN?
YES.
THE LEFT SLEEVE IS MISSING, BUT IT'S STILL BETTER THAN THE ONE YOU HAVE NOW. KEEP IT.

« READ THIS WAY «

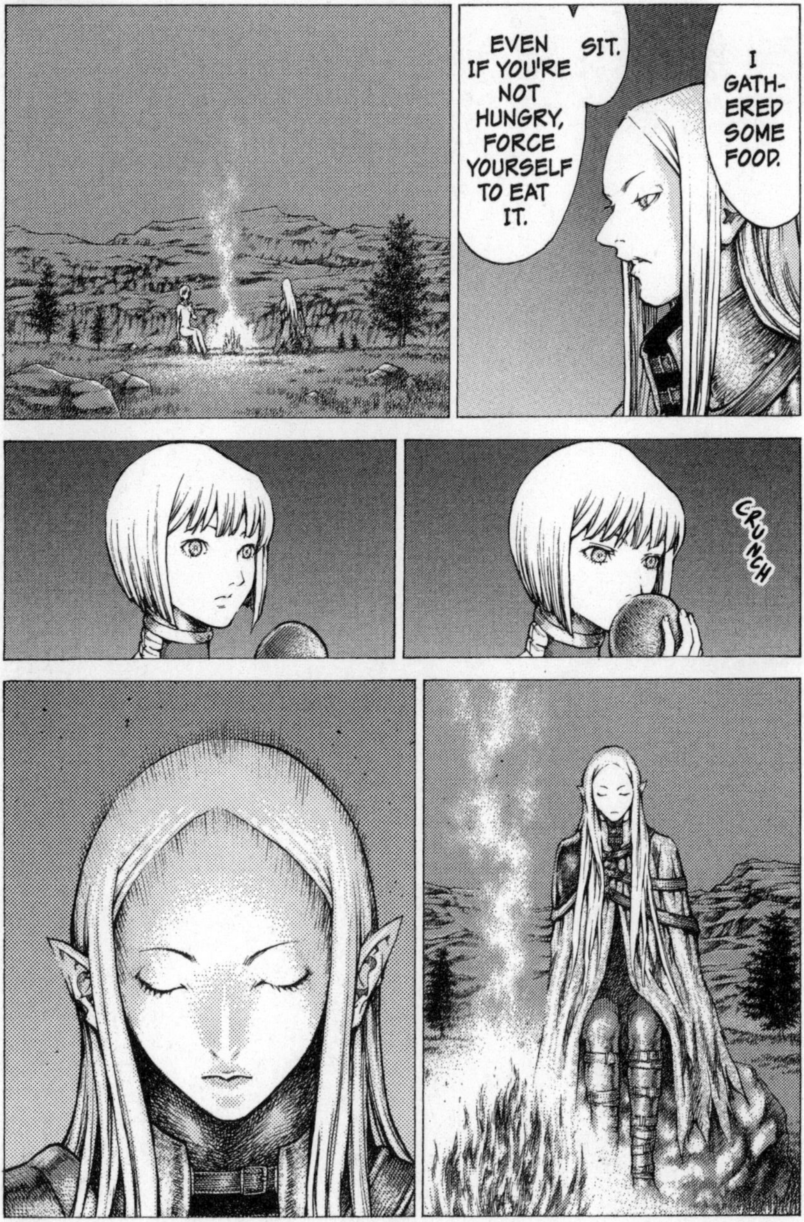
I GATHERED SOME FOOD.
SIT.
EVEN IF YOU'RE NOT HUNGRY, FORCE YOURSELF TO EAT IT.
CRUNCH

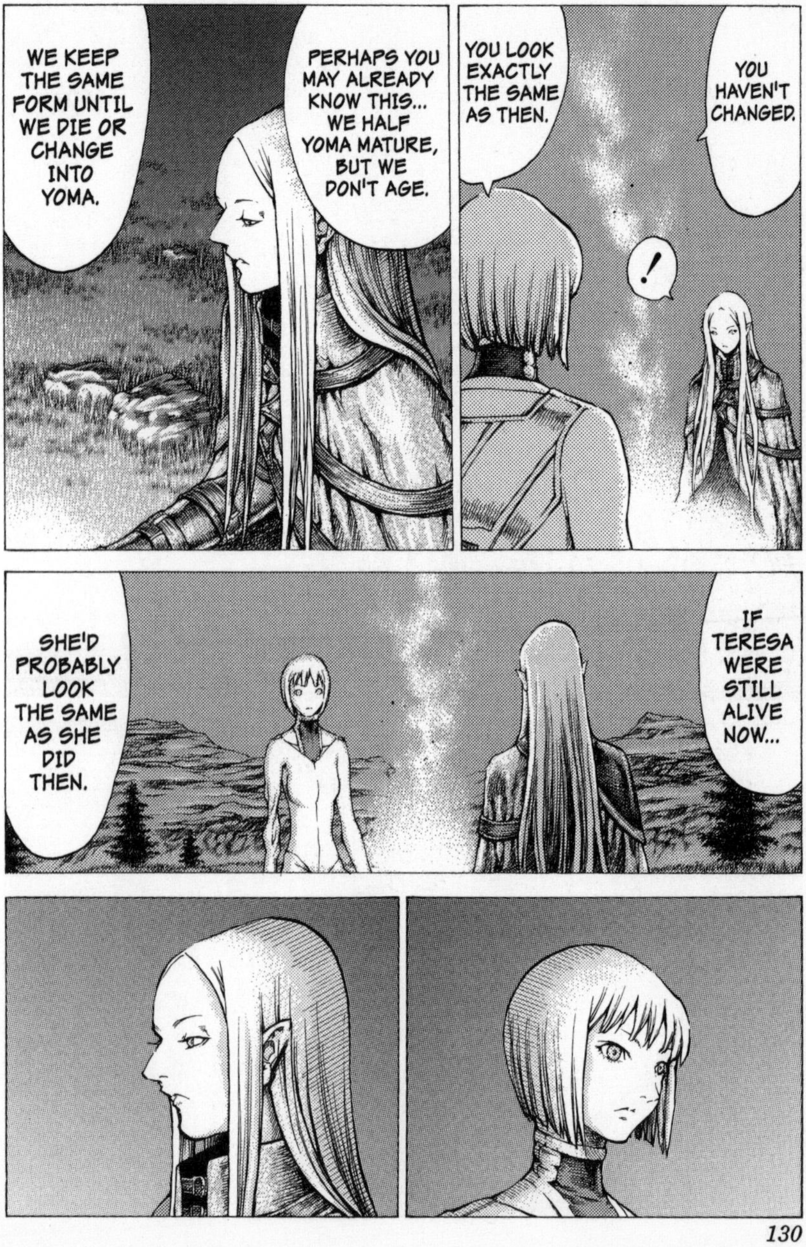
YOU HAVEN'T CHANGED.
YOU LOOK EXACTLY THE SAME AS THEN.
!
PERHAPS YOU MAY ALREADY KNOW THIS... WE HALF YOMA MATURE, BUT WE DON'T AGE.
WE KEEP THE SAME FORM UNTIL WE DIE OR CHANGE INTO YOMA.
IF TERESA WERE STILL ALIVE NOW...
SHE'D PROBABLY LOOK THE SAME AS SHE DID THEN.

READ THIS WAY

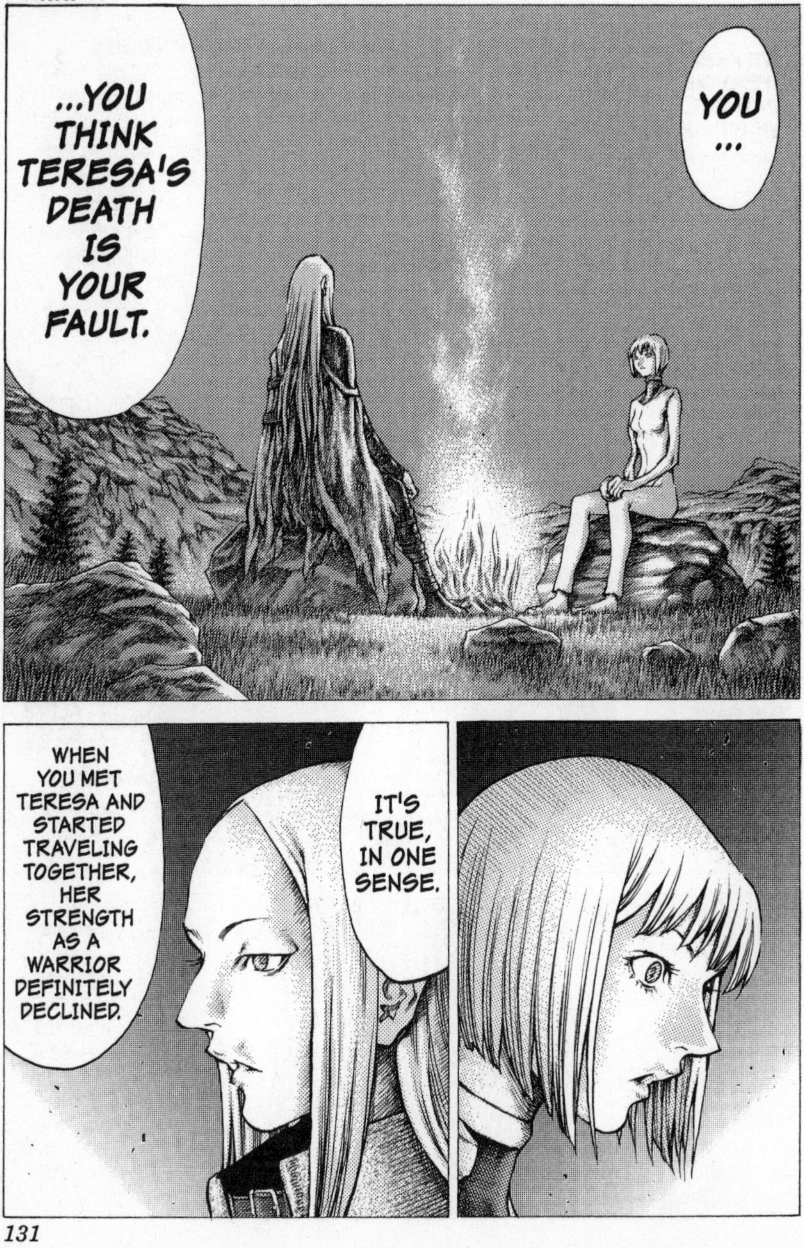
YOU ...
...YOU THINK TERESA'S DEATH IS YOUR FAULT.
IT'S TRUE, IN ONE SENSE.
WHEN YOU MET TERESA AND STARTED TRAVELING TOGETHER, HER STRENGTH AS A WARRIOR DEFINITELY DECLINED.

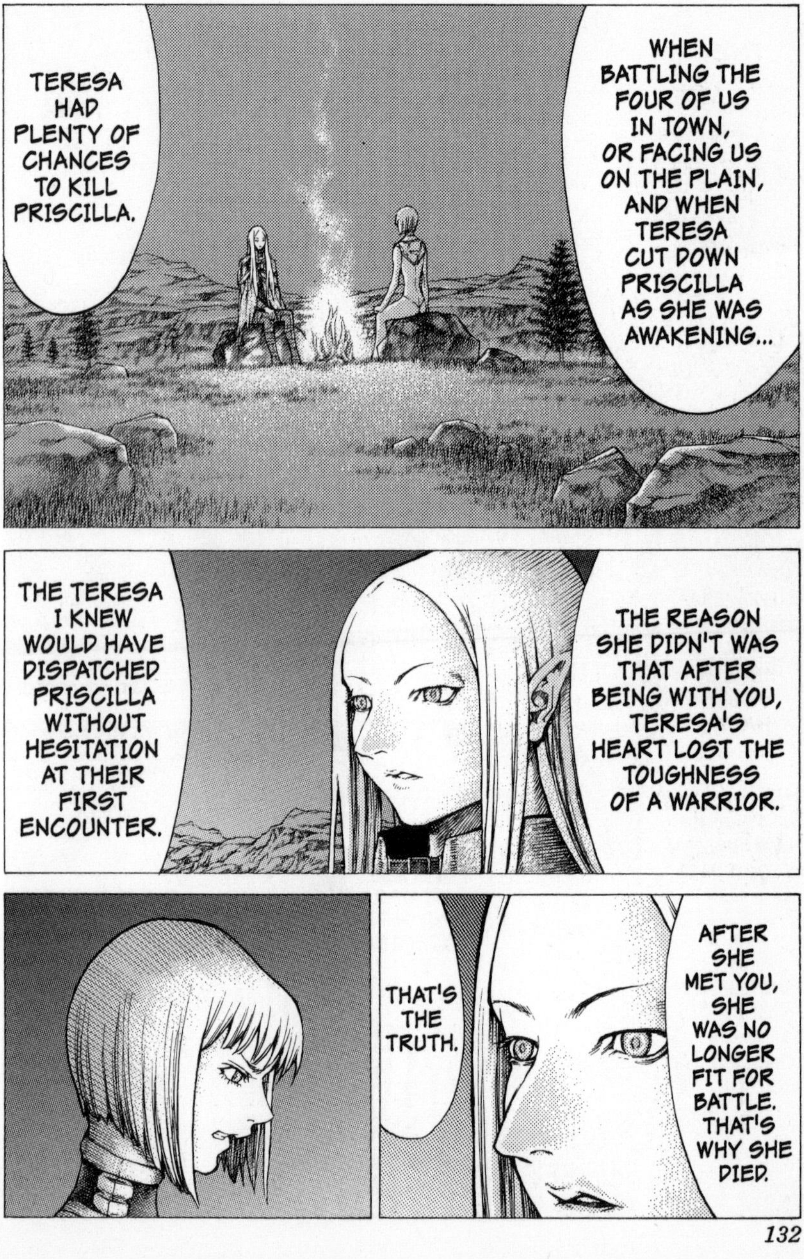
WHEN BATTLING THE FOUR OF US IN TOWN, OR FACING US ON THE PLAIN, AND WHEN TERESA CUT DOWN PRISCILLA AS SHE WAS AWAKENING...
TERESA HAD PLENTY OF CHANCES TO KILL PRISCILLA.
THE REASON SHE DIDN'T WAS THAT AFTER BEING WITH YOU, TERESA'S HEART LOST THE TOUGHNESS OF A WARRIOR.
THE TERESA I KNEW WOULD HAVE DISPATCHED PRISCILLA WITHOUT HESITATION AT THEIR FIRST ENCOUNTER.
AFTER SHE MET YOU, SHE WAS NO LONGER FIT FOR BATTLE. THAT'S WHY SHE DIED.
THAT'S THE TRUTH.

READ THIS WAY

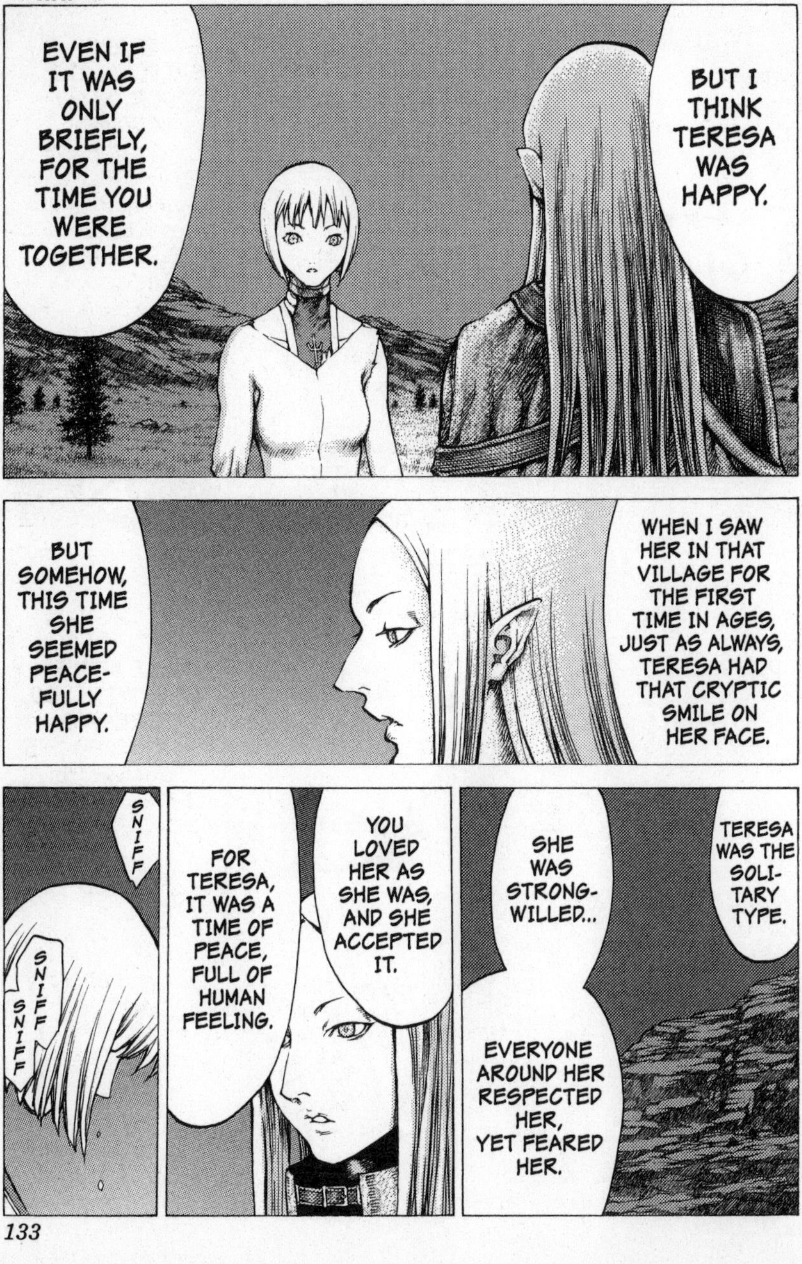

BUT I THINK TERESA WAS HAPPY.
EVEN IF IT WAS ONLY BRIEFLY, FOR THE TIME YOU WERE TOGETHER.
WHEN I SAW HER IN THAT VILLAGE FOR THE FIRST TIME IN AGES, JUST AS ALWAYS, TERESA HAD THAT CRYPTIC SMILE ON HER FACE.
BUT SOMEHOW, THIS TIME SHE SEEMED PEACE-FULLY HAPPY.
TERESA WAS THE SOLI-TARY TYPE.
SHE WAS STRONG-WILLED...
EVERYONE AROUND HER RESPECTED HER, YET FEARED HER.
YOU LOVED HER AS SHE WAS, AND SHE ACCEPTED IT.
FOR TERESA, IT WAS A TIME OF PEACE, FULL OF HUMAN FEELING.
SNIFF
SNIFF
SNIFF

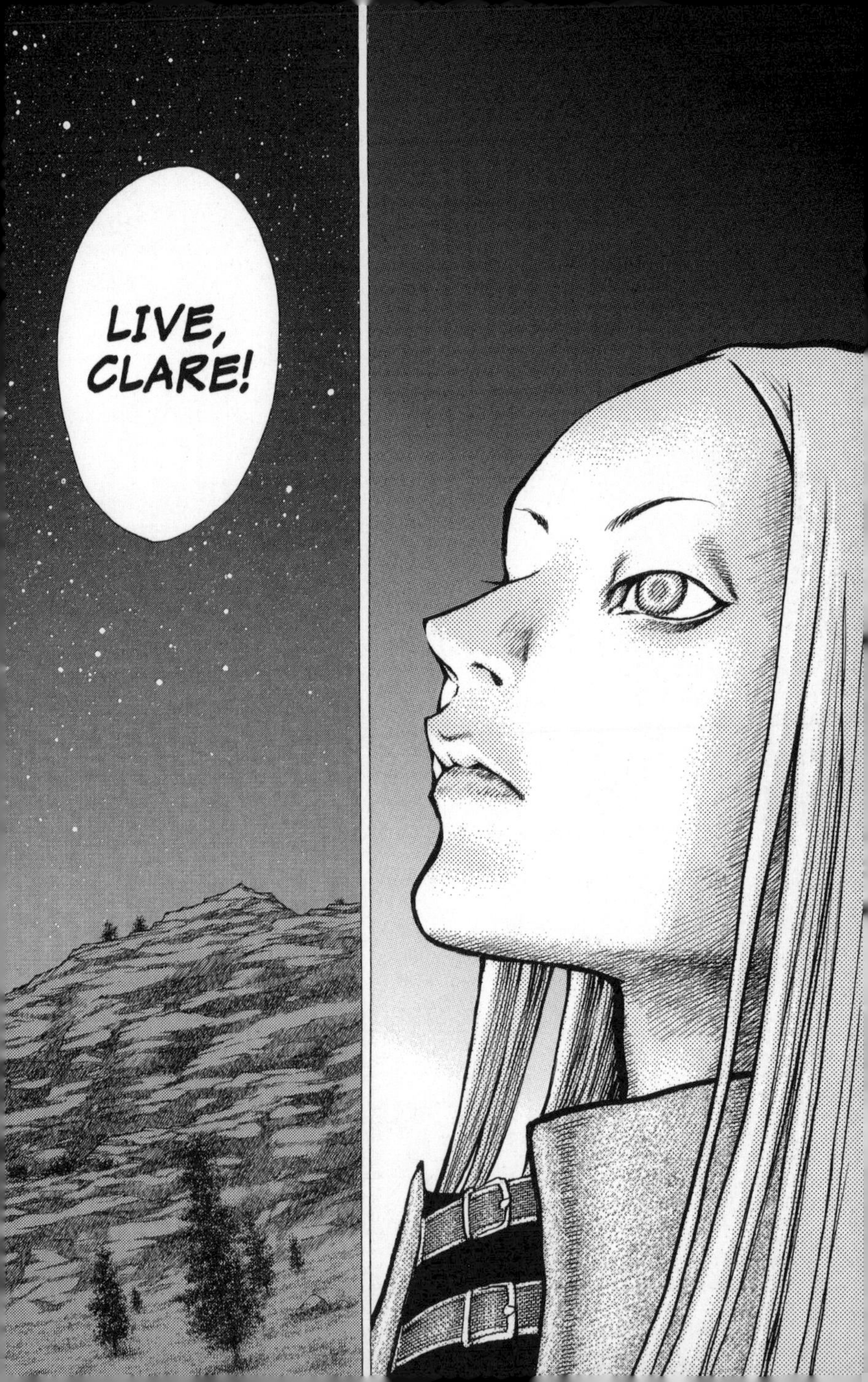
LIVE, CLARE!

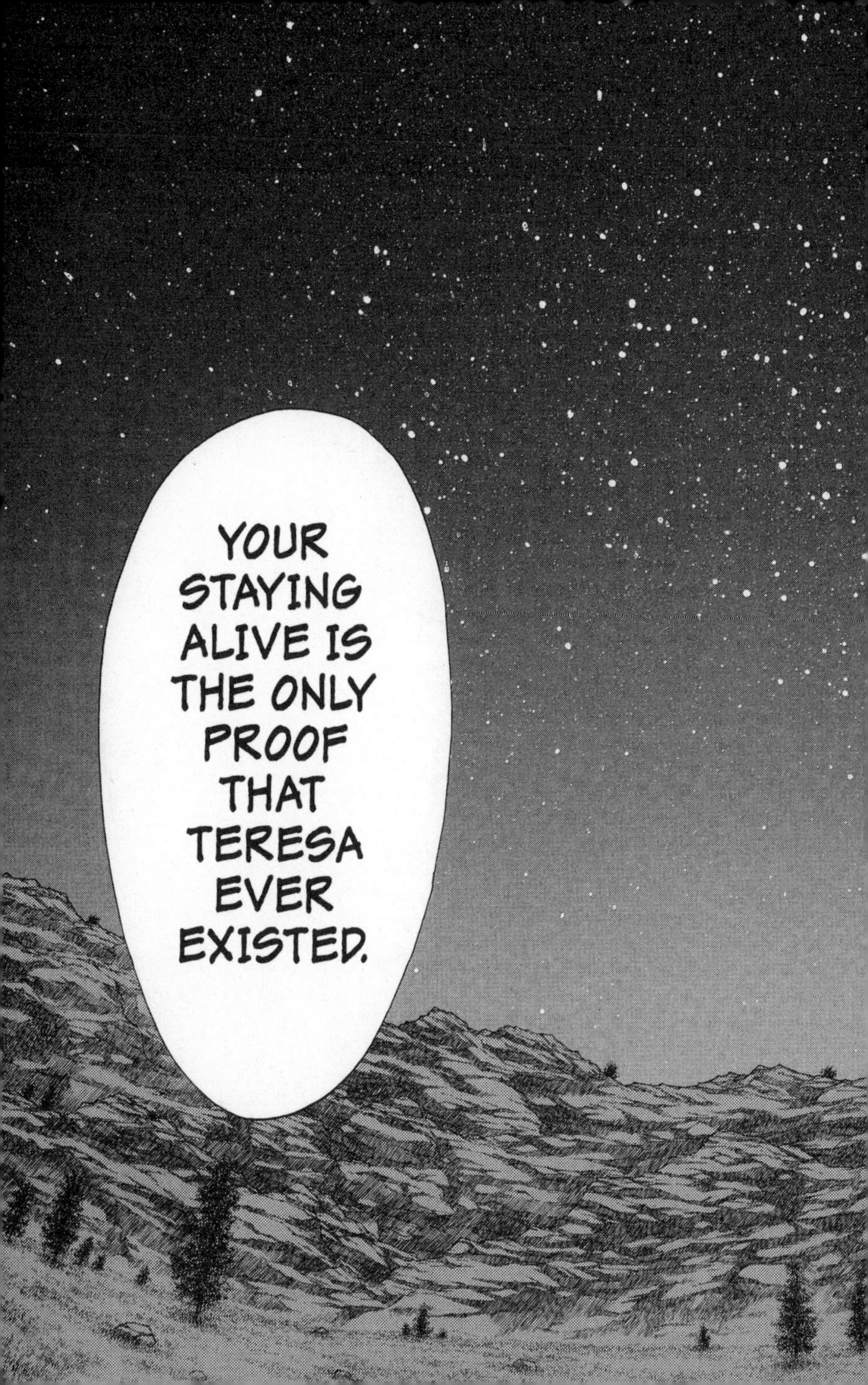
YOUR STAYING ALIVE IS THE ONLY PROOF THAT TERESA EVER EXISTED.

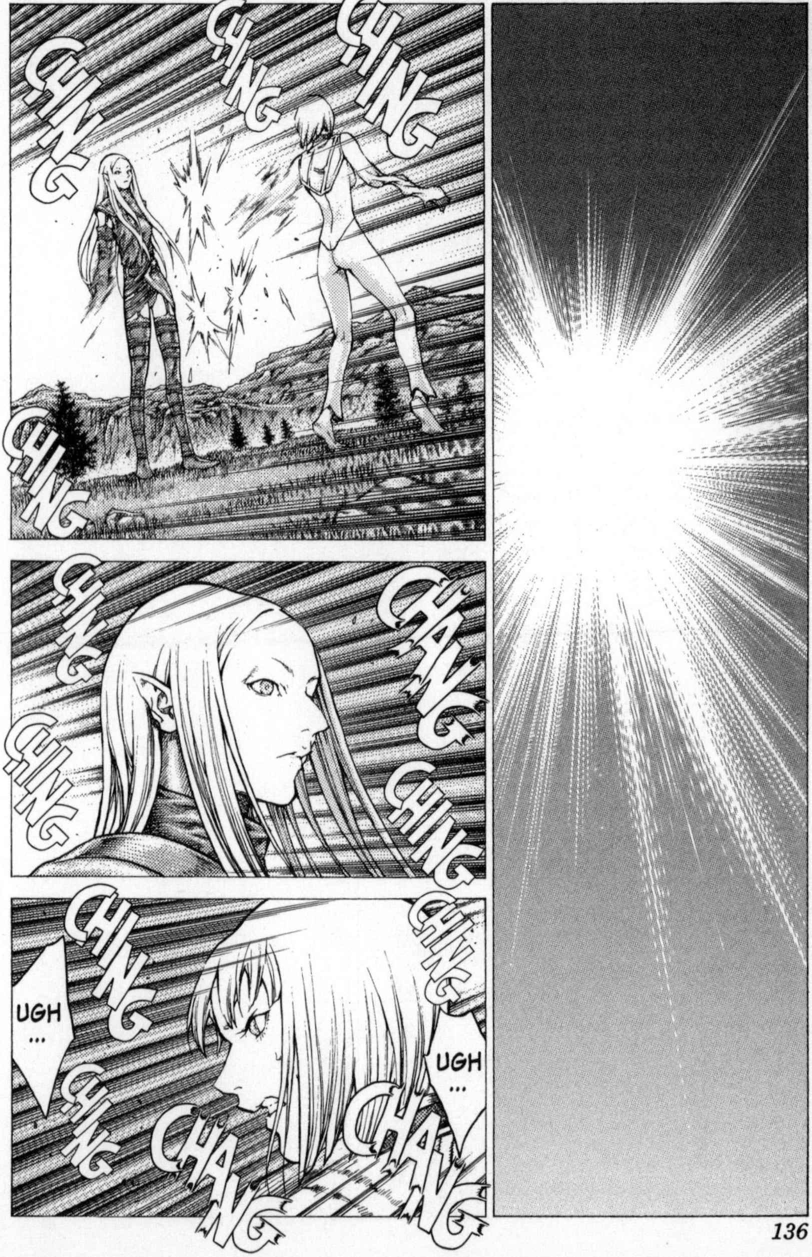
CHING
CHING
CHING
CHING
CHANG
CHING
CHING
CHING
CHING
CHING
UGH...
CHANG
CHANG
CHING
UGH...
CHING

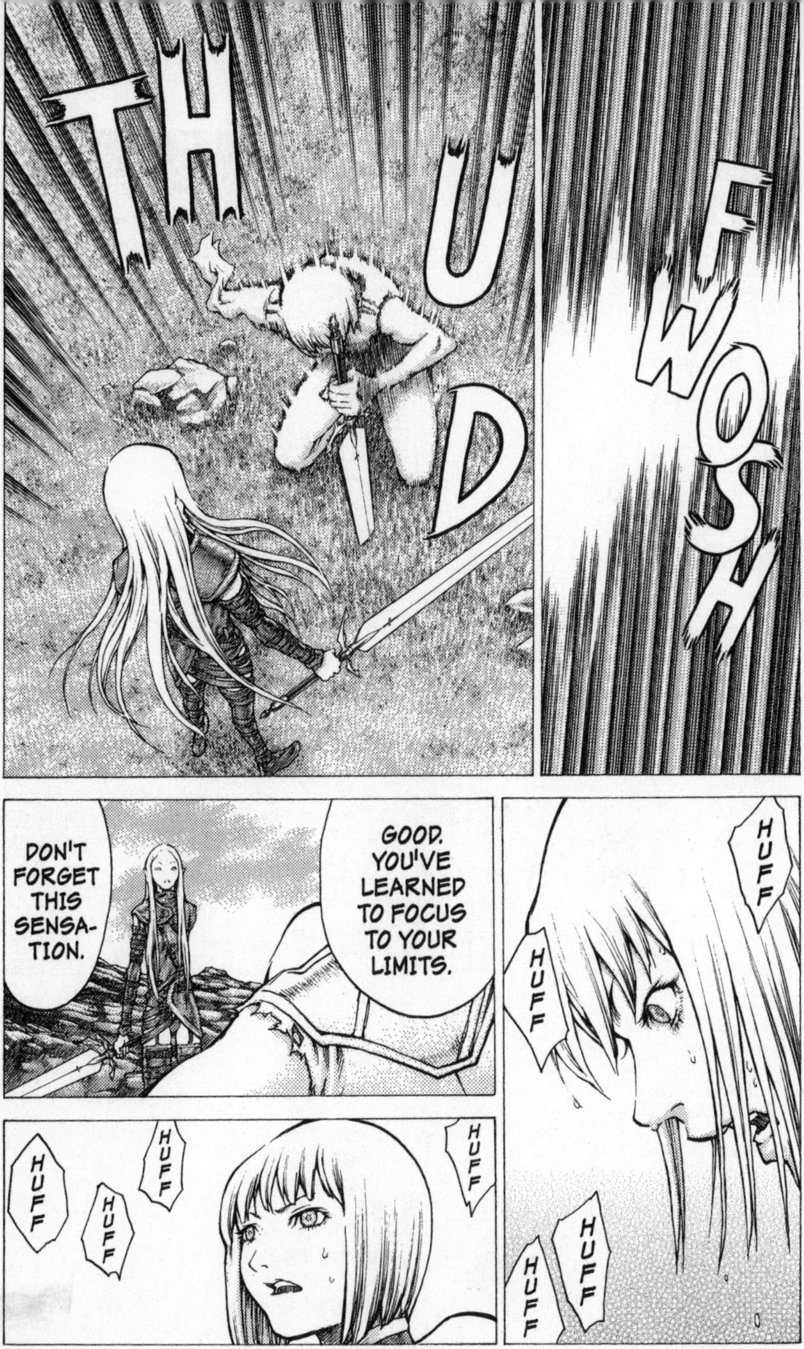
FWOSH
THUD
HUFF
HUFF
HUFF
HUFF
GOOD. YOU'VE LEARNED TO FOCUS TO YOUR LIMITS.
DON'T FORGET THIS SENSA-TION.
HUFF
HUFF
HUFF
HUFF

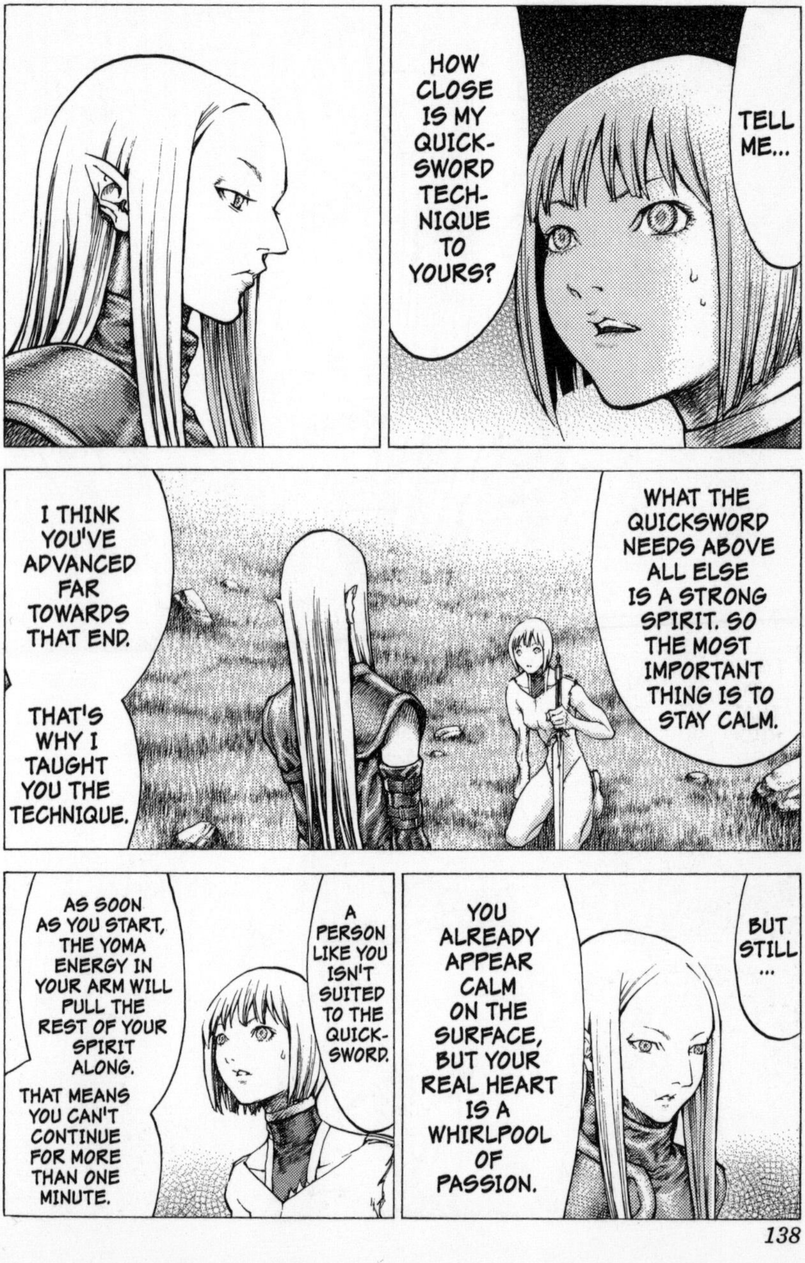
TELL ME...
HOW CLOSE IS MY QUICK-SWORD TECHNIQUE TO YOURS?
WHAT THE QUICKSWORD NEEDS ABOVE ALL ELSE IS A STRONG SPIRIT. SO THE MOST IMPORTANT THING IS TO STAY CALM.
I THINK YOU'VE ADVANCED FAR TOWARDS THAT END.
THAT'S WHY I TAUGHT YOU THE TECHNIQUE.
BUT STILL ...
YOU ALREADY APPEAR CALM ON THE SURFACE, BUT YOUR REAL HEART IS A WHIRLPOOL OF PASSION.
A PERSON LIKE YOU ISN'T SUITED TO THE QUICK-SWORD.
AS SOON AS YOU START, THE YOMA ENERGY IN YOUR ARM WILL PULL THE REST OF YOUR SPIRIT ALONG.
THAT MEANS YOU CAN'T CONTINUE FOR MORE THAN ONE MINUTE.

READ THIS WAY

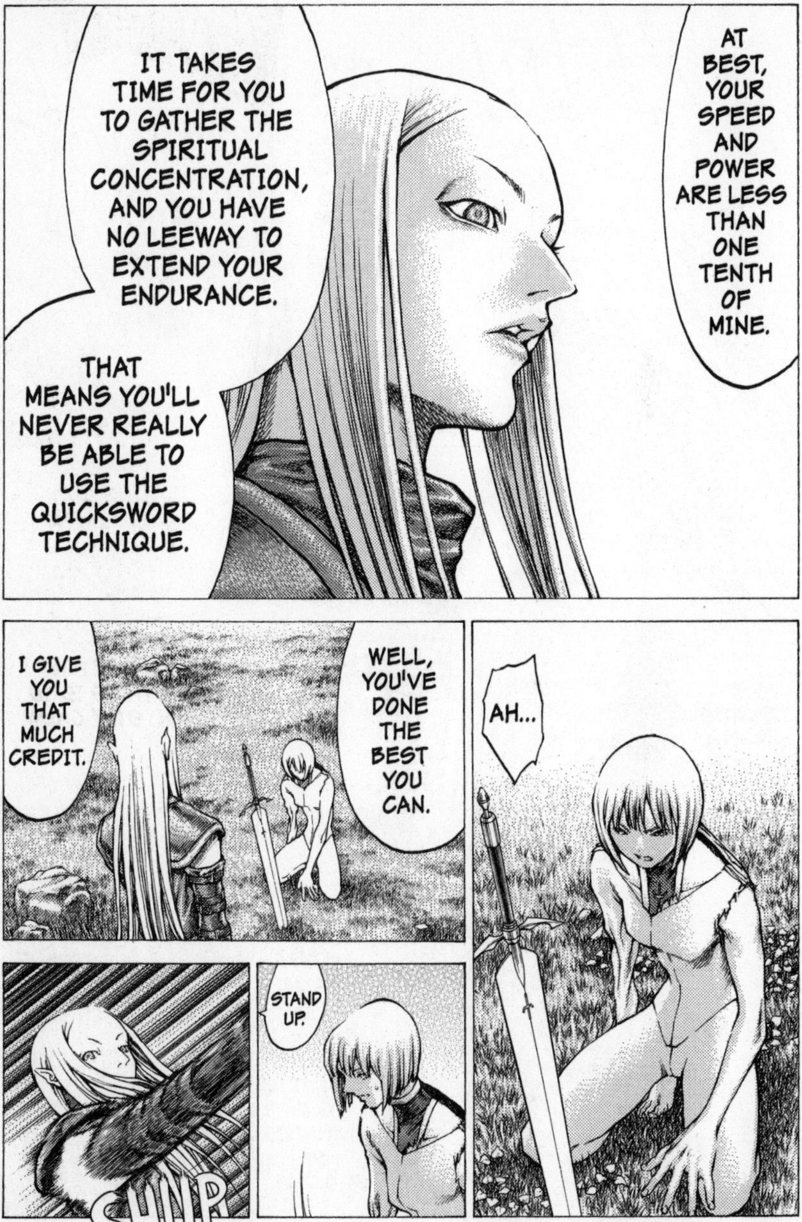
AT BEST, YOUR SPEED AND POWER ARE LESS THAN ONE TENTH OF MINE.
IT TAKES TIME FOR YOU TO GATHER THE SPIRITUAL CONCENTRATION, AND YOU HAVE NO LEEWAY TO EXTEND YOUR ENDURANCE.
THAT MEANS YOU'LL NEVER REALLY BE ABLE TO USE THE QUICKSWORD TECHNIQUE.
AH...
WELL, YOU'VE DONE THE BEST YOU CAN.
I GIVE YOU THAT MUCH CREDIT.
STAND UP.
SHUP

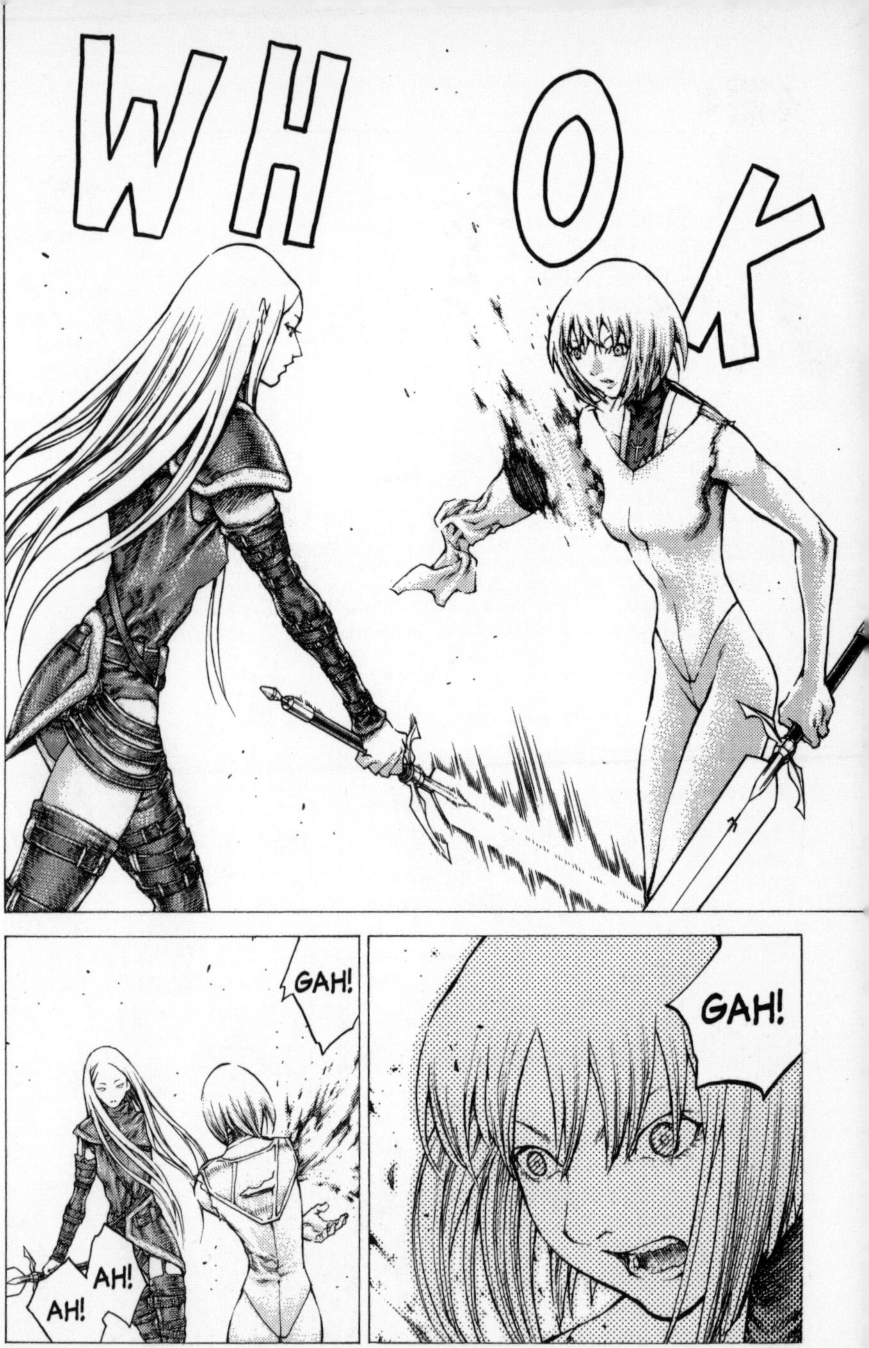
WHOOK
GAH!
GAH!
AH!
AH!

READ THIS WAY

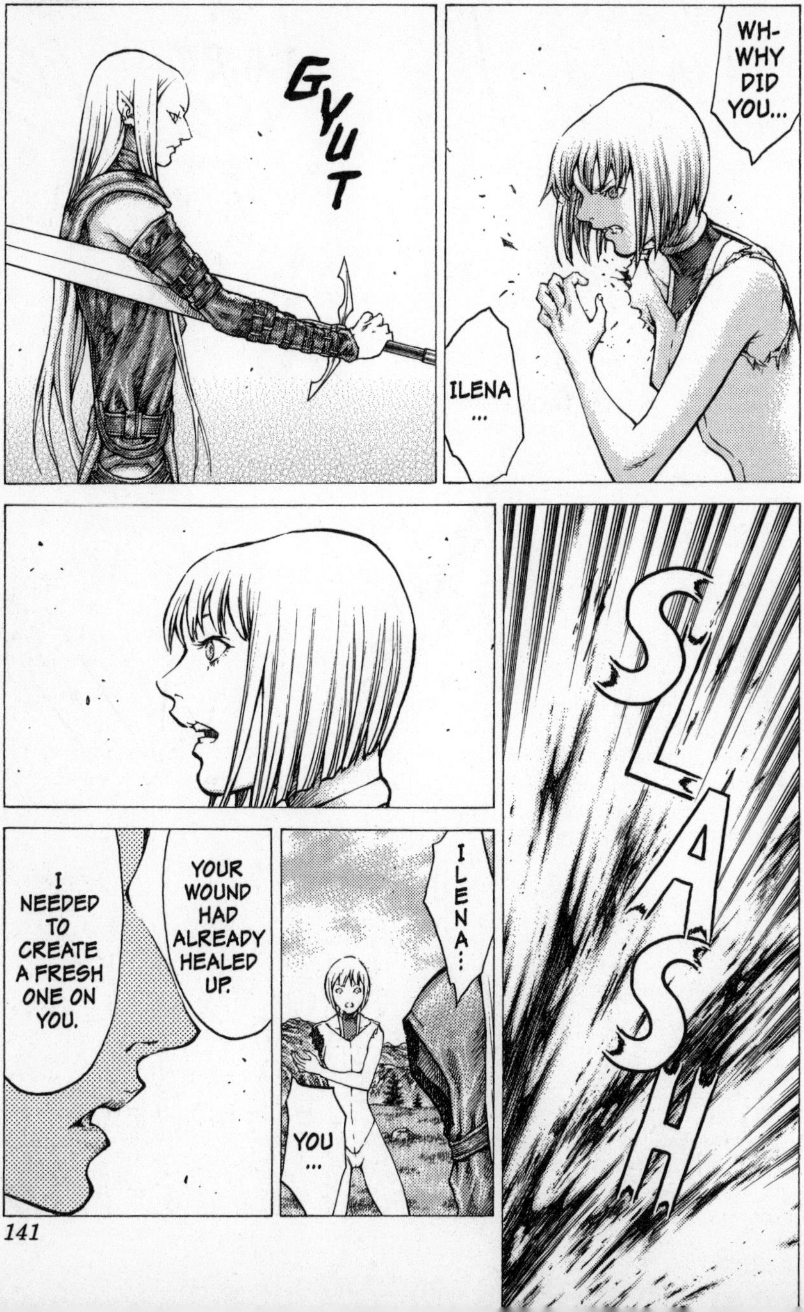

WH-WHY DID YOU...
ILENA...
GYUT
SLASH
ILENA...
YOU...
YOUR WOUND HAD ALREADY HEALED UP.
I NEEDED TO CREATE A FRESH ONE ON YOU.

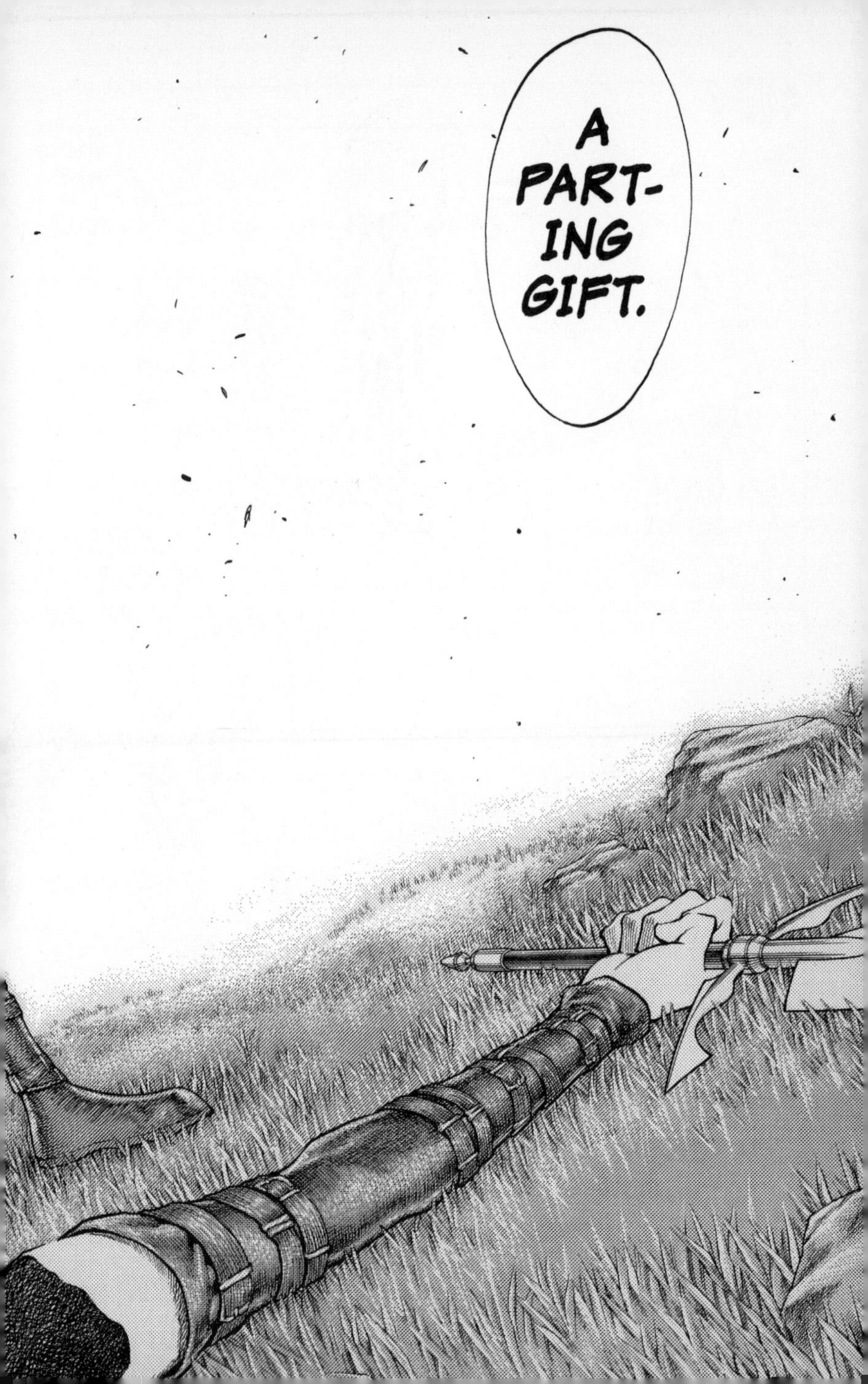
A PART-ING GIFT.

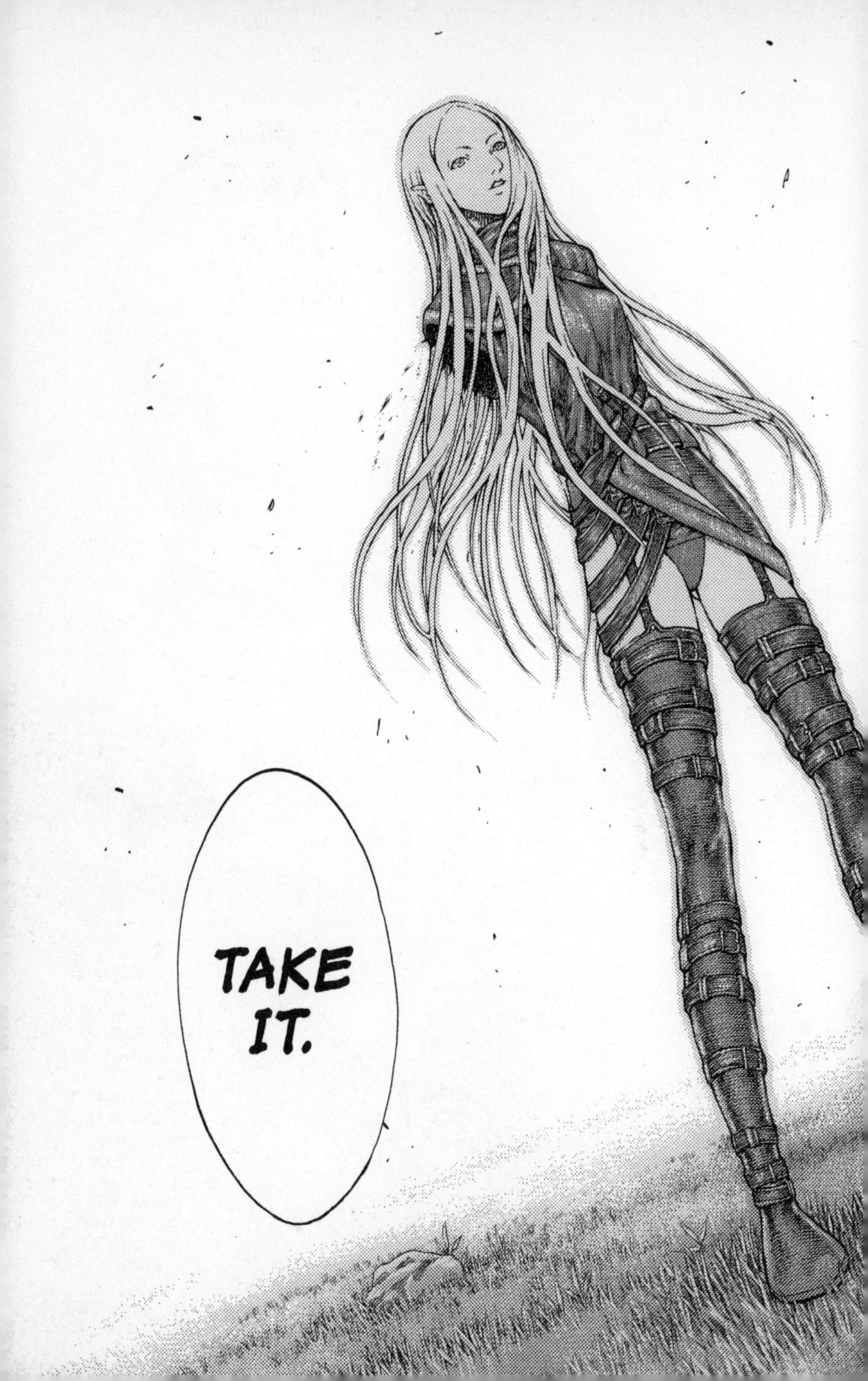
TAKE IT.

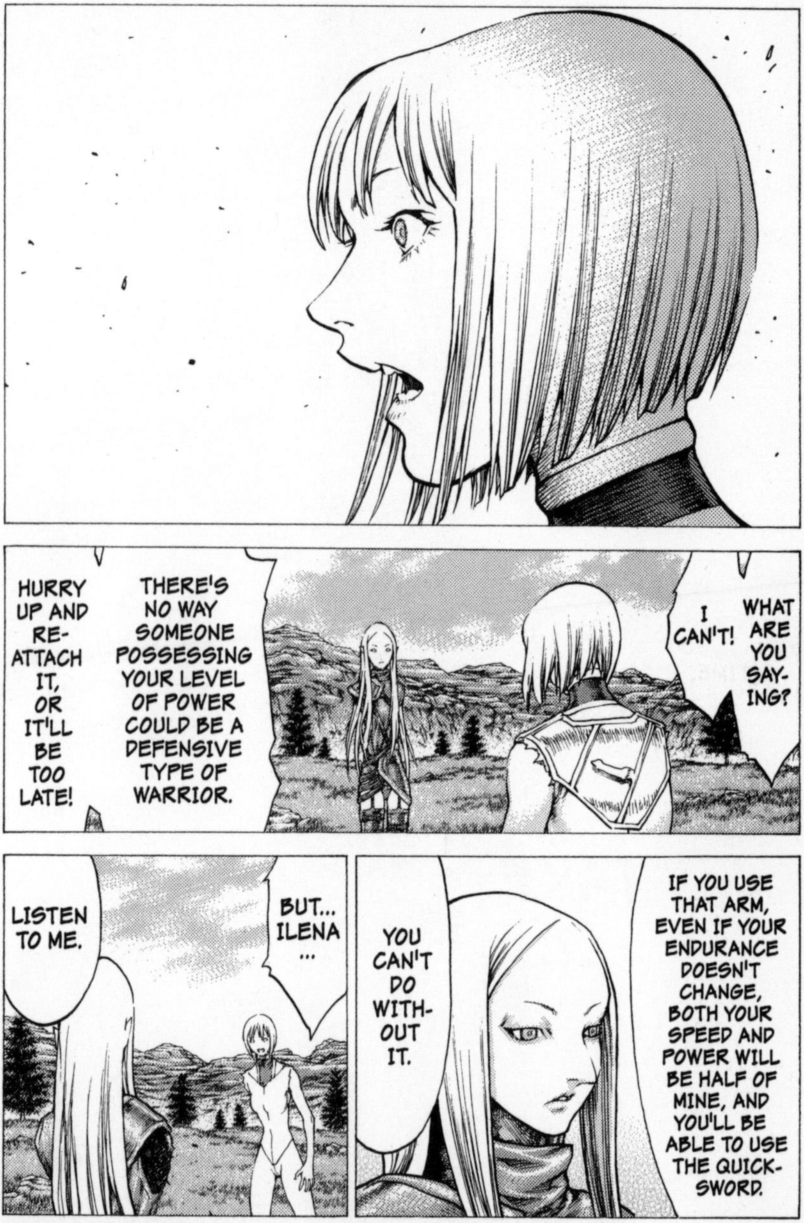
WHAT ARE YOU SAYING?
I CAN'T!
THERE'S NO WAY SOMEONE POSSESSING YOUR LEVEL OF POWER COULD BE A DEFENSIVE TYPE OF WARRIOR.
HURRY UP AND RE-ATTACH IT, OR IT'LL BE TOO LATE!
IF YOU USE THAT ARM, EVEN IF YOUR ENDURANCE DOESN'T CHANGE, BOTH YOUR SPEED AND POWER WILL BE HALF OF MINE, AND YOU'LL BE ABLE TO USE THE QUICK-SWORD.
YOU CAN'T DO WITH-OUT IT.
BUT... ILENA...
LISTEN TO ME.

READ THIS WAY

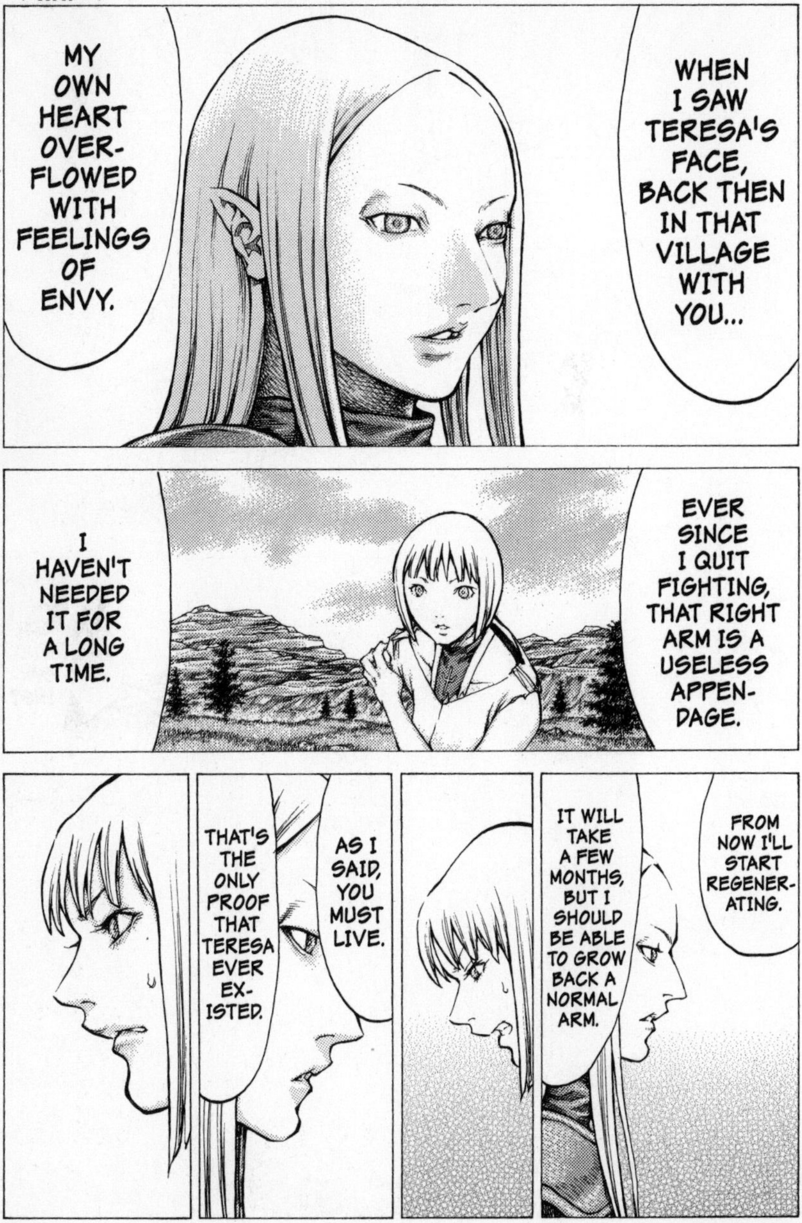

WHEN I SAW TERESA'S FACE, BACK THEN IN THAT VILLAGE WITH YOU...
MY OWN HEART OVER-FLOWED WITH FEELINGS OF ENVY.
EVER SINCE I QUIT FIGHTING, THAT RIGHT ARM IS A USELESS APPEN-DAGE.
I HAVEN'T NEEDED IT FOR A LONG TIME.
FROM NOW I'LL START REGENER-ATING.
IT WILL TAKE A FEW MONTHS, BUT I SHOULD BE ABLE TO GROW BACK A NORMAL ARM.
AS I SAID, YOU MUST LIVE.
THAT'S THE ONLY PROOF THAT TERESA EVER EX-ISTED.

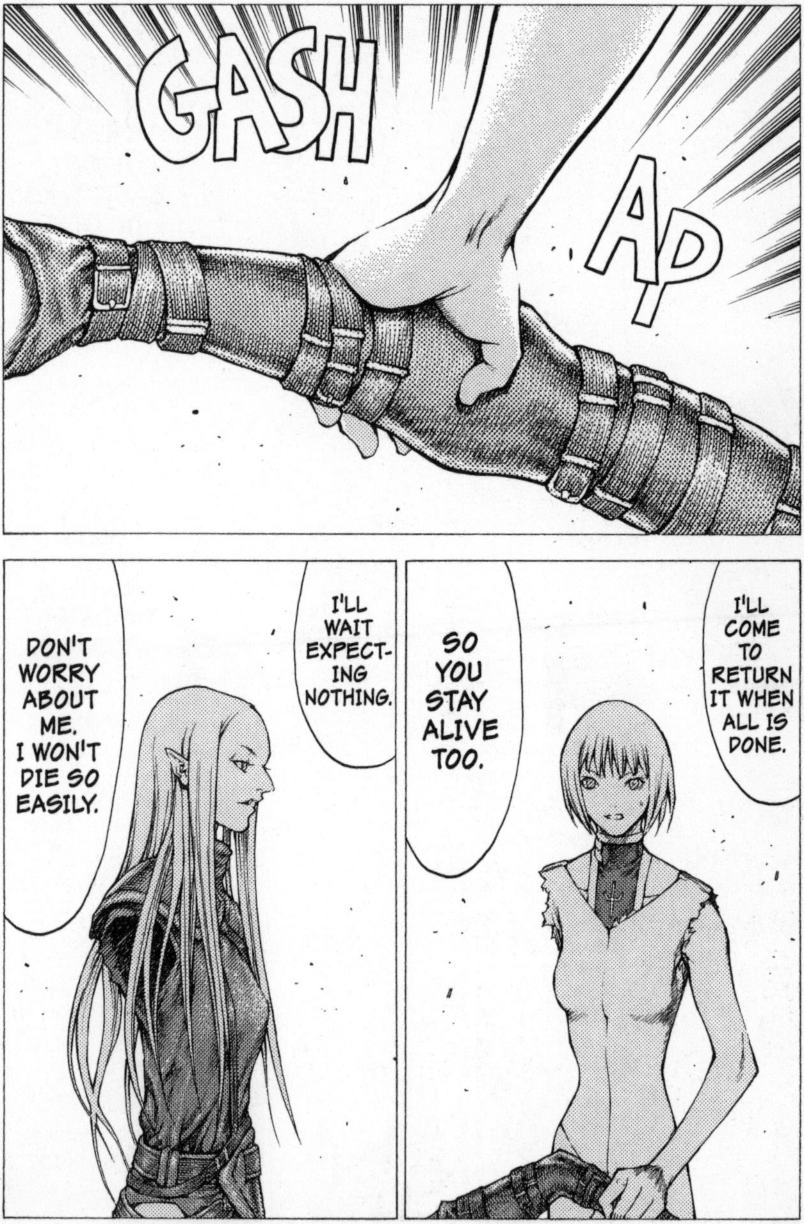
GASH
AP
I'LL COME TO RETURN IT WHEN ALL IS DONE.
SO YOU STAY ALIVE TOO.
I'LL WAIT EXPECTING NOTHING.
DON'T WORRY ABOUT ME. I WON'T DIE SO EASILY.

READ THIS WAY

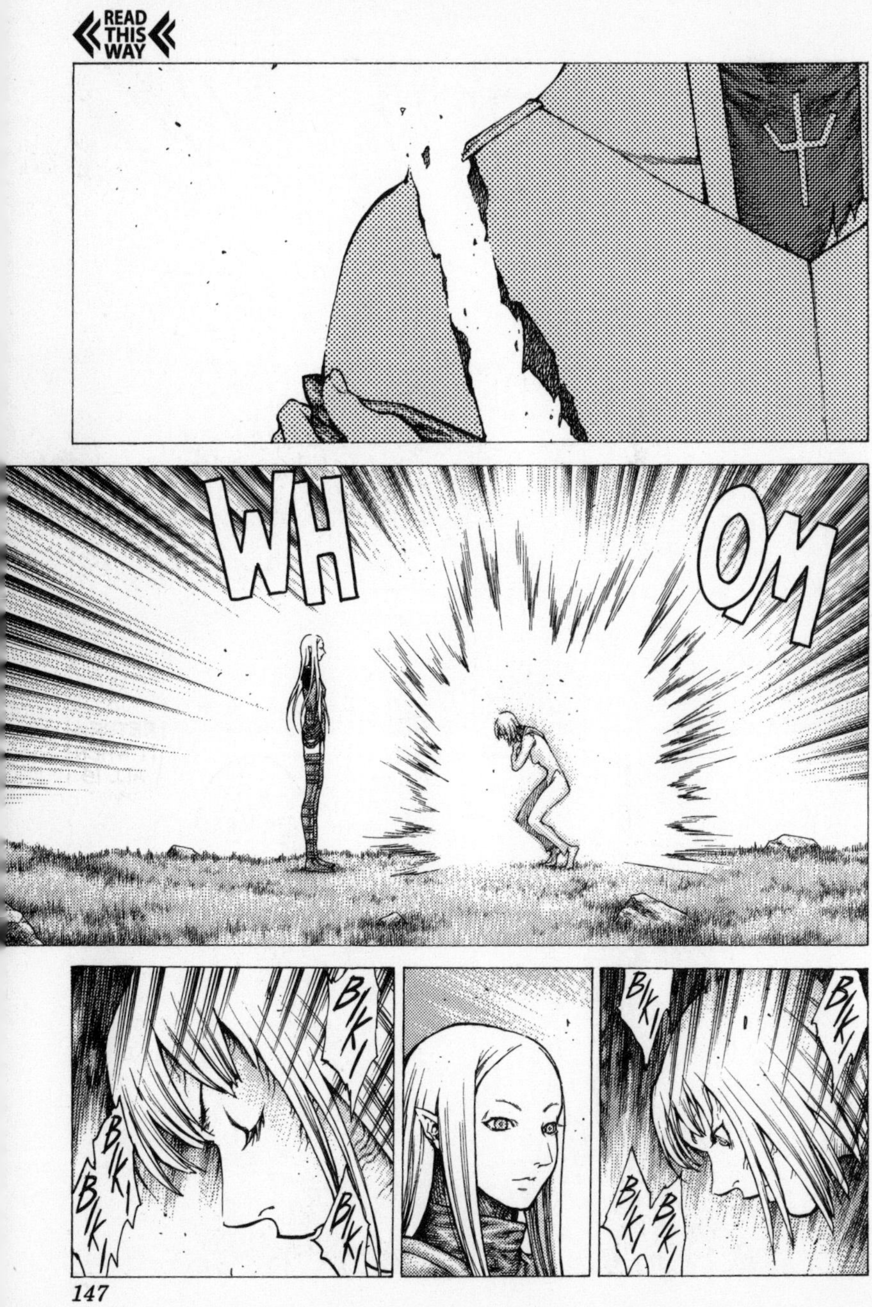
WHOOM
BIKI
BIKI
BIKI
BIKI
BIKI
BIKI
BIKI
BIKI

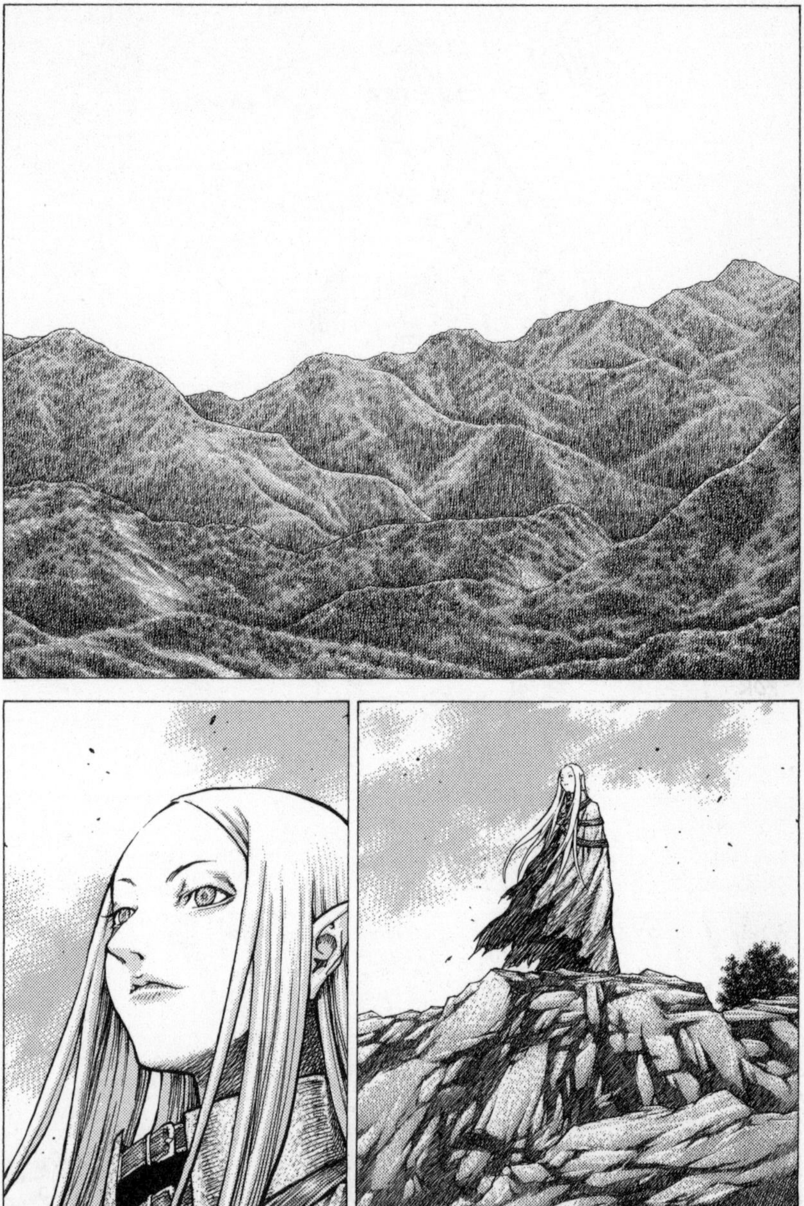

READ THIS WAY

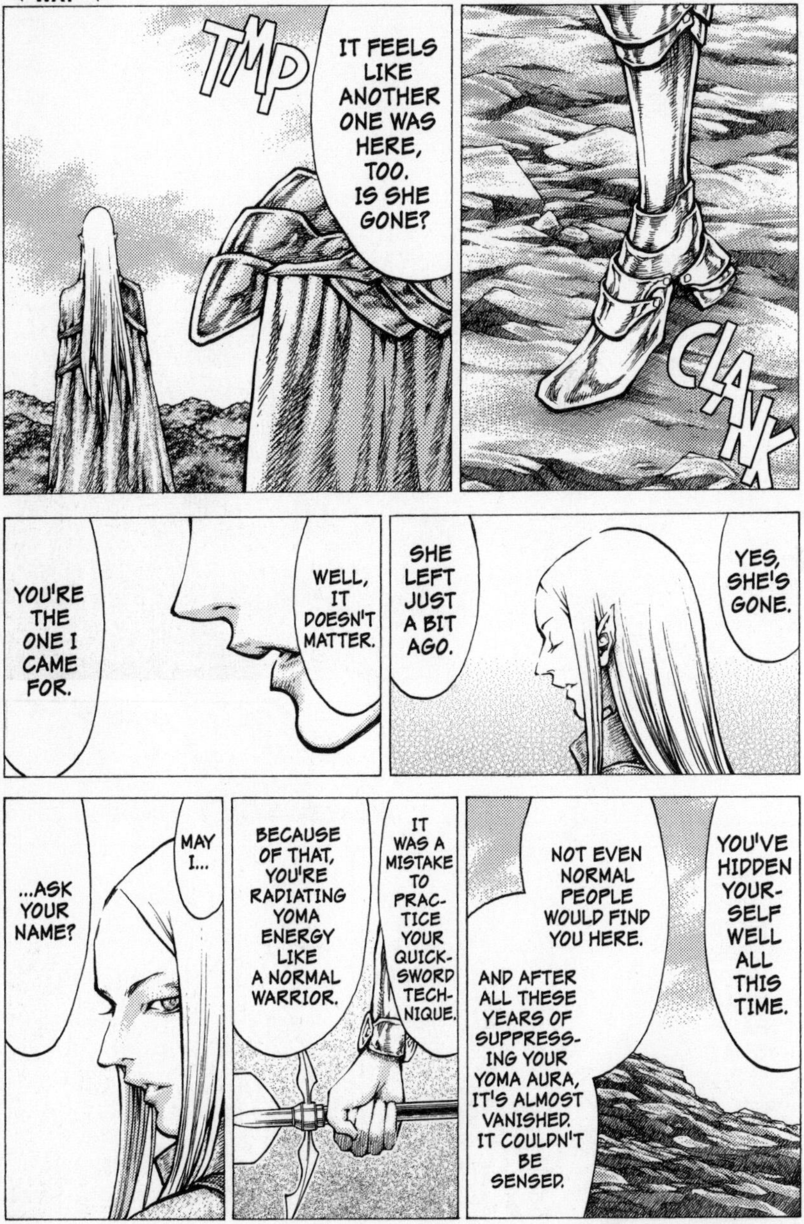
CLANK
TMP
IT FEELS LIKE ANOTHER ONE WAS HERE, TOO. IS SHE GONE?
YES, SHE'S GONE.
SHE LEFT JUST A BIT AGO.
WELL, IT DOESN'T MATTER.
YOU'RE THE ONE I CAME FOR.
YOU'VE HIDDEN YOURSELF WELL ALL THIS TIME.
NOT EVEN NORMAL PEOPLE WOULD FIND YOU HERE.
AND AFTER ALL THESE YEARS OF SUPPRESSING YOUR YOMA AURA, IT'S ALMOST VANISHED. IT COULDN'T BE SENSED.
IT WAS A MISTAKE TO PRACTICE YOUR QUICK-SWORD TECHNIQUE.
BECAUSE OF THAT, YOU'RE RADIATING YOMA ENERGY LIKE A NORMAL WARRIOR.
MAY I...
...ASK YOUR NAME?

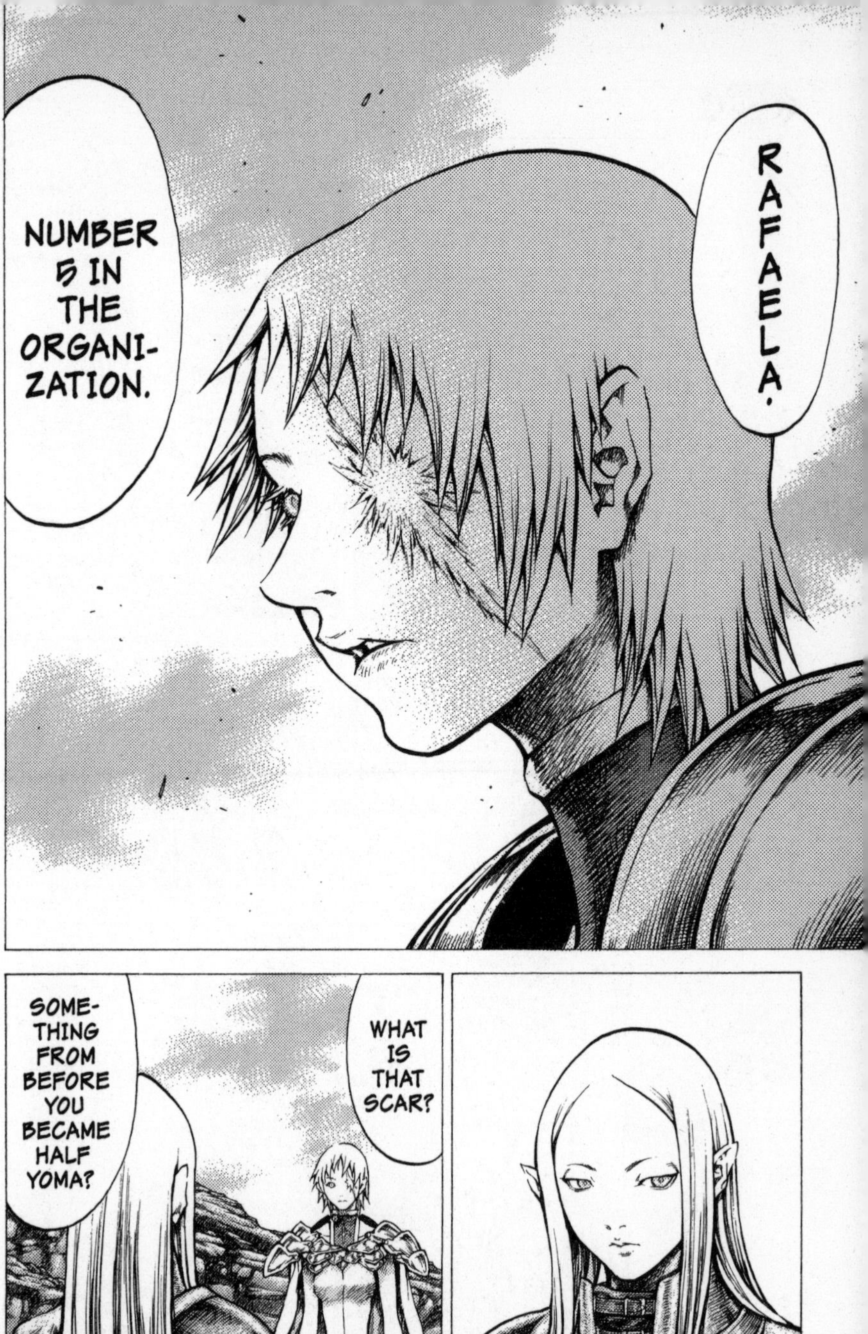
RAFAELA.
NUMBER 5 IN THE ORGANIZATION.
WHAT IS THAT SCAR?
SOMETHING FROM BEFORE YOU BECAME HALF YOMA?

READ THIS WAY

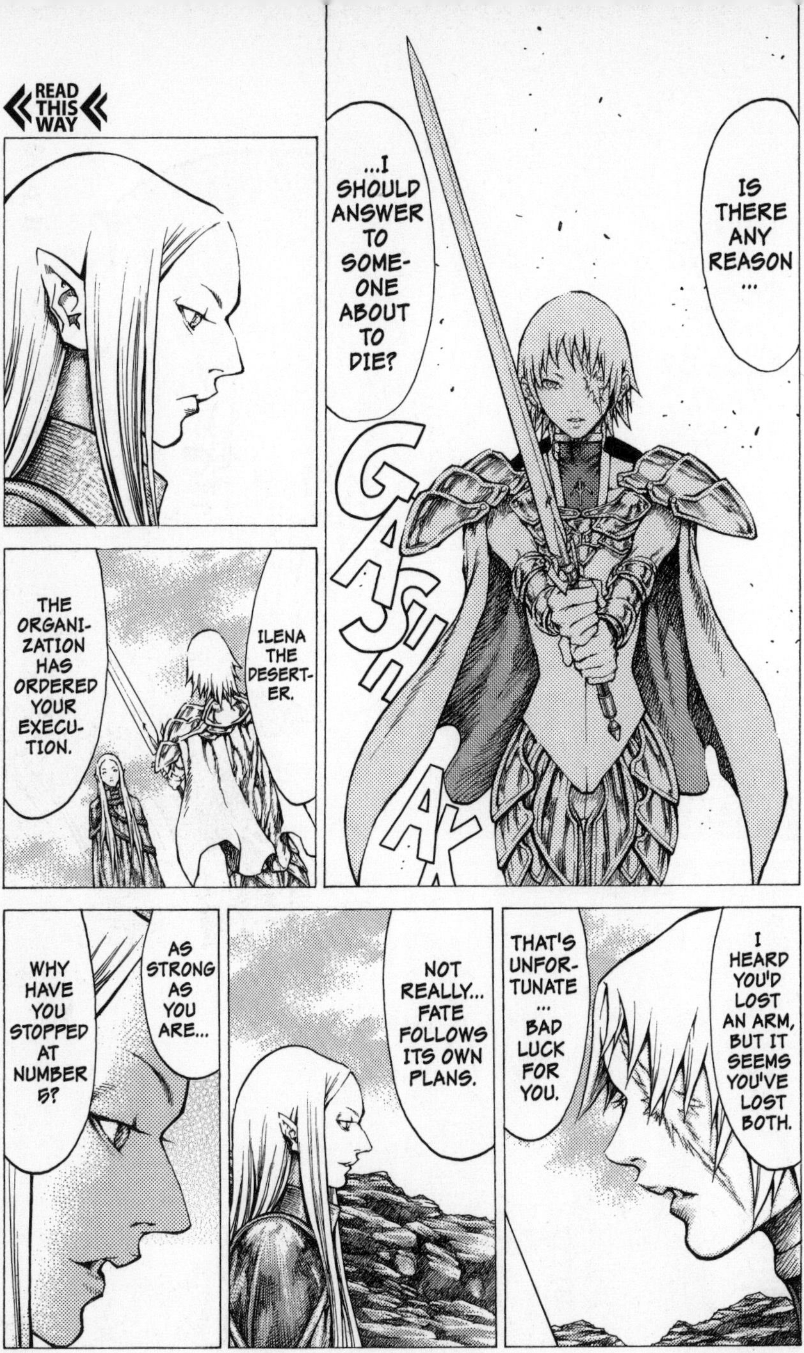
IS THERE ANY REASON ...
...I SHOULD ANSWER TO SOME-ONE ABOUT TO DIE?
GASHAK
ILENA THE DESERT-ER.
THE ORGANI-ZATION HAS ORDERED YOUR EXECU-TION.
I HEARD YOU'D LOST AN ARM, BUT IT SEEMS YOU'VE LOST BOTH.
THAT'S UNFOR-TUNATE ... BAD LUCK FOR YOU.
NOT REALLY... FATE FOLLOWS ITS OWN PLANS.
AS STRONG AS YOU ARE...
WHY HAVE YOU STOPPED AT NUMBER 5?

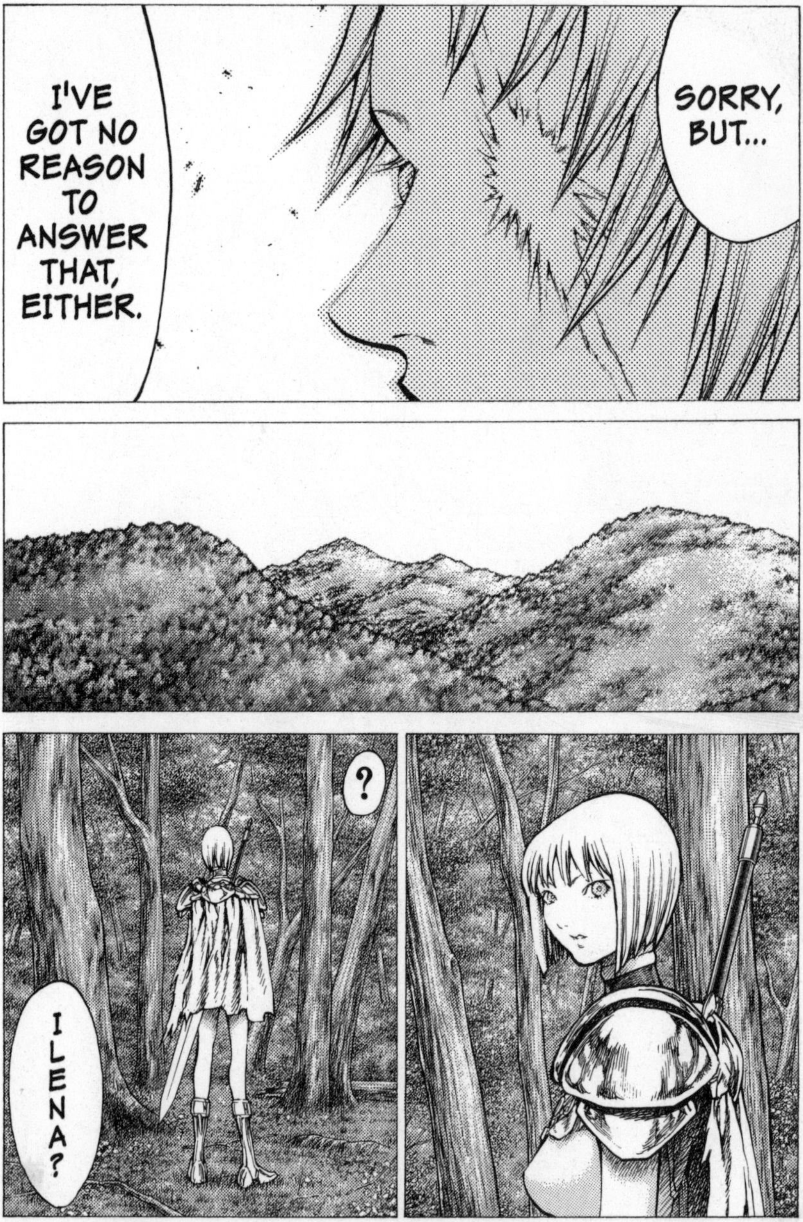
SORRY, BUT...
I'VE GOT NO REASON TO ANSWER THAT, EITHER.
?
ILENA?

READ THIS WAY

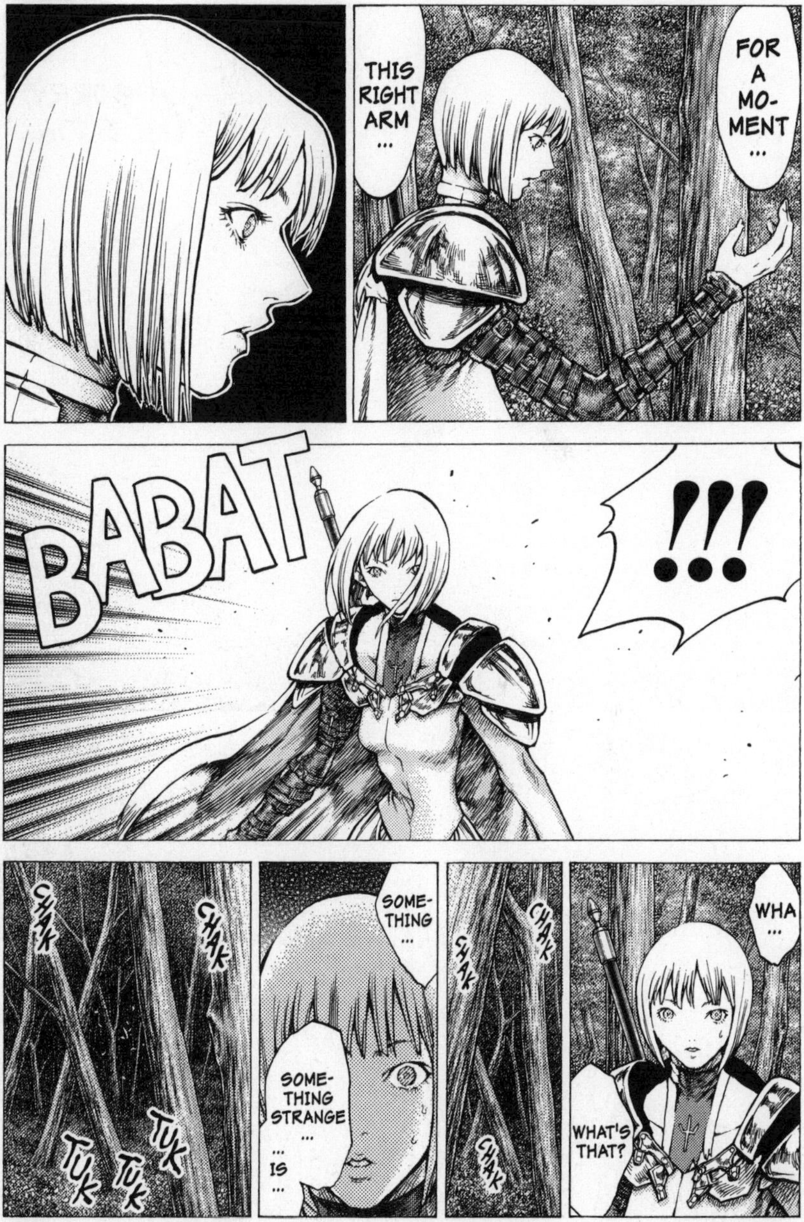

FOR A MO-MENT...
THIS RIGHT ARM...
!!!
BABAT
WHA...
WHAT'S THAT?
CHAK
CHAK
CHAK
SOME-THING...
SOME-THING STRANGE...
...IS...
CHAK
CHAK
TUK
TUK
TUK

クレイモア
Claymore™

Scene 39: Fit for Battle, Part 3

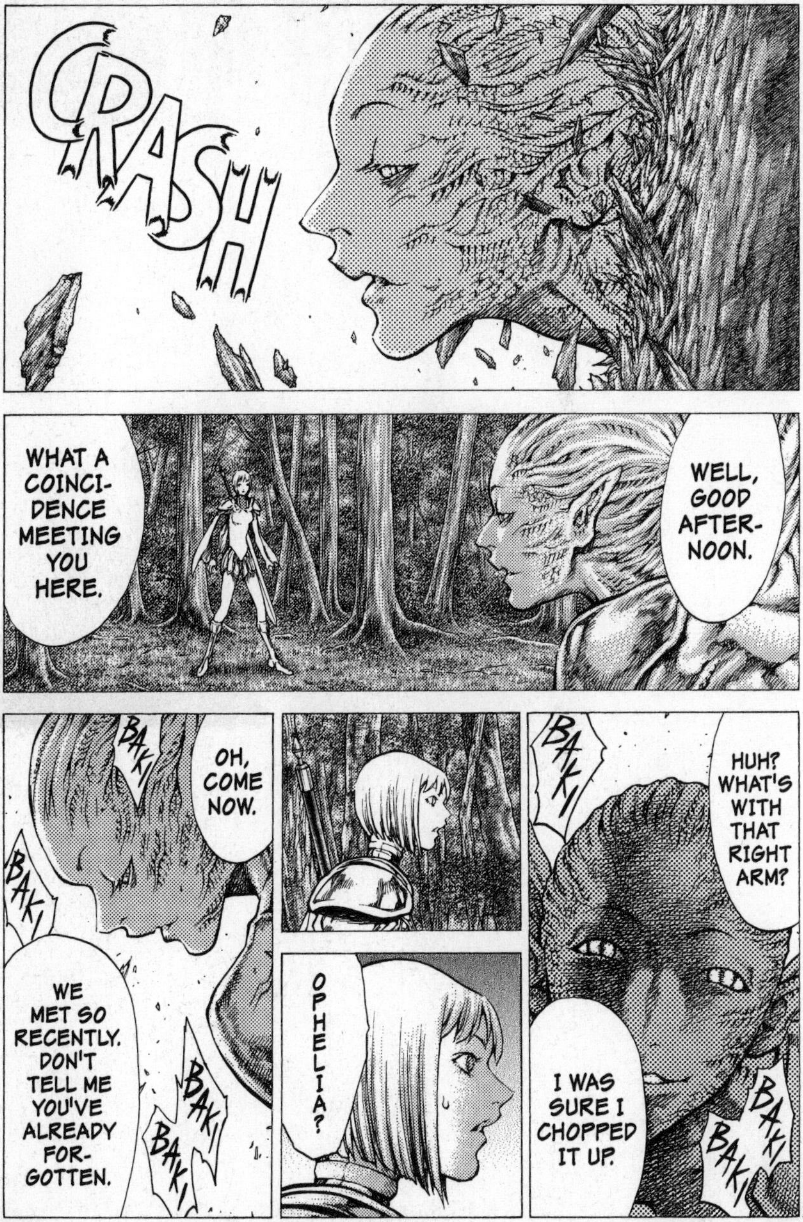
CRASH
WELL, GOOD AFTERNOON.
WHAT A COINCIDENCE MEETING YOU HERE.
BAKI
HUH? WHAT'S WITH THAT RIGHT ARM?
I WAS SURE I CHOPPED IT UP.
BAKI BAKI
OPHELIA?
BAKI
OH, COME NOW.
BAKI
WE MET SO RECENTLY. DON'T TELL ME YOU'VE ALREADY FOR-GOTTEN.
BAKI BAKI

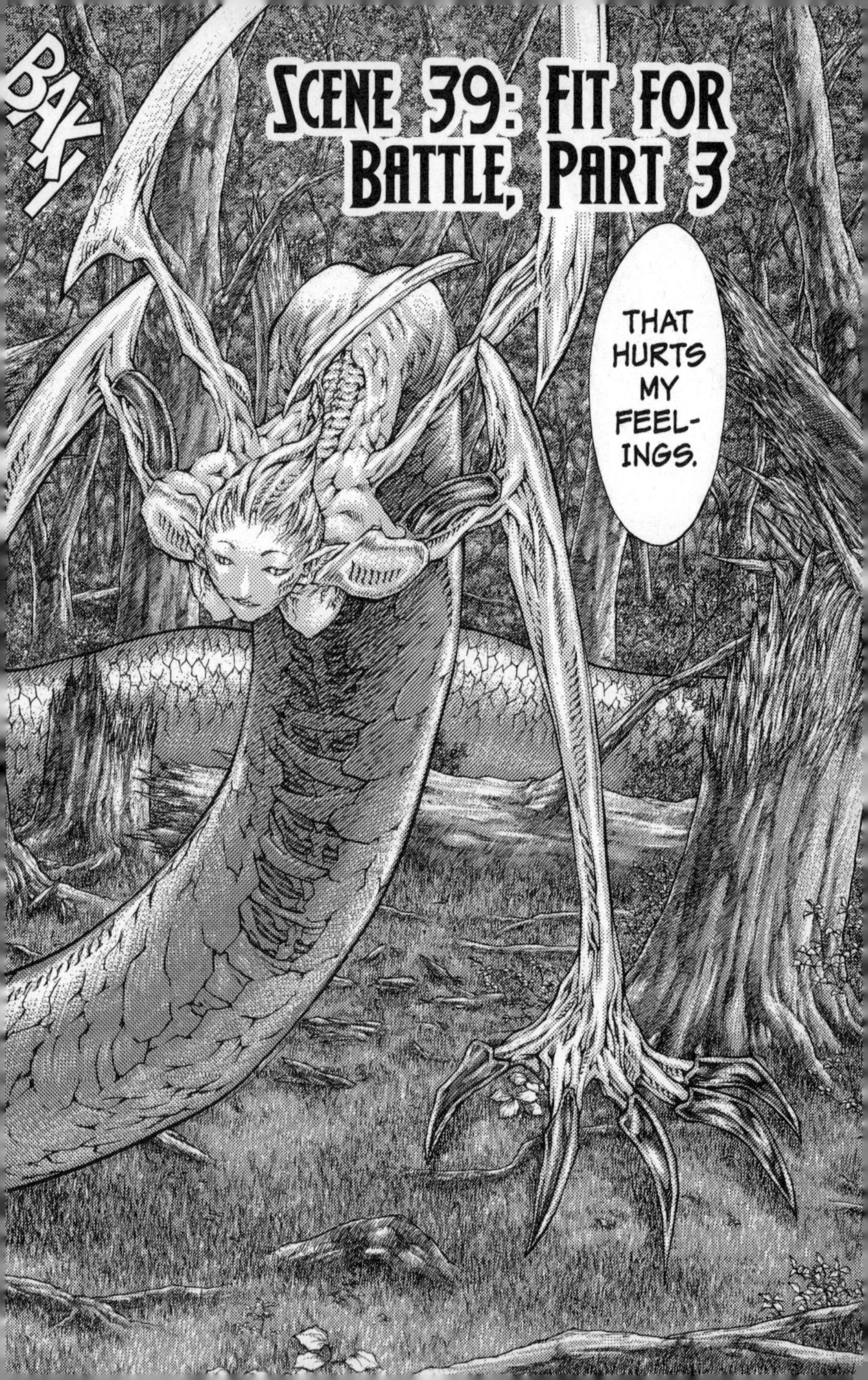
SCENE 39: FIT FOR BATTLE, PART 3
BAK!
THAT HURTS MY FEEL-INGS.

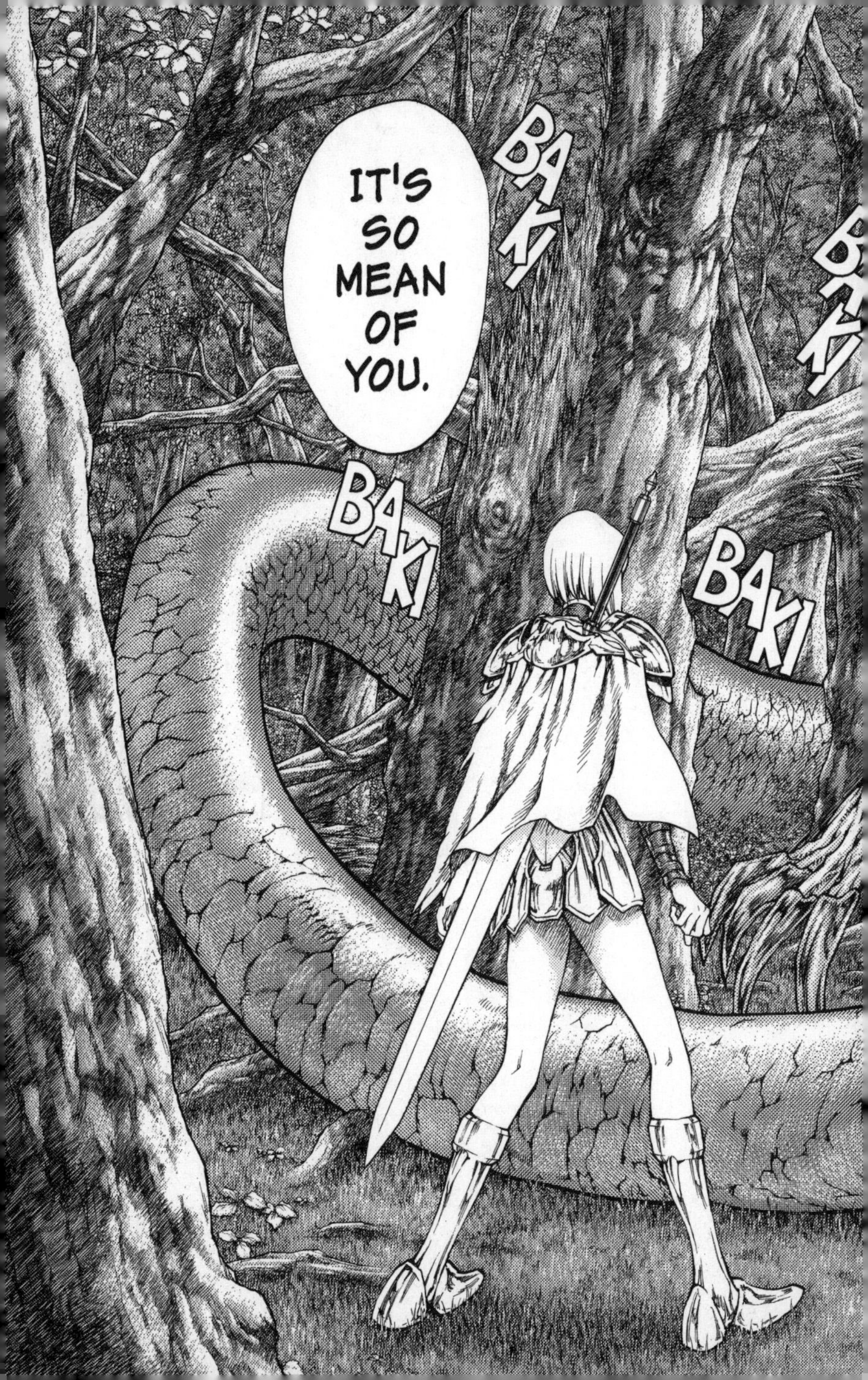
BAKI
BAKI
BAKI
IT'S SO MEAN OF YOU.
BAKI

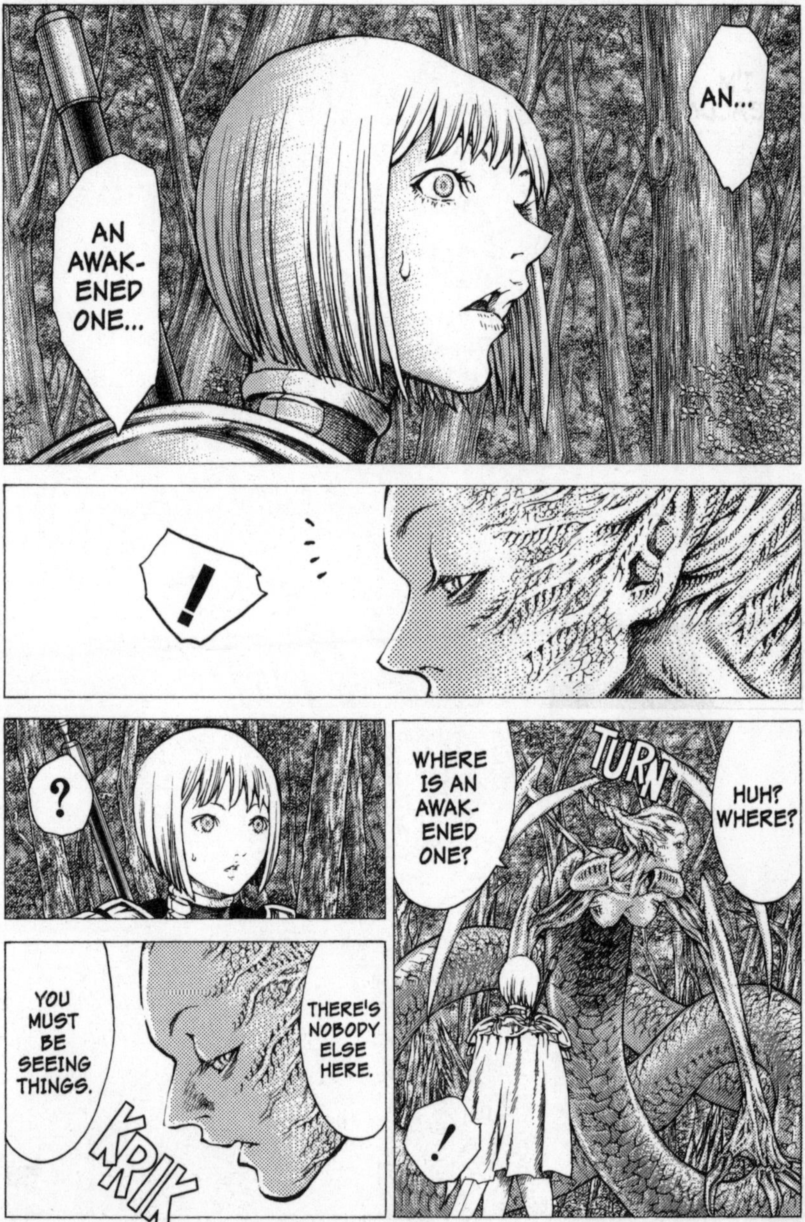
AN...
AN AWAKENED ONE...
!
TURN
HUH? WHERE?
WHERE IS AN AWAKENED ONE?
!
?
THERE'S NOBODY ELSE HERE.
YOU MUST BE SEEING THINGS.
KRIK

READ THIS WAY

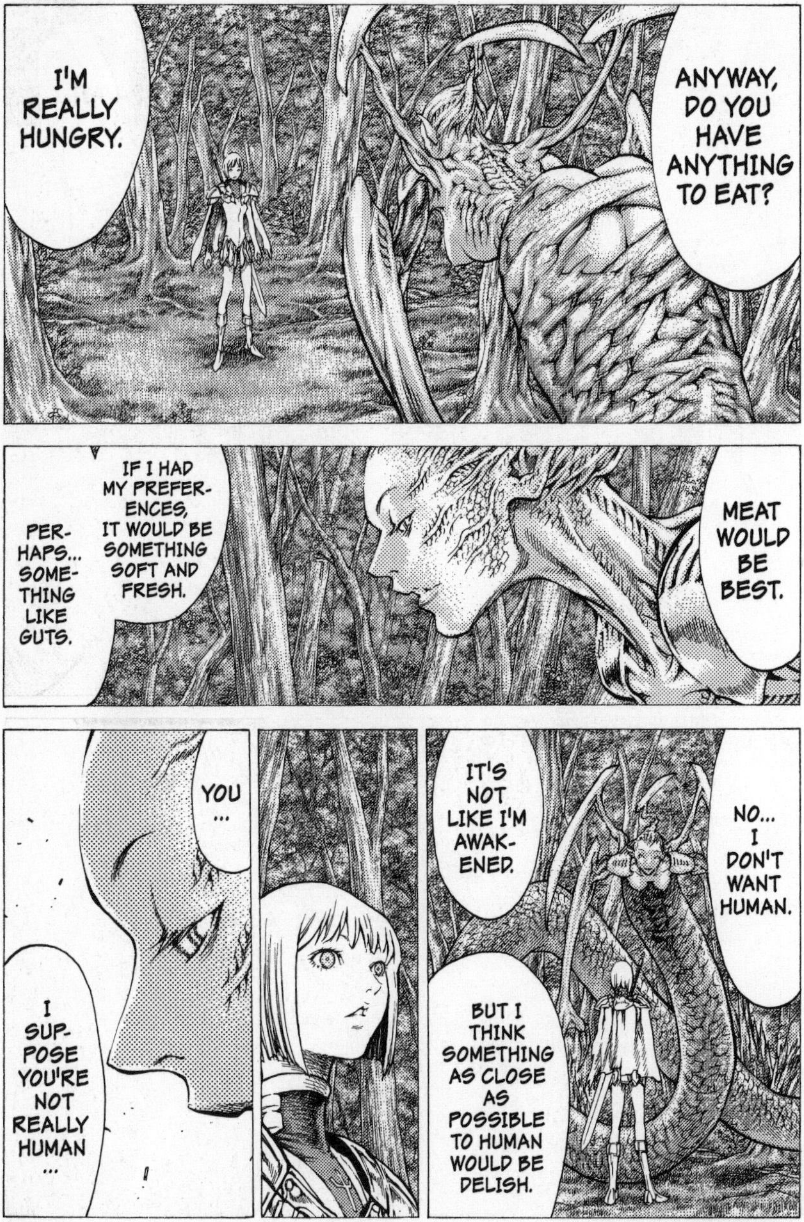

ANYWAY, DO YOU HAVE ANYTHING TO EAT?
I'M REALLY HUNGRY.
MEAT WOULD BE BEST.
IF I HAD MY PREFERENCES, IT WOULD BE SOMETHING SOFT AND FRESH.
PERHAPS... SOMETHING LIKE GUTS.
NO... I DON'T WANT HUMAN.
IT'S NOT LIKE I'M AWAKENED.
BUT I THINK SOMETHING AS CLOSE AS POSSIBLE TO HUMAN WOULD BE DELISH.
YOU...
I SUPPOSE YOU'RE NOT REALLY HUMAN...

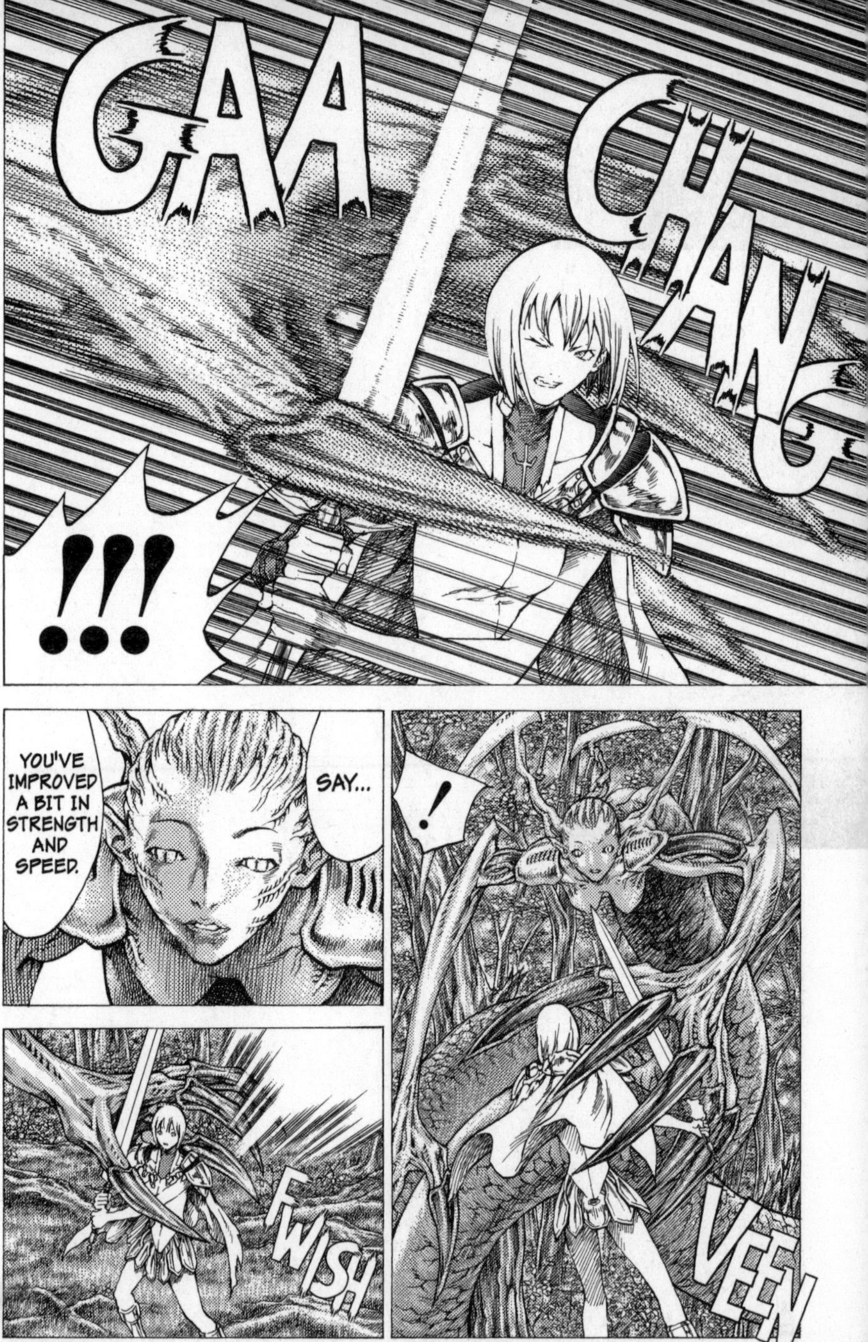
GAA CHANG
!!!
!
VEEN
SAY...
YOU'VE IMPROVED A BIT IN STRENGTH AND SPEED.
FWISH

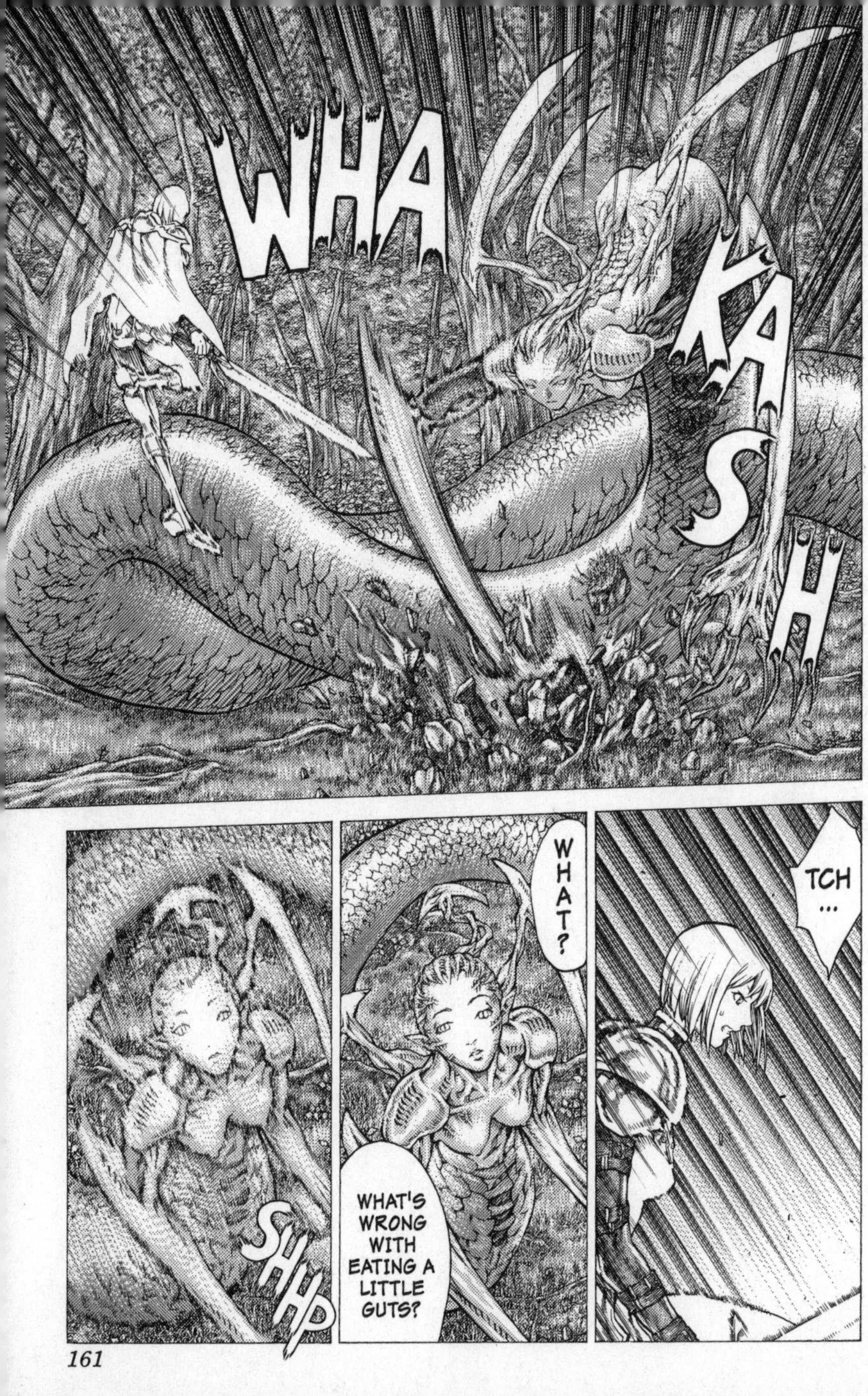
WHAKASH
TCH ...
WHAT?
WHAT'S WRONG WITH EATING A LITTLE GUTS?
SHHP

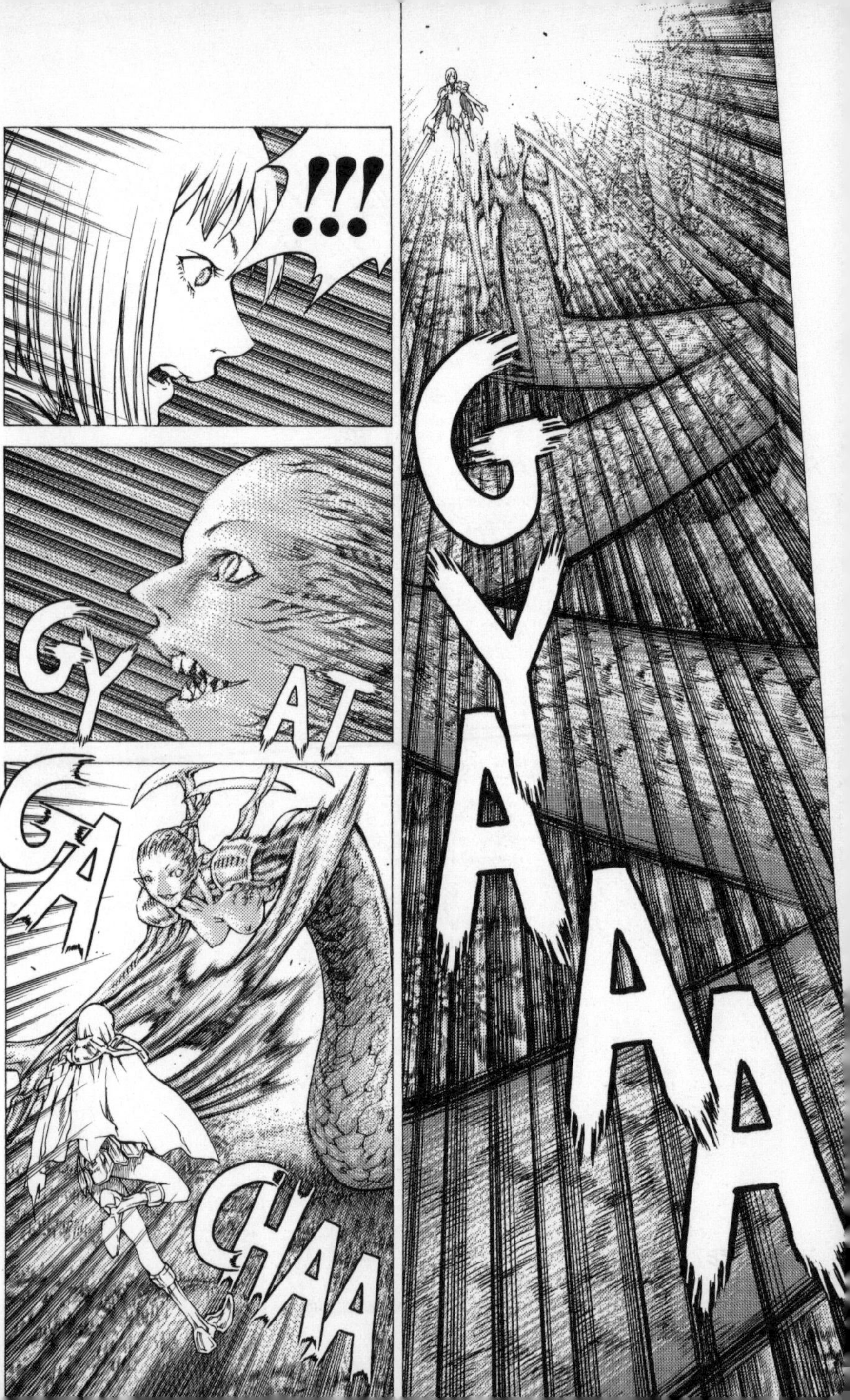
GYAAAA
!!!
GY
AT
GA
CHAA

READ THIS WAY

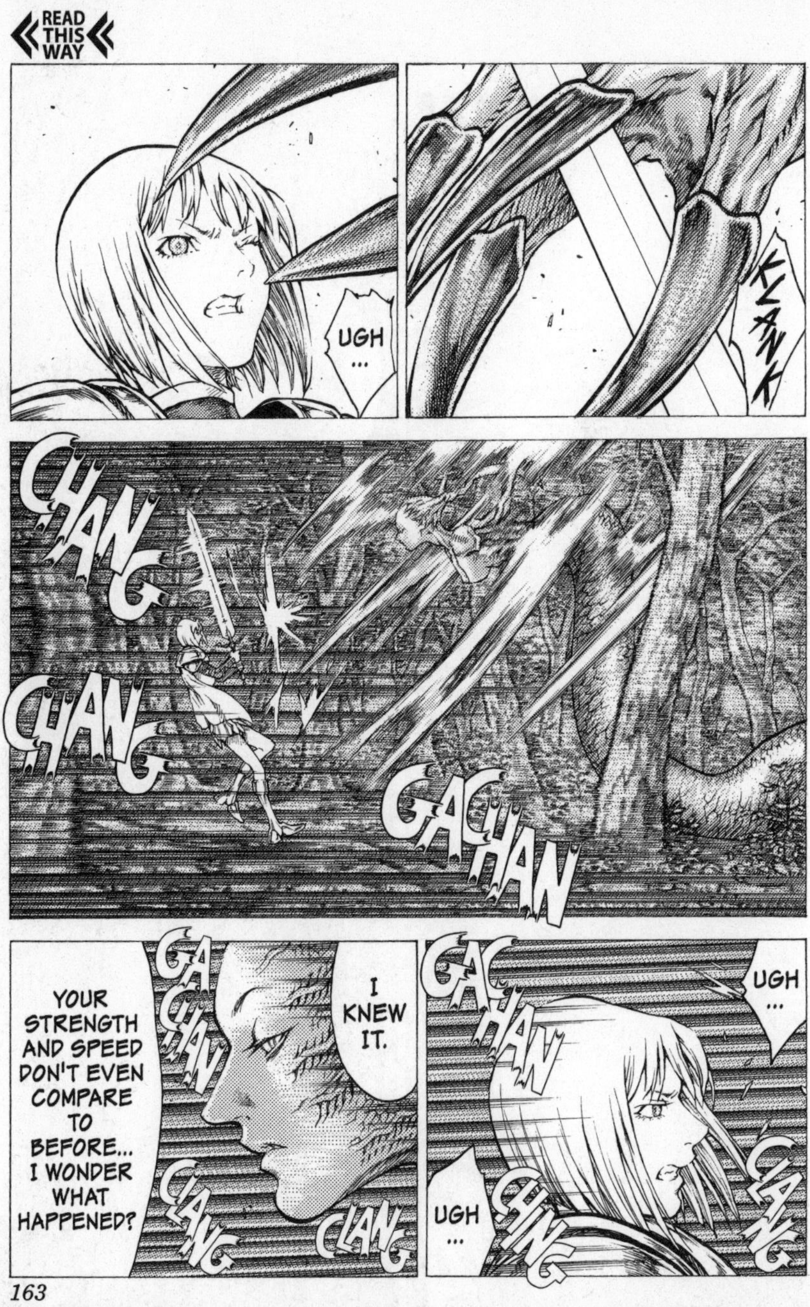
KLANK
UGH...
GACHAN
CHANG
CHANG
UGH...
GACHAN
CLANG
CLING
UGH...
I KNEW IT.
GACHAN
YOUR STRENGTH AND SPEED DON'T EVEN COMPARE TO BEFORE... I WONDER WHAT HAPPENED?
CLANG
CLANG

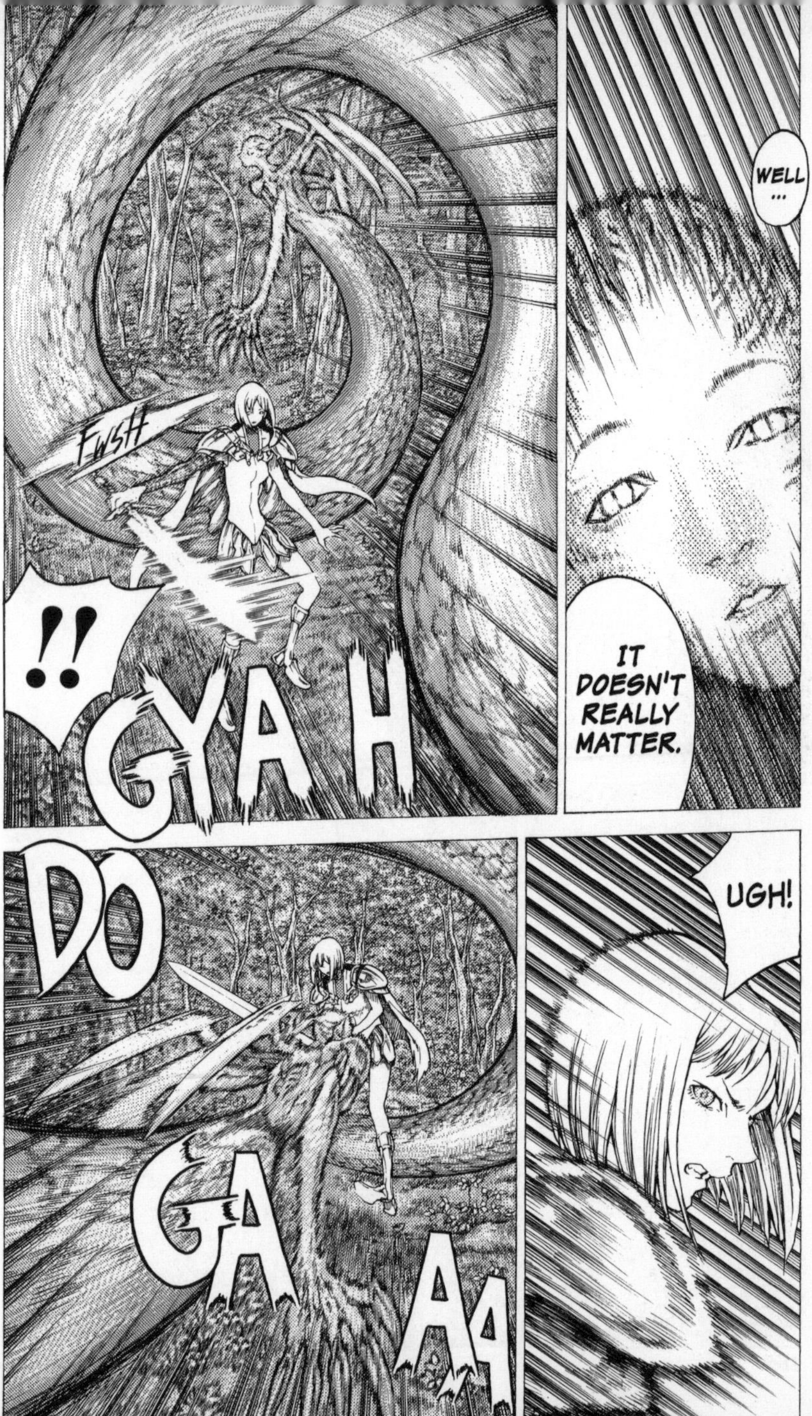
WELL ...
IT DOESN'T REALLY MATTER.
FWSH
!!
GYAH
UGH!
DO
GA
AA

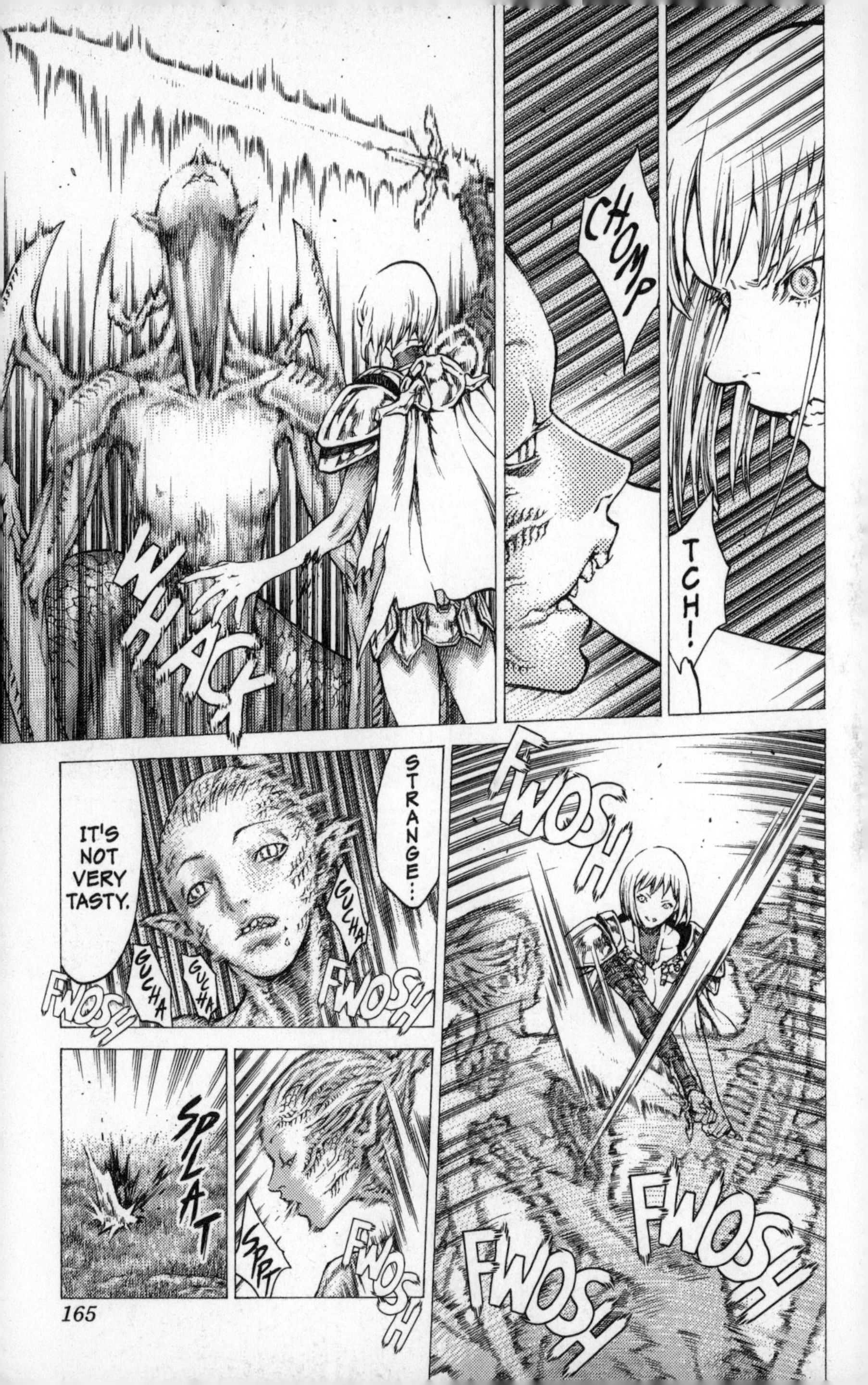
TCH!
CHOMP
WHACK
FWOSH
FWOSH
FWOSH
STRANGE...
IT'S NOT VERY TASTY.
GUCHA
GUCHA
GUCHA
FWOSH
FWOSH
SPIT
FWOSH
SPLAT

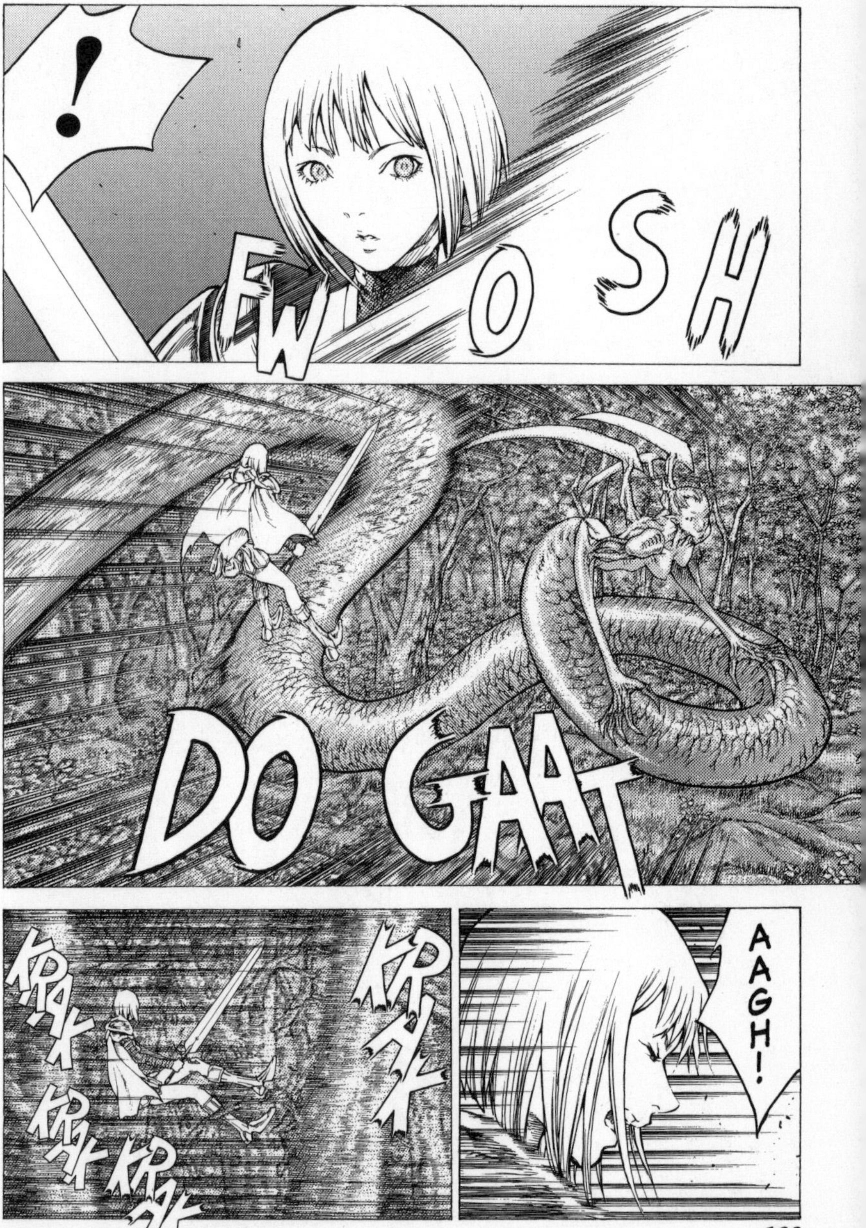
!
FWOSH
DOGAAT
AAGH!
KRAK
KRAK
KRAK
KRAK
KRAK

READ THIS WAY

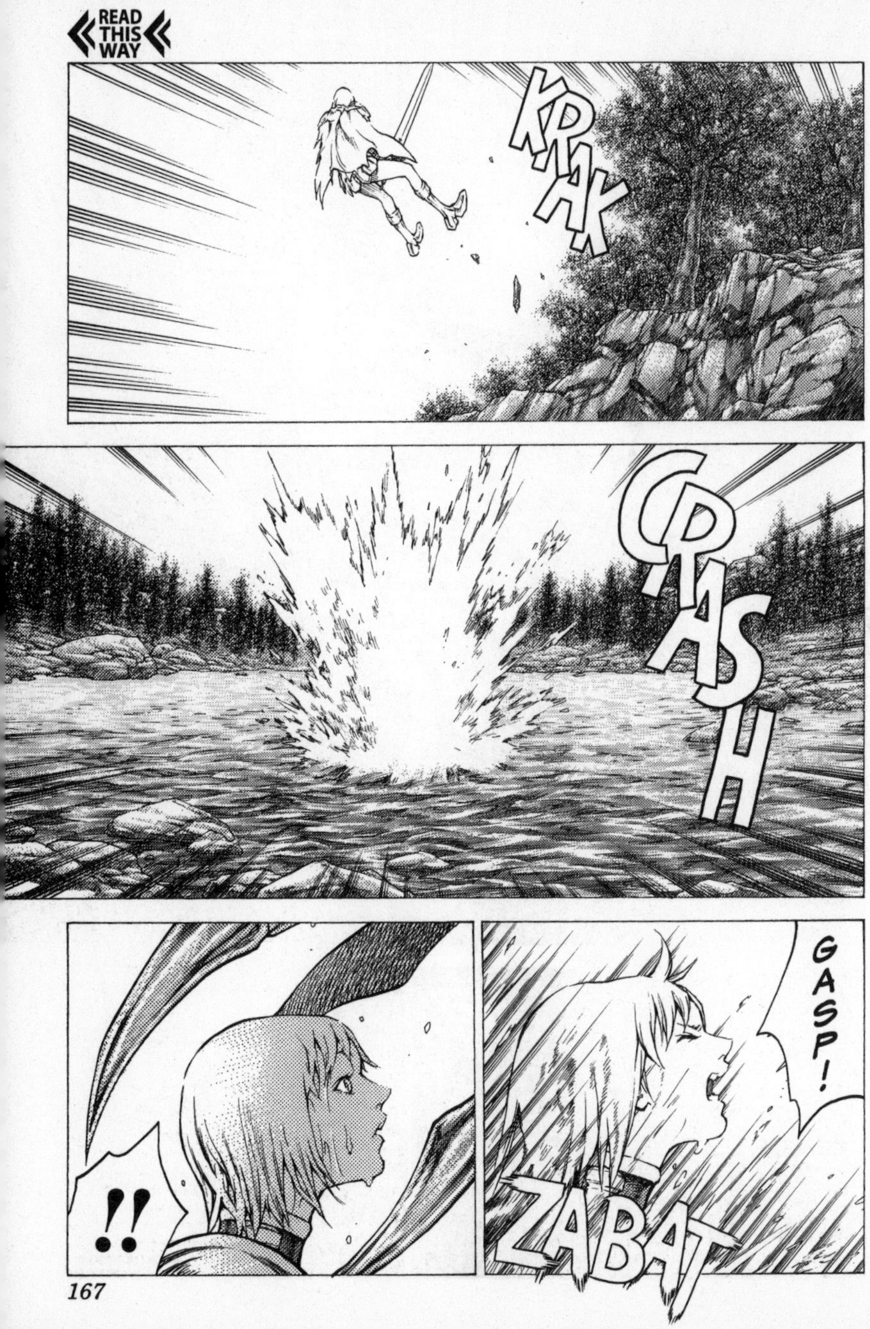
KRAK
CRASH
GASP!
ZABAT
!!

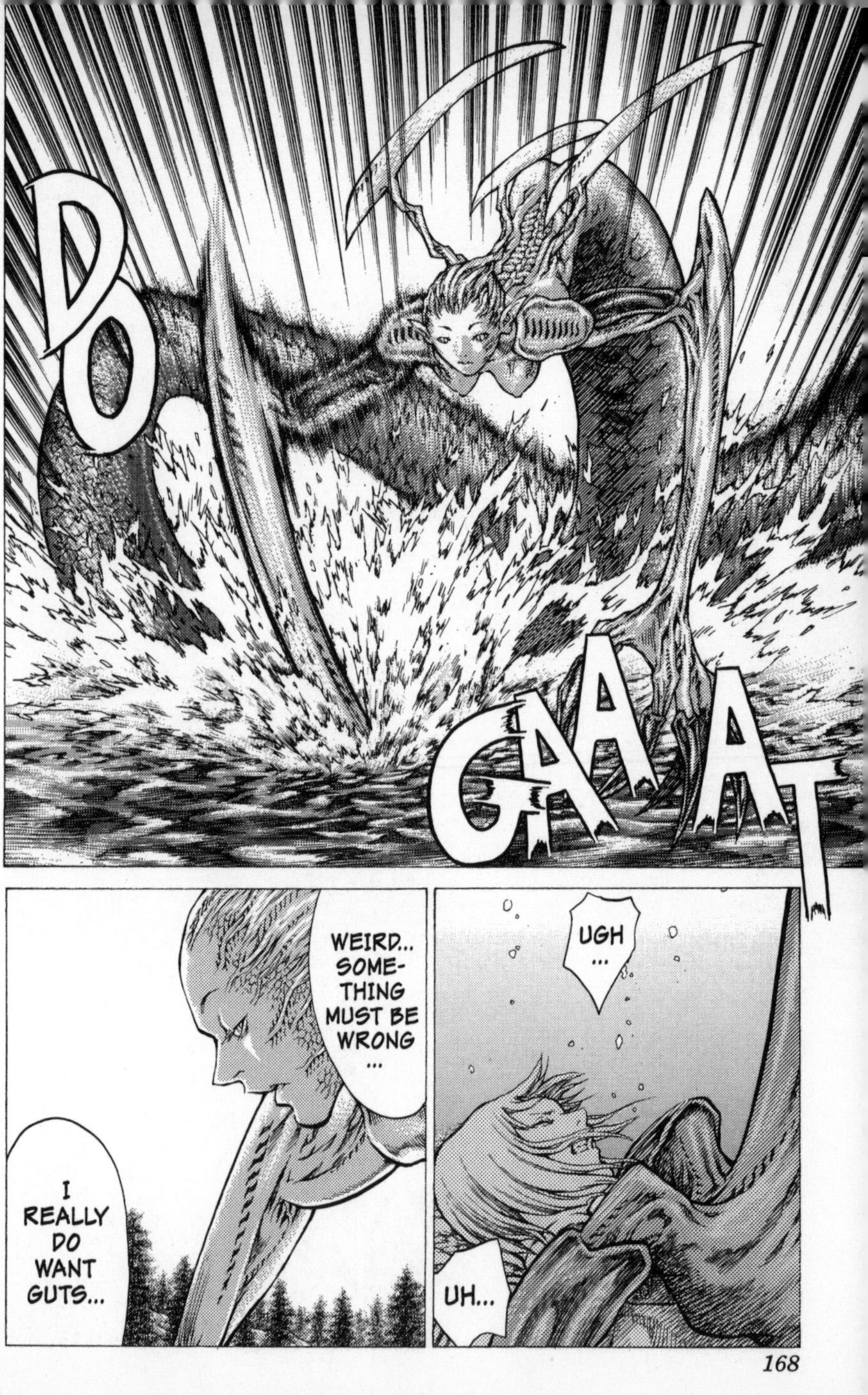
DO
GAAAT
UGH ...
UH...
WEIRD... SOME-THING MUST BE WRONG ...
I REALLY DO WANT GUTS...

READ THIS WAY

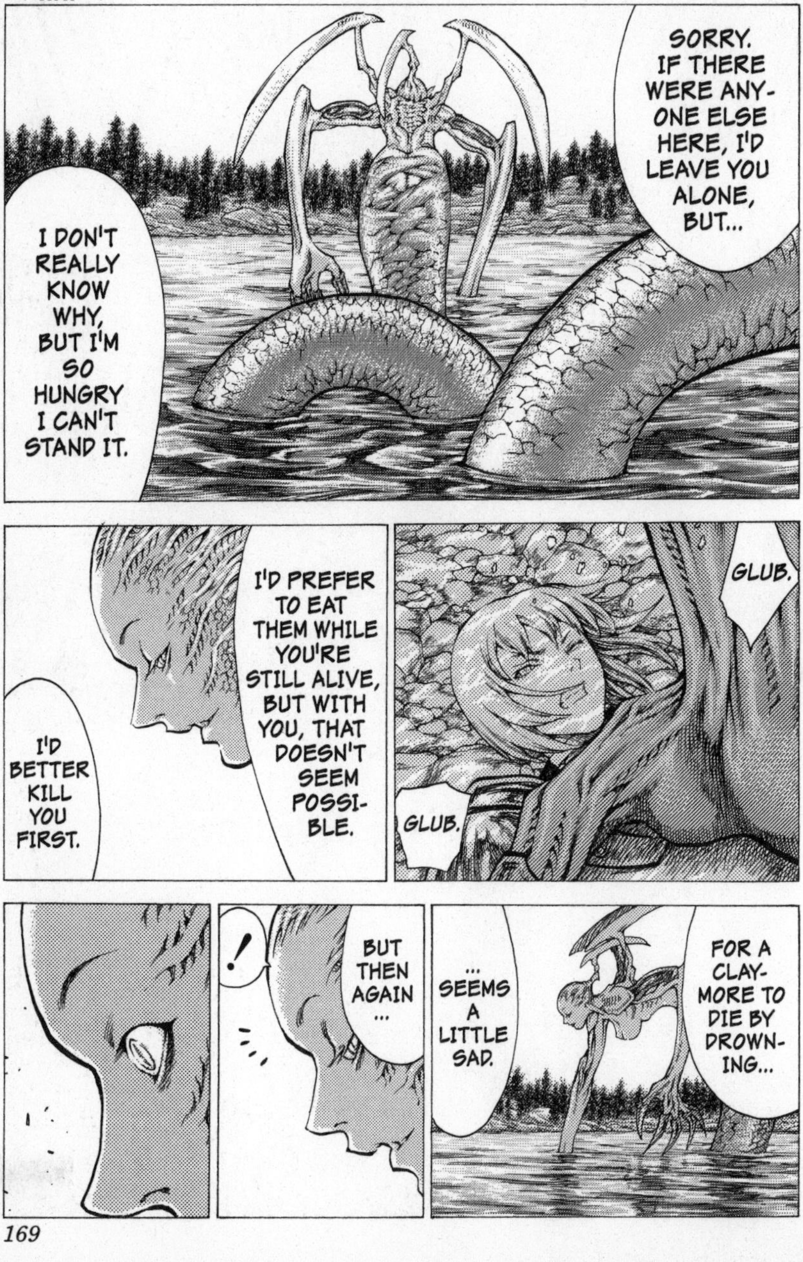
SORRY. IF THERE WERE ANY-ONE ELSE HERE, I'D LEAVE YOU ALONE, BUT...
I DON'T REALLY KNOW WHY, BUT I'M SO HUNGRY I CAN'T STAND IT.
GLUB.
GLUB.
I'D PREFER TO EAT THEM WHILE YOU'RE STILL ALIVE, BUT WITH YOU, THAT DOESN'T SEEM POSSI-BLE.
I'D BETTER KILL YOU FIRST.
FOR A CLAY-MORE TO DIE BY DROWN-ING...
... SEEMS A LITTLE SAD.
BUT THEN AGAIN ...
!

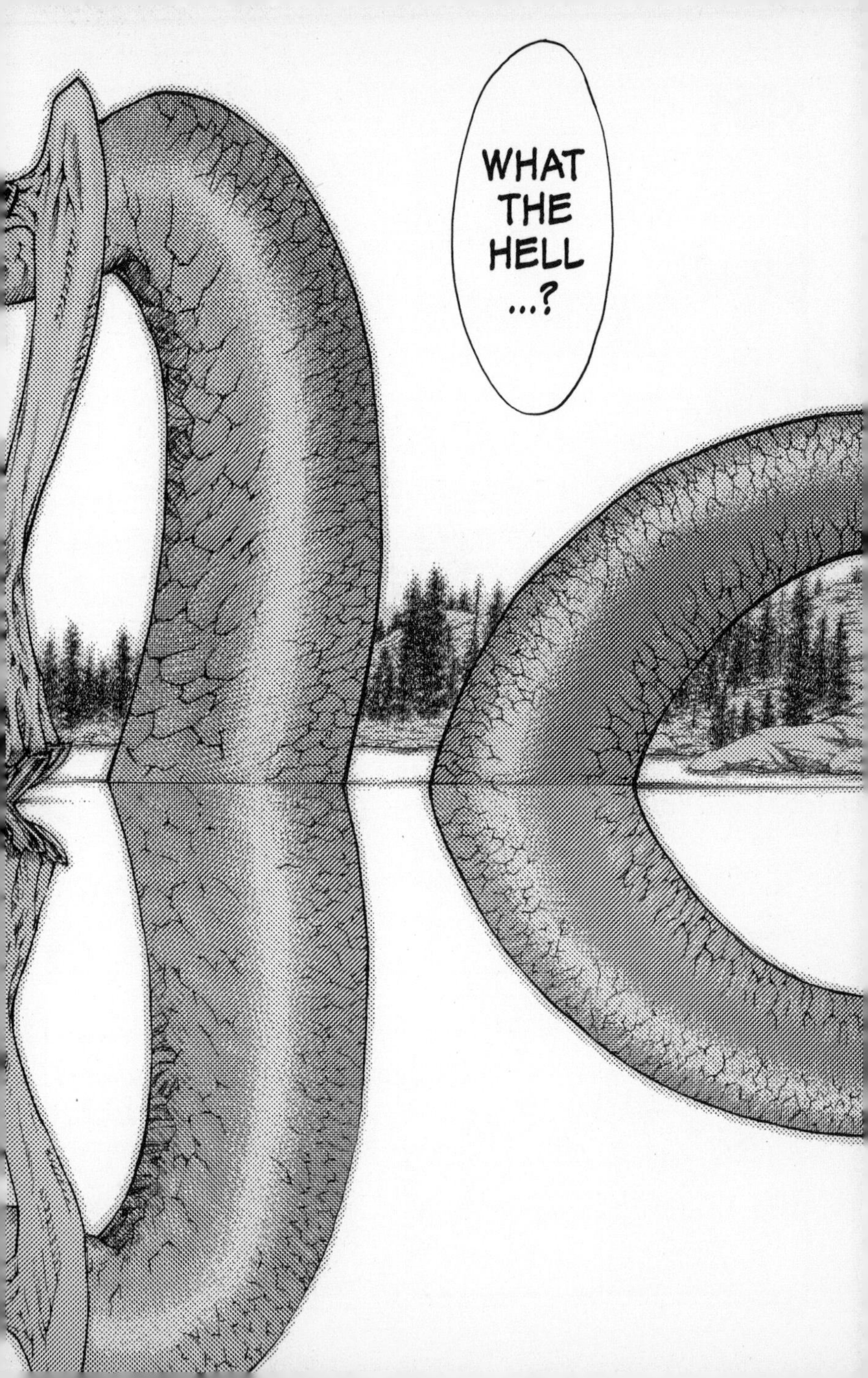
WHAT THE HELL ...?

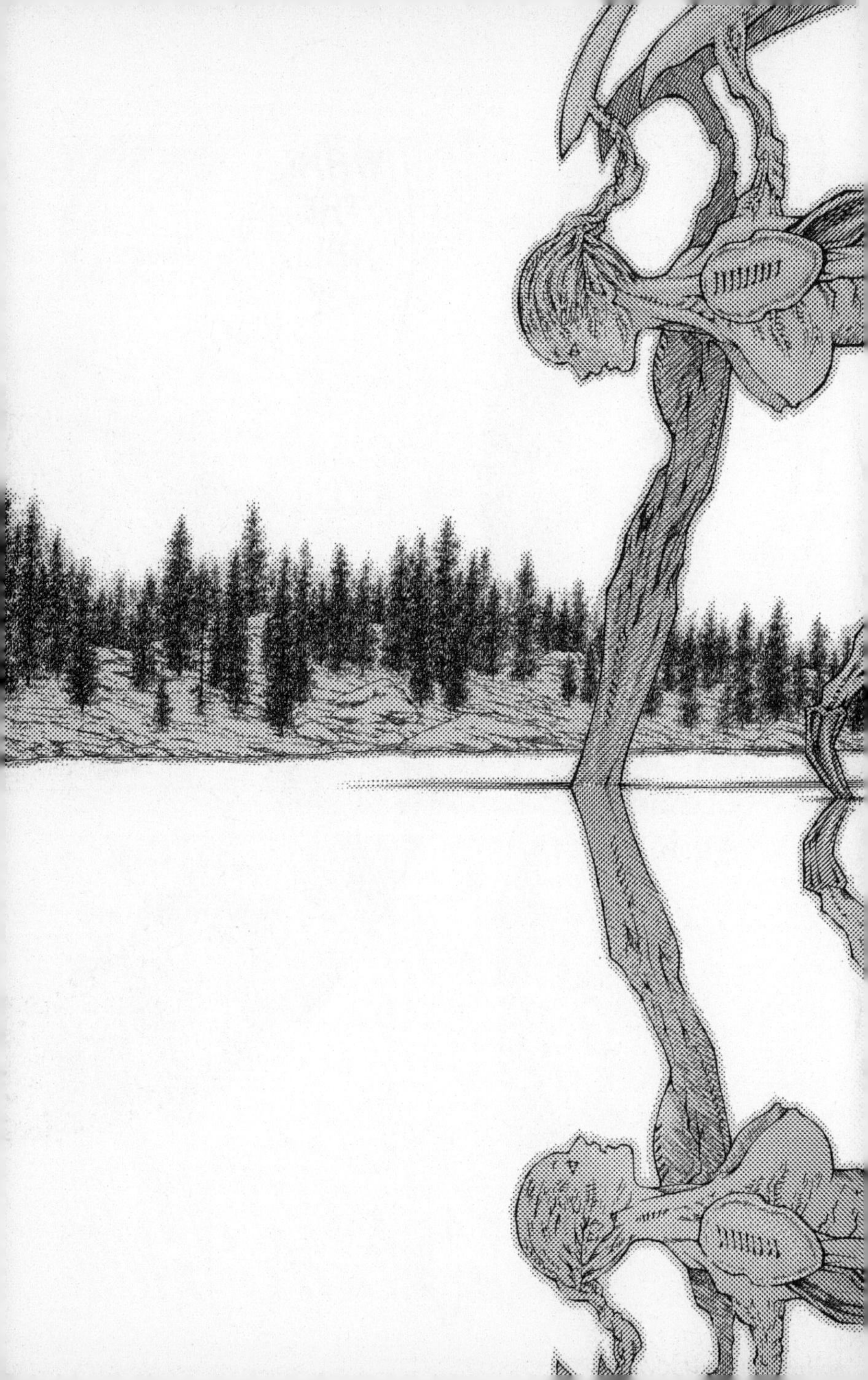

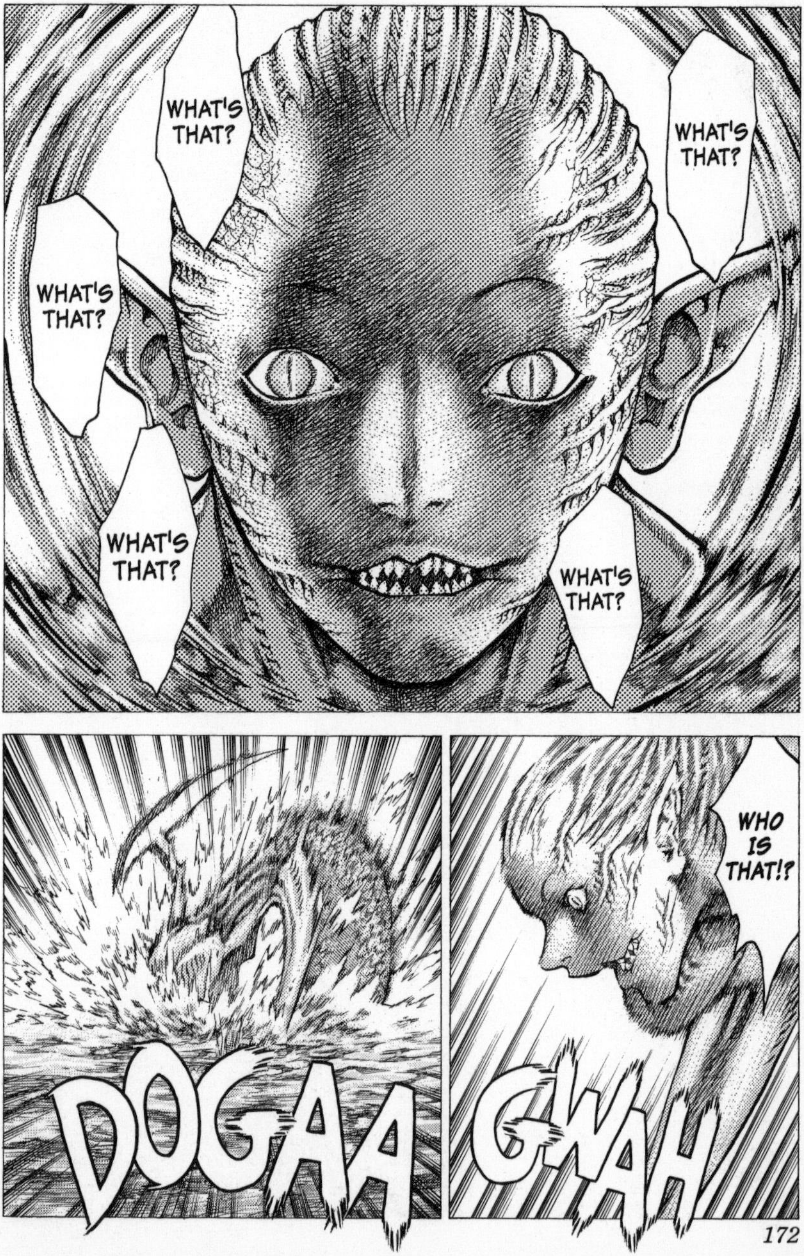

WHAT'S THAT?
WHAT'S THAT?
WHAT'S THAT?
WHAT'S THAT?
WHAT'S THAT?
WHO IS THAT!?
GWAH
DOGAA

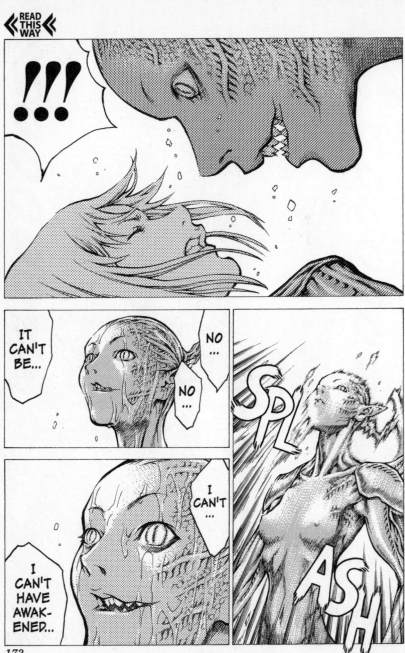

!!!

IT CAN'T BE...

NO...

NO...

I CAN'T...

I CAN'T HAVE AWAKENED...

SPL

ASH

173

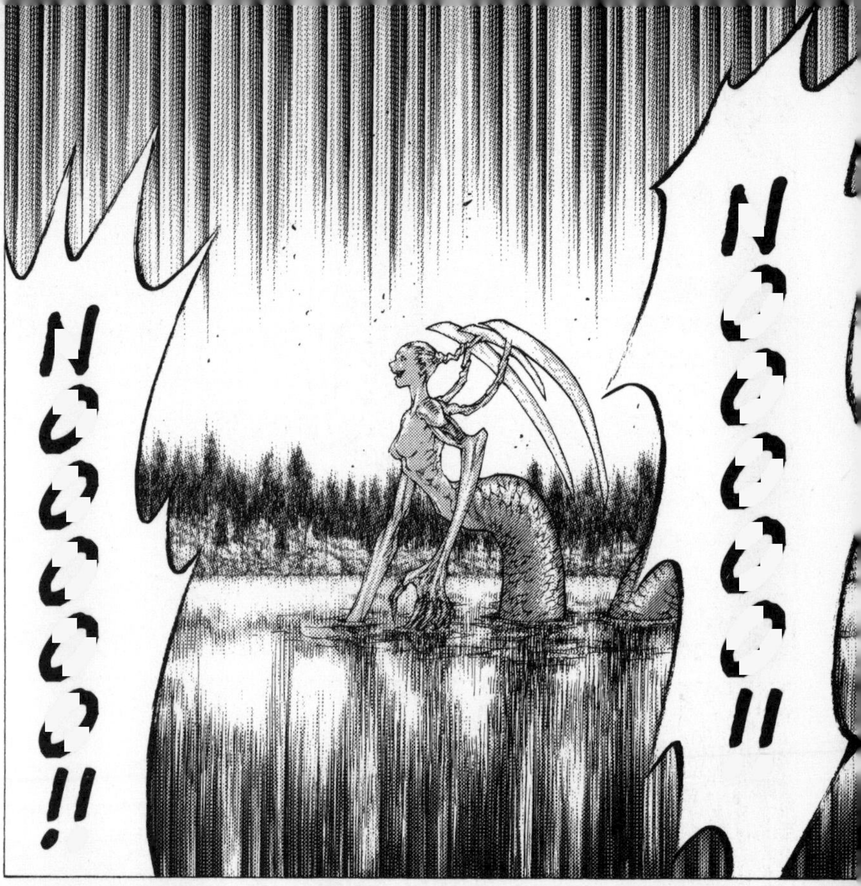
NOOOOO!!
NOOOOO!!

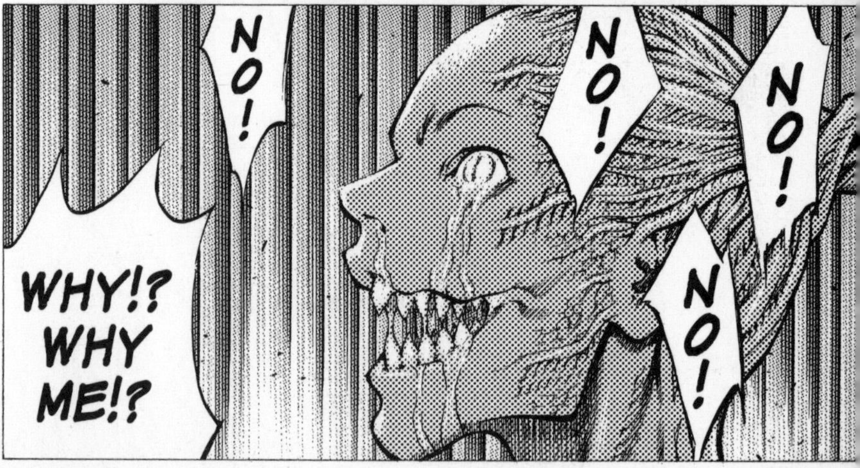
NO!
NO!
NO!
NO!
WHY!? WHY ME!?

READ THIS WAY

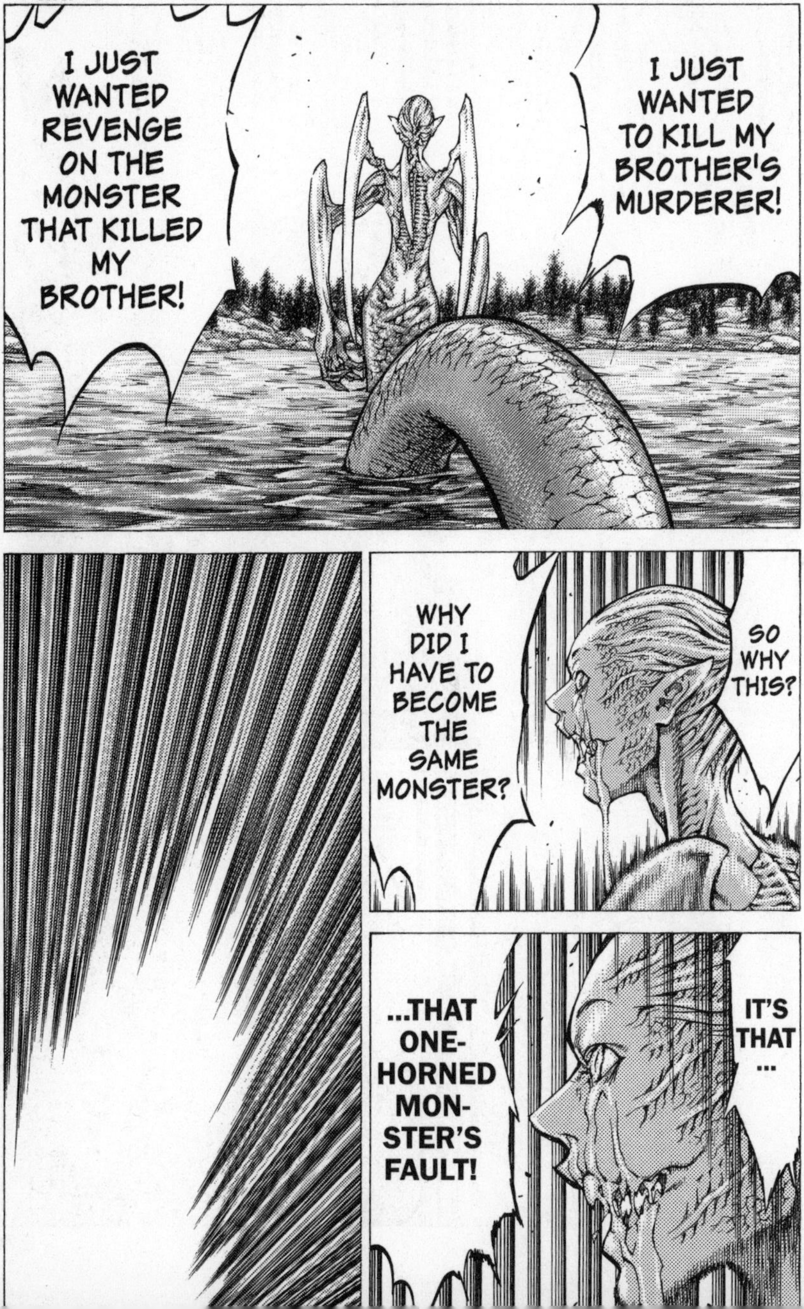

I JUST WANTED TO KILL MY BROTHER'S MURDERER!
I JUST WANTED REVENGE ON THE MONSTER THAT KILLED MY BROTHER!
SO WHY THIS?
WHY DID I HAVE TO BECOME THE SAME MONSTER?
IT'S THAT...
...THAT ONE-HORNED MON-STER'S FAULT!

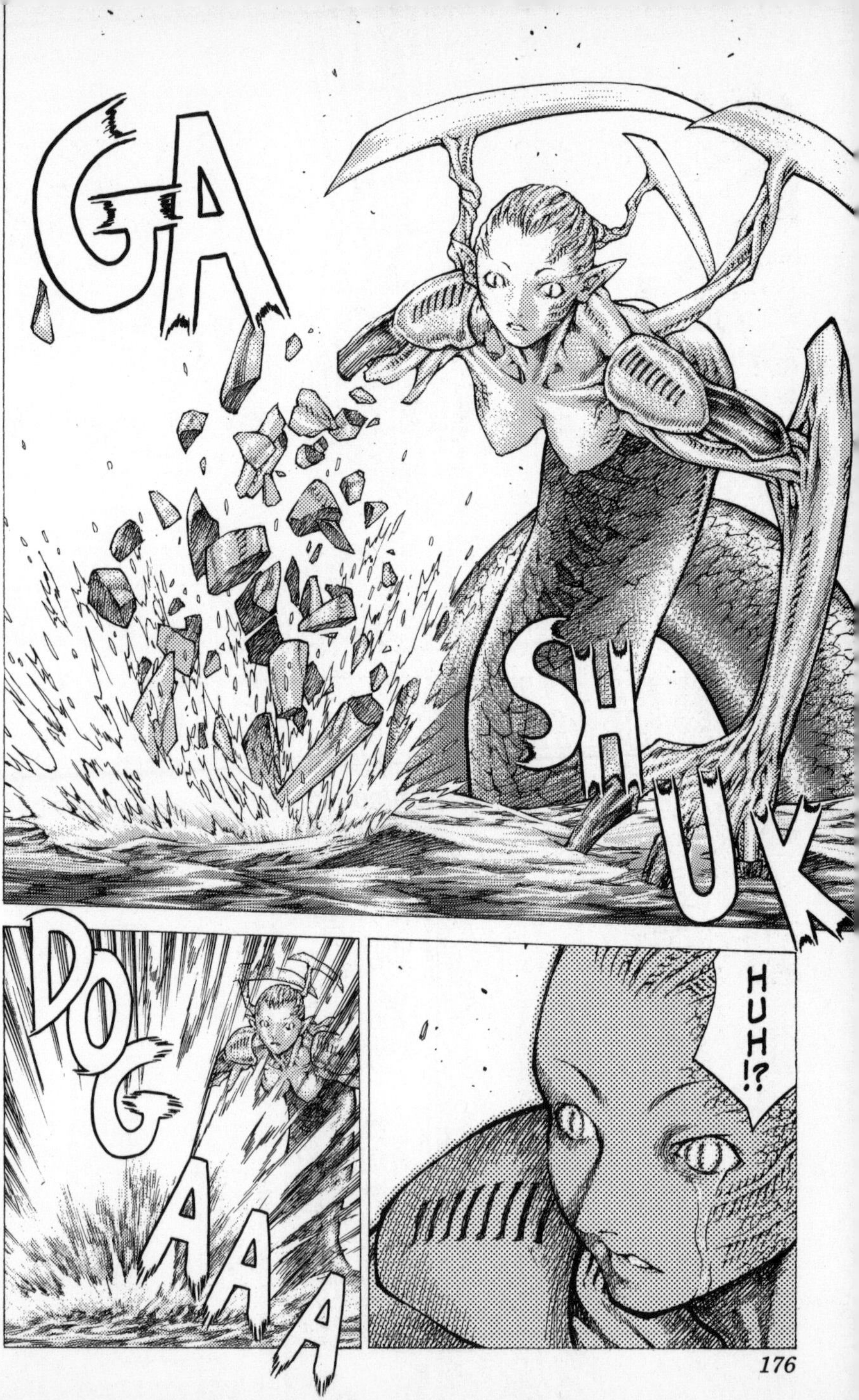
GA
SHUK
HUH!?
DOGAAA

READ THIS WAY

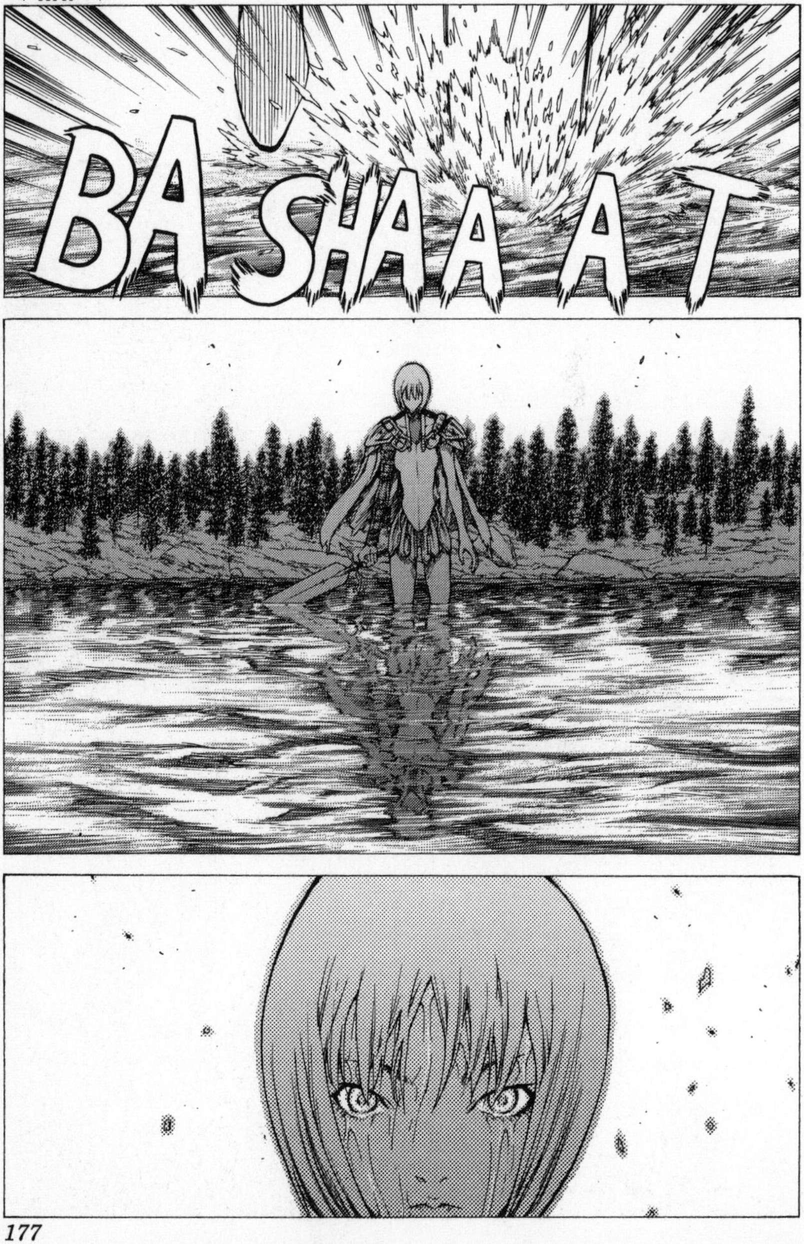
BA SHAA A A T

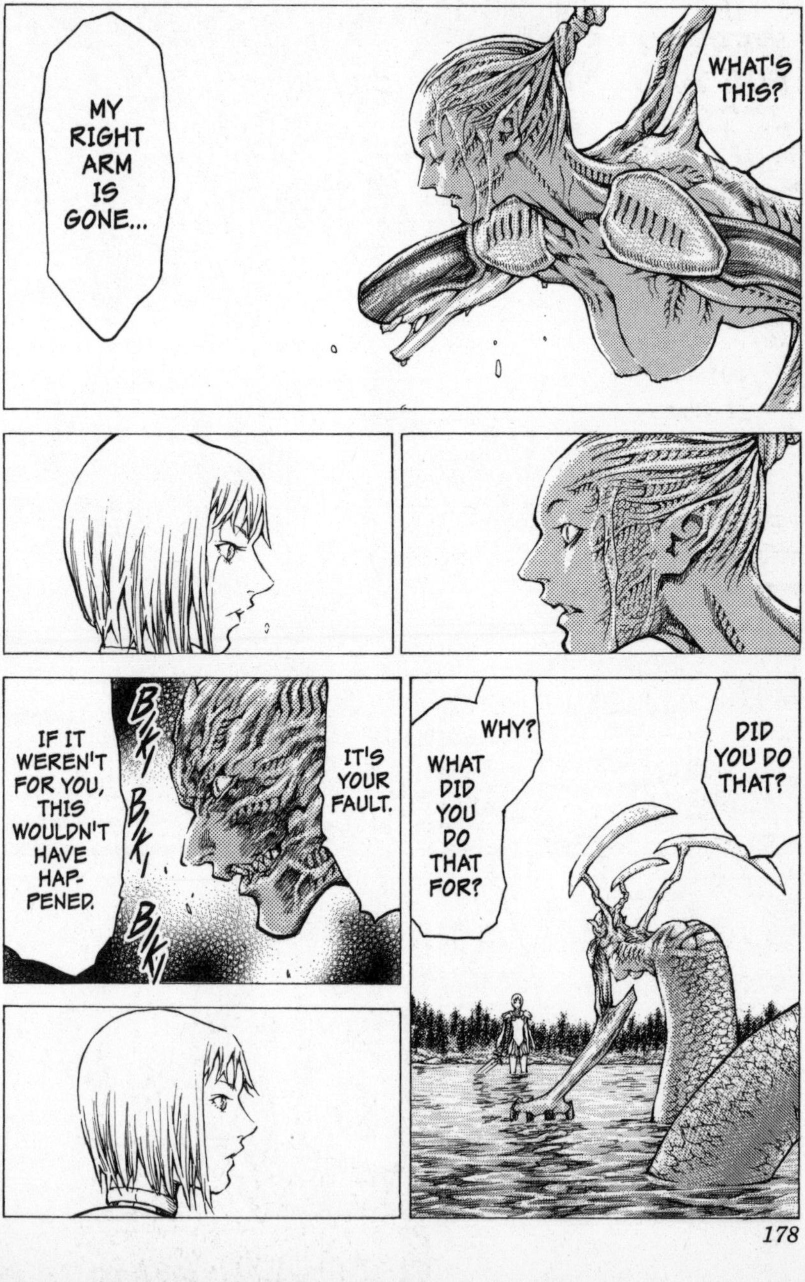
WHAT'S THIS?
MY RIGHT ARM IS GONE...
DID YOU DO THAT?
WHY? WHAT DID YOU DO THAT FOR?
IT'S YOUR FAULT.
BIKI BIKI BIKI
IF IT WEREN'T FOR YOU, THIS WOULDN'T HAVE HAP-PENED.

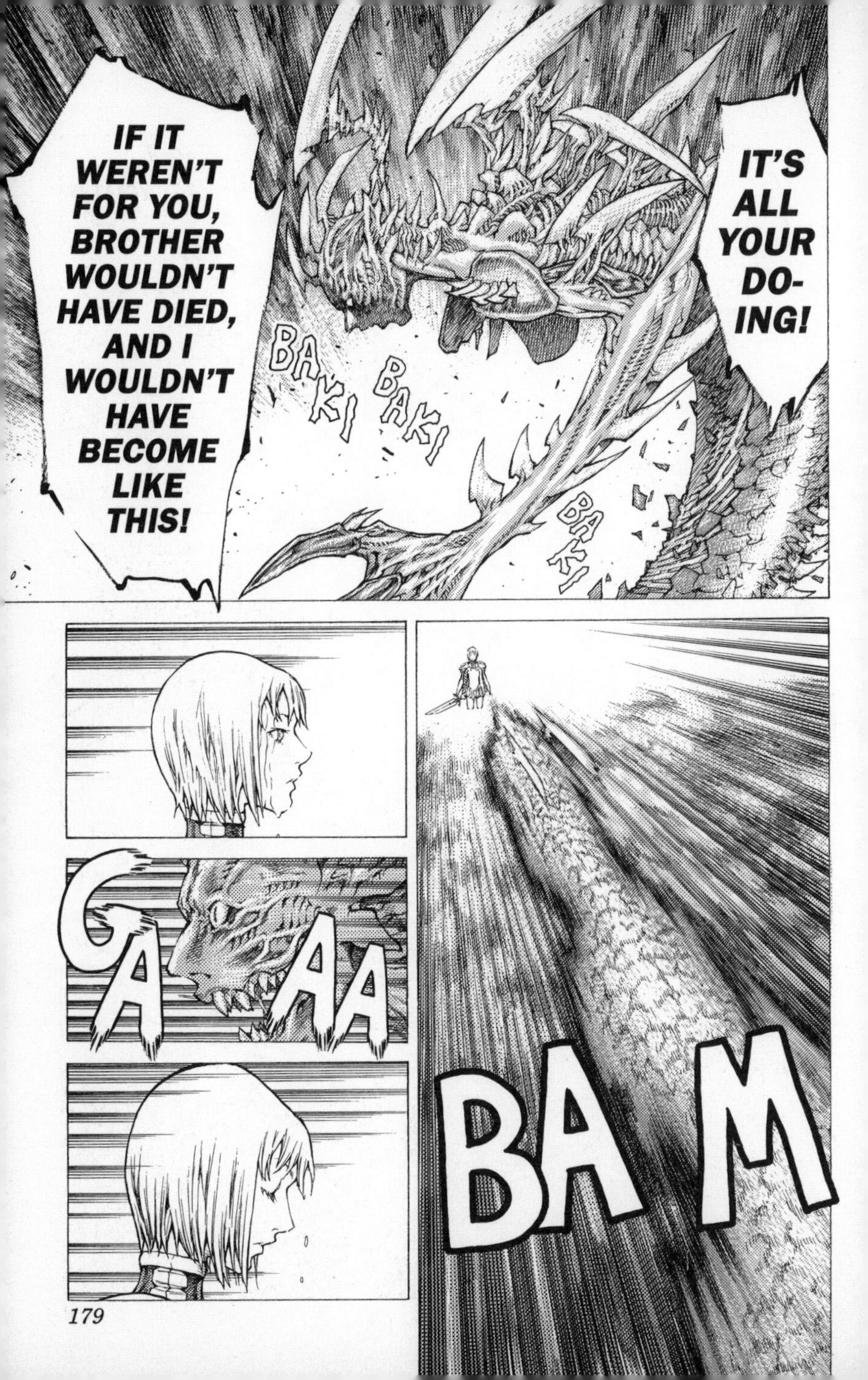
IT'S ALL YOUR DO-ING!
IF IT WEREN'T FOR YOU, BROTHER WOULDN'T HAVE DIED, AND I WOULDN'T HAVE BECOME LIKE THIS!
BAKI BAKI
BAKI
BAM
GAAA

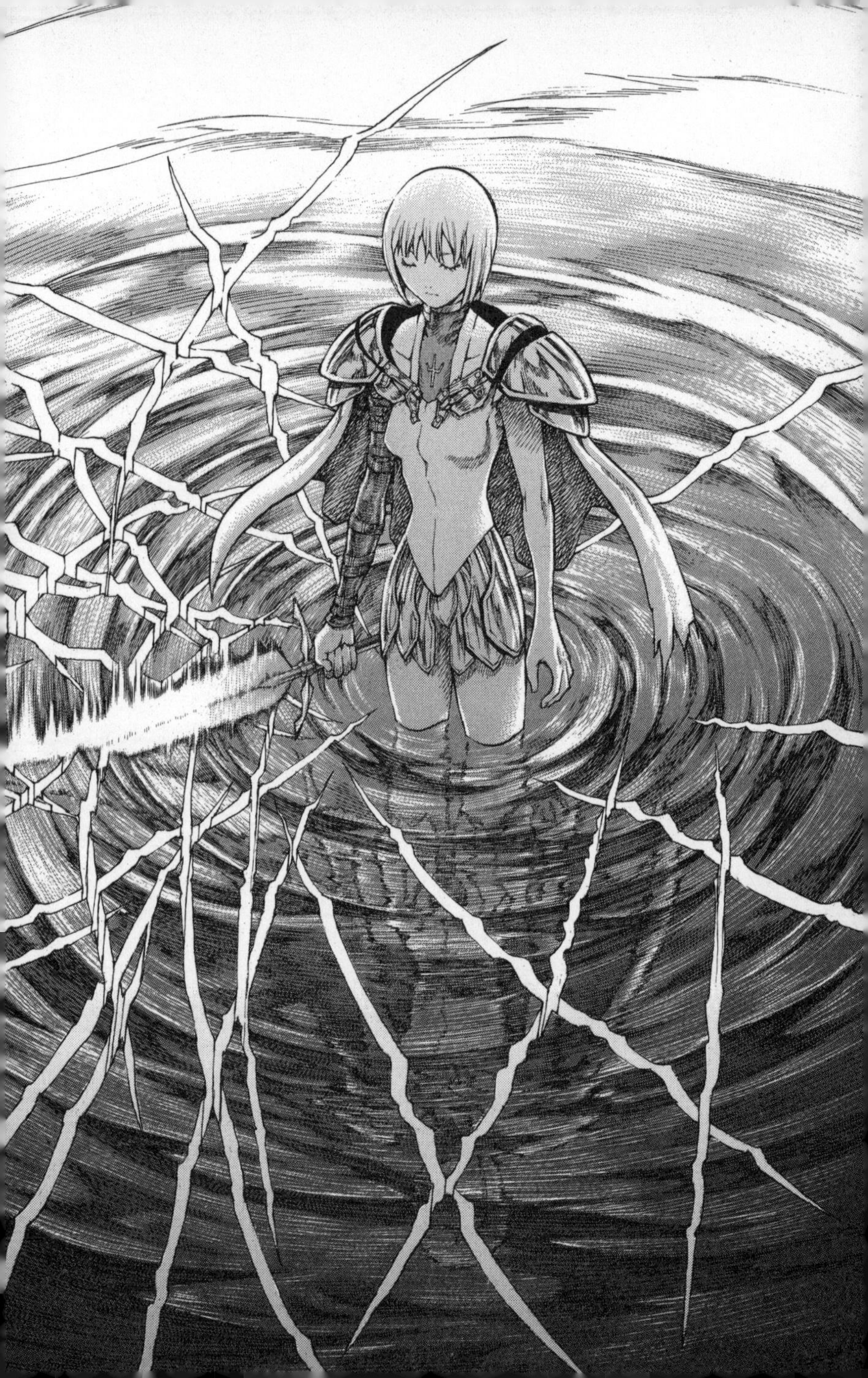

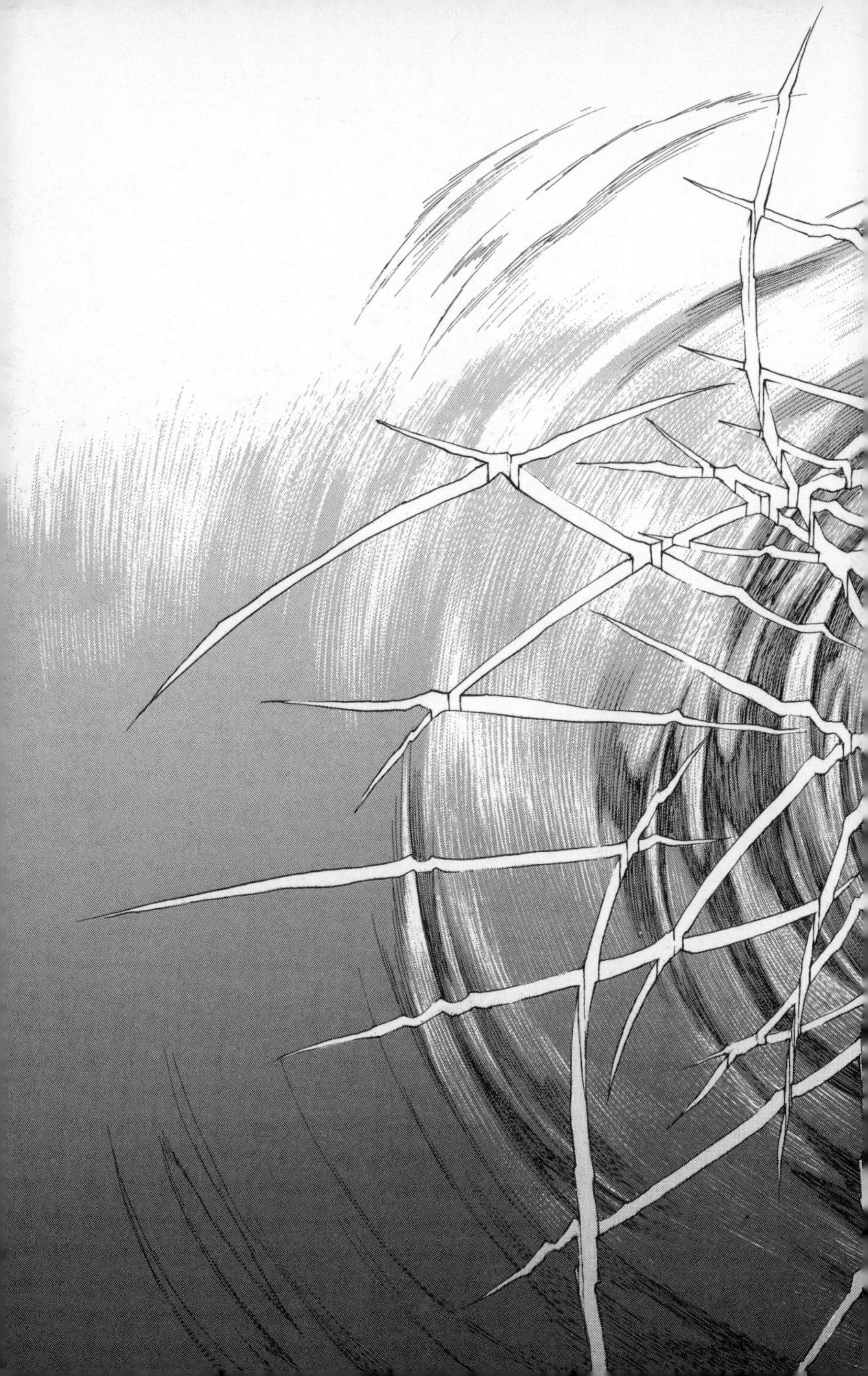

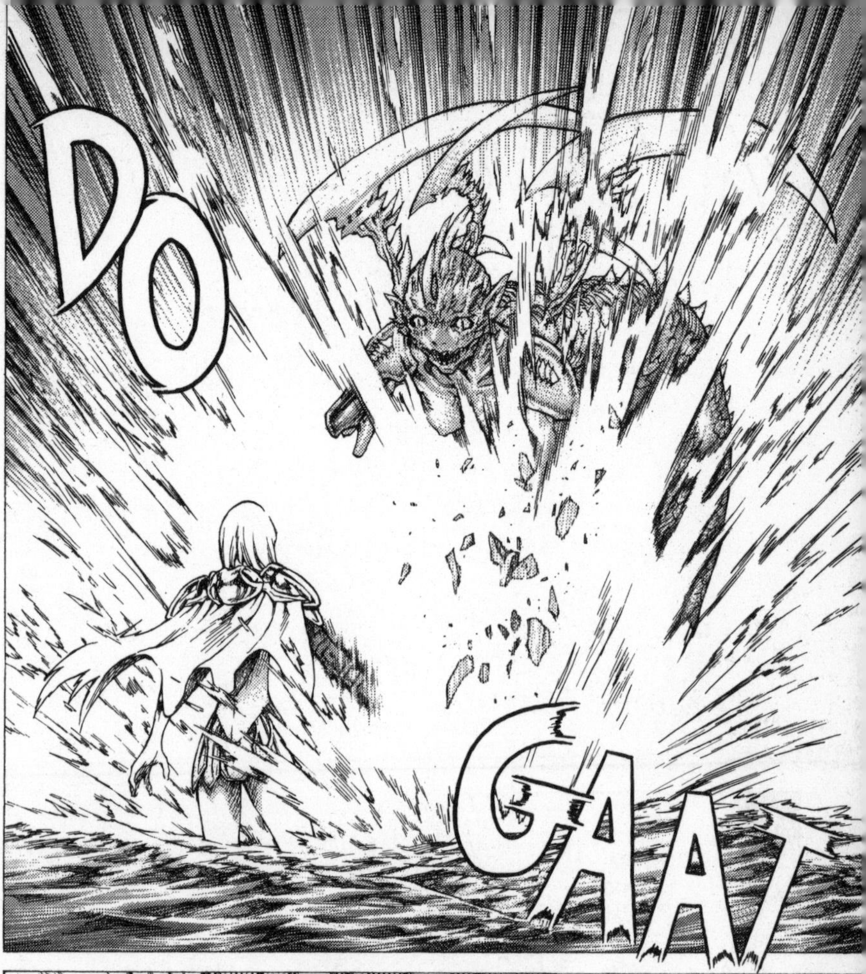
DO
GAAT
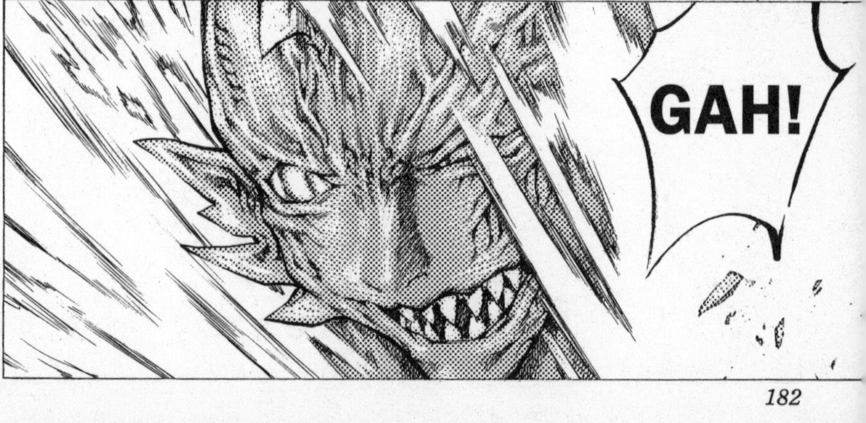
GAH!

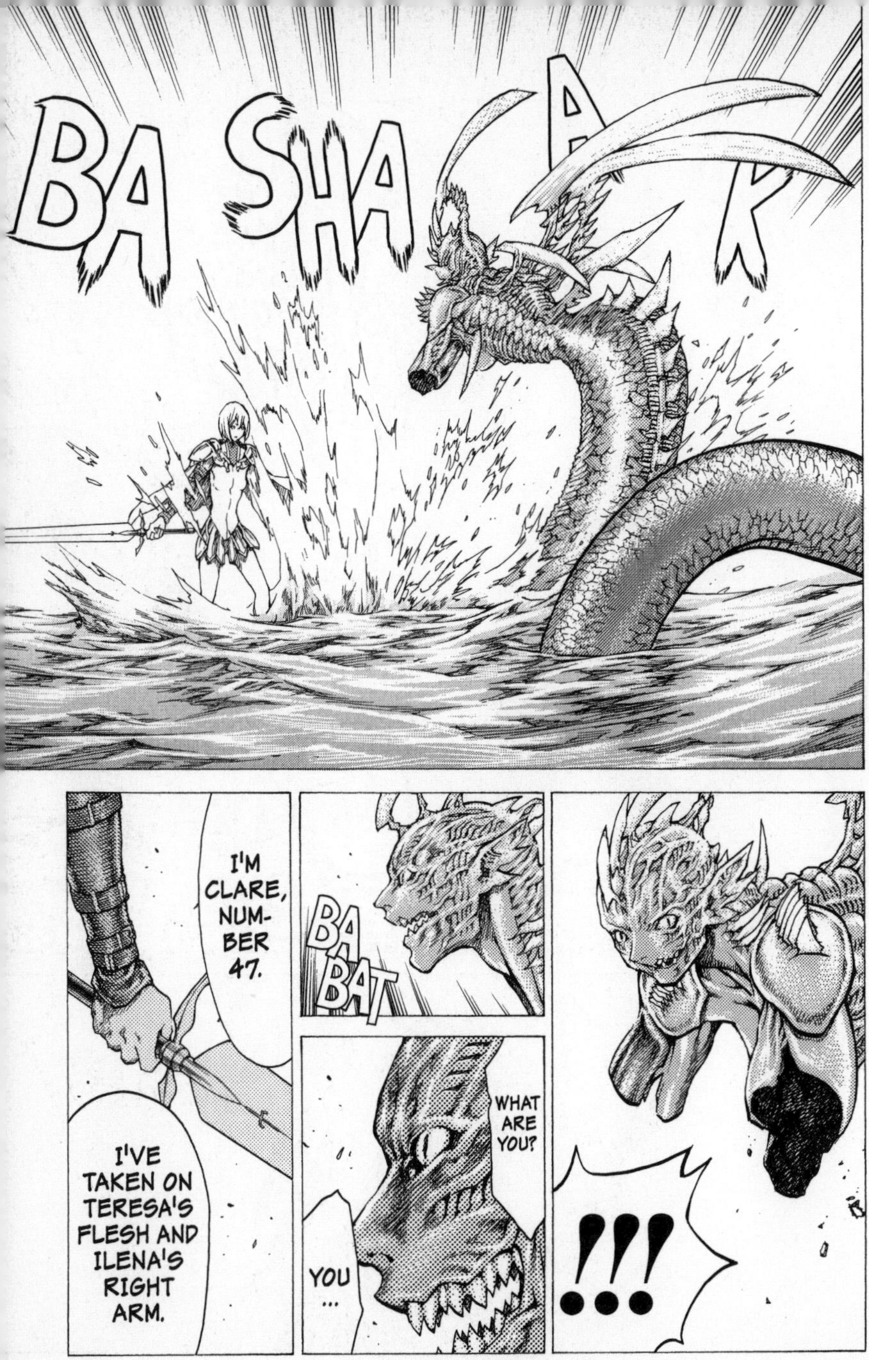
BA SHA A K
!!!
BA BAT
WHAT ARE YOU?
YOU ...
I'M CLARE, NUMBER 47.
I'VE TAKEN ON TERESA'S FLESH AND ILENA'S RIGHT ARM.

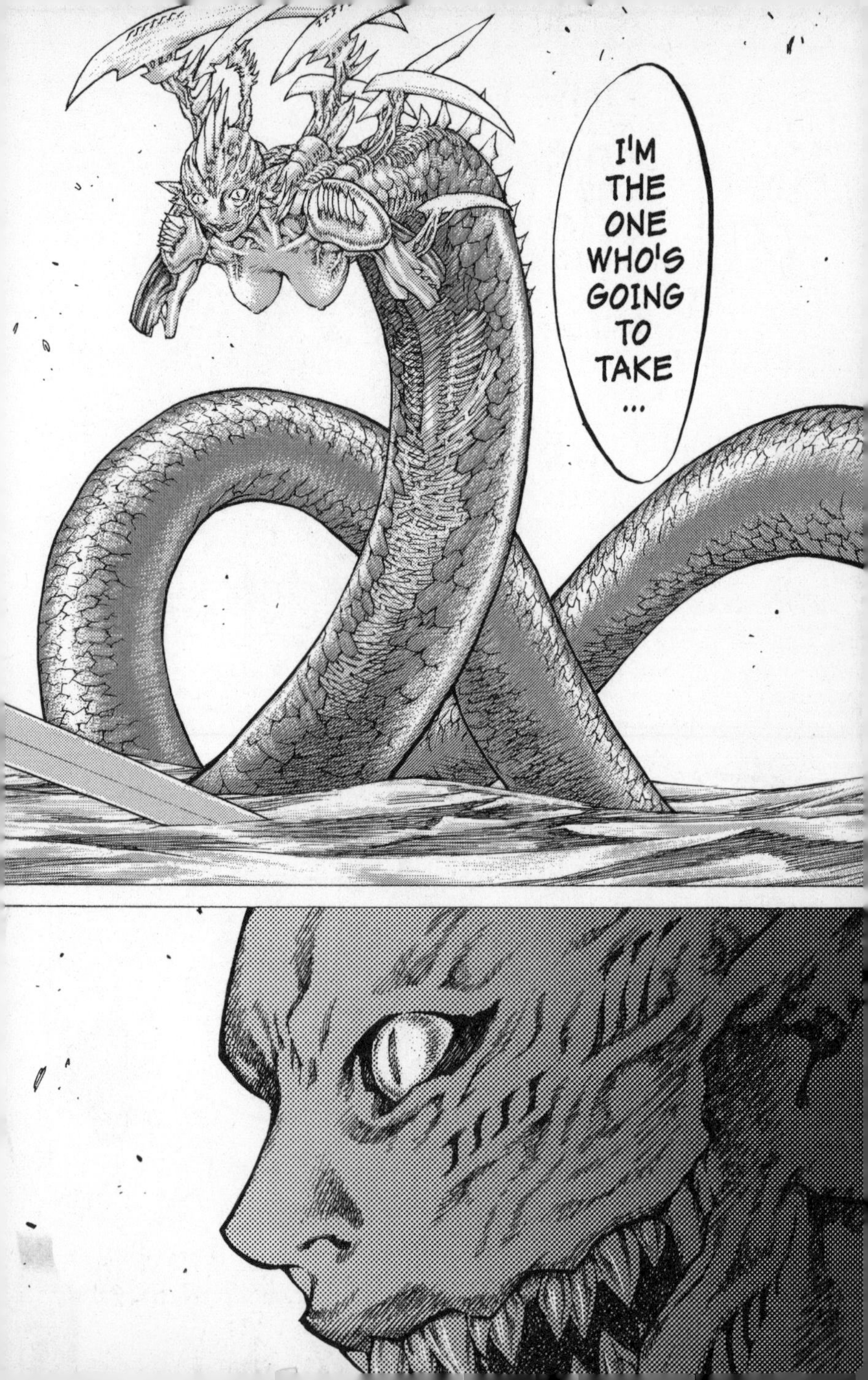
I'M THE ONE WHO'S GOING TO TAKE ...

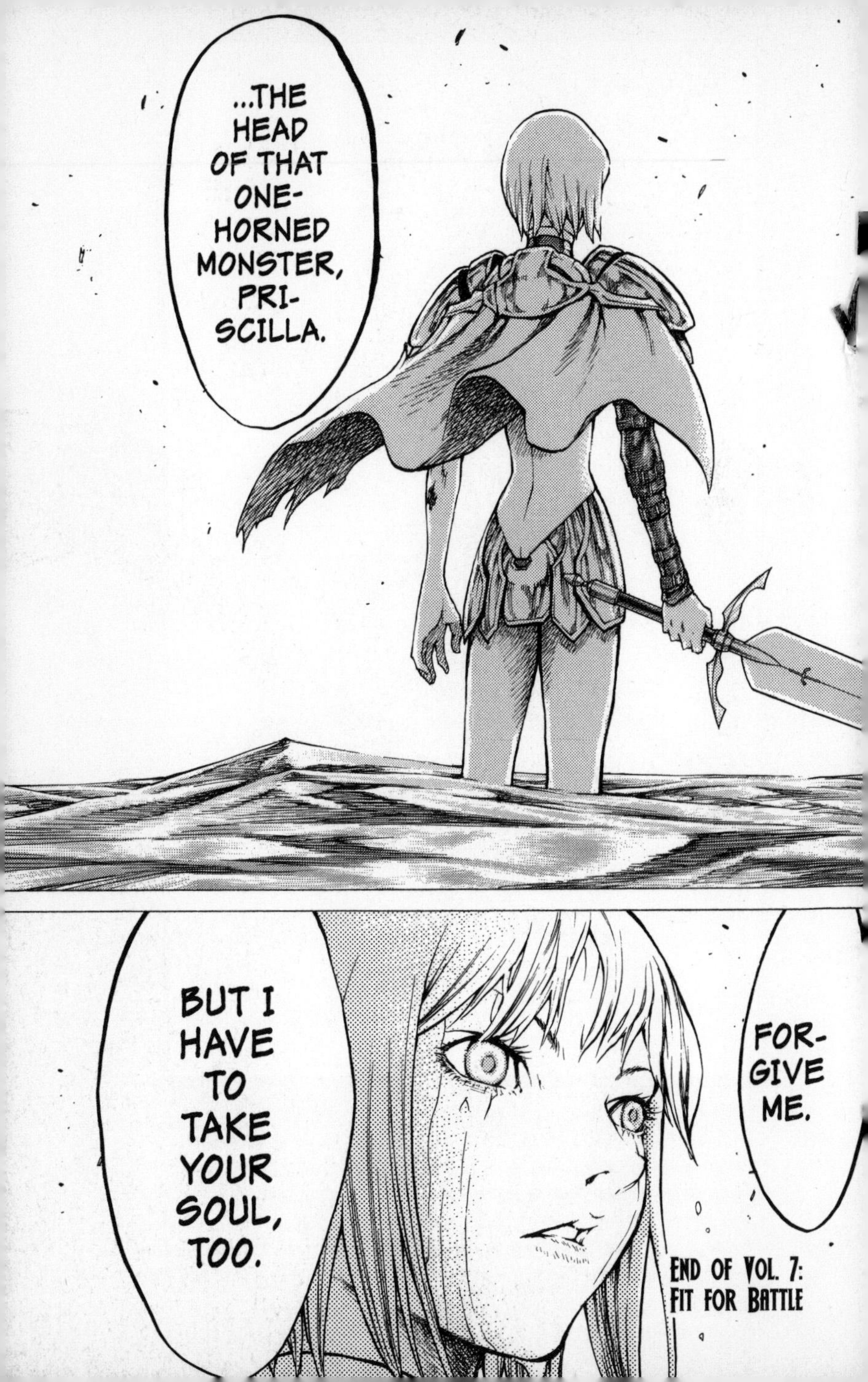
...THE HEAD OF THAT ONE-HORNED MONSTER, PRI-SCILLA.
FOR-GIVE ME.
BUT I HAVE TO TAKE YOUR SOUL, TOO.
END OF VOL. 7: FIT FOR BATTLE

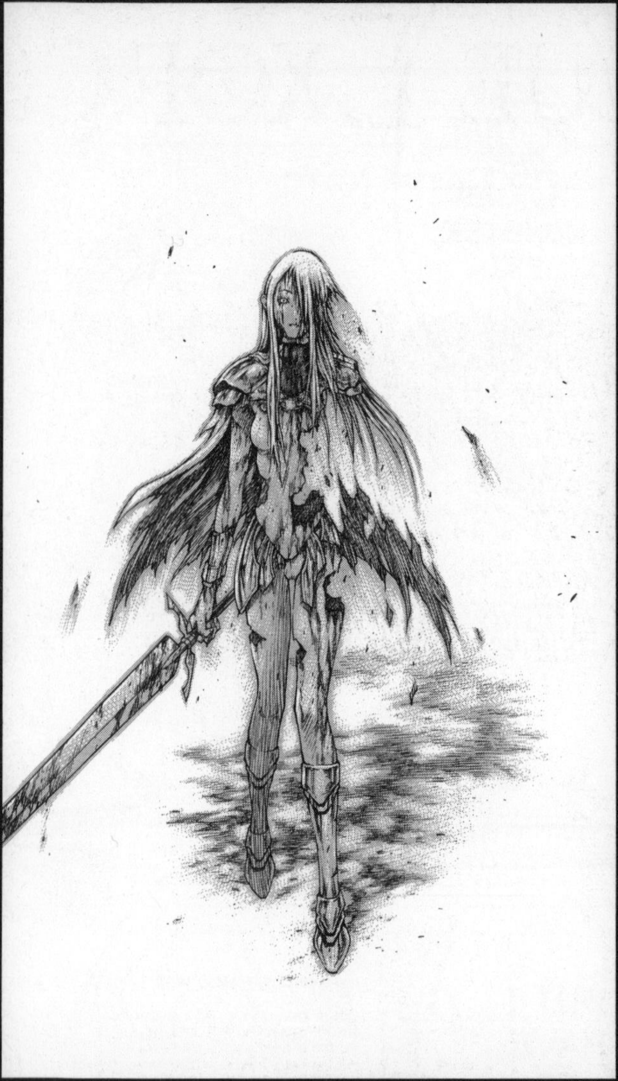

IN THE NEXT VOLUME

The organization is shocked to find that the usually solitary Yoma are not only joining forces, but also appear to be preparing for battle. When Clare goes to investigate, she gets taken captive by an Awakened Being that is holding Claymores in a dungeon. Who is her captor, and what does he want?

Available Now

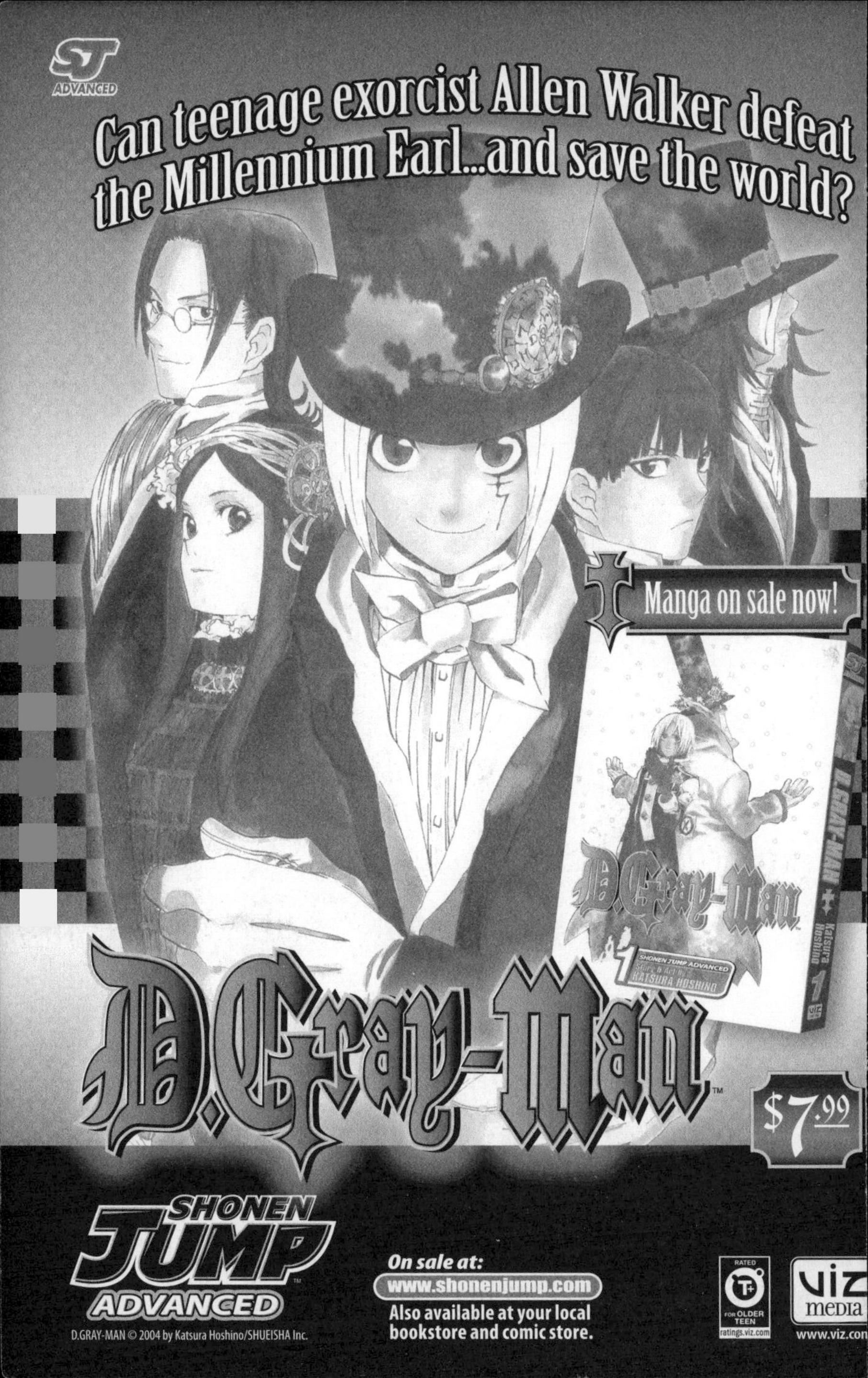

SJ ADVANCED
Can teenage exorcist Allen Walker defeat the Millennium Earl...and save the world?
Manga on sale now!
D.Gray-man™
$7.99
SHONEN JUMP ADVANCED
D.GRAY-MAN © 2004 by Katsura Hoshino/SHUEISHA Inc.
On sale at:
www.shonenjump.com
Also available at your local bookstore and comic store.
RATED T+ FOR OLDER TEEN ratings.viz.com
viz media
www.viz.com

SUBSCRIBE
and you'll get...

48 issues per year!

Weekly SJ Alpha will have 48 issues published per calendar year.

The BEST Manga!

Each issue of *Weekly SJ Alpha* will have chapters from some of the world's most popular manga such as *Bakuman*, *Bleach*, *Naruto*, *Nura: Rise of the Yokai Clan*, *One Piece* and *Toriko*.

A TON of Manga each month!

Four issues per month of *Weekly SJ Alpha* will deliver up to a staggering 480 pages of manga for your reading enjoyment.

The FRESHEST official content!

You'll get chapters from each of the six series just **TWO WEEKS** after they first appear in Japan!

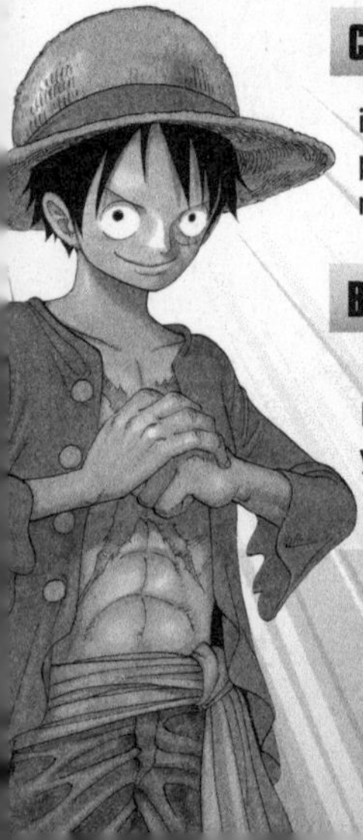

CHEAPER cost at $0.54 per issue!

At $25.99 for an annual subscription, each issue of *Weekly SJ Alpha* is an incredible bargain at $0.54 per issue with 52 weeks of access. Single issues of the digital magazine will cost $0.99 with four weeks of access.

BETTER Access!

You'll be able to read your *Weekly SJ Alpha* issues on practically any device with an internet connection at VIZManga.com. For those with an iPad® or iPhone® or iPod® touch, you can download the VIZ Manga app to read your issues.

To learn more, visit SJAlpha.com.

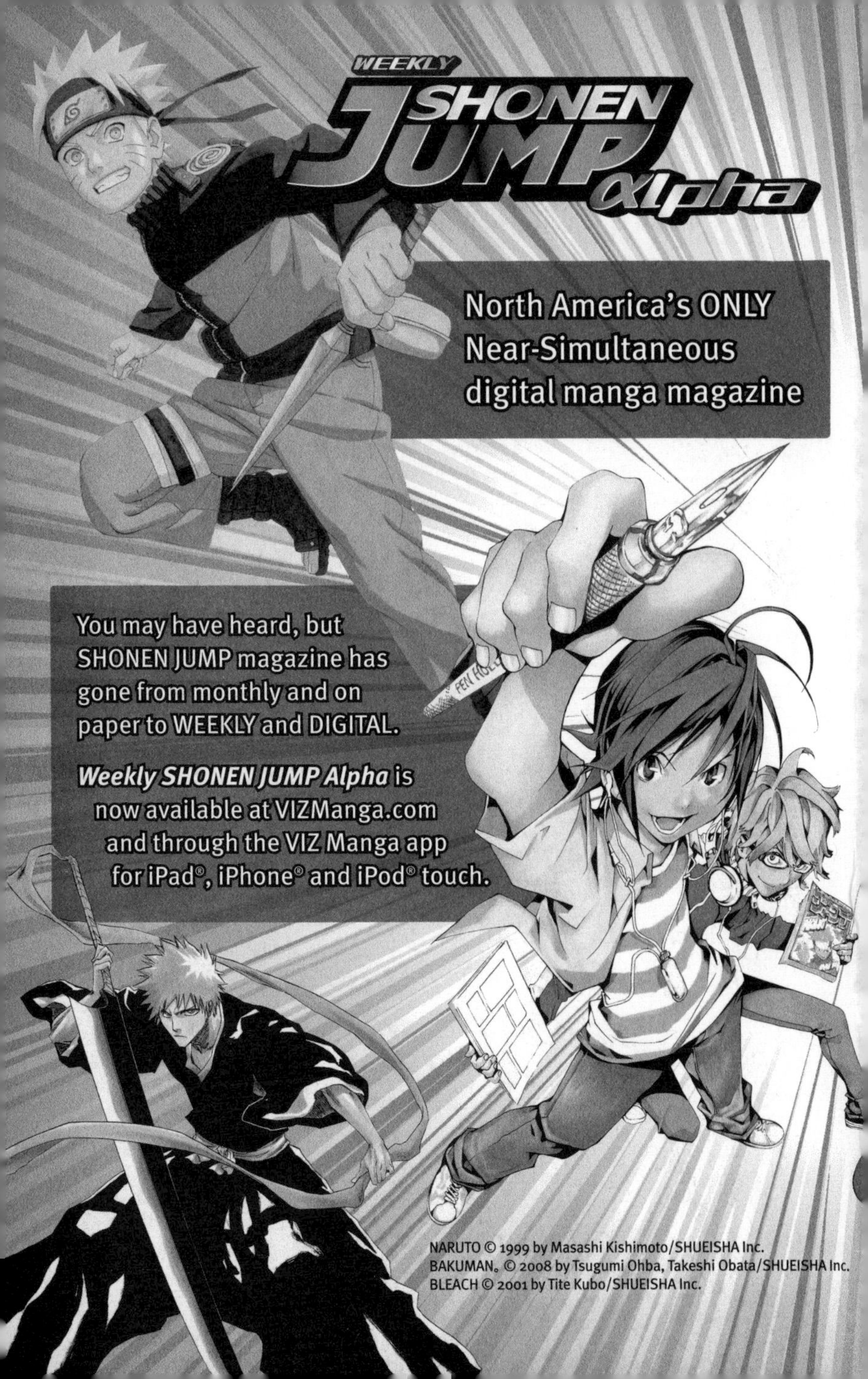
WEEKLY
SHONEN JUMP
αlpha
North America's ONLY
Near-Simultaneous
digital manga magazine
You may have heard, but
SHONEN JUMP magazine has
gone from monthly and on
paper to WEEKLY and DIGITAL.
Weekly SHONEN JUMP Alpha is
now available at VIZManga.com
and through the VIZ Manga app
for iPad®, iPhone® and iPod® touch.
NARUTO © 1999 by Masashi Kishimoto/SHUEISHA Inc.
BAKUMAN。 © 2008 by Tsugumi Ohba, Takeshi Obata/SHUEISHA Inc.
BLEACH © 2001 by Tite Kubo/SHUEISHA Inc.

You're Reading in the Wrong Direction!!

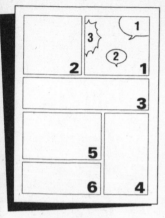

Whoops! Guess what? You're starting at the wrong end of the comic!

...It's true! In keeping with the original Japanese format, **Claymore** is meant to be read from right to left, starting in the upper-right corner.

Unlike English, which is read from left to right, Japanese is read from right to left, meaning that action, sound effects and word-balloon order are completely reversed... something which can make readers unfamiliar with Japanese feel pretty backwards themselves. For this reason, manga or Japanese comics published in the U.S. in English have sometimes been published "flopped"—that is, printed in exact reverse order, as though seen from the other side of a mirror.

By flopping pages, U.S. publishers can avoid confusing readers, but the compromise is not without its downside. For one thing, a character in a flopped manga series who once wore in the original Japanese version a T-shirt emblazoned with "M·A·Y" (as in "the merry month of") now wears one which reads "Y·A·M"! Additionally, many manga creators in Japan are themselves unhappy with the process, as some feel the mirror-imaging of their art skews their original intentions.

We are proud to bring you Norihiro Yagi's **Claymore** in the original unflopped format. For now, though, turn to the other side of the book and let the adventure begin...!

—Editor